Poetry
&Protest

Poetry & Protest

A Dennis Brutus Reader

Edited by
Lee Sustar
& Aisha Karim

Haymarket
Books
Chicago, IL

Compilation and additional materials © 2006 Lee Sustar and Aisha Karim

For a complete list of original sources, see pages 394–401.

First published in 2006 by Haymarket Books
P.O. Box 180165
Chicago, IL 60618
773-583-7884
www.haymarketbooks.org

This book has been published with the generous support of the Wallace Global Fund.

Cover design by Ragina Johnson
Interior design by David Whitehouse

Printed in Canada

10 9 8 7 6 5 4 3 2 1

Library of Congress Cataloging in Publication data
Poetry & protest : a Dennis Brutus reader / edited by Aisha Karim
and Lee Sustar.
    p. cm.
  Includes bibliographical references and index.
  ISBN-13: 978-1-931859-22-6
  ISBN-10: 1-931859-22-1
  1. Brutus, Dennis, 1924- 2. Poets, South African--20th century--
Biography. 3. Protest poetry, South African (English)--History and
criticism. 4. Apartheid in literature. 5. South Africa--In literature.
I. Title: Poetry and protest. II. Karim, Aisha, 1968- III. Sustar, Lee,
1961-
  PR9390.93B7Z82 2006
  821'.914--dc22
                                        2005034855

Contents

Acknowledgments

This book would have been impossible to produce without the collective efforts of many people, most of all the team at Haymarket Books. Julie Fain supervised the project from beginning to end, enduring numerous delays and handling multiple tasks ranging from suggestions on content to final production. Bill Roberts helped turn materials from scattered sources into a manuscript and helped keep the process moving at every stage. Anthony Arnove, who first proposed this project, provided professional advice on organizing the source material and arranged the cover photography. Lance Selfa's editorial comments and suggestions were key to shaping the final form of this book. Sherry Wolf and Deborah Roberts meticulously proofread the entire manuscript. Jeff Bale and Katherine Dwyer graciously agreed to transcribe recorded interviews. Danyal Rizvi, Alivia Moid, Syed Karim, and Tamiz Haiderali helped prepare out-of-print material for republication. Annie Zirin generously agreed to help locate materials at Worcester State College. Jesse Kindig took on similar tasks at the New York Public Library's Schomberg Center for Research in Black Culture. David Whitehouse created the book's excellent interior design, and Ragina Johnson designed the striking cover.

Thanks are also due to those who read this book in manuscript form at various stages. Patrick Bond offered not only comments and suggestions, but pointed us to numerous resources and gave us the benefit of his vast knowledge of South African society today. William Keach's expertise in editing poetry and his comments on the manuscript were invaluable. Bernth Lindfors, who edited and originally published several of the documents in this book, kindly gave us permission to reuse that material, while providing critical suggestions and much encouragement.

In addition, we were fortunate to be able to build upon the work of others who have edited and published Dennis Brutus's work and collaborated with his political projects. These include Wayne Kamin, who provided us with a recording of Brutus's powerful tribute to Steve Biko and gave us permission to reuse material he previously edited and published, and Hal Wylie, who helped us fill gaps in the bibliography and likewise granted us permission to republish. We also benefited from the critical analysis of Brutus's work by Simon Lewis, as well as the tribute to Brutus in the magazine Lewis edits, *Illuminations*. Another key resource was Craig W. McLuckie and Patrick J. Colbert's edited collection, *Critical Perspectives on Dennis Brutus,* which provides biographical data, a detailed bibliography and a range of critical views.

We are greatly indebted to others' work in publishing Brutus's political commentary. Michael Albert, David Barsamian, Linda Barton, Beverly Bell, Ben Cashdan, Ted Glick, lamont b. steptoe, and the IndyMedia South Africa collective generously allowed us to use previously published material.

The work of Brutus' collaborators in the global justice movement has been especially important, in particular Njoki Njehu and Soren Ambrose of the 50 Years is Enough campaign, and the authors and activists Jeremy Brecher and Kevin Danaher.

A number of people supported this project through their work in their respective institutions. Kathy Alaimo, Dean of Arts and Sciences at St. Xavier University supported this project through a generous research grant. The Northwestern University Archives staff spent years organizing Dennis Brutus's papers, making our research possible. We would like to thank in particular University Archivist Patrick M. Quinn, Assistant University Archivist Janet C. Olson, Associate Archivist Kevin B. Leonard, and Assistant Archivist Allen J. Streicker. Also at Northwestern, the Herskovits Library of African Studies staff generously allowed use of their facilities. We would like especially to thank Curator David Easterbrook and Matthew Teti of the library's staff.

At Worcester State College, Dr. Henry Theriault, Coordinator of the Center for the Study of Human Rights, gave us permission to access the center's Dennis Brutus Collection; Worcester's Library Director Donald Hochstetler sorted through the material and made it available to us. A similar valuable service was provided to us at Yale Divinity School Library by Archives Assistant Joan R. Duffy. In South Africa, Andrew Martin, of the National English Literary Museum, located original source material unavailable elsewhere; we also found his *Poems of Dennis Brutus: A Checklist, 1945-2004* to be indispensable. Glenn Cowley at the University of KwaZulu-Natal Press deserves special mention for making this the first time that a volume of Dennis Brutus's work is being published in South Africa.

For advice on resources on the history of the South African left we would like to thank Ted Crawford, Allison Drew, and Hilel Ticktin.

We would also like to acknowledge our debt to our parents, Zeenat Karim, the late Syed Letafat Karim, Gloria Sustar, and Frank Sustar.

Through the entire process, we've enjoyed the collaboration and friendship of Dennis Brutus. We would like to thank him for sitting through interviews and reviewing manuscripts despite a schedule crammed with speaking, teaching, and organizing on a world scale. In his eighth decade, Dennis Brutus remains a troubadour for global justice.

Introduction
Dennis Brutus's "Ticking Explosives"

"The struggle continues": This well-known slogan of the left certainly characterizes Dennis Brutus's life's work. Shot by the apartheid South African police in 1963 and imprisoned for eighteen months alongside Nelson Mandela, Dennis Brutus was exiled from his homeland for twenty-five years. It was during this exile that he burst onto the international stage with a simultaneous debut as a world-class poet and effective political organizer, who led the successful campaign to expel apartheid South Africa from the Olympic Games. Four decades later, Brutus continues to organize, speak, and write with the aim of global social transformation. Through this period his politics and poetry have continued to be welded together. Thus, the selection of articles, speeches, and interviews in this book, spanning half a century, not only document struggles of the past, but also inform the perspectives for those to come. Also included is a substantial selection of Brutus's poetry, much of which has been long out of print despite the widely acknowledged literary significance of many of the works included in this volume.

Brutus's work consciously contends with the dilemma of the artist-activist. In a characteristically untitled poem, we see a poet complaining: "I must lug my battered body" across the globe, reciting "wear-shined clichés" of poetry.[1] The poem ends with the poet claiming: "in my baggage I bear the ticking explosives/of reproach, and threat, and challenge" (10–11). If these "ticking explosives" are the words of reproach that the poet carries in his luggage, and if this luggage is at the same time the very body of the poet, an act of superimposition has taken place: by the end of this poem, the body of the poet and the words of reproach—the poetry—have become one. To put it another way, the word and the act, history and the text, politics and poetry, have melded together to the extent that they have become indistinguishable. In this sense, Brutus's poetry is representative of contemporary Third World writing. If there is a generalization that can be made about such literature, it is that its creation is itself a political act. And Brutus belongs to that tradition of contemporary Third World writers whose writings have consciously grappled with the inescapably political nature of such literature. Another of Brutus's poems overtly gestures towards this superimposition of literature and politics as a historical necessity: "In a country which denies that men/ and women are human... /the creative act is an act/ of dissent and defiance" (1–5) and of the "assert[ion] of one's/ Humanity" (8–9).[2] The very act of writing under apartheid, then, becomes an act of resistance.

Our aim, here, is to trace, in microcosm, not only the continuity between literature and politics, but also the process of broadening of social struggles. In other words, this work explores how a national movement against apartheid broadens itself into the movement for global justice, and what place an individual life, on one level, and literature, on another, may have in this expansion of social struggle. Accordingly, this volume is also an oral, documentary, and artistic history of decolonization, national liberation, anti-apartheid, and global justice movements, told through the work of Dennis Brutus as an oppositional figure and a grassroots participant in those struggles. In this respect, Brutus's position recalls another participant in such struggles, Frantz Fanon, whose essays in the National Liberation Front (FLN) newspaper, *El Moudjahid*, mobilizing for the struggle against French rule in Algeria, warn of what awaits the decolonized countries. Fanon calls for a second, post-nationalist stage of struggle, which, in contrast to the nationalist stage, would be internationalist in character.[3] Brutus's struggles, in keeping with the Fanonian tradition, do not stop after liberation from apartheid in South Africa, but continue and are broadened into the movement for global justice, or, in South African President Thabo Mbeki's phrase, against "global apartheid."

It is this process of the expansion of struggles—and their connections with Brutus's political and literary work—that we wish to document in this book. Although, as with any narrative, chronology is integral to Brutus's story, we have prioritized thematic over chronological organization; we have followed chronological order only insofar as it helps highlight the development of Brutus's work as an activist-poet. Accordingly, the book consists of three parts that deal, respectively, with the conditions that made for the radicalization and emergence of the poet-activist, the necessary intertwining of cultural and political liberation, and the possibility of a national movement maturing into a global struggle. Each part begins with a memoir, based on a series of interviews conducted between April 2004 and September 2005 by Lee Sustar.[4] These memoirs establish Brutus as a key political actor in the history of the anti-apartheid struggle, and as chronicler, storyteller, strategist, and analyst of the movement. The memoirs record a life inextricably linked with the political struggle and with many of its leading figures including, most notably, Nelson Mandela, whose transition from a twenty-seven-year imprisonment to the South African presidency symbolizes the dignity and resolve of the liberation movement. These memoirs introduce and provide the organizational principle, and the historical crux, for each of the three parts.

In addition to the memoirs, we have included a range of documents: essays on sports and apartheid; speeches at historical occasions; and interviews that explore the complex interplay between literary texts and social movements, culture and politics. Each part concludes with a selection of poems that engage with the thematic concerns of the respective sections. We see the poems, here, as that realm of culture that is indispensable to, and inextricable from, the political: the poems provide that space in the imaginary where Brutus's social and political concerns are thought through and find artistic expression.

The poems are selected for each part of this volume not necessarily because they were composed during the historical period in question, but more importantly because these poems, even when composed years later, deal with the historical events and concerns of that period. For example, in Part 1 we juxtapose the poems written in prison, "Letters to Martha," with poems written later—"Still the sirens,"—about the experience of repression and imprisonment. This juxtaposition produces stark results when, in Part 3, we put

"Train Journey," written in 1968, side by side with "Picture of a young girl dying of aids," written in 1991. What is produced is not only a picture of the tragic continuity of life under apartheid, but also the premonition of a questionable liberation. Similarly, the juxtaposition of two poems—"In a country that denies that men and women," written in 1989 and ostensibly about apartheid, and "Mumia," written in 1999—poignantly brings together the experience of apartheid with the post-civil rights struggles of African Americans in the United States. The result is a vision of internationalization of the anti-apartheid struggles. In this way, poems are presented to the reader in the framework in which Brutus produced them—as integral to, and enactments of, political struggles.

Part 1 includes Brutus's account of growing up in one of South Africa's "colored" ghettos under apartheid—surrounded by the kind of poverty that, as Brutus points out, has persisted in the post-apartheid era. His writings about race, sports, and apartheid included here highlight the contradictions between sports' notion of fair play and apartheid's institutional white supremacy. Brutus's powerful account of imprisonment on Robben Island, never before published, and edited specifically for this volume by Aisha Karim, details both the horrors of a sadistic prison regime as well as the efforts by political prisoners to maintain a measure of dignity and respect.

For Brutus, who was introduced to socialist politics as a young man by South African followers of the Russian revolutionary Leon Trotsky, the struggle to overthrow apartheid became one element in an even greater endeavor. "The significance of the Southern African liberation movement is that it goes beyond resistance," he said in a 1974 speech:

> It is not resistance to oppression; it is not even liberation merely in the sense of freedom to govern yourself. It has penetrated beyond that to an understanding that what we are engaged in is a struggle against imperialism. It is not a local, nor even a national struggle. We see ourselves as an element in the global struggle against imperialism. This seems to me the truly revolutionary element in our struggle for cultural liberation.[5]

It is this concern with the relationship between politics and culture that forms the basis of Part 2. Divided into three sections, this part details Brutus's launch into the world of international sports, literature, and politics. First, we deal with Brutus in exile: operating from Britain and then from the United States, Brutus led the successful campaign to expel racist South Africa from the Olympic Games. This material focuses on Brutus's involvement in the sports world, including a memoir that details how Avery Brundage, head of the U.S. and International Olympic Committees, was pressured and maneuvered into expelling from the Games both South Africa and the white minority regime in Rhodesia (now Zimbabwe). A selection of letters and documents provide insight into the campaign to isolate apartheid sports, an effort that involved activists and athletes internationally, including such well-known figures as boxing champion Muhammad Ali, tennis great Arthur Ashe, and baseball pitcher Jim Bouton.

Second, we chronicle Brutus's emergence as a poet and a pivotal figure on the literary and academic scene. Among the articles and speeches included are Brutus's remarks to the first Pan-African Cultural Festival in Algiers in 1969, where he spoke as a representative of the Southern African liberation movements. This section also includes selections of Brutus's own writings on literature, as well as an interview on poetry and art conducted by Bernth Lindfors, a leading critic of African literature and close collaborator of Brutus's. These documents and poems, covering an era when social movements had a far-reaching impact on the academic world, remain signposts for those seeking to understand art in its historical and political context—more specifically, art as an inextricable part of social movements. This section also documents Brutus's central role in the African literary scene that he helped to establish within academia as a teacher of English literature; his collaborators have included such luminaries as the Nigerian writers Chinua Achebe and Wole Soyinka and the Kenyan author Ngugi wa Thiong'o.

The dramatic and bitter last phase of the anti-apartheid struggle in the 1980s concludes Part 2. Included are documents from Brutus's successful campaign against a deportation order from the adminstration of President Ronald Reagan. The effort to deport Brutus came as he played an increasingly high profile role in the movement to compel U.S. corporations to divest from holdings in South Africa. Several of Brutus's speeches and articles from this period are included here, among them pieces detailing U.S. and Western economic, military, and political support for the apartheid regime.

Part 3 covers the post-apartheid years. It includes Brutus's speeches, interviews, and poems that trace the rise of the global justice movement, which developed as the international Left contended with a new world order after the Cold War. In the post-apartheid era, Brutus helped to initiate campaigns against the International Monetary Fund, the World Bank, and the World Trade Organization. These campaigns laid the cornerstones for the global justice movement and the annual gatherings of the Left at the World Social Forum. The selections in Part 3 underscore the continuity between the liberation movements of previous generations and those of today. These selections record Brutus's activism; for example, his support for such activist groups as the Soweto Electricity Crisis Committee, formed to stop service cutoffs to poor residents. Included here are articles and speeches by Brutus on why he was among the protesters at two high-profile international events hosted in South Africa: the United Nations World Conference Against Racism in Durban in 2001 and the World Summit on Sustainable Development in Johannesburg in 2002. These articles and poems demand reparations from companies that profited from apartheid, trace the continuity between the anti-apartheid struggle and the struggle for racial equality in the U.S., and attempt to envision the possibility of a different world.

While Brutus sees the Group of Eight industrialized countries, the World Bank, and the International Monetary Fund, as institutions forming the core of the world system and its problems, he also becomes equally critical of the post-apartheid South African government, which he views as having collaborated with an imperialist agenda:

> where we marched against the oppression of a minority racist regime in the past, we now have to march against the people we put in power. The people who were elected to serve us, are now serving instead the World Bank, the IMF, and the whole corporate global agenda. And so we are now in the position once again, of having to march. And some of us will be beaten, and some of us will be jailed, and some of us may end up in prison, as I did on Robben Island [prison], when I broke stones with Nelson Mandela many years ago.[6]

Many of Brutus's former comrades, now part of the post-apartheid government, have responded to these criticisms harshly. Essop Pahad, a minister in President Thabo Mbeki's office and member of the South African Communist Party (SACP) who once worked with Brutus in the South African Non-Racial Olympic Committee, criticizes Brutus for having "disappeared without trace from the anti-apartheid struggle many years before 1994, and re-emerged in the last few years to hurl invective at the democratic government and programs for Africa's recovery." Pahad continues:

> However, to the extent that on some issues such as eradicating global inequality, we may agree, perhaps there is hope for cooperation. Welcome home Dennis the Menace! Hope this time you will stay, the better to appreciate that we cannot not allow our modest achievements to be wrecked through anarchy. Opponents of democracy seek such destruction. But if you intend once more to leave for demonstrations elsewhere, we can only retort: et tu Brute! Good luck.[7]

Such a dismissal of Brutus's contributions to the anti-apartheid movement, however, contradicts the historical record as laid out in this book and elsewhere. More significantly, Pahad's criticisms of Brutus reflect an irreconcilable difference between the internationalism that Brutus has always upheld and the African National Congresses's (ANC's) view of national liberation in South Africa— the achievement of a non-racial government—as an end in itself. On the one hand, Pahad stresses the possibility of "cooperation" between Brutus and the "democratic government" of South Africa on the issue of "eradicating global inequality." But on the other hand, Pahad seems to ignore the possibility that Brutus's "leav[ing] for demonstrations elsewhere" might be part and parcel of this fight against global inequality—and that Brutus's continued activism in South Africa and his challenges to the ANC government are part of that same struggle for global justice.

Indeed, it is precisely Brutus's ability to mesh the political and the cultural, the local and the global, that prompted the acclaimed South African novelist Nadine Gordimer, in a tribute on his eightieth birthday, to characterize Brutus as "a freedom fighter who never thought it necessary to give up being an intellectual, but combined both in the campaign that has been his life so far and there is no doubt will be as long as he is with us." Commenting on Brutus's move to extend the national into an international struggle, Gordimer continues: "His passion for justice in our African continent has now long extended to the whole world where the abyss between rich and poor countries grows instead of closing."[8]

Editorial note: Dating Brutus's poems

Dennis Brutus seldom titles or dates his poems. When he does provide the date of composition, we have included it next to the left margin; those dates need to be seen almost as part of the poem, as significant to the valence of the poem. As such, these composition dates stand in as the last lines of the poems. The dates on the extreme right are the original publication dates.

Aisha Karim and Lee Sustar
Chicago, Illinois
January 2006

[1] This untitled poem begins with "I must lug my battered body." The subsequent in-text line numbers refer to this poem, included on page 126 in this volume. Henceforth, we will identify all of Brutus's untitled poems by their first lines.

[2] These lines refer to the untitled poem, "In a country which denies that men," included on page 370 in this volume.

[3] These essays are collected in Frantz Fanon, *Toward The African Revolution: Political Essays*, ed. Francois Maspero, trans. Haakon Chevalier (New York: Grove, 1967). See especially the essay, "The Algerian War and Man's Liberation," first published El Moudjahid, No, 31, November 1, 1958, also in *Toward the African Revolution*.

[4] Dennis Brutus reviewed and approved all interview texts as Lee Sustar edited them for clarity.

[5] See page 199 of this volume.

[6] See page 359 of this volume.

[7] Quoted in Patrick Bond, "Geopolitics of the Johannesburg Protests," September 2, 2002. Available on the Znet Web site.

[8] Nadine Gordimer, "Tribute to Dennis Brutus: Brighter Than Their Searchlights," *Illuminations* 20 (August 2004), 34–35.

Part 1

Early Years: Radicalization and Rebellion

when my mother talked to me
about her mother and slavery
evoking images of persons bound
to wagon wheels and whipped
it was mere narrative:
perhaps I was too young a boy
to be stirred to rage, too weak
to think of changing the world.
But when I came to adulthood
I challenged myself to
confrontation,
to admission and action

May 9, 2002   2005

From racial segregation to institutionalized white supremacy and the denial of political rights for Africans and "non-whites": this was the transformation of South Africa in the late 1940s. Like other blacks and "coloreds" of his generation, Dennis Brutus was confronted with a choice of whether to adapt to the highly restrictive and humiliating conditions of the system of apartheid— "separateness" in Afrikaans, the language of the descendants of Dutch settlers. Public resistance meant the near certainty of repression and quite possibly death.

Brutus, born November 28, 1924, in Rhodesia (now Zimbabwe), grew up in a ghetto for coloreds in the South African industrial city of Port Elizabeth. His memoir in Part I describes how his family's efforts helped him to achieve the education needed to become a teacher—a choice that would propel him into the center of anti-apartheid activity in South Africa's Eastern Cape.

Imposed by the largely Afrikaner Nationalist Party in 1948, apartheid drew upon both the race laws of Nazi Germany and the Jim Crow racial segregation laws of the U.S. South. There were already longstanding traditions of resistance against British colonial rule—the African National Congress (ANC) was founded in 1912, and Mohandas K. Gandhi was first arrested for his protest activities in South Africa in 1908. Moreover, the economic boom of the Second World War had opened the way for black labor to organize in unions on a serious scale, raising the possibility of challenging the entrenched racism under British rule. Deeply involved in these efforts was the South African socialist Left, albeit one divided between the pro-Moscow South African Communist Party (SACP) and smaller but influential Trotskyist organizations.

A wave of resistance met the 1948 apartheid laws, which included the creation of the Colored Affairs Department (CAD).

Aimed at institutionalizing a collaborationist layer of "colored" South Africans—people of mixed race background—the imposition of CAD also entailed their forcible removal from areas designated as white. This struggle against apartheid laws brought Brutus into organized political activity.

A new phase of resistance began with the 1952 Defiance Campaign, in which the ANC defied apartheid laws with civil disobedience and mass protest. During one such protest, Nelson Mandela, who would become the ANC's leader and one of the world's best-known political prisoners, was arrested. The apartheid regime retaliated with mass arrests, setting the stage for the 1956 Treason Trial, in which Mandela and other leaders were accused. It was in this period when Brutus initiated the South African Sports Association, to challenge apartheid's rigid racial divisions in sports.

This phase of anti-apartheid resistance came to an end with the Sharpeville Massacre of March 19, 1960, in which police shot sixty-nine protesters to death. A new crackdown ensued, including "banning" orders on individuals that prohibited them from attending meetings and, in some cases, publishing. Brutus himself was banned in 1961 and arrested for violating that order in 1963. He escaped twice—and was shot the second time by police on a crowded Johannesburg street.

Part 1 begins with Brutus's memoir of his youth and the first political activity. Also included are documents and articles from the efforts to challenge apartheid in the sporting world, as well as a further memoir of Brutus's experience on Robben Island prison. The poetry selection in Part 1 includes several pieces from the first two books, the widely acclaimed Sirens Knuckles Boots *and* Letters to Martha, *which was largely composed while on Robben Island. In addition, this selection incorporates several poems written later, especially those reminiscing about prison and repression under apartheid.*

L.S. and A.K.

Memoir
From Protest to Prison

Growing up "colored"

I was born in 1924 in Rhodesia, now Zimbabwe, a British colony, in the capital, Salisbury, now called Harare. My father and my mother had gone there from South Africa, and were both teachers in a missionary school.

We came back to South Africa when I was maybe a year old. Zimbabwe, or Rhodesia, had no significance for me. But I was going from one colonial setup to another colonial setup—both, of course, part of the British Empire. And you must remember that these were the days of great imperialism. The British were so proud of their empire, they said ["the sun never sets, or from where it rises, to where it sets, the color is red."] And Cecil Rhodes was dreaming of Britain running from Cape Town to Cairo—of building a railroad across the continent. It was all going to be British. So you have this incredible imperial dream, and it's out of that context that I come.

But you must remember that my parents were both what are legally called "coloreds," which is not an unusual situation in South Africa, because the Dutch settlers who landed in the 1650s encouraged intermarriage as a way of penetrating society. The first black-white marriage took place in 1664, of an African woman who had been a servant of Dutch governor Jan van Riebeeck in the fortress in Cape Town. Before the first African woman married a settler, she had to be baptized, because marriage is a Christian institution. So they baptized her Eva, because she was to be the mother of the new human race—Adam and Eve, sort of.

There are people who have a notion—if they grew up in the United States, for instance—that black-white marriages in South Africa were romantic, interracial, daring, breaking the law. Well, it was nothing of the sort. Only in 1950 does South Africa pass a law called the Mixed Marriages Act, so that more than 200 years later it became illegal for blacks and whites to marry. The miscegenation laws of the U.S. are much older.

By the 1920s, the British had established "reserves" in South Africa—really not unlike the racial segregation that was happening in the U.S. So I grew up in Port Elizabeth in a segregated area for coloreds—one of the first in the entire nation where there was an actually segregated housing scheme, like a project, for coloreds, that separated them from Africans—blacks, if you like. Blacks at that time were called Natives, which is interesting because when you say "native" you're really conceding that these are the indigenous people of the country. "Native," however, became a term of contempt—like "red Indian" would be in the United States.

On the one side we had a white segregated community, and on the other side, a black segregated community. And in between, the coloreds' segregated community. And some of the sociologists of the time, including Americans, were coming to South Africa and writing about how it would be good to have a buffer community separating white from black. So again, you had these interesting echoes between South Africa and the United States.

The one advantage of growing up in a segregated community was that you were protected from the kind of racism that you might have encountered in a multiracial community. Within the community one was not conscious of racism, because one was not exposed to it. But it was always on the periphery, and you would meet it periodically. All the colored townships were supervised by a white person from the municipal body, so you had that kind of control. Once a month, you would meet someone who treated you like dirt, when you paid the bills. But within the community, there was a marvelous extended family approach. People were interdependent. They helped each other if someone had a need—if someone wanted to borrow a cup of sugar, for instance, or the baby was sick and you needed medicine, you went to a neighbor. There was all this kind of wonderful communal assistance.

There were jealousies, of course, and now looking back I understand that there really was prostitution going on around me, but I was too young and too naïve to perceive it. That was one of the ways women survived. Other women were washerwomen, or looked after babies, or they were cleaning women—domestics, we called them.

The men were in the factories. Ford came into Port Elizabeth, and then General Motors (GM). You had kind of a Detroit of Africa. All the cars that were going all over the continent were being produced in my hometown. And the people in my community were working in the factories nearby. On my way to school I had to pass both Ford and GM; the school, interestingly, was set up by nuns in the white community. The white kids went to better schools and moved up. The colored students didn't, and attended the whites' old school. It was a scale.

"Future Springboks"

There was a seminal moment in my life connected to this school. On Saturdays and Sundays, we had nowhere to go—there were no playgrounds. So we would go back to the school, even though it was in a white area, and kick a ball around. One Saturday afternoon, as we were kicking a ball around, it bounced out of the school yard, into one of the gardens of one of the white, middle-class houses around there. The husband and the wife and everybody else were sitting on the stoop in the sunny, warm Saturday afternoon, listening to a radio broadcast of a rugby match between South Africa and New Zealand, the two great rugby rivals. As the ball bounced in the garden, I went and got the ball.

And the man says to his wife "Ah, future Springboks"—meaning future members of the South African rugby team. But he's saying it cynically because no non-white ever gets onto the team! I'm not sure, but his wife says to him, "You know, sarcasm is the lowest form of wit." So I'm maybe twelve or thirteen, listening to this. And it strikes me, this guy's saying that coloreds—blacks—won't ever get onto the team. I think it stuck with me, until years later, when I began to challenge the whole barrier—questioning why blacks can't be on the team. I remember both the cynicism with which the possibility was dismissed, and the woman alerting this man to the fact that maybe he's not as smart as he thinks he is.

So I went to a colored school. And if you were poor, you ended up in either a car factory or a shoe factory. Port Elizabeth was also the capital of the shoe industry on the continent. It was called the Northampton of Africa, because Northampton in Britain was the largest shoe producer in the empire at that time. My brother, for instance, ended up in a shoe factory.

Once you finished grade school, you didn't really go to high school—you went to junior school, and after junior school, you'd go to work. If you were very fortunate, or if your parents were moderately well off, comparatively, you might have gone to a high school at that point.

I went to junior school. I was fairly bright, and I was also encouraged for what I think is a rather interesting reason: The nuns and the priests thought that I was potentially seminary material. But by the time I finished junior school to go to high school, my mother couldn't afford to pay for it because my parents had already separated, largely for economic reasons. The family broke up in 1937, and attempts at repair did not work.

White students, as far as I know, didn't have to pay, but coloreds did. However, an old friend of my mother's was on the school board—a kind of parent-teacher supervising committee. I think what happened was that he recommended that she should fake my age, because if you were fifteen you had to pay, but if you were fourteen, you didn't. This enabled me to go high school, at least for one year. I then won a scholarship, which paid for me for the last two years of high school.

And then—this surprised me—I won a scholarship to university, and in South Africa you generally didn't get those. They were a lot less commonplace than in the United States. It went by grades, and you had to be number one or two out of 100 students or whatever. So it was an achievement. Although I didn't pay much attention to it then, I realize now that without it I would never have gone to university. A Catholic priest had volunteered that if my mother could not find the money to send me to university, that they would send me. Winning the scholarship meant that I did not need their money. I was relieved, because I didn't want to be committed to anyone.

I attended the South African Native College—later Fort Hare

University College—the only black university in South Africa, and indeed in Southern Africa. So people from Kenya, even from West Africa, Nigeria, were sending their students to Fort Hare. After four years I won a scholarship for a Master of Arts degree—but as a Catholic, I was disqualified. Nevertheless, I graduated with distinction with a double major, English and Psychology. And it was at Fort Hare that I first became conscious of outstanding black athletes and began to make the comparison between those who are on the South African Olympic team and those who are kept off because of their color.

After I graduated, I started teaching, from 1946 to 1948, at Paterson High School, the same school from which I had matriculated. When the apartheid government came into power in 1948, the differences that had existed before were suddenly exacerbated. You had a new system—virtually a Nazi system—imposed by people who supported Hitler during the Second World War. They were now running the country. So even had I chosen not to be in collision with the system, the system was in fact becoming so much worse that you could not avoid collision with it. I began to challenge apartheid in education, because there was black education, white education, and brown education, and each one was different. And the brown one was much worse than any white one, and slightly better than any black one. So again, you had this variation. Eventually of course, I was banned from teaching and the government decided that I was a dangerous person. Their own language was, "unfit to teach young minds." Obviously because they wanted a different kind of teaching for young minds!

"Do you have the stamina?"

After the apartheid government came to office, it passed a law saying that all cities have to be white and any non-whites living in the city must get out. They were called black spots—they had to be bulldozed flat. Blacks entering the city at night were arrested. The phrase was "white by night." So you have this blatant racism and the whole notion of an *übermensch* coming straight out of Nazi Germany—and these types had inherited this.

So there I was confronting apartheid in sports, confronting it in education, and finally, even in housing. It was an inevitable collision. It came for me at a meeting in the City Hall, where people were called and told, "You know, you're going to have to get out of the city. But don't worry, we'll find housing for you out in the boondocks." Sadly, there were blacks who'd been found and been promised that they'll get the best houses in the boondocks. So they were ready to be used to sell the project to the other blacks.

I was in the hall, where this whole business was taking place, and I walked up to the front and demanded to be heard. I went to the stage and I took the mic and I took over the meeting. It's the same city hall where I made my first public speech. I had been active in various ways, but this was a major event. The following day was a Sunday, the day I regularly played chess with another teacher. He said to me, "I heard you last night, and you were good. I've got only one question." He said, "Do you have the stamina?" I liked that, because it really was a challenge. Of course, one couldn't answer then. You didn't really know how long you would be going. You could only say, "Well, I think I have it, you know." There was no certainty about it.

We led a quite successful opposition. We were able to mobilize the people, especially through the Parent Teacher Associations, the PTAs, to challenge the government and get them to retreat on some issues. Unfortunately, there were sell-outs in our own ranks, and there were always a few compromisers as well.

But in a curious way, it's through sports that I became aware of the discrimination that existed by law, as opposed to day-to-day interactions. I got marvelous insight from a colleague who was a Marxist and quite important—Erik Ernstzen. He was a colored, of course, but he had been educated at Cape Town University, which at that time admitted some coloreds.

Trotskyism vs. Stalinism

When I was growing up, South Africa already had a pretty strong Trotskyist movement, which coexisted with a pretty strong Stalinist movement. In the 1920s, people came from Britain to form labor unions in South Africa—such as Bill Andrews, a leading Communist. This was the heyday of the Labor Party in Britain, with Ramsay McDonald as prime minister. It was also the era of Bernard Shaw, and the Fabian socialists, Beatrice and Sidney Webb. Plus, you had Marxists coming to South Africa, who had fled from Eastern Europe and the pogroms. This led to an exciting injection of two kinds of Lefts—a Trotskyist Left and a Stalinist Left.

The Communist Left, interestingly, decided to target white mineworkers. But there was a logic behind it. The theory was that the way to win workers to communism was an alliance with white labor. But when white labor said, "We don't want black labor to be promoted to skilled jobs," this created a crisis in the Communist Party that persisted throughout the 1920s.

Later, a Trotskyist group emerged that was bucking the Communist International on other issues. There was a strong Trotskyist faction around Cape Town University, which later initiated the NLL, the National Liberation League. They had very stimulating seminars—very open, so that Stalinists could participate. They published a paper that was quite exciting.

These were people who were studying not just Marx, but also conflict—ideological conflict. It was quite a sophisticated Left, and I was not only reading Marx, but also Trotsky's *Revolution Betrayed*, Isaac Deutscher's biography of Trotsky, and Mao as well. There was a lively debate that actually extended over a period of twenty to thirty years. By the time I came into it as a student under the influence of high school teachers, it had already been going on for a long time.

Allison Drew's book *Discordant Comrades* traces the 1930s split between the Communist League of South Africa and another group, the Spartacus Club. They developed a thesis and a conflict about the relative importance of the proletariat versus the peasantry. This was a major ideological debate on the Left. In the 1930s, the groups had sent their thesis to Trotsky, exiled in Mexico, asking him to adjudicate the conflict—and he responded. Here's where it gets sticky, because some people say he came down on the side of the peasantry, others say he came down for the proletariat, and the third party says his adjudication document was tampered with in the process of returning it. This bred all kinds of conflict on the Trotskyist Left. The South African Trotskyists were further separated organizationally as a result of segregation. One group was colored; the other was African, because communications were difficult.

The significance in South Africa was that people took sides, either on the side of Trotsky and the Fourth International, or with Moscow and the Stalinist thesis—and this is where the South African Left is from thence forward always dominated by a Stalinist line. If you challenged this line, you were expelled from the South African Communist Party. Edward Roux's book, *Time Longer than Rope,* is a fair account of what happened. The ANC essentially took a Stalinist position.

What this meant in South Africa in political terms is that the Trotskyist Fourth International adopted a policy of non-collaboration with the government at the time when the ANC adopted entryist politics—that is, that you would collaborate with apartheid and try to get power. This debate played out in a hundred different ways over many months, many years.

I was part of the Trotskyist Fourth International movement via the Anti-CAD movement, to which the Teachers League of South Africa was affiliated. It was called Anti-CAD, because it opposed the Colored Affairs Department, through which the government was systematizing the division between colored and African. Many organizations had not had that barrier previously.

The African Stalinists in the South African Communist Party went into the ANC. But briefly there was a combination of the two currents called the AAC—the All African Convention, which tried to merge the Stalinists and Trotskyist groups by more of a loose coalition than anything else, but which later became part of two different groups.

There was a third organization active in education, the overtly collaborative Teachers' Educational and Professional Association. Their approach was: "We get the jobs, we get the principalships, we get the promotions, we work with the government." The ANC's was a political position. They said, "We collaborate with these guys, not as sell-outs, but as ways of challenging them." Ours was a non-collaboration position—that we would challenge them by not collaborating.

The wing of Anti-CAD that I belonged to had two subdivisions. One was specifically for teachers, the TLSA, and the other one was called Parent Teacher Associations, the PTAs. The PTAs would bring in a lot of workers that were not coming via a union.

There was quite a good labor group, trade unions, plus a good ed-
ucational group. We had a body of unions, which then came to-
gether under the Fourth International rubric—though they were
never called the Fourth International. Others were together under
the ANC. In each of them, there would have been educational
groups, labor groups, even church groups. In 1950, right about the
time when I made the speech at City Hall, I joined for the first time
the Teachers' League, which had branches all over the country. I
became editor of the journal of the branch of the Teachers' League
in Port Elizabeth, which gave me something of a role. The journal,
Education News, became a voice for the local radical position.

Working with the ANC

In the early 1950s, the ANC suddenly assumed the ascendancy.
They did so by two things. One was the 1952 Defiance Campaign,
which was really initiated by the South African Indian Congress,
the SAIC, as a faction of the Congress Alliance, which insisted that
the Gandhian method was the one that would build the movement.
The other factor was the 1955 Freedom Charter.

The ANC was becoming strong, not as a Stalinist body, but
more as a Gandhian one. The Gandhian tactics of the Defiance
Campaign brought them membership, gave them exposure and visi-
bility. Plus, it was a reasonable approach. It didn't use arms—it was
a nonviolent approach to change people's hearts. All of this meant
that the Stalinist wing gained the ascendancy, and the Trotskyists
continued to decline.

If the Trotskyists had engaged in their own campaign of a simi-
lar sort, they might have been equally visible. That wasn't the case.
They did create the Anti-CAD to fight what they saw as the cre-
ation of a new colored Bantustan. So they did have a campaign,
but it was really a very narrow one. It was mainly focused on the
Cape, rather than the Transvaal or Natal, whereas the ANC was
engaging in a national campaign.

Anti-CAD was led mainly by teachers, because the first thing
the government did was to create a colored Bantustan and call the
colored teachers together, to say, "We are going to use you to cre-
ate this Colored Affairs Department. You will be well paid, get
promotions, become principals of all the schools." All of the perks

were there. This meant that the Trotskyist group had to exhaust all
of its energy fighting the betrayal in its own ranks. So while the
ANC was engaging in a national campaign, the Trotskyists were
engaging in a provincial campaign. That is one explanation for
their decline—there are others as well.

When the ANC and Anti-CAD met, the debate was over a sin-
gle issue: non-collaboration. The Trotskyists would say, "You don't
collaborate with the government;" the ANC would say, "You col-
laborate if it gets you your aims, whatever your aims may be." So
there was no blanket dismissal of collaboration on their part.

The other issue, rather absurdly, was structure. The ANC in-
sisted on a unitary structure and central discipline. Anti-CAD al-
ways insisted on a federal structure, on the grounds that you would
be less vulnerable to attack. Any unit could be attacked without de-
stroying the whole struggle. We had incredible, hours-long debates
going on over these two issues.

There were two groups, the *Torch,* and the TLSA journal,
which had very sophisticated critiques of the South African politi-
cal situation—what the government was doing, what people in the
townships were doing. Out of that would come these definitions
and dismissals—they dismissed the Defiance Campaign earlier, as
just another adventure.

The Trotskyist groups also defined the Freedom Charter as
phony, and said it didn't mean anything. I found myself in disagree-
ment with them. They were, I regret to say, quite academic. For
them it was heavily theoretical. For real activism, you had to look
to the ANC.

I helped organize these debates in Port Elizabeth. An Indian
businessman bought a hall, hoping to turn it into a dance hall and
make a lot of money. But it stood idle on Sundays. So he came to
me and said, "Find a way of using it on any Sunday." So I started
the Twentieth Century Club, with meetings on jazz, Buddhism,
whatever. I was also working with the ANC, the Pan-Africanist
Congress (PAC), and Anti-CAD, and would invite people from
these different camps.

Once, I got a marvelous speaker from the ANC, Themba
Mqota. He said, "I will speak to you on: 'Political Consciousness,
Its Use and Abuse.'" I said, "What the hell is he going to talk

about?" He gave a brilliant lecture attacking the Trotskyists. Not so much from the Stalinist point of view, but about consciousness. He said, "You guys are bright, and you've got all the theory, but you never get to do anything. So your consciousness is wasted. You are academic theorists, armchair activists." Unfortunately, he was right.

What I am trying to say is that I was keeping an open house. I was open. I was neither Trotskyist nor Stalinist—although I was with Anti-CAD, I didn't feel I was locked into that position. I was open to all ideas. So when the Freedom Congress of the People came along, and with it the notion of a Freedom Charter, I was not opposed to it. I was not wholly bought into it, but it was evidence of my openness. I was open to anything that would help the struggle.

Drafting the Freedom Charter

My closest contact with the ANC for a long time was Govan Mbeki, because we lived in the same town, Port Elizabeth. We had a very friendly relationship. When I came out of Fort Hare University, I went back there and renewed my connection with him. Mbeki had been a teacher, but was thrown out of education by the government. He then set up a little store in a rural African area that was run by his wife. He had a degree, a B.A. in economics, from Fort Hare, which he received prior to my own time there. Govan would go up to Johannesburg regularly, for meetings of the SACP Central Committee.

It was through Mbeki that I got involved in drafting the ANC's Freedom Charter, though I make no claim to being a major player in the process. I was in Port Elizabeth, and we had a whole slew of proposals to send. I participated in selecting and improving the language—adding demands for more jobs, better transport, etc. I saw it as a very good way to define what the struggle was about. People now allege that the charter was really written by the SACP. My view—and I was part of the process—was that we were drafting proposals to be incorporated in the charter. To me it was a genuine process. I was working with Mbeki and Z.K. Matthews, who was a member of the central executive of the ANC, but not the SACP. To me, it was a purely legitimate exercise.

My other connection with the ANC and the South African Communist Party came through a classmate at Fort Hare who was

involved with Stalinist politics—Alfred Hutchinson—who was
black. He majored in English and graduated with distinction a year
after me. And I had graduated with distinction in English also. We
had a kind of affinity that was literary. But he came out of a much
tougher environment—an African ghetto, as opposed to the col-
ored ghetto. He had long been associated with the SACP in the
Transvaal in the Johannesburg area, whereas I was from the East-
ern Cape. The one friend we shared was Ruth First, a leading
member of the SACP who was the editor of *Fighting Talk*. When
he said to her that she should print something by me about sports,
the people on the editorial board said, "Sports really has nothing to
do with politics. We don't have to waste our time with it." But
Hutch, as we called him, kept nagging Ruth. So eventually, and
rather reluctantly, I appeared in *Fighting Talk*. But the board itself
was not very enthused. They thought sports were going nowhere.

I also wrote a sports column for the Communist Party (CP)
newspaper. Of course, it wasn't known as the CP newspaper, and it
had to change names each time it was banned: from the *Guardian*
to the *Clarion* to *People's World* to *Advance* to *New Age* to *Spark*.
I wrote under the name of A. de Bruin—"a brown" in Afrikaans—
over a three-year period before I was banned in 1961. The column,
which appeared on the back page, was ostensibly about sports re-
sults, but also about the politics of race and sports as I was build-
ing the South African Sports Association (SASA).

In 1961, I wrote an article for the ANC's *Fighting Talk* called
"Sports: Threat to the Security of the State." The interesting thing
is that I was approached by the ANC to write it—and then re-
proached for it. The reason they gave was: "You are giving away
the game—this is our strategy." It is a light piece. I actually chal-
lenged the boss of the Olympic committee to speak at a meeting of
SASA. He attended, and was so confident—he said, "You guys are
never going to get into the Olympics." I replied, "Mr. Honey, de-
spite your name, things are going to get very bitter." I was alerting
people in the community. A lot of people didn't see the significance
of that issue, and that's still true today.

Hutchinson became a member of the ANC executive. He intro-
duced me to Ruth First, Walter Sisulu, Nelson Mandela, and Albert
Luthuli, who was then the president of the ANC. They, along with

Hutch, were among those arrested in 1956 and made defendants in the Treason Trial.

During the trial, friends of the accused were allowed to travel with them to court on buses that were escorted by the police. We may or may not have really belonged there, but we sneaked onto the buses anyway, and we would chat.

Along the way, Luthuli had a game where he would ask people what they would do with the Voortrekker monument to the Afrikaner pioneers in Pretoria. It is a huge thing, like a cathedral—and horrifying, with a sort of socialist realism in reverse. There is something of an altar in the middle. One day each year, the sun strikes the hole in the roof on the altar—on the 16th of December, the anniversary of the day in 1838 when the Dutch massacred the Zulus at the Battle of Blood River.

As the buses went past the monument, Luthuli would say, "When we take over, what are we going to do with it?" Hutchinson said, "It should become a slaughterhouse." Someone else said, "I want it to be a jail, and I want to be the chief jailer and administer the whippings." Someone else said, "It should be a creche—a nursery, to become a contrast to what it was under apartheid."

Hutchinson escaped while on trial. Although the ANC policy was to go through the trial to expose apartheid, the organization did permit some of the accused to escape. At that stage, he may have defied the ANC and escaped without their permission. He was in love with an English woman named Hazel Grant. She drove him across the border in a car without brakes—that's a remarkable story by itself. I wrote about them in a story called "Walking Home to Mofolo" that was published in *Fighting Talk*. Hutchinson later died of alcoholism in Ghana. Many exiles drank themselves to death. Alcohol was a panacea for them.

Quite separately from all this, I was formally offered membership in the CP by Govan Mbeki, and again by a man called Naphtoli Bennun, who was known as Toli. He said to me that he had been authorized by the Central Committee to offer me membership in the party. I declined. This was after Sharpeville—in 1961. Everyone was underground, and I was part of the ANC underground.

It was in that period that Nelson Mandela was a fugitive. During some of that time, he hid in my house. He was confined to one room to make sure that no one could see him through the window. To kill time, Nelson—who had been a very good amateur boxer— taught my sons to box.

I had differences with the ANC leadership from time to time— for example, when the ANC decided to put up white candidates in parliament to represent blacks. Of course the right to vote had been taken from blacks as early as 1936. Along about 1956 came the idea of having whites in parliament representing blacks, and the government agreed. What is very interesting—and very reveal- ing—is that the SACP agreed to the deal.

Govan Mbeki came to discuss this with me when I was sick in bed. My wife, May, let him into the bedroom, and he sat down in a chair and started lecturing me. He said, "You must understand, we are going to have whites representing blacks. It has been offered by the government and we are going to accept it." I said, "I am going to oppose it—blacks should be represented by blacks. It's a bad deal." So he said to me "We're going to do it anyway. This is going to be the party line and the Congress line."

So I opposed them. And for a long time, I was on a kind of blacklist of both the ANC and the SACP, because I was known as someone who was undisciplined—insubordinate. And I didn't mind it. I kept doing my thing. With Govan, it was not personal. We agreed to disagree.

I had a similar dispute with the ANC in 1962, after I discovered that Avery Brundage was refusing to reply to any letters from SASA, because he said that he only replied to letters from Olympic com- mittees. When I proposed that we change the name of SASA to in- clude the word "Olympic," I got a message from the ANC saying, "Don't do it." The argument was: "SASA is so well known and so well respected, why give it a new name? Who ever heard of South African Non-Racial Olympic Committee (SANROC)? It's going to have to start all over again educating people."

They were adamant about another argument as well, but I main- tained that was the way to go. Again, they sent me a message that, "We're going to have to discipline you for not following the line." I went ahead and did it anyway. Again, I bucked them. My own atti- tude has been consistent. And I still remained friendly with Govan. Of course, I could only join the ANC when I was in Britain. Prior to that, no non-Africans were allowed to join the ANC. I could only give donations.

At what point did I actually make the break? When did I say, to heck with the Anti-CAD—from now on, I am solidly ANC, even when I am unhappy with what they are doing? Sharpeville. The day in 1960 when sixty-nine people were machine-gunned to death. After that, I said, "Well, I'll go all the way." To me, at that time, prison was irrelevant. It was not so much ideological. It was a matter of social injustice.

Sharpeville

After Sharpeville, the ANC went from passive resistance to armed struggle with the formation of the Umkhonto we Sizwe group. But it should be remembered that Sharpeville was not generated by the ANC, but by the PAC. The PAC had been a branch of the ANC that broke away, because they alleged that the ANC was dominated by the Communist Party, whereas the PAC was interested in the black bourgeoisie.

When the ANC called for a national demonstration against the Pass Laws for March 30, 1960, the PAC called for a demonstration on the same issue for March 21, preempting the ANC. The sixty-nine people who were killed that day had been called out by the PAC. Preempting the ANC was, I think, bad politics on the PAC's part—cynical politics. I am not taking sides, but this is the evidence. Today, if you read the history, you get the impression that it was ANC members who were the victims of Sharpeville, and that they were the actors in Sharpeville. Neither was true.

Sports—a threat to apartheid?

I was beginning to challenge apartheid in education, because there was black education, white education, and brown education, and each one was different. And the brown one was much worse than any white one, and slightly better than any black one. So again you had this variation.

Parallel to this, I was interested in the sports issue, and actually developed a sports organization. The sports thing—and this is true of most everything I've done—dropped in my lap. We had a typically colored education system, rather like your black schools in the U.S., and each school supposedly had a bit of sports. Of course you had sports activities, as was the case of Paterson High School, where I had been a student and returned as a teacher in 1946. But they didn't have any teacher who organized sports, although they were supposed to have a sports master. I found myself doing it because of the absence of anybody else.

One of my colleagues, Aldridge Adamson, had just come back from Europe, where he had been working. He had been in London at the time of the Empire and Olympic Games, the first Olympics after the war. This was 1948, and the Helsinki Olympics of 1952 were approaching. I was beginning to be aware of the whole race and sports issue and its significance. Also on the same staff was another teacher who was a Marxist, Harry Jeftha, who also was a strong influence on me. He pointed out the fact that the Olympic charter makes it illegal for any participating country to discriminate on the grounds of race.

I put the pieces together. The facts of apartheid in South Africa were in contradiction with the Olympic governing rules. That got me into the Olympic issue, for which many people know me chiefly, having pretty much spearheaded the expulsion of South Africa from the Olympic Games in 1970.

I was never a good athlete. Let's not kid ourselves about that. But I was reasonably good at organizing, so I'd arrange interschool matches. That's how it began. My team against your team, this high school against that high school. Eventually it expanded and, very significantly I think, it encouraged colored kids to play against African schools. So really I was crossing that barrier—breaking out of one ghetto to get into another ghetto. The political component was there, but it was not defined as such. I ended up coaching the school team that won a trophy in softball—an American sport, ironically. From that, I began to make connections. There's soccer matches, then there's cricket, there's rugby, there's track, once-a-year track meets, and so on. Out of that came association with a number of schools and a number of programs for sports.

Gradually I had more work to do. I was not really looking for power—it's just that the work was accumulating. You had the city sports union, and then you had a provincial union, and then you had the national union, so I found myself being elected to various positions, ending up on about seven national boards of sport—tennis, cricket, and others. This created one person who knew what was happening in several sports, who could coordinate at both the provincial level with five provinces or at the national level. Usually I opted for a secretary's position. I am not interested in the prestige positions, because there is no real work there. The real work is with the secretary—or if you have a good assistant secretary, you really can get a lot done.

I ended up with a reputation of being the most efficient secretary in any sport—but it's actually my assistants who did most of the work. I just got the credit for it. I couldn't have done it without their help. The secret was not to create organizations, but to find what was there and to coordinate—to try and resolve clashes about ego and so on. That was important, because blacks of all shades were so demeaned in that society, one of the few bits of prestige you could get was in sports—to be the chairman of the sports body, or the chairmen of provincial sports, and finally, president of the national sports body. But observe what was happening: You had colored national cricket, African national cricket, Indian national cricket. Malays even had a subdivision. So one of the problems was to find a way to get these people to work together without anyone having to surrender the prestige they had gotten out of their position.

Eventually we ended up with a meeting of twenty of these national bodies, all presidents, all very protective of their egos. I'm rather proud of the solution I came up with. I proposed someone who was from a minor sport, whom everybody disregarded. They all settled on him as the president, provided they were all the vice presidents. So we had twenty vice presidents, and a president who happened to be a weight lifter, which was not a highly regarded sport by the other guys. They didn't feel any competition from him. The organization became SASA—the South African Sports Association, with Chris de Broglio as its first president. I was offered the presidency, but I said no, thank you. I wanted to be the secretary. I knew that was where the work was to be done, provided I got a good assistant secretary. I was very lucky. I got a marvelous man, Arthur Latchman, who was self-effacing and who could do everything that needed to be done. We used to send out minutes twenty-four hours after there had been a meeting. Some of our success, certainly, was bound up with our efficiency.

Ultimately, I did become president of an organization—oddly, as the result of my banning in 1961. I got a letter from the minister of justice ordering me to resign from all organizations—sports, politics, you name it, even church organizations. I had to resign from everything, and I did. At this point, SASA was without a president; it had a vice president who really didn't do any work, and twenty vice presidents all over the country. They had prestige in their own sports, but they were not really doing anything for SASA.

Meanwhile, SASA had been writing to Avery Brundage, president of the International Olympic Committee (IOC), about racism on the South African Olympic team. But we were ignored, and we didn't know why. I asked Rabbi Andre Ungar, a friend of mine, to talk to Brundage, while he was in Europe. Ungar, a Hungarian who had been in Budapest during Nazi rule, was sympathetic to our cause. Later, he got into trouble in South Africa for comparing the ghettos of South Africa to the ghettos of Hungary and was ordered to leave the country, and his visa was withdrawn. The chief rabbi in South Africa thanked the government for expelling him, because he was an embarrassment to the Jewish community in South Africa.

Ungar was sympathetic to our cause. He asked Brundage, "Why are you not replying to any letters from South Africa?" And Brundage gave an excellent answer: "I only write to any organization which is an Olympic association. Anything else I ignore."

My response was to say, "Let's become an Olympic committee. If that's what we need, then that's what we'll be." Now the IOC said there was already an Olympic committee in South Africa—all white, of course. We said, "That's all right, we are the non-racial Olympic committee." That's how SANROC came into being—the South African Non-Racial Olympic Committee. Immediately, ironically, the president of the all-white Olympic committee contacted me and said, "You can't do this. How can you have a non-racial Olympic committee? There's no such thing in the world." I said, "Fine, if you will admit us, then obviously we don't need a non-racial Olympic committee." We got nowhere, of course, so we went ahead and formed SANROC.

Here's the irony. Just about that time I was banned. It was therefore illegal for me to belong to any organization. I suggested to SASA: "Form SANROC, and make me be the honorary president." It's just a name—I won't do any work, because I'm banned, but they might as well give me this link. So I became honorary president, with no work to do, no function, nothing. I wrote the minister of justice to ask if it would be a contravention of my banning order if I were elected an honorary president with no work to do. His reply was one line, a letter from his secretary. It says, "The minister of justice does not dispense free legal advice, yours truly." That was it.

I chose to read this as meaning that the SANROC presidency was not something I was forbidden to do. So I was elected honorary president with no work. Later, fortunately, I had legitimacy to operate all over the world as the president of SANROC, because I had been formally elected. But it was pure accident. It was a result of trying to get around the banning order.

Banned, shot, imprisoned

I was banned in October 1961 under the Suppression of Communism Act. I was arrested in 1963, sentenced in 1964, and released in July 1965, so it was just an eighteen-month sentence. I spent some time in the hospital, of course, because I'd been shot. It was about a year in Robben Island prison in the same section as Nelson Mandela, breaking stones together.

First, I was arrested by the secret police and charged with the crime of contravening a banning order. I had helped arrange a meeting at the official South African Olympic Committee offices, and planned to leave before it began. But it was a setup—I was arrested on the spot and accused of having been at the meeting.

I was released on bail on the condition that I sign the police station register daily to prove that I was in town, because I was not allowed to leave Johannesburg. But then they passed a new law, called the Indefinite Detention Act, which said the government could jail you for 180 days, and then upon release you could be re-arrested and jailed for another 180 days. It went on and on.

I was strongly urged to leave South Africa. I was told, "This time, when you go in, they're going to keep you. So you better get out." Some people were getting out—members of the Communist Party and so on were getting out. So I escaped by signing the book on a Sunday morning at the police station. Then, John Harris, a colleague in SANROC who was white, drove me across the border to Swaziland, a British colony. The officials told me, "You have to be out in thirty days. We don't care where you go. But you're not going to be here, or we're going to throw you out." They would have sent me back to South Africa.

To avoid that, I made the arrangements to try and get to a meeting of the IOC to present the SANROC case. The meeting was originally scheduled for Nairobi but was moved to Baden-Baden in Germany, a sort of holiday resort. To try to get to Baden-Baden, I went to Mozambique, then a colony of Portugal, and planned to fly from what used to be Lourenço Marques, now Maputo. But when I got to the border, I was arrested. I said, "I have a ticket, all I have to do is get to the airport and get on a plane."

But the Portuguese secret police told me, "We have an arrangement with the South African police. They catch our fugitives and we catch their fugitives." I was kept in Lourenço Marques for three days and interrogated. I was photographed by INTERPOL, and my fingerprints were taken—the whole works. When I said, "I want to go to court, why are you arresting me?" they said, "Don't waste your time trying to go to court. We are the court."

I then went on a hunger strike. I was kept in a very comfortable cell, but I refused to eat. After the third day, I was interrogated by the top man in the PIDE—their secret police. They said, "All right, we don't know what to do with you. We'll return you to Swaziland, because that's where you came from. So we're just going to dump you there." But the guards who were sitting in the back of the police wagon, black guys with machine guns, said, "you're going to South Africa."

I was handcuffed in the back of a Toyota truck with these guys sitting beside me. They drove me to the border—not the Swaziland border, but a place on the border between South Africa and Mozambique. The guys who had arrested me at the South African Olympic offices were there to meet me.

I was interrogated and taken to a little court in Middleburg, near the border, and charged with various crimes, including leaving the country without permission. Then I was taken to Johannesburg.

The police showed me their armpit holsters and guns. They said, "Look, we're not going to handcuff you, because we're hoping you'll <u>try to escape</u> and <u>we'll kill you.</u>" One sat in the back of the car and chatted with me while the other was driving. Eventually, the two cops were up front, and I was sitting in the back. They drove back to Johannesburg via the capital, Pretoria, in order to present me to the head of the Bureau of State Security (BOSS) General Hendricks van der Bergh. He took a look at me and said, "OK, take him away."

That was the end of it. He was the head of the secret police, roughly the equivalent of the head of the CIA. He was not your regular police. He was right at the top, the boss of bosses. They had their own headquarters in Pretoria, which is called Waghuis—the watch house.

After they presented me to van der Bergh, they took me to Johannesburg. I was in the back seat; they were in the front. I checked the door handles, and they had them locked, so there was no way out of there. But I really wasn't thinking at that stage of escaping. I was more anxious about disappearing into prison with no one even knowing about it. For me, the problem was how to let people know I was back in the country. Because in Swaziland, I read the reports that the people in Soweto were celebrating my escape.

To get out word of my arrest, I tried to pass messages on the backs of a cigarette packs until I realized that it wasn't working. So I decided to escape at 5 o'clock in the afternoon in Johannesburg, when the streets were busy with thousands of people—commuters and workers—when we were right in the center of town. Of course, the police guarding me had guns, but I figured they couldn't shoot me in a crowd—it would be too risky.

I took a chance there, thinking I could get away with it. They gave me my suitcase, which I had taken to Swaziland and Mozambique. As I got out and walked to the police station where I had originally been kept in John Vorster Square, I limped along as if I were struggling with a heavy suitcase. Then I went down into a crouching position, like a sprinter, and it caught them by surprise. Before they knew it, I was gone, into the crowd.

They pursued, but I actually got away—two blocks, maybe as much as four blocks ahead. But I made a stupid mistake. Somewhere nearby was a little Indian restaurant where I knew the folks and knew they would hide me, because they were part of the resistance. I doubled back on my tracks in order to get to the restaurant, the Taj on Commissioner Street. I thought I'd shaken off the police, but I hadn't. One of them, Warrant Officer Helberg, was pretty elderly, but he had a gold medal in marksmanship. As I rounded the corner, I ran into him. And he shot me—instantly, with no hesitation at all.

An ambulance came, but when they took a look at me, they put the stretcher back in the ambulance and left—it was a whites-only ambulance, and they refused to take me. I had to wait, bleeding, for a non-white ambulance to take me to the hospital.

The bullet entered my back and came out of my chest. A "through and through wound," as the doctors called it. I collapsed and lost a lot of blood, of course, and ended up in the hospital. The shot was just below the lung. The lung collapsed, but the bullet didn't penetrate it. It went through the intestines three times, which led to adhesions, which still bother me.

I think the gamble was a justified one, and I might even have gotten away with it. But I think I was trying to be overly clever— doubling back was not a smart thing to do. So I ended up first in the hospital and then in the Fort, the old prison, and eventually on Robben Island.

There I was kept in a single cell. I was with Mandela and about twenty-two others in the maximum-maximum section that was a particular part in the center of the prison. There were over 1,000 of us. Most were kept in big cells, about sixty to a cell. But some of us were kept in single cells.

Talking was prohibited. Once a week, when we had a shower— we had to run through the water, a kind of fire hose—we were able to talk. Of course, we spoke in spite of the guards. It was just a matter of not being caught, because if you were caught, you lost your food. Three meals would be taken away.

But that was in the 1960s, and conditions become much better later on. In fact, by the 1980s, they were actually having classes on Marxism. They had come a long way.

Documents

Letter from Balthazar Johannes Vorster, minister of justice, to Dennis Brutus
1961

NOTICE IN TERMS OF SUB-SECTION ONE OF SECTION NINE OF THE SUPPRESSION OF COMMUNISM ACT, 1950 (ACT NO. 44 OF 1950), AS AMENDED

WHEREAS in my opinion there is reason to believe that the achievement of the objects of communism would be furthered if you were to attend any gathering in any place within the Republic of South Africa or the territory of South-West Africa;

NOW THEREFORE, I, BALTHAZAR JOHANNES VORSTER, in my capacity as Minister of Justice for the Republic of South Africa, by virtue of the powers conferred upon me by sub-section one of section nine of the Suppression of Communism Act, 1950 (Act No. 44 of 1950), as amended, do hereby prohibit you from attending during a period of five years as from the date that this notice is delivered or tendered to you, any gathering in any place within the Republic of South Africa or the territory of South West Africa other than gatherings

a. of pupils of the Paterson High School, Port Elizabeth, assembled for the sole purpose of being instructed by you in the ordinary course of your duties at the said High School; and

b. of personnel of the said High School assembled for the sole purpose of dealing with the affairs of the School.

Given under my hand at _____ on this the _____ day of 1961.

Minister of Justice

To: Dennis A. Brutus,
20 Shell Street, Port Elizabeth.

Silent poets, strangled writers

Fighting Talk, January, 1963 (under the pseudonym, J.B. Booth)

In 1962, a fresh barbarism was perpetrated in South Africa. While the civilized world has repeatedly been shocked by revelations of the inhumanities committed here in the name of racial supremacy, the "Gagging Clause" of the Sabotage Act should move all humans to the profoundest disgust. It is a disgust which must find expression in action.

What does the Gagging Clause mean? And what can be done about it?

The General Laws Amendment Act—to give the Sabotage Act its official name—was aimed at those who seem in ANY WAY to change a state of society intolerable to the majority and portending destruction to all. A special clause in the Act enabled the Minister of Justice to gag those who might speak or write against the system of oppression which the world knows as apartheid. To date, the Minister has listed 102 persons. Nothing they say or write may be quoted or printed. Anyone printing whatever they say (or are purported to have said!) is liable to imprisonment. If they cause anything to be printed, they will be imprisoned themselves.

Silent poets

Among the 102 gagged are journalists, many of whom made their living by writing. They are no longer able to do so. Among them were numbered, too, novelists, short story writers and poets. All these people have been silenced. They may not utter, print or publish a single word in their own country. If their writings are published outside, the publications on entry into South Africa have to be mutilated and their words torn out.

Strangled throats

If the Act itself is directed against sabotage of the structure of apartheid, the gagging clause is itself a sabotage of the human spirit. Men and women are dammed to silence without a trial. They are forbidden to communicate their emotions, experiences and visions to their fellow men. Protest is strangled in the throat. The creative outpouring which could enrich the community is blasted.

True, in the context of the overall savagery and barbarism which "General Law" means in South Africa, this is a trifle. But no one in the world who cares for freedom of thought, speech and the human spirit can permit this particular act of barbarism to pass in silence.

It is important to know what Sabotage Act and the "Gagging Clause" in particular mean. It is more important that something should be done about them.

It would be unreasonable to look to the gagged for protest. But there are many more who are free to speak. They should speak out now.

Greasy smoke from the gas ovens drifted across bustling towns in Germany. It swirled across playgrounds and into classrooms and through the studious closes of the Universities. The atrocities went unheeded. We remember now with shame the absence of vigorous protest. No one who cares about freedom of the human sprit or the freedom of creative talent can remain silent before this ugly imitation of Nazi ugliness.

Writers in particular—a notoriously vocal tribe—should be the first to declare their opposition. Writers in South Africa should be in the lead. But the whole international community for all those who care for the arts or are in any way connected with them should register their protest.

Writers outside South Africa are in a particularly strong position. There are numerous ways in which they can demonstrate their disgust. It would be especially shameful for them if South Africa were allowed to preserve its disgustingly hypocritical façade of culture while at the same time perpetrating this rape on the human spirit.

Writers' action

What does this mean in practical terms? What can writers do? There are several possibilities. South African writers, and writers throughout the world, should first of all declare their opposition and contempt for this measure. They must go further and hold up this disgusting gallows to the contempt of the entire world.

And then, to demonstrate the genuineness of their opposition, they must both as individual writers and as a community of artists take action against the barbarians.

They must refuse to have their books sold in South Africa: they must refuse to grant performing rights for their works in South Africa's apartheid theaters, cinemas and concert halls: they must refuse to have any truck with apartheid in South Africa: and there must be a concerted international explosion of disgust against the cretinism and prostitution of the human spirit which exist in South Africa.

But this means turning South Africa into a cultural desert?

The alternative is to provide compost for the dungheap where noxious and strangling weeds proliferate.

What of profits? Of prestige? Of those with crusading zeal to bring humanism to the new Neanderthalers?

We shall see. We shall see how many high-sounding phrases are belied by a low greed for profits or prestige. We shall see how much crusading is mere cant.

How is it to be done? There are P.E.N. clubs throughout the world; there are Writers' and Artists' Guilds; there is the Congress for Cultural Freedom; most important of all there is the great international agency of UNECSO. If all these can be mobilized, a telling impact can be made.

It will not bring the "Baasskap" barbarians to their senses. But it will establish the contempt and opposition of the world. And it will hearten those who are trying to keep alive the flicker of human values in South Africa as we go down into the Pit.

It is a small flicker. But if the flame of freedom is ever to burn again in South Africa, it will have to start with small beginnings. It will have to start in the conscience of a few individual writers in South Africa and all over the world.

It will have to start soon.

Negritude, literature and nationalism: A word from South Africa

Fighting Talk, October, 1962 (under the pseudonym, J.B. Booth)

At the Mbari conference at Ibadan recently—a milestone in the development of literature on our continent—no subject evoked livelier discussion than Negritude—the expression of a peculiar blackness or African-ness in literature which is related to matters like the development of an African personality and the cultivation of a recognizably African literature.

It is a subject on which the writers from the French-settled parts of Africa are most vocal and vehement—they have also supplied vital examples in both theory and practice.

But on this subject, South African writers are strangely silent. True, the trio of Lewis Nkosi, Zeke Mphahlele, and Bloke Modisane, effectively punctured the mystical aura which surrounds the concept—and in his "African Image" Zeke drove a truck through it. Yet it seems hardly adequate to dismiss the subject by pungent criticism: if it can excite the lively interest of a sizable proportion of the writers on our continent it surely deserves a little more careful analysis.

The origins of Negritude and its associated concepts are not hard to find: it might be easiest to sum them up in the typical Gallic tendency to ratiocination and the abstraction of theory from a small number of observed facts. It can also be partly explained by a reaction against European-ness or whiteness, the assertion of the black man's pride in his ancestry and blackness in defiance of the superiority and disdain which he encountered in many white circles—including the literati.

But certain aspects of the problem expressing Africa in literature are genuinely problematical. They amount, among others, to these: how does one express the atmosphere and customs of the people of Africa?: how does one avoid slavish imitation of "European" models?: to what extent should one conform to the standards set by "European" writers?: and how does one achieve a literature which is genuinely and peculiarly expressive of thought, custom and ideals in Africa?

At the risk of sounding charlatan, I begin my answers with the

assumption that the life of people on this continent is indeed differ-
ent in certain respects from that of people on other continents, and
that to express this life and the peculiar vitality of Africa is not only
a feasible but laudable aim, and that it is possible for Africa to
make its own contribution to world literature but offering a litera-
ture as great and universally human as that of any other continent.

Underlying the statement of the problem, and my partial reply
is a further assumption: that we can think of concepts such as
African nations and African nationalism.

This, it seems, to me, lies at the heart of the matter and it is the
failure to recognize its existence which makes discussion of subjects
like negritude and an African literature sterile and unfruitful.

But we had better have some clarity on what we mean by "na-
tionalism" in relation to literature.

Two quotations will help. The first is from the late Lionel For-
man, writing in *Liberation* in 1959: "The best way to achieve a fu-
sion of national cultures in the future into one culture, is to favor
the blossoming of many cultures first."

The second is from a recent publication by the African Na-
tional Bureau of Political and Social Studies: "African Nationalism
is evolutionary, dynamic and progressive (because) we recognize
that it is in itself restrictive and exclusive but as it evolves and pro-
gresses its dynamism makes it less restrictive and more inclusive
and finally becomes all-embracing."

This, it seems to me, is a good point to start from: that we must
recognize and accept the existence of nationalism—and be prepared
to use it and give expression to it—but that we must always be aware
that it is evolving into something more all-embracing in which we
can find the expression and ultimate fusion of many diverse cultures.

What does this mean in terms of literature?

I suggest that the writer make use of the material at hand—ma-
terial he knows and understands and loves. It means that the West
African, the Kenyan and the South African alike can depict in their
writing the milieu they know—and make it available to the world.
It means to write with understanding of the remnants of tribal cul-
ture where they exist, and the bustling life of the South African
proletariat—a peculiar fusion of European culture and the vestiges
of a tribal culture.

It means that we can speak freely and understandingly of what we know, and share our knowledge with the world. It means too that we must be sufficiently catholic to have a keen eye for and assimilate the diverse cultures which make up life on the African continent.

For the South African it means moving familiarly through the glassy exurbia of Nadine Gordimer with its surface glitter, as well as the missionary plaints of Paton's "Cry the Beloved Country;" through Peter Abrahams' faded stores of over-simplified images as well as the garbage of Zeke Mphahlele's "Second Avenue." They are all part of our continent—our own special world.

Finally, it means that out of this rich and varied soil will come the literature which will be Africa's special contribution to world literature.

Little has been written or said on this subject: it is uncharted waters and one sets sail perilously: but it is time that we struck out and began to fix a course.

the literature, one contribution

In a Cape packing shed

Fighting Talk, August, 1961 (under the pseudonym, D.A.B.)

[Editors' note: This article is deliberately vague because of state repression. It describes the first National Convention of the Colored People, an organization aligned with the African National Congress. Banned from being held in Cape Town as scheduled, the Convention met on a tobacco farm, July 8–10, 1961.]

We drove the 400-odd miles through the cold night although the banning of Convention had come through that morning. We talked of many things, but chiefly of how to persuade the organizers to set the alternative date of Convention as early as possible. For we knew that the sponsors—and this was one of the most significant things about the Convention movement—came from the section of "respectable" coloreds; professional people mostly, who had none of the experience of bannings, raids and general police persecution familiar to those long in the political struggle: they were people who had gone on hoping for a change of heart, or simply for something to turn up. Certainly the grim business of defiance of the government was new to them. We thought they would need persuading, and planned for it.

We were soon to discover how wrong we were.

We got to Cape Town, grubby and travel-groggy, to be revital-ized almost immediately by the news that efforts were being made to hold Convention, in spite of the ban, on a mission station outside the prescribed area. Details would be given to us at a rendezvous.

Off we went, to find a large number of others chatting appar-ently aimlessly outside a hall in Athlone. There was a relaxed air about the little social knots that did not auger well. They came from various areas—Durban, Johannesburg and Worcester were singled out for us, but they tended to group according to political leanings. So we found ourselves—reputedly fire-eaters—regarded with interest and some little suspicion. The conservative elements (those we feared would set a limit on our demands) seemed in the majority. Periodically, there were rumors of arrangements, only to be countermanded by others, and still we stood around in the bleak sunlight, scuffing the sand.

Hopefield, the mission station outside Malmesbury on which we pinned our hopes, fell through, as the booking of the Malmesbury townhall had earlier. Finally, the word was passed: "kalbaskraal!" We drifted to our cars and haphazardly formed a convoy.

Hopes picked up then but not much. Also, the distrust had been dampening.

So out on the national road to Malmesbury, through the rolling lands clothed with the dark green of sprouting wheat under a bright sun quite without warmth.

We turned off to a dirt road, the dust billowing in red clouds behind us until we came to a fork. Then out into the waist-high grass to scout around for some indication. There was a plot with rusted wire around it and inside a few rough wooden crosses; the farm cemetery we had been told to look out for. So we turned and arrived at a building red-brown with mud and bricks, under the pale gray shadows of some scraggy trees. But there were no other cars there, and we knew with a sinking anxiety that we had taken the wrong road. If anything happened, we would be out of it.

A small farm boy who turned up was taken aboard after he had agreed to show us "the place."

Back along the dirt road, then along another, and so passed a tree with a board nailed to it: "Dassenberg." Perhaps, I mused, the name would still be famous. A turn off the road through the long grass, then a low out-building and beyond it a sudden concourse of cars, at ease and glittering in the cold sunlight. We had arrived.

Already, in the circular depression in the grass, the crowd was gathering, boxes and chairs were being planted shakily in the grass, a chair and table were being brought for the chairman to sit squinting into the sun.

Then, with a prayer and a little initial fumbling in procedure, we were off, papers were being read and discussed, resolutions were being formulated.

At the back of our mind was the thought: we've pulled it off! For now at any rate. There might still be police interference. Some other law might still be invoked (Riotous Assemblies or what-not) but at any rate we were at Convention and it was under way.

Once it got under way, it moved at top speed. In retrospect, the degree of understanding and cooperation was to prove unbelievable. Above all, the economy of discussion (on the whole), the businesslike approach, the grasp of the bare bones of our problems, brushing aside the frills that clothe and disguise them.

Twice, on the first day and on the second day, Convention steered dangerously close to shipwreck. On the franchise, it was a small right wing, pledged to a qualified franchise; on nationalization, it was the vocal left. Each time we hammered out a formula which was accepted as the true expression of Convention and which did not abate our demands for a democracy one jot.

From the first discussion came the immediate understanding: We are South Africans and our concern is with South Africa and all South Africans. After that, as the records of Convention will show, there was no looking back.

So the afternoon raced away with the sun sinking, the shadows lengthening across the chill grass, and the evening so cold that it seemed that liquid cold was being poured into our depression from the edges of the mountains. Fatigue and nervous strain might account for some of the sensation, but the next day Hetty, most acid of hecklers, was in bed and a doctor diagnosed pneumonia and pleurisy.

As the gathering dusk made further business impossible, we instructed the Commissions to deal with specific issues and closed. There was no certainty whatever that we would meet again.

The cars drove off in a long stream, their tail-lights bright pathfinders ahead of us into the advancing gloom.

The word for the Monday rendezvous, "Rondberg," was passed around in the cathedral hall after the BCESL meeting the Sunday night. (One of the six Special Branch police, thinking he was not known, sidled up to ask when I would be leaving the next day. I played safe—and dumb!)

Back towards Malmesbury the Monday, but to a different farm, we were told early that the police were out scouring the roads—and aided by army trucks. So we drew up opposite a car with its bonnet open and people busy underneath. A shirt-sleeved delegate came over to warn us: the police are around; cars must not be seen in groups. Just beyond the rise was a turn-off and we could see the hood of a car flashing as it traveled through the grass. Then it was our turn, and we drove up to the large out-building.

Inside, Convention was already discussing raising money for the defense of the eleven delegates who had been arrested at a house the previous afternoon. Outside loitered members of the Security Police who had discovered that they needed a warrant. Some had gone off to Malmesbury for it. An army truck was drawn up to block egress from the farm.

In the gloomy packing-shed, the air blue with cigarette smoke, the Convention got under way with cut and thrust of argument: all minds bent to the task of shaping a free South Africa.

In the later afternoon, the great doors were flung open and van der Westhuizen, head of the Cape Security Police, strutted, swaggered in, for all the world like a Nazi gauleiter as he stood silhouetted against the blinding sunlight, his eager pack at his heals.

Convention thrust on. Nonplussed, they stood around (did they hope for panic or confusion?) and then stood at a large box taking notes and looking sheepish.

So, we moved to the end, with votes of thanks (a thunderous and prolonged ovation for our hosts of the farm bringing tears to the eyes) a prayer and a hymn. It had grown dusk in the shed, but there was brightness in the eyes of the delegates and in the place that came from a sense of a job well done. Of having labored manfully to lay the foundations of a great future where all men would stand up free and equal.

So, with hand-shakings and munching sandwiches, with the Special Branch members still hanging around aimlessly, and our hearts steeled in democratic resolve, we left the Malmesbury farm to take our pledges for freedom across the country.

Sports: Threat to the security of the state
Fighting Talk, December 1961/January 1962

It is not generally realized how serious a threat sports are, or how vigilantly they are watched by the prime guardians of the security of our state—the Special Branch (SB). The fact is that a large body of men have been detailed to keep an unsleeping eye on our sports fields and that thousands of man-hours are spent on studying subversive movements in the field.

Of course you will say that I am "shooting a line" and will ask for evidence. There are lots of others, though, who would support my statements with amply documented evidence. I will confine myself to my own limited range of experience and let it justify my claim.

In September of 1958 there was a small press announcement that the Weightlifting Federation (non-white or non-racial—the papers weren't fussy) was to set up a coordinating body to fight against racialism in sports. So for weeks before the championships took place in East London, members of the Special Branch haunted non-white sports fields brandishing the clipping and making ominous noises. By the time sportsmen had converged on East London for the show it was evident that there were going to be very few East Londoners at the preliminary meeting: the "Fighting Port" was a very frightened port. The limit was reached when the chairman of the Border Union was visited and questioned about one Brutus— with the chairman frantically disclaiming all knowledge! I phoned the police, asked to speak to the head of the Special Branch and demanded an interview. Eventually we saw the second-in-command— Lt. Schoombie—who apologetically explained that it was his duty to investigate strangers to ensure that they were not "suspicious characters." I didn't ask for a definition!

In the meantime another detective, whom I remember for his remarkable resemblance to a potato, called at our hotel room to ask permission to attend the meeting. As a formality, we stated that it had to be referred to our executive.

Sunday morning bright and early, Schoombie and Hattingh arrived and pressed to enter the meeting room: firmly we barred the door. They hung around, offering us gumdrops, arguing, and trying to peek around the door. We all got impatient. They threatened us with a warrant. We threatened to blast the story in the newspapers. Reluctantly they drifted from the hotel lounge. Later they were seen hanging around the kitchen cadging tea.

But they had not failed, as we discovered later.

Govender, the friendly well-wisher who had traveled down from Durban, later appeared in a press photograph escorting an emergency detainee to a funeral: Special Branch! And Selepe, who traveled down from Krugersdorp with an elaborate credential and who made a virulent—and irrelevant—attack on apartheid was found to come from a non-existent body. His real organization: Special Branch.

This Selepe turned up again at our South African Sports Association Conference in Durban three months later—with six members of the Special Branch at the back busily taking notes. This time we threw him out—though there were some who sportingly called out "Give him a chance!"

The six in Durban in January were to become an accepted feature. I list only a few other occasions:

October, 1959, Port Elizabeth: Sports Conference. White and non-white SBs occupy front seats in the hall.

May 1960, Port Elizabeth: Homes of SASA officials—president, secretary, assistant secretary, and executive member raided: all SASA paper—including blank letterhead sheets—seized. Returned only several months later after protest.

October, 1960, Johannesburg: I arrive at Jan Smuts airport at 6:30, at weightlifting show at 7:30. Find Special Branch has already been inquiring about Brutus and Ragansamy. I insist that Taylor (SB) explain why he claims he is investigating crime. I offer to see his chief following morning. Offer declined. The home where I was supposed to be staying is visited by SB.

May, 1961, Port Elizabeth: Home of secretary raided.

October, 1961: Secretary banned under Suppression of Communism Act.

All of this, while no doubt deadly serious to the SB has not been without its lighter moments. The day after the SASA stuff had been seized we trotted off to demand an interview with the chief. Major Heiberg was very busy, but we persevered. We saw him two days later and asked, naively, for the return of all our material. He feigned ignorance. But the files were spread out on his desk. He refused to return them. Gently, servilely, we probed him. Why? There was a State of Emergency. But why take our stuff? He was only doing his duty. But surely his were *police* duties? He had to protect the state from all dangers! But how were sports a danger? So it went on. We probed too long and too incisively: he blew up.

"Kyk hierso, *ek* is die man wat die vrae vra. J't my mos nou onderkruis-verhoor!" (Look here *I'm* the man who asks the questions. You've got me under cross-examination!) His face turkey-red, he bundled us out. (So SASA was born under the watchful eyes of the Special Branch—and has enjoyed their attention ever since!)

There are, as well, unofficial guardians of the security of the state—holding official positions in the big all-white sports bodies.

Massive Ira Emery, until this year secretary of the South African Olympic (and Commonwealth) Games Association and the man who boasted that for eight years he saved South Africa from being thrown out of the Olympics because of her racial policies, is a case in point.

When I saw him he complained: "If you've got a good boy, why don't you send him to Tanganyika[1] or Uganda (I don't think he added Timbuktu) instead of causing us trouble?" And in an expansive moment he added: "You know, in the mines, when there's a good black who does the 100 yards in very good time, they give him a watch or ten bob." Triumphantly, "That makes him a professional!" This is admittedly a rather different method but no doubt it is equally effective in preserving the security of the state.

Military man Algy Frames, boss of all-white cricket for endless years, was more menacing. After the gruff "Sit down, my boy" and "What do you want, my boy?" came the forbidding question: "Have you ever heard of MI5?"[2] Nervously I admitted that I had. "Well, we've got our own MI5. We know your cricket is in a mess.

We know you haven't got one boy who's good enough to play for South Africa. Besides, you know that if there's one black boy on our team to England, there'll be trouble." My parting shot was that there would be trouble if there wasn't, and there *was*. Boycotts and demonstrations and a loss of 17,000 pounds in England!

God-fatherly Reg Honey, Q.C.,[3] until this year boss of the most powerful sports association in the country—the Olympic Association—was more subtle in his means, but the ends were the same. But let the definitive comment come from someone else. It is by James Fairbairn, reporting in the *New Statesman* on an interview with Honey—a classic article called "The Olympic Swindle": Mr. Honey said at the end of an unrewarding interview: "Of course, we can't let the blacks have equality. All this nonsense about one man one vote. Once that happens, the country will go down the drain."

And in a sense they are right. When there is equality on the sports field, or when it becomes impossible to stave it off, or when our sportsmen are deprived of the drug of sports and look at the country beyond the sports field, then apartheid South Africa will go down the drain.

[1] Now called Tanzania.

[2] The British domestic intelligence agency.

[3] Q.C.: Queen's Council, a high ranking title for lawyers associated with the British Crown.

Walking home to Mofolo

Fighting Talk, May, 1959 (under the pseudonym, D.A.B.)

Inevitably we had stayed too long. After an inept supper—much was forgiven her because she confessed her inefficiency with much frankness—Hazel produced some dry wine and we settled down to talk. Secure in her little backyard room in a classy suburb, tolerated but suspected, we shut out Johannesburg and South Africa and talked, by turns lightly and seriously, of many things. Hazel, who was white, yet had cast off her whiteness and belonged nowhere in a white society of privilege and dominance she had scorned and which was revenging itself on her: myself, from the crepuscular no-man's land of what are generally called colored people, and Hutch, who was generally agreed to be African, but whom even officialdom had failed to classify. Husky and shrewdly obtuse, he shouldered his way through all categories, remaining in the last resort, only the elusive and enigmatic man that artists persist in being. He had just come through a shattering mental and physical experience in which I had supported him with a strength I only managed to find because of his compelling need, but now no trace of it showed, except in the languor of his speech. For Hazel, his presence, after his ordeal and her own recent grilling by the police, meant a delight that she tempered with uneven firmness. With blonde hair curled in crisp unruliness and trimly silken legs she moved about the small room, trying to be unfussy and put us at ease. After she had produced the wine from under the bed, the dishes stowed, we settled down at last.

We were at once strangers, and old acquaintances, and intimates. Thinking of it now, it seems to me we were like patterns in figured cloth. Dissimilar each in his own way, yet woven together by so many threads of knowledge and shared pleasures and lively reminiscences that linked us over many years, over hundreds of miles.

And so, after the talk of frustrations and danger, of oppression and tension, of how long it would endure or be endurable, of our own breaking down under the system, of Ghana and flights across the border, we came to our common love, poetry. Always it was just one more, though it grew later, and at the back of our minds was the peril of the return to Mofolo, in the dark and in danger of our lives.

There were snatches of Eliot and Spender—Dylan Thomas and MacNiece for me—and for Hutch, a little démodé, Browning and Dobson's "Cynara." And then more.

Finally, the brief, brittley lovely period of parting, and then we were off. Leaving the embattled security of the gracious homes around Zoo Lake, we worked our way towards the station. Beside me walked Hutch, sniffing at the keen night air. Some classically pedigreed bull, expensively bred on a Spanish estancio might be like Hutch, rampaging into the bull-ring with lumbering grace and exquisite sensitivity.

We passed the bright modern facade of Park station and entered the dim rear maze of barriers and fences which was the Non-European entrance. Already they crowded the station, the throng who were waiting for the last train. The bearded watchmen with their great kieries, the roistering toughs with their clubs, the silent men with their heavy sticks, the suede-shoed city slickers with their ominous bulge at hip or armpit. Offence or defence? No-one could tell but many died each week on the train, and few questions were asked. The tired elderly workmen, the anxious women, the servant-girls in their finery huddled in nervous knots. A young spiv dragged a girl along the platform, whimpering. He cuffed her savagely and she cried aloud, but no-one interfered. Wisely, numbly, we looked the other way. African policemen, never far away, moved officiously among the thickening crowd which now blocked the platform. Sensibly, never able to gauge the measure of hostility which existed among the people, they studiously avoided the area of the disturbance.

For me, new and ignorant, it was exciting: it was a fresh experience, with the tang of danger and adventure. But Hutch, speaking in a somber undertone, did not conceal his fear. He had seen death come too swiftly, too easily and too often. Sometimes it was for a pay-packet, or for protection, or after an argument. And sometimes for no reason at all. He was afraid. Afraid of the crowd, afraid of the journey, and afraid of the long walk at the end of the journey. He gestured surreptitiously at a tough, identified a gangster with so many killings to his credit, chose some bearded watchmen with heavy staves and edged me into the radius of their possible protection.

An electric train hurtled into the station, and I moved to it but it did not stop. It was going through, going somewhere else into the darkness. Then we gathered ourselves for the scrambling rush for the train as it rumbled in. A brief pause, with a wild clutching at doors and then we jerked off, with dozens racing after and taking flying leaps into the train. We stood pressed against each other—there was no seating room, but not too far near the door—"Not safe," Hutch explained laconically. We crashed into the suburban stops, falling pell-mell against each other. All round were villainous characters, but it did not do to scrutinize them closely. It might give offense.

It was then in that long headlong flight, surrounded by those violent and terrified people that I realized the perils of that long walk from Dube to Mofolo.

"Is there no station at Mofolo?" Hutch shook his head dumbly.

We thundered into another station. Above the crash and rumble I heard the noise of scuffling further down the long carriage. A sharp cry, smothered or drowned in the stampede of a fresh crowd of passengers boarding.

"Can't we take a taxi?" I asked desperately.

"No." Hutch said morosely. "When we get off, keep with the bunch, it's safer."

Then we were alighting, scurrying along the platform, through fenced barricades up a flight of steps that led off from the station. At the top I paused in the jostling crowd. On the right hand, the lights stretched away. On the left hand, so far off that they formed a single yellow line, another stretch of lights. But ahead, the way we had to go, a great expanse of darkness and gray shapes, its reaches emphasized by an occasional solitary light—a feeble glimmer, as of a sputtering candle.

At the foot of the steps we split into two groups. It seemed to me that what we followed was by far the smaller group. We huddled together. At my shoulder was the gaunt giant with the livid scar that I had noticed eyeing me on the station. Behind me I made out the dim form, and the club he carried half-upraised. I trod on the heel of a city slicker ahead of me. He never looked back and I realized that here identification would be futile. Hutch was an admired Congress leader, I thought. But he had discounted it. Here it counted for nothing. I shrank into the silent crowd.

Suddenly a car swung round in a wide arc, its headlights sweeping the group like a searchlight. "A taxi," I whispered eagerly to Hutch.

"No use," Hutch grunted. "Might be gangsters. They'll strip you naked. You'll be lucky if they leave you alive."

In the silent starless night the cold and fear poured down on us. Fear froze us in silence. Bright metal glinted briefly beside me, a knife perhaps. Helpless, locked in fear like solid ice, we plodded on. Stumbling over the uneven ground, squelching in the slush, we plodded on. I bowed my head, seeking the anonymity of complete darkness, my shoulders hunched. Naked and unprotected. Cold.

Behind me a man's voice gasped, someone slithered in the mud, fell. No-one looked back.

Cold fear piled on us, mounted like a huge iceberg which crushed down on us. My mouth was dry, my thighs aching with fatigue and tension.

And then suddenly we were among the first houses and the tension relaxed. As we reached a solitary streetlight and moved into its pool of wan light, the tension snapped audibly. Speech began, first in muttered undertones, then in pointless but loud conversation. Someone laughed uncertainly, we were there.

Ahead the long indistinguishable streets stretched, and there was a long way to go to our place still, but we had reached Mofolo. We were home.

"You've come to Hell Island": A political prisoner under apartheid
Autobiographical notes, 1974

I was sentenced, as I remember, on the eighth of January 1964, 'round about midday. Having been kept in a cell with the other convicted prisoners, I was put in the prison truck, taken to the Fort prison, stripped, and dressed in prison uniform, and then, barefoot for the first time in prison, made my way painfully down to the section of the prison where I was to be kept as a convicted prisoner. It was some distance from the administration block, and I remember the pain and discomfort I felt walking down to my section of the convicted prisoners, and being met now by the guards who had seen me as a prisoner awaiting trial and sentence and who now met me as a convict. I thought that was a particularly grim day, but I shan't linger over it now. I want to go rapidly on to something that happened that evening and which to me seems in retrospect very fortunate.

I was put in a kind of underground section of the prison, a type of basement prison section containing an enormous pile of soiled and dusty blankets, from which I was expected to select some, and a mat, for myself. I found a number of prisoners there. But that night we were not subject to very close surveillance, because the other prisoners there were those who were back in the Fort from other prisons for further charges. They were being sentenced for additional crimes, some of these having been discovered subsequent to their being imprisoned on particular charges.

On the mat adjoining mine that night was a prisoner who had

come from Leeuwkop. He talked to me about this prison, which I never expected to see. I assumed I would serve out my sentence—which was a short one of eighteen months—at the Fort as most other prisoners did if their sentences were less than a year. He told me about the prison he had come from, Leeuwkop (Lion's Head), which was near Pretoria, and I think situated in an exclusive suburb called Bryanston. He described it as the worst prison he knew. He spoke of the beatings and particularly of one peculiar indignity to which prisoners were subject on arrival, and often thereafter, and this was being made to strip and stand naked facing a wall with your palms stretched above you and placed on the wall, and your legs apart, and then a warder would come along and put on a rubber glove and insert his fingers and almost his entire hand into your anus, allegedly in search of hidden money or tobacco or marijuana—dagga, as it is called—or weapons. And he spoke of the almost constant beatings there and the intense surveillance prisoners were subject to, especially those known as D Group prisoners, the worst group.

This was the group into which prisoners with political offenses automatically fell. Though the South African administration denies that it has any political prisoners and insists that all of the prisoners in South Africa have been convicted of what are criminal offenses, it is true that the political prisoners are in fact treated differently. For one thing, they cannot earn remissions, as other prisoners can; for another, they tend to be classified invariably in the D Group, which is the severest disciplinary group of the fewest prisoners [who are] kept in separate sections of the prison. I listened with fascinated horror that night to his stories, and felt secure in the knowledge, the comforting knowledge, that I would never have to go to Leeuwkop. The next day I discovered I was wrong.

In the morning I was brought out like all the other prisoners; I had my head shaved, which in fact was not strictly necessary, because one is supposedly permitted to have a quarter-inch of hair on your head in prison, and later in the day I was called out with one or two other prisoners and told I was being transferred, and discovered by overhearing a conversation that I was going to Leeuwkop. I did in fact go and had it not been that I had been warned by the knowledge the previous evening of the kind of expe-

rience I was going to be exposed to, I think I would have found it
even more terrible than I did....

"The notorious Brutus"

On arrival there at the entrance and being taken through recep-
tion and booked in—my body was in fact delivered over to the new
prison administration—I was then made to run in the large prison
courtyard with a crowd of others, a kind of aimless circular running
where you were beaten at random by the warders who were either
black or white. From a kind of parapet or catwalk surrounding this
courtyard the guards gathered to look on, because word had
reached the prison...that I was due to arrive; some of them looked
at me in some astonishment and disgust on arrival because I was the
notorious Brutus, who...must have looked rather like a plucked
hen. [I] certainly didn't look the reportedly dangerous and daring
saboteur that I suppose they had heard of, or the kind of thing that
had been reported in the press, and the kind of image it might have
created of me.

I was stripped, made to face a wall and had someone rummage
in my anus like all the others, and given a torn shirt and trousers
and hustled off to a cell, being beaten again en route: it was a rou-
tine. Batons were used, sometimes straps of thick leather, sometimes
simply fists. But even this fairly minor beating was nothing to what
was to come later in Leeuwkop, and...later on Robben Island. I
spent the night in one of the prison sections in a large cell with some
twenty or thirty other prisoners, mainly Africans, and assumed that
this was to be my future cell; again I was wrong.

The next morning breakfast was served. It consisted in my case
of a bowl of porridge without sugar and with no spoon, so that I
had to eat it with my fingers. We were [then] marched out, rather
than forced to run that day, but I was separated from the group
and taken to another section of the prison. This, though I did not
know it at the time, was the D Section. And I was told to stand or
sit against a wall, facing a long row of cells, large ones, of which I
could only see the high windows—and I sat there with skinny and
cold shanks, cold feet, torn khaki shirt and pants, eating porridge
with my fingers in the cold, pale blue dawn. I must have looked a
pretty miserable and disconsolate figure, and indeed felt that way.

But perhaps the intention was for the guards to put me on display for all the D prisoners in that section, political prisoners, so that they could see this pitiable object, who was Brutus: the man who had been recaptured, brought back from another country, gunned down, and finally safely incarcerated. It was, I suppose, some kind of object lesson to the other prisoners. Ruth First, in her book, *117 Days* (which tells of her own detention without trial), [tells of the kind of shock she felt at that moment when] a guard, male or female, came to her cell one afternoon and told her, "They've just shot and killed Brutus."

Later in the day I was taken into one of the cells, a large one, in which I was to spend the next two months. The cells at Leeuwkop are large and airy. It is, after all, regarded as one of the finest prisons in the South African prison system. The ceiling is high and slopes from the back at a steep angle forward and then level with the ceiling at its lowest point is a catwalk running the entire length of the building of perhaps five large cells, with windows all along the catwalk. [A] guard patrolling a catwalk can see down and have an excellent view of all the cells as he passes them, of the prisoners in them, and can keep them under observation all the time.

The prison is in fact called an observation prison, where prisoners are classified into categories after a period of observation; but for the time being they are all in category D and indeed are liable to remain in category D. One relief in the cell was that the bricks on one wall—the one [between] the adjoining cells—were burnt brick, exposed to various temperatures and various chemicals, so that they came out differently colored and one had a wall of fascinatingly varied subtle changes in color: reds, oranges, ochres, blues, greens, blacks—which was colorful for me, at least, and gave immense relief in the monotony of the cell. I could look across from my mat on the floor at night, to this colored wall and count the bricks and use them as images of the weeks and months and days of [my] sentence, and indeed use it as a calendar and mentally check off each day as it passed....

Minister of culture in Leeuwkop prison

The time I spent in Leeuwkop was curiously rewarding for me, though looking back it may be that I attempted to dominate the

ministries

cell too much. I was asked to act as a kind of minister of culture. We had different responsibilities [that] we called ministries: a ministry of health whose job was to keep the cell clean; a ministry of justice, which was the disciplinary group [that] ruled on behavior and discipline. If necessary, [this group] applied sanctions for people who got others into trouble by talking too loudly or behaving recklessly and thus getting all the members of the cell punished. The punishment mainly [meant] loss of food, perhaps for the entire day, which was called "threemeals," pronounced pretty much as one word. Of the things I remember with pleasure, there were many in that cell. We played draughts [checkers] with a homemade board drawn on the surface of the cell with a piece of tar, rubbing black lines, then taking little bits of tar and rolling them into balls and using them to play games of draughts.

I'd also undertaken to teach the others to play chess, but I'm afraid I kept postponing this. In the evenings in the dusk, 'round about the time when the guards had their meals and changed the guard, it was possible to have a period to tell stories, particularly if you huddled close to the wall where the window was so that the guard...would have difficulty in seeing us clustered together. Technically we were not supposed to be in groups at any time, possibly because we were then suspected of plotting our escape or discussing political matters. During this time in the dusk it was my function as part of the entertainment team to tell stories, and I remember telling all of *Hamlet*. As a [continuation of] the Hamlet theme, I also told all of Sophocles' *Oedipus*, developing the notion of challenge to authority, and particularly the implied Oedipus complex in Hamlet and its explicit articulation in Sophocles' play; I then used *The Brothers Karamazov* by Dostoevsky to explore the theme further. *Karamazov*, I think, took me five days to tell, and I treated it, at one level, as an exciting detective story—not excluding [its sexual aspect]—but pretty much treating it as a detective story. Over the period of about five days in which this story was told, there were bets of bits of meat that we got every other day—an ounce of meat. People were staking and pledging their bits of meat in advance, betting on who...murder[ed]...the old man—whether it was Ivan, or Dmitri, or Alyosha, or anyone else in the story. Great fun. For lighter entertainment I remember telling the story of a Barbara Stanwyck movie,

Sorry, Wrong Number. Towards the end, before I realized I was being moved from Leeuwkop, I told as another five-part serial, *Gone with the Wind.* It was extremely well-received, so much so that when I was moved from Leeuwkop with some of the other prisoners, they insisted, on the journey when we were handcuffed together, that I retell the story of *Gone with the Wind.* And this I did....

"Here one doesn't smile"

One other thing I set in motion was an application to continue my legal studies. And it may be that this was a factor in deciding to send me from Leeuwkop where there were no study facilities—or so they said, although this turned out to be untrue, because others were able to study while at Leeuwkop. But it was decided that I should go to Robben Island where I was supposed to be able to get study facilities. I also appeared before the prison review board at some point in my stay at Leeuwkop. The whole business was inconclusive and is vague in my mind now, but it may have had some bearing on the decision to send me to Robben Island.

I had, through [my lawyer] Ruth Hayman, asked to see a priest. I was adamant about my rights as a prisoner with relation to religion. I felt that this was something where I should assert myself. In addition, this was a period of some religious deepening for me. Indeed, [it] caused many debates in the cell, where I was with the thirty-five or so members of the PAC because their own views were mixed: some were religious and sang hymns on Sunday, so far as this was permitted. In the evenings they would sing the PAC anthem, which at first I refused to join. Subsequently I did join in.

I saw a priest and he undertook to return a week later—this would be at the beginning of March. And then, as far as I remember, on the ninth of March I was suddenly removed from Leeuwkop to another prison. There were rumors that prisoners were being moved. There were also rumors, wholly false, through messages we got from prisoners who were alleged to have returned from Robben Island to Leeuwkop, of how well the political prisoners were being treated—that they were being given magazines, the right to smoke, and things like that. All this, I was to discover, was wildly false. But on the night I was moved I had no idea that my destination was to be Robben Island.

At Leeuwkop we were made to run from our cells each day to a food line. We would be beaten en route to the food line, especially by a burly Zulu guard called Khumalo. And we were required to run at high speed both ways. The food often fell and if we ran past the table or ledge where the plates were flung out and missed catching one, we would be without food for the day; that was just one's misfortune. I remember that as we ran from our cells one day, we passed a line of prisoners who were leaving their cells as we were returning to ours. They were political prisoners—the ANC group—though that probably didn't matter, and in a signal of comradeship I winked at one of them. It was enough for a guard to stop me and to take my porridge from me. "Winking is not permitted at Leeuwkop," was roughly what he said.

On another occasion I smiled [in greeting] at a prisoner as I passed. It was a kind of cameraderie and solidarity one tried to express. And again I was deprived of my food: "Here one doesn't smile," was roughly what the guard said. But the criminal prisoners, the trustees in a sense, who were assigned the job of bringing us our food when we were locked in, would contrive to bring messages, and also to deliver newspaper clippings. This was a dangerous business, because if you were found with a clipping in your possession you could be severely punished for it. They also on occasion managed to smuggle messages written by other prisoners and handed to us as they shoved the food through the metal grill which formed the second door to the cell.

We developed a technique for communicating with the other cells. In each cell in the far wall in the center was a toilet basin, so that one used the toilet basin in the cell and did not need to leave the cell; nor were there the metal buckets such as one found in the cells at Robben Island. Regrettably we were also required to wash our faces in this toilet basin, using the water in the basin, and indeed to brush our teeth, a peculiarly disgusting and humiliating experience, but part of the kind of mentality of the guards at Leeuwkop. We contrived to find a method of communicating through these toilet basins. They were linked in each cell by pipes to the adjoining cells, the pipes running through the back of the wall on the outside; but by scooping out the water one could then shout down the hole in the base of the toilet basin and hear messages back as well, and the pipes acted as reasonably good conductors of sound. And so we were able to hear each other and to send messages of encouragement and even ideas of protesting against treatment there, and against conditions like the denial of facilities to wash, the denial of clean clothes, and the denial of exercise.

I must have been at Leeuwkop quite some time, kept in the semi-dark cell all day, without exercise—not that I was particularly keen to have it. I guess I'd not wholly recovered from the effects of my injury. But when we did eventually get up a deputation of about three of us who stood out of line at inspection time in order to request exercise, we got it with a vengeance. We were brought out and made to run into a circle and to run until we dropped. And as we ran we were beaten by guards who thought we were not running fast enough. The whole idea of running was a test of endurance, with the guards driving you past the point of endurance. In my case this became fairly soon more than I could take, and so I slowed down to a walk and tried to explain to a guard that I was not able to continue because I was suffering pain and discomfort from my injury. But the guards paid no attention to this and I was compelled to keep running and was beaten as I ran until I literally dropped from exhaustion. Unable to continue, I was hauled off back to the cell.

This happened twice as far as I remember, and so rather than face it the third time I demanded to see the prison doctor. The doctor, as far as I remember, came once a week for complaints and to deal with the sick. The following week I was taken off to the hospital section for examination by the doctor. I explained to him my predicament and he asked me to lie down on the couch in the examination room, looked me over, and decided that there was nothing wrong with me. He made a remark which I remember, and which I was to hear repeated on Robben Island: I said I could not keep running, and his reply was, "Brutus, you are the man who wants to get the blacks into the South African Olympic team, so you should be grateful for the opportunity to have this exercise." It was a cynical remark, but as far as I remember he gave some kind of instruction so that I was not required to go through this exercise again....

Punishment in Leeuwkop was pretty arbitrary. We would be talking in fairly low voices inside the cell and suddenly we would hear a guard knock, bang on the door and shout "threemeals."

This meant that we were being punished and being deprived of our next three meals, which generally were for an entire day: morning, midday, and evening meals.

This was the pattern of existence there. Of course I had many fantasies of escape, particularly of a helicopter landing in the prison courtyard and whisking us away. But I had assumed that I was going to stay in Leeuwkop for the duration of my sentence. One day in March we were hauled out of our cells and the cells were searched by some of the other prisoners and guards. Mats were shaken out. By this time at least I had been issued a toothbrush and a spoon—and these were things one treasured. The spoon was a wooden one; metal spoons were not permitted. The toothbrushes were soft and almost useless. And one also was issued a cake of cheap soap, a mixture of soda and washing blue, and one guarded these; they were our only possessions, really. I think in some cases there was a Bible in the cell, but in the case of political prisoners it was assumed that they were all communists and therefore there was no point in their reading a Bible; they were often refused one. We were hauled out and lined up in the sun while our cells were searched and then returned to them. The more experienced prisoners interpreted this as a signal that some were going to be moved.

At three or four the following morning, there was a banging on the door and we were all ordered out. We were ordered to strip and stood in the cold courtyard on the concrete under the stars. Then we were issued new uniforms of coarse white cloth-jackets or shirts, trousers, but no shoes or socks. We were manacled in pairs and herded out of the prison and into a large prison truck. In my truck there were about thirty. We were crowded together in the dark. There was a kind of metal grill at the one end separating the prisoners from the driver's seat and we were supposed, I think, to use a kind of mobile toilet basin, toilet container. I'm not sure if this worked. We were chained at the wrists and at the ankles: handcuffs with fairly extended chains in the case of our legs—manacles, these were. The handcuffs paired us together, left arm to right wrist of someone else. I had a young prisoner with me who had shared the same cell with me. And so we journeyed off in the dark, with an armored car as an escort; the dawn came up, and I began to see the faces of people around me as we lurched against each other, elbows, knees bumping into each other, and rather reluctantly I was retelling the story of *Gone with the Wind*, for the sake of those who wanted to hear it again....

Apartheid's concentration camp

The image of Robben Island in my mind was one of terror. At that time the political prisoners went there for life. I certainly didn't think that I ought to be there as a short-term prisoner; no one under three years went to Robben Island; even subsequently, I was one of the few with a sentence of less than three years. And I had, I'm afraid, the premonition that if I went there I would never return alive. Years before, I had read and written about the way in which this island—which had been a leprosarium, a place for lepers—was being converted by the South African government into a concentration camp. The old hospital section was converted into a prison, and all of it surrounded by barbed wire, searchlights, and guns: South Africa's prototype of a concentration camp. The thought of Robben Island filled me with considerable horror and I remember trying to get a message [out] through someone who had a stub of pencil, scribbling on a bit of paper, "Brutus has been taken to Robben Island." But no doubt that didn't work either.

We stopped again between Kroonstad and Paarl, in the small hours of the night. We probably got there in the evening, were put in cells at Colesberg, the small prison in the Northern Cape, and then hauled out again by sleepy-eyed and irritable warders, at between three and four in the morning, and given our porridge which we ate with our hands, since there were no spoons issued. We were manacled again, placed in the truck, taken on to Paarl, and from Paarl to Cape Town docks to go to the island. And the experience I had at Colesberg, eating porridge under the stars of the Southern Cross in the sky, had a kind of consoling influence on me and still does. In times of desperation I look up at the stars, and if I can find them, somehow things are more endurable—I've recorded that experience in a poem about that event, though it was written some time ago, and fuses several perceptions, including a religious one.[1]

At the Cape Town docks the area was cordoned off and heavily guarded. There were two tugboats at the wharf or the jetty; the first one a kind of decoy, so that you passed from the one boat, through it to the second one where men stood with their guns at the ready, armed, and which was the ferry to Robben Island. The boat may well have been called *Issie*, after the wife of the former prime minister, Jan Smuts, and of which I had just recently read in a report of a fellow prisoner on the island, Mac Maharaj, as we called him.

We were herded aboard the second boat, but first there was a rather nasty experience to be undergone. The first boat, while it was tied up at the quay, was some distance from the landing, and we were required to jump from the land to the boat. This would not have been particularly difficult, except that the boat was heaving and swaying on the tide. We were also handcuffed and manacled together at wrists and ankles and so had to jump in pairs; there was a real danger that if you missed the jump or lost your footing that you would go down the pair of you, into the sea between the land and the boat. I murmured to the prisoner chained to me that we ought to time it correctly—that I would count three, and that we would jump on the count of three. This we did, scrambling onto the ship, and then walking across it, through it to the other one. Herded downstairs, into the hold, we traveled that way onto the island. Some prisoners had never seen the sea, and I had had the humbling experience in Leeuwkop of finding how inadequate language was in describing the sea to someone who had never seen it. On the quay, waiting for our turn to jump, I had looked around at what I could see of Cape Town and the docks, with a kind of sick feeling, quoting to myself lines from a poem, "Look your last on all things lovely," murmuring lines half wryly like "at daybreak for the isles."[2] And these were lines I was subsequently to weave into a poem printed in the *Letters to Martha*.[3]

When we got to the island, there was some difficulty in getting out, getting ashore, and getting organized in a truck and driven over to the reception center, which at that time was a temporary one. Around us there were prisoners working or returning from work—it was pretty late. We arrived when most of them were already locked up, having been fed, and then we were marched over, or run over, to the kitchen. I found myself at the head of the line, and marched with some dignity, refusing to run at the head of the chain of prisoners. This meant that those behind me, even if they wished to run, could not run.

There were guards around me, shouting and threatening and occasionally cuffing me, but I continued to walk and so all those behind me walked. It was a kind of naive and almost simple-minded courage, which I sometimes displayed, for which I don't particularly take credit. But it was a rejection of the kind of animal-like behavior that the guards demanded of us and which I was not prepared to give.

After we had eaten, we were taken to a large cell in a part of the prison just "finished"—so unfinished, in fact, that there was no water in the taps or in the toilets yet. And our clothes were taken from us—the clothes we had arrived with from Leeuwkop. We were not issued other clothes; we were given blankets instead, and so we huddled in the cell, and slept on the floor. I watched the dawn the following morning, the sky turning orange and saffron, and brilliant vermillion, against pale green like green ripening apples. In the morning we were given some clothes, and breakfast, and then taken over to the temporary administration section on another part of the island, where we were issued clothes, and medically inspected, and then, I think, issued new prison cards—ID cards. Mine was a white one, unlike the others, which I think were red or green or blue, depending on the number of years of their sentence. Mine was white because my sentence was under two years; in fact I was the only prisoner on the island with a card like that, and almost certainly ought not to have been on the island, and this was occasionally pointed out to me. One last recollection of that first day was that as we were locked in by the guards in charge of the large cell in which we were to be kept, one guard shouted that we should be silent and went on to say, "You think you've come to Robben Island, but you're wrong. You'll find out that you've come to Hell Island," and that was an ominous threat....

Bright red blood on gray broken flint

When I was seen by a doctor—or rather we'd all been seen—I had pointed out that I was recovering from a bullet injury and had not properly recovered, because of the treatment on Leeuwkop. I was told by the doctor, whose name was Gosling, that I would have to be treated like any other prisoner. We were then locked up in a cell in the administration area, and perhaps this was done deliberately to teach us a lesson: very shortly from our cell windows, we were able to see another batch of prisoners (perhaps as many as fifty, I'm not sure) being brought in from the place where they were working, which was a quarry, apparently, on the beach, where they were digging rocks, or building a wall, hauling rocks out of the sea, or they may have been working somewhere else. They had been brought in for discipline. George Peake was a colored prisoner, a former member of the Cape Town city council, who was serving a sentence for sabotage, and had been on the island for some time, and therefore was knowledgeable, and had managed to get himself some responsibilities as a prisoner, and so could walk around. Peake came to us and told us that the prisoners who were brought in were called the Masondo group, after Andrew Masondo, who was one of the ANC political prisoners, and had been a former lecturer in mathematics at Fort Hare. What had happened was that the guards had consistently ill-treated Masondo, in the place where he was working with his squad. Masondo had protested this, and as punishment he had been tied to a stake in the center of his working group, and denied the opportunity to go to the toilet or to drink water. And he had been left there for some time, in the sun. There had apparently been previous episodes similar to this, and as a result the prisoners in the Masondo squad had all refused to go to work, or to continue their work.

So they were being marched in order to be disciplined. They were lined up, with a row of guards facing them; the guards were armed with batons, or leather straps, and their report was made to a young slim officer called Lt. Frazer, who, after hearing the complaint, had issued a command in a quiet, almost conversational voice and had said, "Carry on." "Carry on" in South Africa is a special term in the language of guards; it is almost the equivalent of the army order, "fire at will," and is a command normally reserved for riots and jail breaks. When the instruction is given to "carry on" it means that the guards are free to do pretty much anything to the prisoners. In this instance they waded in to the prisoners with batons and straps and sticks and then grabbed wooden pick handles and staves from a nearby storing shed. They beat the prisoners, who scattered, and then rained blows on them as they ran; some tried to crawl under a fence in an attempt to escape, some were unconscious, others tried to ward off the blows and were struck over the head, across the arms, shoulders, elbows, beaten to the ground. It was an indescribable kind of fury unleashed, and when we came out of our section a while later, there were still splashes of bright red blood, almost vermilion in contrast, on the gray broken flint that formed the gravel of the ground. I heard that there were guards with special sadistic preferences, who concentrated in striking only at elbows, ankles, or knees, trying to permanently damage joints, and break the bones, and others whose preference was only for striking skulls, so that one guard would plead to the others to hit everywhere else but on the head, and save the heads for him: "Just leave the head for me." This kind of thing was fairly common.

This incident—"Carry on"—would, I expect have taken place anyway, but it probably served a double function for us, in that it was used to give us an object lesson of what was liable to happen to us.

But we were not only to see an example; later in the same day we were ourselves to experience such an example. As far as I remember we were taken back to our cells, in our own new section of the prison, and then fetched out later in the afternoon, to work in what was called a quarry, although this term is used extremely loosely. It's not always a place where people quarry in the earth. In this instance we were required to carry large rocks from one area and dump them in a hole, which I supposed we were being asked to fill up. The stones were of various kinds, and of course if they were fairly small or moderately big you were required to take several; others were much bigger and almost too much for one person to carry. The catch was, first, that we had to carry these stones at a run to the pole where they had to be deposited. Second, as we ran, we were beaten by guards to hurry us along. Third, they also attempted to trip us, and sometimes succeeded, so that we fell heavily, and were then beaten while we lay on the ground, or as we got up and gathered our stone and made off with it. As the work went on, the tempo increased—we were required to run ever faster—the beatings increased, and the number of guards who were beating us was augmented by other guards who were off-duty, and who came along to join in the fun; there were always the long-time prisoners, serving probably life sentences for criminal offenses, who were used as trustees, or busboys, who wanted to get themselves in the good graces of the guards, and therefore joined in these beatings. This was apart from their own sadistic impulses, I guess. So we had a bad time. I saw others fall, get up, their legs and feet bleeding (we had no shoes yet, as far as I remember), their noses bloody.

At least one of the prisoners from Natal, a young Asian boy, literally passed out, fainted, or was beaten unconscious, and it went on until I thought it could no longer be endured. At first, and this may well have been a mistake, I worked energetically, and even cheerfully, and encouraged others and was determined to display this kind of courage which would demonstrate that my spirit, or, our spirits, were not being broken. But this of course attracted even more attention, more violence, more viciousness. By the end of the day, by the time we were taken back to our cells, I was in pretty bad shape. In addition, while you worked, and this was a further goad, if you did not work sufficiently hard, the guard would take from you your identity card, your ticket. By taking it he signified that you were being punished, that you would not receive any food that evening—and by now we were pretty hungry just from the hard work—or perhaps for the entire following day there would be no food for you, and some did in fact get "threemeals," which meant losing three meals the following day. It was my first experience of the arbitrary and almost limitless brutality, the sadism, the malicious glee with which the guards saw people fall and beat them and forced them to their feet again. There's no doubt that we learnt in that first short period just what lengths of brutality we could expect to see on Robben Island, and I suppose it did have some kind of salutary effect.

My next rather gruesome experience took place within a day or two. There may have been a Saturday or Sunday intervening when we didn't do much work, and I had to go and report to the administration, to get my documents, my record, in order. I was assigned to a squad working on the beach. We were at this time issued prison-made sandals, most of which were badly fitting and painful to wear, and we would be marched out to the kitchen, a large prison kitchen, and sat down in rows on the ground, and given our porridge there. Often the wind blew in from the sea, carrying the fine

sea sand onto our porridge, so that it formed a fine layer on the sur-
face. And after we'd had our breakfast of porridge and coffee, (col-
oreds got bread at lunchtime, Africans got crushed corn—I'm not
sure, we may have got bread in the evening, it all seems far away,
and then we were lined up in squads after breakfast and the squads
were marched off to work. Some of the PAC members were anxious
to be in squads which would take them marching where [Robert
Mangaliso] Sobukwe was being kept. He was leader of the PAC,
who, after he served his present sentence on Robben Island, was
confined there under preventive detention for a number of years,
subsequently released and placed under house arrest. At this time he
was on the island, under preventive detention. The PAC prisoners
were anxious to work in a direction that would take them marching
past the cottage where he was confined behind barbed wire, and
guarded by police. One of the things I noticed in the morning was
that when the squads were being made up, the senior criminal pris-
oners who had positions of some authority in organizing the squads
would come along with the guards and select the prisoners they
wanted for their squads—particularly the new young political pris-
oners who would come in, and whom they wanted for homosexual
purposes, and the guards would cooperate with them in this.

I was sent out to work on the beach with a squad. My job in
the early part of the morning was carrying rocks out of the sea to
the shore where they were used to build a wall around the island
alongside a road which was to run the entire periphery of the is-
land and which was part of its defense program. The rocks were
slippery and large, many of them covered with seaweed, extremely
heavy. One kept one's footing with enormous difficulty, swearing
at the smooth leather or composition material of the badly made
sandals; in fact it was more dangerous walking on these rocks
along the shore while wearing the sandals, slipping and sliding on
the slippery, slimy seaweed, and in order to work more efficiently I
took the sandals off. This was a mistake, because the rocks were
also sharp at the edges, and slashed my feet; I saw little ribbons of
red blood in the pools of water on the sand, where the waves broke
and gathered. I worked there but was not very efficient, and in any
case, they had brought in a group of criminal prisoners whose job
it was to beat us and goad us. It was hard work, but I thought at
that time that the sight and sound of the sea, the smell of the brine,

the sparkle of spray in the air, the sight of the low, blue, luminous horizon—these things were compensations for the hard work. As the day went on and the mood of the guards became uglier, beatings became more common. And when a prisoner slipped and fell into the water, was floundering around, a guard would come along, stand over him on a rock, put his foot on his neck, and keep the prisoner underwater until he fought for air, and bubbles came to the surface in pools where he was being kept. The mood grew uglier and the work harder.

But about lunchtime the chief sergeant or senior officer came along; one of the things he'd come about, it seemed, was the application I had made while at Leeuwkop for permission to continue my studies. He instructed the guards that I was one of those prisoners who were to be given special treatment. No doubt there were others. Because we were the kind of prisoners who wished to be educated and wanted to take over the country from them, the consequence was that I was taken off the rock carrying and made instead to push a wheelbarrow loaded with rocks. This was difficult because the wheelbarrows had to be pushed on the sea sand and when they were heavily loaded the single wheel of the wheelbarrow tended to sink into the sand making it extremely difficult to push; but this was my work and I attempted to do it except that the guards, in almost every instance, decided that I was not carrying enough rocks on my wheelbarrow; so they would instruct the criminal prisoners to pile even more rocks onto it. These were piled on until the wheelbarrow wheel was sunk into the sand almost to its axle, and this made it literally immovable or nearly so.

I'm not physically particularly strong and after the Fort and the hospital, and the lack of exercise, I was probably less strong. But I will say that I made just about every effort I could to move the wheelbarrow on these occasions and would in fact go down in front of the wheelbarrow and turn the wheel itself, painfully hauling it forward. This did not satisfy the guards who beat me persistently as I worked. And then to cap it, one of the prisoners, a particularly unpleasant one, I'm afraid, kicked me by a kind of karate kick, leaping into the air and then lashing into my stomach—he was wearing boots. I may have exaggerated the pain, but it certainly was acute at the time, my stomach still was in pretty bad shape, and for many days thereafter I suffered various pains, which I attributed to this kick in the stomach. In addition, and these were minor pains by comparison, the entire length of my body on the back, from the nape of my neck, down to the heels, was a mass of bruises from the repeated blows I had received. I don't know how many days—it couldn't have been many—I worked on the quarry; but one morning at breakfast, when we were being issued our porridge, and there was some kind of medical inspection, I reported that I was suffering the consequences of this injury. So I was taken out of the squad and put to work in the prison yard where my job was to drag some kind of mat back and forth across some area which I think they were going to cultivate, possibly lay grass, and turn it into a football field. I believe they did so later, when I was away, or even while I was there, but kept in the maximum security single cell section, where I was not able to see what was happening in the other part of the prison where I'd worked, which was called the zinc prison, or the sinktronk. I worked in the sinktronk area but my feet were enormously blistered by these badly fitting sandals, so that I worked in considerable pain. This was near the hospital section and indeed I was checked into the sinktronk hospital and stayed there for a while.

From prison hospital to knife-stabbers' camp

This hospital section was made of galvanized iron; there were rows of beds in it and beside each bed was a mat. And though I thought I was now going to sleep on a bed, it was explained that the beds were only there for inspection purposes; that one stood beside them in the morning when the senior officer passed through the prison, but that one slept on the mat beside a bed. And this indeed is what happened, in all the time I was there, with one exception: on one day there was a visitor from the Red Cross who was sent to Robben Island to investigate conditions; that day we were allowed to get into the beds in the morning, and then after he'd passed about midday we were required to get out of the beds and return to our mats on the floor.

This Red Cross episode was a curious one. Information had been smuggled out of Robben Island about conditions there, and so an investigator was sent. Up to that time I was without shoes— my order of events may be mixed up—but it was decided that I

ought to be issued shoes in case the Red Cross investigator asked to
see me. In fact he did not. I got the impression that he did not try
very hard to establish the facts, but this impression is also compli-
cated by the fact that the prisoners were not sure who the Red
Cross man was, and were not told that he was coming. Also, when
he happened to question prisoners in the presence of guards, the
prisoners were afraid to speak frankly, because he might, for all
they knew, have been a member of the prison administration in
plain clothes, and any statement they made would be used against
them, and they would subsequently be punished.

The specific issue which was getting some attention outside,
was a thoroughly unpleasant one, which, as far as I remember, in-
volved the Kleinhans brothers, who were reputedly among the
most sadistic guards on the island. They had instructed a particular
prisoner to dig a hole on the land where he was probably planting
something in the area where some crop was grown, and ordered
him to dig a deep trench, and get down into the trench. Other pris-
oners were instructed to fill the trench until he was buried into the
sand with only his head showing from it. At that point, the guards
instructed him to open his mouth and they urinated in his face and
mouth. This gave them great pleasure and amusement. News of
this episode was smuggled out.

I was also 'round about this time able to see Barney Zackon,
who came to the island to see me with regard to my appeal, and
technically we were supposed to be in a place where we could not
be overheard by guards. But Zackon—who was a member of the
Liberal Party and himself under considerable pressure from the po-
lice—was not very enthusiastic about receiving information from
me about prison conditions. He insisted that he had come entirely
with regard to my case, and not about prison conditions. The Red
Cross visit, I think, was a failure, because the kind of evidence
which should have reached the Red Cross on the outside did not
reach them through this visit. My own experience with the hospital
beds is an example of this.

When I was working in the section at the sinktronk (Afrikaans
for zinc prison), the prison hospital, I was summoned because I
had made a complaint about the prisoner who had kicked me in
the stomach. Very cleverly, I was escorted from my cell in the hos-

~ Villa Grimaldi

pital section to the complaint section by the very prisoner who had assaulted me. He made it quite clear that if I testified against him he would simply proceed to assault me afresh. I was thus in a position where, while I could testify to the assault, I was unable or unwilling to identify the prisoner who had committed the assault, and it was the same prisoner who escorted me back to my section. It was decided the following day to move me to a section near the old administration where I would be in solitary confinement. The purpose of this was twofold: one, I would be unable to communicate with any other prisoner, so that if I laid a charge against the prisoner who had assaulted me, I would not be able to contact any other prisoners who could act as witnesses and confirm the assault.

The second, and more dangerous one, was that in the isolated situation I was in, it would be possible for the same prisoner who had previously assaulted me to enter my cell and assault me with the connivance of the guards but without the knowledge or the awareness of any other prisoner, who would not be able to see it happening. I was kept in this area for some time, mainly with other prisoners who were being held on other charges; they were regarded as among the most vicious and were segregated at work as well in a barbed wire area where they sat with two-pound hammers breaking stones. This section was known as the knife-stabbers' camp, for especially those prisoners who were guilty of assaults and stabbings on the island itself; some of them were men with multiple murders, some committed outside prison, some of them inside prison. And while we worked, on the occasions when we were able to talk, they would sometimes narrate the murders they had committed both inside and outside prison. They were a curious bunch. For them I was a kind of simpleton who had gone to prison for a political offence, something wholly incomprehensible to them. This was a camp for sadistic prisoners, and sadistic guards. The Kleinhans brothers were there, and also a senior guard called van Kreunen, who happened to be one of those who singled me out for particularly vicious treatment.

Once I was brought out of the knife-stabbers camp—because of a brutal fight that developed among them, in which they clubbed each other with hammers and struck each other with pick axes—I was taken to my cell. The guards were going to be enter-

knife-stabbers camp

tained by allowing the knife-stabbers to fight each other until they were literally senseless. I watched this from my window; it was a kind of entertainment, bloody and almost animal, which the guards delighted in arranging.

Breaking rocks with Nelson Mandela

It was while I was in the solitary section of the old prison that the decision was made to send me to a hospital at a prison in Cape Town so that I could receive treatment for my stomach. On my return from Retreat, which is where this prison was, Tokay prison, in a suburb of Cape Town, I found a number of new people there. I heard their voices, but did not see them. Two batches of people who had been awaiting trial had arrived on the island: one group was from the Cape and was led by Neville Alexander and his group, which was called the YCC (Yu Chi Chan club) and was allegedly a Chinese-inspired group that had engaged in guerrilla activity. It included not only Neville Alexander but Don Davis, Fikile Bam, and others.

The other group included Nelson Mandela, who had been taken to Johannesburg for the conclusion of the Rivonia trial, and also all of the others in the trial. This group, which included old friends of mine besides Nelson, was due to come to Robben Island: Walter Sisulu, with whom I had worked closely in Johannesburg with the National Action Committee Council—formed after the ANC was banned—was a dear friend and is now serving, like the others, life sentences on Robben Island; Govan Mbeki from my home town, Port Elizabeth, with whom I had been associated for many years; Ahmed Kathrada from Johannesburg, in whose apartment on Market Street I had stayed many times in Johannesburg and with whom I had worked closely on various sports issues; Raymond Mhlaba, from Port Elizabeth again; Andrew Mlangeni, whom I had not met before; and the rest of the Rivonia party.

Andrew Mlangeni was there already and I was to meet him later when we were all put in the maximum security section which at this time was not complete; in fact when I had been carrying stones on arrival at Robben Island it was for part of the process of completing the new maximum security section immediately behind the administration block. In June of 1964, I was taken off the island, accompanied by two other prisoners who required medical treatment as well; we were taken on the ferry to Cape Town and then to Caledon Square prison and from Caledon Square prison to the prison in Retreat. It was from Retreat that I traveled for several days to the Victoria Hospital in Wynberg for treatment and where my brother and my sister-in-law, Martha, contrived to see me illegally. Martha had also come to visit me on the island, and brought me a handsome cake that was eaten by the guards; I was not permitted to receive it because I was now a sentenced and convicted prisoner rather than an awaiting-trial prisoner.

After treatment in Wynberg, I also requested and saw a priest while in the Retreat prison. I had contemplated escape and had been dissuaded by him from undertaking it. And indeed there was no reason why I should escape, since I only had approximately another year to serve, except that even now there was no certainty that I would be permitted to leave prison after I had served my sentence.

Around June 24—the feast of St. John the Baptist—I was permitted a Missal, the Roman Missal of the Catholic Church. I returned first to the isolation section on the old zinc prison and then we were all marched down or brought down to the newly completed, much more sturdy stone building built of the gray flintstone found on the island, which was the new maximum security prison. It consisted of eighty-eight single cells built in a square around a courtyard, over which there was a catwalk patrolled by a guard with an automatic rifle at all times. In this courtyard we worked first clearing the ground and later breaking stones. For a brief time, when we were visited by a journalist from a British paper, we were given the job of mending torn police clothes with needles and thread; we were duly photographed doing this and the picture appeared in the British press and has been printed widely elsewhere. After the photograph was taken, the following day we were returned to breaking stones.

I spent the remainder of my time on Robben Island breaking stones. This was because I was held to be not strong enough and not well enough to undertake hard work. The other prisoners—Mandela, Sisulu, Mbeki, the rest, and Neville Alexander and his group—were sent off each day to work in a limestone quarry where they dug lime out of the earth and returned at about four in the afternoon covered with dust, as I've described in one of my poems. I was left to break stones, except for perhaps the last two weeks of my sentence when I was given the much lighter chore of being a prison window cleaner. Perhaps this was part of the process of rehabilitation and preparing me for normal existence once again; this would have been about June of 1965, a year later. But the period of breaking stones was in fact a period of immense psychological action rather than external physical action.

At no time was it absolutely certain that I would be released from prison. In fact the contrary might have been more certain, to the extent that at the time that I was due to be released from prison, it was discovered that all my clothes—my shirt, my jacket, my trousers, and my shoes had been sold by a guard. This was fairly common practice in the case of people who were serving life sentences, so it must be assumed that at least one guard, and perhaps more, thought that I would never again need civilian clothes. By some curious twist or very complicated process, it was discovered that this guard was engaged in running a secondhand clothes business and was busy retailing clothes of the convicts.

While I was breaking stones there was a pail in the middle of the area where we broke stones, which one was required to use as a toilet, and one needed permission to approach the pail. The guards would conveniently be distracted or concerned with other things whenever one needed to attract their attention to go to the pail. I remember on one occasion walking over to the pail without permission, and being threatened with punishment for disobedience. In addition, the guard engaged me in a discussion during which he said that I ought not to complain about being in prison or the hardships of prison life for I had brought it upon myself. I had brought myself to prison; no one else had done it. I agreed with him and said, "Yes, I agree that it is for the prison system to imprison me for opposing them," that if I were free I would be working to imprison the prime minister, whom I regarded as a criminal, and I mentioned his name, Dr. Verwoerd. The guard, of course, was outraged, and reported me for this insubordination, which was almost approaching heresy, and it was proposed that I should be tried in the prison court for this offense. The punishment would be lashes. There were milder punishments: I could have been deprived of my food or put on spare diet, which would have meant drinking rice water 3 times a day for a period of six or twelve or eighteen days; but it was predicted that I would receive lashes. [South Africa is one of the countries where corporal punishment is still inflicted as part of the law.] The system is to strip a prisoner naked, and then strap him to a large metal triangle so that his hands are outstretched, and then to use bamboo canes, usually six feet in length and sometimes dipped in salt, I am told. The prisoner is literally assaulted with these, and the marks they inflict—and I have seen them—are marks you carry for life. What the cane does is literally to cut out a slice of flesh from the buttock, leaving an open wound, which looks rather like a freshly bitten plum, a great red fleshy pulp wound. Six lashes would mean six of these gashes, and for days after the prisoner is unable to either sit or lie on his back because of the injury. Faced with the prospect of lashes for having spoken disrespectfully about the prime minister, I demanded that I should be allowed legal defense and that a lawyer be brought to defend me. Rather than get involved in this kind of legal hassle, which would involve exposing what the charge against me was, this particular charge was dropped.

Traps and new charges

But it was not the only time I got into trouble. While I was still in the old jail in solitary, I had been approached by a prisoner who undertook to smuggle letters out of the prison for me, and to give them to a guard who would post them on the island or in Cape Town and to whom replies could be addressed. I could make appeals for money or anything else, and they would be given to me, provided the guard got a slice as well. I was a new prisoner and the notion attracted me. I wrote a letter to John Harris—strange how our lives were linked—and asked him to send me some money, though I never saw it. I did get a letter back from John, and a prisoner brought me sweets, and cans of beans, but perhaps a guard originally bought it. For a day or two I lived high on the hog worth perhaps one-tenth of the money that was sent to me. The kind of sterile existence, the unappetizing and almost inedible food in prison, made this a very welcome relief. I might well have done it more often, except that I was going through a spiritual trauma.

The further complication was, when I returned from the mainland and the prison there, where I had again been contemplating escape, I found a letter from John Harris waiting for me from the same prisoner who had acted as a go-between before. It was mainly about sports and it must have been written sometime before, because 'round about the time the letter reached me, the news also reached me that John Harris had been arrested for sabotage on the main railway station in Johannesburg and a bomb explosion had killed one woman and injured others. John Harris had been captured, been beaten up and tortured by the police, and was facing the death sentence.

I then received a message from George Peake, my fellow prisoner in the maximum security section where we were all in single cells, warning me that the prisoner who was bringing me the letter was part of the an elaborate trap—what in prison parlance is called a bomb, or a scheme by which either a prisoner or a guard is trapped in a conspiracy and gets into serious trouble. George alerted me that Garibaldi—as we called him in code, because he was a prisoner who wore a red shirt—was part of an elaborate trap to plant a bomb for me. The letters were being transmitted for me as part of this process to trap me into something extremely dangerous, the outcome of which would be that I would get a further charge, a further sentence of a number of years, insuring that I remain in prison.

So that was part of the kind of uncertainty and anxiety I was living through in prison. I had one other: One day I was summoned to the office of the chief, and he confronted me with a copy of Sirens Knuckles Boots. It was, I think, the first time I ever saw the book in print, and he asked me if I was the author. I confirmed this, and he told me that I would formally be charged with the crime of publishing poetry when this was a criminal act for me and I was liable to a sentence of a further three years. This is part of the rather curious situation I was in. I cooperated with him in preparing the information about the book to establish my guilt, except that he insisted on knowing the exact date on which the manuscript had been transmitted, but I found I could not tell him.

I wracked my brains; I tried desperately to remember the exact date, so that it could be entered into the indictment, and I could be charged and convicted. I was going through a period of agonizing

guilt and of agonizing attempts to be honest and truthful, and so I
genuinely tried. But part of the process of agony was that my mind
was becoming extremely unreliable and particularly my memory. I
could remember things exactly, but not remember the order in
which they had happened, and so I was unable to supply the infor-
mation, and the charge was eventually dropped. Looking back I
can see how the series of pressures worked on me simultaneously—
the possibility of never ever getting out of prison, facing first a
charge of insubordination, and then the knowledge of a plot to en-
snare me, and then of course I had clearly broken prison regula-
tions at least in terms of smuggling letters out and receiving letters
back. All of this combined to create a state of tension, heightened
by the kind of spiritual anxieties I was going through, which set up
a wholly new phase of near-insanity and certainly of hallucina-
tions, ending in attempts at suicide.

Like a tattooed lady in a circus

Let me just add two footnotes which fill out some of the exter-
nal experience. It was in the section in the zinc jail where I was in
the temporary hospital with other prisoners lying on the floor that
I first discovered the systematic use of sexual assault as a method
used by the guards in prison. The exchanges would go something
like this: a guard would ask one of the lifers who was there and
who was known to have several mistresses or wives, as it was
called, "How many political prisoners have you fucked today?" Or
"How many *poqos* have you fucked today?" Clearly there was a
system by which prisoners were rewarded for sexual assaults on
the political prisoners, and *poqo* was a term used for all political
prisoners regardless of whether they were ANC, PAC, YCC, or, as
in my case, belonged to no specific organization. The outcome of
this I saw in at least one instance—and I have written about this—
of a young boy, no more than a school boy, who was first starved
into submission, and then beaten to compel him to submit, beaten
until he wept and cried, urinated, and generally messed up his cell.[4]
After this he would continue to be starved to the point where
he himself begged for sexual assault. This was the great "achieve-
ment" of the lifers: if they could reduce a prisoner to the point
where he did not only submit, but out of hunger and out of pain

and innumerable beatings, he also actually begged for sexual assault. I heard innumerable tales of this, in addition to occasions when I myself witnessed beatings, or the systematic denial of food and exercise to a prisoner in order to starve him into submission. All this of course happened in the larger context of homosexual relations which were established, independently of beatings or political implications. And one of the things I came to understand, or began to understand, in prison was the possibility of forming valid emotional relationships. I am not sure that I thought it through in prison. I was merely beginning to question my own hostility to the notion, the sense of the unnaturalness of it. And by the time I left prison, homosexuality was still offensive to me, both morally, for everybody, and specifically for myself. But even this generated tensions of a curious kind, which I will discuss.[5]

Although I was never sexually assaulted myself, there were numerous occasions when I was threatened, particularly when I was in solitary, and particularly and most graphically 'round about December 1964 when I was removed to a more distant section of the maximum security prison and threatened by prisoners who were doing life. One specific occasion, when the other prisoners expressed a particular sexual interest in me, was when I reported to the hospital in the zinc jail after I had been assaulted on the beach in the quarry, and I was complaining and requesting treatment. I had, as I have said, been beaten continuously, and my back, the entire back from my neck down to my ankles, was a mass of bruises. These turned purple and green and became quite a spectacle, so that in the section where I was kept with the other prisoners, guards would come over and request me to strip in order that they could see these bruises that formed a continuous pattern, like a carpet, over my body. I myself became something of a spectacle, almost like a tattooed lady in a circus. Standing in line at the hospital, where allegedly I was going to be attended to and where I was eventually put for treatment, and given suppositories, they suggested I was simply constipated when I was complaining of these stomach pains. Standing naked in the line there, awaiting treatment with the other prisoners, there were prisoners who expressed a sexual interest in me and threatened to deal with me at some future date. But nothing came of this.

At the maximum security section I was kept at various times in four different cells: first, in one near the entrance, later, in one down the corridor on the same side, and then in one on the opposite side of the corridor, slightly further up, and eventually, to this remote one on the other side of the quadrangle, where I remained, as far as I remember, most of my time. I also had a brief interlude in a cell in the far side of the quadrangle. From the window in my cell where I first arrived, I had the fortune, if I stood on my lavatory pail and rolled up my blanket and put that on top of the lavatory pail and then stood on the blanket, delicately balancing on the rim of the pail—I had the fortune to reach up and look through a window high up in the wall of my cell. From the window I could see the sea and a few fir trees, green and black. But of course I wasn't in my cell all that much. I was out breaking stones. And if I was in the cell it was an offense for me to look through the window: if I was caught by the guard passing along in a corridor, I would be punished for looking through the window.

The sea gave me pleasure on the rare occasions I was able to see it. There was a road that wound down, one running from the administration block and security section down to the jetty, another one which wound by, going to the part of the island where the guards lived and they had their cinema and gymnasium, and sometimes one even saw civilians, men and women, walking by there. I never did see the stars, though I made the attempt once when I was in Side 2 of the maximum security and directly opposite the catwalk where the guard patrolled all night with his automatic rifle. Roughly on the corner where Sides 1 and 2 joined, there was a machine gun post and a lookout on the wooden stilts raised above the ground, and I remember another one near the section where I originally was put, as well as one near the prison yard at the kitchen where we were issued our food.

I was visited in prison. At first it was ruled that I was a D category prisoner; I was allowed a visit once every six months, and a letter once every six months. I disputed my classification because I carried a white card and I had a sentence of under three years; eventually the rules were re-jigged in my favor so that I was visited at various times on the island; once by Martha, my sister-in-law. When she came again on a second time I was going through my traumatic period; it was 'round about the first of November, and I refused to see her. At least once I was visited by my wife, May, who came to the island and brought with her Gregory, still a baby in arms. We were able to communicate through a fence with two sets of fences separating us, and the guards of course in attendance and all the prisoners on the one side of the fence shouting simultaneously to their relatives on the other side of the fence, who were also shouting. It was a kind of bedlam and not very much conversation took place.

At first, in the maximum security section, we were not allowed to work or to go out at all, until there were protests from people like Nelson [Mandela] and Walter [Sisulu], and they then agreed to allow us to exercise once a day for half an hour. We walked in a circle and were not allowed to talk, rather like the images one sees of prison yards in an American prison. At first there were no showers and washrooms in the maximum security section because the water was not working. Eventually there was a section at the far end, where there were showers and washbasins. But for the start we were made to strip in the maximum security section and then run all the way over to the old zinc jail and shower there, either under extremely powerful jets of water, almost like fire hoses, or else the water would be turned off abruptly while we were in the process of a shower.

I think it was there that for the first time going over to the shower that I was able to talk to Nelson [Mandela], Walter [Sisulu], Kathy [Ahmed Kathrada], Raymond [Mhlaba], Lionel [Davis], Andrew [Mlangeni], and Elias Motsoaledi, the other member of the group. I remember with much pleasure that Walter Sisulu's greeting to me was by the code name that I had used when working for the National Action Council, a name which he and perhaps one other person knew—she is now in Britain. The secret police tried a great deal to discover to whom the name belonged. Walter's answer, as Ruth's had been, that the man to whom the name belonged had already escaped from the country and there was no point in trying to find out who he was. But I take pleasure in the extremely effective concealment of my alias, something I did much more skillfully than people in more responsible positions who failed to conceal their identities.

In the maximum security section with its eighty single cells, as far as I remember, we were mostly political prisoners. Occasionally, a criminal prisoner would be brought in because he was going to be given some extra punishment, and a few of them were kept there in order to bring us our food while we were in our cells, and also to act as informers and spies. Of these I will mention a couple, because they were the people who were involved in my own various complications in prison. One of the things that I learned from the non-political prisoners was their wonderful matter-of-factness, their understanding of the nature of the South African system as an oppressive system, and their rather contemptuous attitude towards us, particularly those of us who thought of change by nonviolent methods. And, of course, the folly of going to prison for an ideal rather than for a bank robbery was something that caused them endless amusement.

But I learned for myself to work out how much those who were made criminals by the violations of the criminal code were themselves victims of injustice in another form, that the racism and oppression which we challenged and which denied us our human freedom was in other ways operating to destroy their human dignity and their freedom. They were outlaws and proud of it. They stood outside the law, and they had very few illusions about the justice of the system under which they lived. They spoke frequently about their exploits outside, many of them perhaps boasting, and they were extremely curious to know what the politicians would do about them when they came to power. The notion that they would be excluded from justice when we took over was one that appalled them. It antagonized them, of course, because they saw no reason why they should support us when we were liable to imprison them as well; that may simply be because they had a better understanding of the conditions which produced their predicament than we had.

This raises an interesting idea: I believe that if the liberation movement came out with a clear statement on this issue, it would be able to enlist a far greater measure of support from a section of the South African public which does not now support us. They include the criminals, the tsotsis,[6] the riff-raff—the people compelled to live outside the law because no opportunity exists for them inside the law, or simply because they've lost their documents and there is no way of reestablishing their identity. This would entail an announcement directed at the reexamination of the South African legal system so that fewer people will be made criminals by the system, apart from those who become criminals by challenging the section of the law dealing with political activity and racial justice, but simply in terms of the economic relations, opportunity, the right to function in a society, and work within it, and live comfortably within it.

I think such a challenge, and statements along these lines, would elicit a great deal of support from a very large and significant section of the South African population. It is not enough for us to think of our reforms simply in terms of legislation which affects racism, equal opportunity, the right to vote, and the right to form trade unions and things like that, some of which is necessary and some of it merely reformist. It is also necessary to attack, to go to the heart of the South African system and define the degree to which the system creates criminals, and to make the statements indicating that we will reject and overthrow that system so that the present conditions will no longer obtain. I think that one could make not only an important contribution to the transformation of the society and declaration of one's objectives, but one would also elicit an extremely significant measure of support of the kind that we need very badly. This is also the lesson of the Algerian Revolution, but it is the kind of support at this time we simply do not have. This issue, I believe, deserves a special comment—a memorandum perhaps addressed to the ANC, with a copy to Albie Sachs, who I think would be responsive to this notion as a result of his study on justice in South Africa.

[1] Brutus is referring to an untitled poem, "Cold," that was written en route to Robben Island; the poem works through the juxtaposition of a series of images: a "grizzled senior warder" who considers these prisoners "Things" that "are worse than rats/you can only shoot them"; to the "large frosty glitter of stars; to the chains on the prisoners' ankles and wrists that also "jangle/glitter…like the stars." The poem was first published in *Letters to Martha: and Other poems from a South African Prison* (London: Heinemann, 1968), 48–49.

[2] A reference to Lawrence G. Green's *At Daybreak for the Isles* (Cape Town: Howard B. Timmins Publishers, 1950), a popular book about seafaring in the islands off the South African coast.

[3] Here Brutus is referring to his untitled poem, "At daybreak for the isle," published as the thirteenth in a series of eighteen poems in *Letters to Martha*.

[4] Brutus describes this instance in an untitled poem, "Perhaps most terrible are those who beg for it," the seventh among the eighteen poems published in *Letters to Martha*.

5 Brutus recalls that his perception of homosexuality changed while he was in prison; he later became a supporter of gay and lesbian liberation: "Growing up, I had the homoerotic experiences that many people do, but then went through the typical Western Christian phase of believing that homosexuality was repugnant. In prison, although homosexuality was often used as a means of domination, I began to see that gay relationships could be emotionally genuine." [Interview with editors, November 12, 2005.]

6 A South African term for scoundrels and gangsters.

Poems

Waiting
(South African style):
"Non-Whites Only"

1

At the counter an ordinary girl
with unemphatic features and
a surreptitious novelette
surveys with Stanislav disdain
my verminous existence and consents
with langorous reluctance—
the dumpling nose acquiring chiselled charm
through puckering distaste—
to sell me postage stamps:
she calculates the change on knuckly fingertips
and wordless toothless-old-man mumbling lips.

2

Was ever office-tea-colored tea as good as this
or excited such lingering relishing ever?
Railway schedules hoot at me derision
as trains run on their measured rods of time:
But here in this oasis of my impotence
the hours dribble through lacunae in my guts:
Stoic yourself for some few hours more
till the Civil Service serves—without civility:
["Arsenic and Old Lace"]andantes through my head.

1963

The mob

*The white crowd who attacked those who protested
on the Johannesburg City Hall steps against the
Sabotage Bill*

These are the faceless horrors
that people my nightmares
from whom I turn to wakefulness
for comforting

yet here I find confronting me
the fear-blanked facelessness
and saurian-lidded stares
of my irrational terrors
from whom in dreams I run.

O my people

O my people
what have you done
and where shall I find comforting
to smooth awake your mask of fear
restore your face, your faith, feeling, tears.

May 1962   1963

Sharpeville

What is important
about Sharpeville
is not that seventy died:
nor even that they were shot in the back
retreating, unarmed, defenceless

and certainly not
the heavy caliber slug
that tore through a mother's back
and ripped through the child in her arms
killing it

Remember Sharpeville
bullet-in-the-back day
Because it epitomized oppression   ←———
and the nature of society
more clearly than anything else;
it was the classic event

Nowhere is racial dominance
more clearly defined
nowhere the will to oppress
more clearly demonstrated

what the world whispers
apartheid declares with snarling guns
the blood the rich lust after
South Africa spills in the dust

Remember Sharpeville
Remember bullet-in-the-back day

———7   And remember the unquenchable will for freedom
Remember the dead
and be glad

                                                        1973

Zulu defeat
_(1838)_

Blood River Day
For Daphne Edmondson

Each year on this day
they drum the earth with their boots
and growl incantations
to evoke the smell of blood
for which they hungrily sniff the air:

guilt
drives them to the lair
of primitiveness
and ferocity:

but in the dusk
it is the all pervasive smell of dust
the good smell of the earth
as the rain sifts down on the hot sand
that comes to me

the good smell of the dust
that is the same
everywhere around the earth.

December 16, 1965   1968

The impregnation of our air
with militarism
is not a thing to be defined
or catalogued;
it is a miasma
wide as the air itself
ubiquitous as a million trifling things,
our very climate;
we become a bellicose people
living in a land at war
a country besieged;
the children play with guns
and the schoolboys dream of killings
and our dreams are full of the birdflight of jets
and our men
are bloated with bloody thoughts; inflated sacrifices
and grim despairing dyings.

1968

Their behavior

Their guilt
is not so very different from ours:
—who has not joyed in the arbitrary exercise of power
or grasped for himself what might have been another's
and who has not used superior force in the moment when he could,

(and who of us has not been tempted to these things?)—
so, in their guilt,
the bared ferocity of teeth,
chest-thumping challenge and defiance,
the deafening clamor of their prayers
to a deity made in the image of their prejudice
which drowns the voice of conscience,
is mirrored our predicament
but on a social, massive, organized scale
which magnifies enormously
as the private deshabille of love
becomes obscene in orgies.

Blood River Day, 1965   1968

In memoriam: I.A.H.*

Being dead
it does not matter
how guilty or innocent he died

we are free to speak
though because he chose not to speak
he died.

Being dead
it does not matter
how well or ill he died

—now they can touch him not
though it was under their pulping boots
he died.

Yet the living
for whom he put out tendrils of self
must live miasma-ed by his death

and the flowers he put forth for them
are now pale wreaths of terror
with the sick-sweet smell of death.

Being dead
we might pay him tribute
but it was for the living he died

and we must content ourselves in saying
"it was for our cause he died"
and inwardly know for what cause he died.

* Imam Abdullah Haroun, "found dead of natural causes" in his cell
in Cape Town, after being held without trial for four months by the
Secret Police.

1969

Robben Island sequence ←———

I

neonbright orange
vermillion
on the chopped broken slate
that gravelled the path and yard
bright orange was the red blood
freshly spilt where the prisoners had passed;
and bright red
pinkbright red and light
the blood on the light sand by the sea
the pale lightyellow seas and
in the light bright airy air
lightwoven, seawoven, spraywoven air
of sunlight by the beach where we worked:

where the bright blade-edges of the rocks
jutted like chisels from the squatting rocks
the keen fine edges whitening to thinness
from the lightbrown masses of the sunlit rocks,
washed around by swirls on rushing wave water,
lightgreen or colorless, transparent with a hint of light:

on the sharp pale whitening edges
our blood showed light and pink,

our gashed soles winced from the fine barely felt slashes,
that lacerated afterwards:
the bloody flow
thinned to thin pink strings dangling
as we hobbled through the wet clinging sands
or we discovered surprised
in some quiet backwater pool
the thick flow of blood uncoiling
from a skein to thick dark red strands.

The menace of that bright day was clear as the blade of a knife;
from the blade edges of the rocks,
from the piercing brilliance of the day,
the incisive thrust of the clear air into the lungs
the salt-stinging brightness of sky and light on the eyes:
from the clear image, bronze-sharp lines of Kleynhans laughing
Khaki-ed, uniformed, with his foot on the neck of the convict
    who had fallen,
holding his head under water in the pool where he had fallen
while the man thrashed helplessly
and the bubbles gurgled
and the air glinted dully on lethal gunbutts,
the day was brilliant with the threat of death.

II

sitting on the damp sand
in sand-powdered windpuff,
the treetops still gray in the early morning air
and dew still hanging tree-high,
to come to the beginning of the day
and small barely-conscious illicit greetings
to settle to a shape of mind, of thought,
and inhabit a body to its extremities:
to be a prisoner, a political victim,
to be a some-time fighter, to endure—
find reserves of good cheer, of composure
while the wind rippled the tight skin forming
    on the cooling porridge
and sandspray dropped by windgusts depressed it:

to begin, at the beginning of a day, to be a person
and take and hold a shape to last for this one day....

(afterwards the old lags came along
with their favorite warders, to select
the young prisoners who had caught their eye,
so that these could be assigned to their span)

III

some mornings we lined up for "hospital"
—it meant mostly getting castor oil—
but what a varied bunch we were!
for all had injuries—but in such variety
split heads; smashed ankles, arms;
cut feet in bandages, or torn and bloodied legs:
some, under uniform, wore their mass of bruises
but what a bruised and broken motley lot we were!

                                                      1978

Still the sirens

Still the sirens
stitch the night air with terror—
pierce hearing's membranes
with shrieks of pain and fear:

still they weave the mesh
that traps the heart in anguish,
flash bright bars of power
that cage memory in mourning and loss.

Still sirens haunt the night air.

Someday there will be peace
someday the sirens will be still
someday we will be free.

                                                      1989

Endurance

"...is the ultimate virtue—more,
the essential thread
on which existence is strung
when one is stripped to nothing else
and not to endure is to end in despair."

I

Cold floors
bleak walls
another anteroom:
another milestone behind
fresh challenges ahead:
in this hiatus
with numb resolution
I coil my energies
and wait.

II

Stripped to the waist
in ragged pantaloons
long ago I sweated over bales,
my stringy frame—strained—
grew weary but sprang back
stubbornly
from exhaustion:
the lashes now,
and the labors are different
but still demand,
wound and stretch to breaking point:
and I still snap back, stubbornly.

III

All day a stoic
at dawn I wake, eyelids wet
with tears shed in dreams.

[IV] ←——

My father, that distant man,
gray hair streaked with silver,
spoke of St. Francis of Assisi
with a special timbre in his voice:
loved him not, I think, for the birds
circling his head, nor the grace
of that threadbare fusty gown
but for his stigmata: the blood
that gleamed in the fresh wounds
on his palms and insteps:
in my isolation cell in prison,
the bullet wound in my side still raw,
those images afflicted me.

V

[he's in Athens 24 years later]

When we shook hands in the Athenian dusk   ny ?
it closed a ring that had opened twenty-four years before
when a wisp of off-key melody had snaked into my gray cell
whistled by a bored guard in the sunlit afternoon outside:
it circled the gray walls like a jeweled adder
bright and full of menace and grew
to a giant python that encircled me, filling the cell
then shrank and entered me where it lay
coiled like my gut, hissing sibilantly
of possession;
twice I breathed death's hot fetid breath
twice I leaned over the chasm, surrendering
till some tiny fibre at the base of my brain
protested in the name of sanity and dragged me
from the precipice of suicide that allured
with its own urgent logic

Our hands meeting, uncordially, your gaze
quizzical, perhaps affronted
sealed a circle in the gathering dusk,
like the ring of dark waves advancing
on the island's jagged shore
and the dark enclosure of wire   ‖ ←——
whose barbs are buried in my brain. ‖

VI

Wormwood gray shadows take shape
as night drains from the moon:
objects assume outlines
and some backdrop is suggested
and still the noose of time's expiring closes in

shapes, like bats-upended
hover and circle
holy men chanting their mantras
as darkness dissolves
in a purgatorial stasis.

VII

In the air pungent with asepsis
the raucous guards swagger
their uniforms and holsters bulk
in a perennial twilight
the sweat of newly dead corpses
makes rigid the smoke-laden fug
the collapsed lung labors stertoriously
strained iterations of emergencies
thread the air like steel bobbins
stitching towards finality, mortality
corpselike, in the gloom
bodies clutter the floor in rows
a gloom threaded with sighs
yearnings, griefs and lusts
overhead, the silhouette of guard and gun
prowl against the discolored glass
men's hungers, tears, groans

tall expanses, concrete brick, glass
encircle the harsh cement
dull gray against fresh blood
and a circle of gaping mouths
the faces swallowed away
life bleeding away, the blood pooled

only redeeming this crepuscular acesis
one bright voice, bright eyes, welcoming flesh
one bright ribbon in the encircling gloom
long torn, long lost and tattered
but still cherished at the center of the brain

No, it redeems nothing
cannot stave off the end
nor offer any relief from this
encompassing gloom

1993

Letters to Martha

1

After the sentence
mingled feelings:
sick relief,
the load of the approaching days
apprehension—
the hints of brutality
have a depth of personal meaning;

exultation—
the sense of challenge,
of confrontation,
vague heroism
mixed with self-pity
and tempered by the knowledge of those
who endure much more
and endure...

2

One learns quite soon
that nails and screws
and other sizeable bits of metal
must be handed in;

and seeing them shaped and sharpened
one is chilled, appalled
to see how vicious it can be
—this simple, useful bit of steel:

and when these knives suddenly flash
—produced perhaps from some disciplined anus—
one grasps at once the steel-bright horror
in the morning air
and how soft and vulnerable is naked flesh.

3

Suddenly one is tangled
in a mesh of possibilities:
notions cobweb around your head,
tendrils sprout from your guts in a hundred directions:

why did this man stab this man for that man?
what was the nature of the emotion
and how did it grow?
was this the reason for a warder's unmotived senseless brutality?
by what shrewdness was it instigated?

desire for prestige or lust for power?
Or can it—strange, most strange!—be love, strange love?
And from what human hunger was it born?

4

Particularly in a single cell,
but even in the sections
the religious sense asserts itself;

perhaps a childhood habit of nightly prayers
the accessibility of Bibles,
or awareness of the proximity of death:

and, of course, it is a currency —
pietistic expressions can purchase favors
and it is a way of suggesting reformation
(which can procure promotion);

and the resort of the weak
is to invoke divine revenge
against a rampaging injustice;

but in the gray silence of the empty afternoons
it is not uncommon
to find oneself talking to God. ‖

5

In the grayness of isolated time
which shafts down into the echoing mind,
wraiths appear, and whispers of horrors
that people the labyrinth of self. ⎤

Coprophilism; necrophilism; fellatio;
penis-amputation;
and in this gibbering society
hooting for recognition as one's other selves
suicide, self-damnation, walks
if not a companionable ghost
then a familiar familiar,
a doppelgänger
not to be shaken off.

6

⎡Two men I knew specifically⎤
among many cases:
their reactions were enormously different
but a tense thought lay at the bottom of each
and for both there was danger and fear and pain—
drama.?

One simply gave up smoking
knowing he could be bribed
and hedged his mind with romantic fantasies
of beautiful marriageable daughters;

the other sought escape
in fainting fits and asthmas
and finally fled into insanity:

so great the pressures to enforce sodomy.

7

Perhaps most terrible are those who beg for it,
who beg for sexual assault.

To what desperate limits are they driven
and what fierce agonies they have endured
that this, which they have resisted,
should seem to them preferable,
even desirable.

It is regarded as the depths
of absolute and ludicrous submission.
And so perhaps it is.

But it has seemed to me
one of the most terrible
most rendingly pathetic
of all a prisoner's predicaments.

8

"Blue champagne" they called him
—the most popular "girl" in the place;
so exciting perhaps, or satisfying:
young certainly, with youthful curves
—this was most highly prized.

And so he would sleep with several
each night
and the song once popular on the hit-parade
became his nickname.

By the time I saw him he was older
(George *saw* the evil in his face, he said)
and he had become that most perverse among
the perverted:
a "man" in the homosexual embrace
who once had been the "woman."

9

⌈The not-knowing⌉
is perhaps the worst part of the agony
for those outside;

not knowing what cruelties must be endured
what indignities the sensitive spirit must face
what wounds the mind can be made to inflict on itself;

and the hunger to be thought of
to be remembered
and to reach across space
with filaments of tenderness
and consolation.

And knowledge,
even when it is knowledge of ugliness
seems to be preferable,
can be better endured.

And so,
for your consolation
I send these fragments,
random pebbles I pick up
from the landscape of my own experience
traversing the same arid wastes
in a montage of glimpses
I allow myself
or stumble across.

10

It is not all terror
and deprivation,
you know;

one comes to welcome the closer contact
and understanding one achieves
with one's fellow-men,
fellows, compeers;

and the discipline does much to force
a shape and pattern on one's daily life
as well as on the days

and honest toil
offers some redeeming hours
for the wasted years;

so there are times
when the mind is bright and restful
though alive:
rather like the full calm morning sea.

11

Events have a fresh dimension
for all things can affect the pace
of political development—

but our concern
is how they hasten or delay
a special freedom—
that of those the prisons hold
and who depend on change
to give them liberty.

And so one comes to a callousness,
a savage ruthlessness—
voices shouting in the heart
"Destroy! Destroy!"
or
"Let them die in thousands!"—

really it is impatience,

November 11, 1965

12

Nothing was sadder
there was no more saddening want
than the deadly lack
of music.

Even in the cosy days
of "awaiting trial" status
it was the deprivation
and the need
that one felt most.

After sentence,
in the rasping convict days
it grew to a hunger
—the bans on singing, whistling
and unappreciative ears
made it worse.

Then those who shared one's loves
and hungers
grew more dear on this account—
Fiks and Jeff and Neville
and the others

Strains of Eine Kleine Nachtmusik
the Royal Fireworks,
the New World,
the Emperor and Eroica,
Jesu, joy of man's desiring.

Surreptitious wisps of melody
down the damp gray concrete corridors

Joy.

13

"At daybreak for the isle,"
and
"Look your last on all all things lovely,"
and
"So, for a beginning, I know
there is no beginning."

So one cushions the mind
with phrases
aphorisms and quotations
to blunt the impact
of this crushing blow.

So one grits to the burden
and resolves to doggedly endure
the outrages of prison.

Nothing of him doth change
but that doth suffer a seachange...

14

How fortunate we were
not to have been exposed
to rhetoric

—it would have falsified
a simple experience;
living grimly,
grimly enduring

Oh there was occasional heroic posturing
mainly from the immature
—and a dash of demagogic bloodthirstiness

But generally
we were simply prisoners
of a system we had fought
and still opposed.

15

Extrapolation
is the essential secret of our nature
—or so one may call it:

the capacity
to ennoble
or pervert
what is otherwise
simply animal
amoral and instinctual

and it is this that argues for us
a more than animal destiny
and gives us the potential   humanity
for the diabolic
or divinity.

16

Quite early one reaches a stage
where one resolves to embrace
the status of prisoner
with all it entails,
savoring to the full its bitterness
and seeking to escape nothing:

"Mister,
this is prison;
just get used to the idea"

"You're a convict now."

Later one changes,
tries the dodges,
seeks the easy outs.

But the acceptance
once made
deep down
remains.

17

In prison
the clouds assume importance
and the birds

With a small space of sky
cut off by walls
of bleak hostility
and pressed upon by hostile authority
the mind turns upwards
when it can—

—there can be no hope
of seeing the stars:
the arcs and fluorescents
have blotted them out—

the complex aeronautics
of the birds
and their exuberant acrobatics
become matters for intrigued speculation
and wonderment

clichés about the freedom of the birds
and their absolute freedom from care
become meaningful

and the graceful unimpeded motion of the clouds
—a kind of music, poetry, dance—
sends delicate rhythms tremoring through the flesh
and fantasies course easily through the mind:
—where are they going
where will they dissolve
will they be seen by those at home
and whom will they delight?

18

I remember rising one night
after midnight
and moving
through an impulse of loneliness
to try and find the stars.

And through the haze
the battens of fluorescents made
I saw pinpricks of white
I thought were stars.

Greatly daring
I thrust my arm through the bars
and easing the switch in the corridor
plunged my cell in darkness

I scampered to the window
and saw the splashes of light
where the stars flowered.

But through my delight
thudded the anxious boots
and a warning barked
from the machine-gun post
on the catwalk.

And it is the brusque inquiry
and threat
that I remember of that night
rather than the stars.

December 20, 1965   1968*

    * All poems 1-18 were originally published as "Letters to Martha" in 1968.

Postscripts

1

These are not images to cheer you
—except that you may see in these small acts
some evidence of my thought and caring:
but still I do not fear their power to wound
knowing your grief, your loss and anxious care,
rather I send you bits to fill
the mosaic of your calm and patient knowledge
—picking the jagged bits embedded in my mind—

partly to wrench some ease for my own mind.
And partly that some world sometime may know.

2

There are of course tho' we don't see them
—I cut away the public trappings to assert
certain private essentialities—
some heroic aspects of this all
—people outside admire, others pity—
but it is not of these I wish to speak;

but to pin down the raw experience
tease the nerve of feeling and expose
it in the general tissue we dissect;
and then, below this, with attentive ear
to hear the faint heartthrob—
a flicker, pulse, mere vital hint
which speaks of the stubborn will
the grim assertion of some sense of worth
in the teeth of the wind
on a stony beach, or among rocks
where the brute hammers fall unceasingly
on the mind.

3

The seagulls, feathery delicate
and full of grace when flying
might have done much to redeem things;

but their raucous greed and bickering
over a superflux of offal—
a predatory stupidity

dug in the heart with iron-hard beak
some lesson of the nature of nature:
man's ineradicable cruelty?

4

The wind bloweth where it listeth
and no man knoweth whence it came

And we poor temporary mortals
probationary in this vale of tears
damned and blissful in due course
must wait some arbitrary will
to determine our eternal destiny.

5

There were times in my concrete cube
—faceless both the nights and days—
when the arbitrary wind gusted
and I, desolate, realized
on how other things I hung
and how easily I might be damned.

6

A studious highschoolboy he looked
—as in fact I later found he was—
bespectacled, with soft-curved face
and withdrawn protected air:
and I marvelled, envied him
so untouched he seemed to be
in that hammering brutal atmosphere.

But his safety had a different base
and his safely private world was fantasy;
from the battering importunities
of fists and genitals of sodomites
he fled: in a maniac world he was safe.

1968*

* All poems 1-6 were originally published as "Postscripts" to "Letters
to Martha" in 1968.

On the island

1

Cement-gray floors and walls
cement-gray days
cement-gray time
and a gray susurration
as of seas breaking
winds blowing
and rains drizzling

A barred existence
so that one did not need to look
at doors or windows
to know that they were sundered by bars
and one locked in a gray gelid stream
of unmoving time.

2

When the rain came
it came in a quick moving squall
moving across the island
murmuring from afar
then drumming on the roof
then marching fading away.

And sometimes one mistook
the weary tramp of feet
as the men came shuffling from the quarry
white-dust-filmed and shambling
for the rain
that came and drummed and marched away.

3

It was not quite envy
nor impatience
nor irritation
but a mixture of feelings

one felt
for the aloof deep-green dreaming firs
that poised in the island air
withdrawn, composed and still.

4

On Saturday afternoons we were embalmed in time
like specimen moths pressed under glass;
we were immobile in the sunlit afternoon
waiting;
[Visiting time:]
until suddenly like a book snapped shut
all possibilities vanished as zero hour passed
and we knew another week would have to pass.

1968

For Daantjie—[on a New Coin *envelope]*

On a Saturday afternoon in summer
grayly through net curtains I see
planes on planes in blocks of concrete masonry
where the biscuit factory blanks out the sky

Cézanne clawing agonizedly at the physical world
wrested from such super-imposed masses
a new and plangent vocabulary
evoking tensions, spatial forms and pressures
almost tactile on the eyeballs,
palpable on the fingertips,
and from these screaming tensions wrenched
new harmonies, the apple's equipoise
the immobility of deadlocked conflicts
—the cramp, paralyses—more rich
than any rest, repose.

And I, who cannot stir beyond these walls,
who shrink the temptation of any open door
find hope in thinking that repose
can be wrung from these iron-hard rigidities.

1967

This sun on this rubble after rain.

Bruised though we must be
some easement we require
unarguably, though we argue against desire.

⌈Under jackboots our bones and spirits crunch⌉
forced into sweat-tear-sodden slush
—now glow-lipped by this sudden touch:

—sun-stripped perhaps, our bones may later sing
or spell out some malignant nemesis
Sharpevilled to spearpoints for revenging

but now our pride-dumbed mouths are wide
in wordless supplication
are grateful for the least relief from pain

—like this sun on this debris after rain.

[sewed up]   1962

Off the campus: Wits

Tree-bowered in this quaint romantic way
we look down on the slopes of sunlit turf
and hear the clean-limbed Nordics at their play.

We cower in our green-black primitive retreat
their shouts pursuing us like intermittent surf
peacock-raucous, or wracking as a tom-tom's beat;

so we withdraw from present, place and man
—to green-clad Robin with an iron beak
or Shakespeare lane-leaf-hidden from a swollen Anne.

So here I crouch and nock my venomed arrows
to pierce deaf eardrums waxed by fear
or spy, a Strandloper, these obscene albinos
and from the corner of my eye
catch glimpses of a glinting spear.

                              Sharpeville   1963

A common hate enriched our love and us:

Escape to parasitic ease disgusts;
discreet expensive hushes stifled us
the plangent wines became acidulous

Rich foods knotted to revolting clots
of guilt and anger in our queasy guts
remembering the hungry comfortless.

In drafty angles of the concrete stairs
or seared by salt winds under brittle stars
we found a poignant edge to tenderness,

and, sharper than our strain, the passion
against our land's disfigurement and tension;
hate gouged out deeper levels for our passion—

a common hate enriched our love and us.

                                                             1963

---

why?

The rosy aureole of your affection
extends beyond our urban bounded knowledge
to tangled undergrowths of earlier time:
subtly obscure lymphatics of the flesh
proliferate bright labyrinths of mind
and cobweb-shadow them with primal dusk.

Beyond our focussed shaped projection
to immensities of tenderness defined
like blind protrusion of these searching nipples
shut-eyed in luminous rooms of lust I nuzzle,
loom shadows darker than the dusk of passion
that turn our pinks dust-gray as spider's back.

Beyond your open hungering embrace
yawn other older mouths from oozy shores
and over me, enormous, straddles
the ancient fetus-hungry incubus
that leaves me sprawling, spent, discarded
dry-sucked and shattered as a spider's shard.

                                        1963

Light, green-yellow luminescent, tender
seeps through these deep-foliaged weeping willows
to filter streams and runnels of soft glow
suffusing enclaves of green and somber gloom,

and all my frantic and frustrated sorrow
dribbles from me in a pith-central tenderness
extracted by awareness of the charm
that graces this distraught and mourning land.

Oh lacerating land that pulps out anger's
rancid ooze from my resisting heart
now, with this loveliness you distill in me
a balm that eases and erases all my hurt.

Zoo Lake: Johannesburg   1970

Erosion: Transkei

Under green drapes the scars scream,
red wounds wail soundlessly,
beg for assuaging, satiation;
warm life dribbles seawards with the streams.

Dear my land, open for my possessing,
ravaged and dumbly submissive to our will,
in curves and uplands my sensual delight
mounts, and mixed with fury is amassing

torrents tumescent with love and pain.
Deep-dark and rich, with deceptive calmness
time and landscape flow to new horizons—
in anguished impatience await the quickening rains.

1962

Miles of my arid earth
rasping dry as smoker's cough and craving
heat, hunger ache in your dusty haze
sighing, heaving, tremulous;

all my seared eyes caress your miles—
boulders that blister, scald and rust—
ranging parched reaches of rutted sands;
coax pastels from your dun and dust

and know the tenderness
of these my reaching hands
can conjure moisture, gentleness
and honey sweetness from your yearning hollows.

1971

Milkblue—tender the moonlit midnight sky;
receive me now my sleeping love.
Lovelaughter—gentle, a luminous glow
arches from circling horizoning hills
to this plain your tremulous breast exposes:

So, gentle and tender I brood and bow
over your scent, your hid springs of mirth
and know
here in this dusk, secret and still
I can bend and kiss you now, my earth.

1970

I might be a better lover I believe
my own, if you could truly be my own:
trafficked and raddled as you are by gross
undiscerning, occupying feet,
how can I, the dispossessed, achieve
the absolute possession that we seek?
How can we speak of infidelity
when, forced apart, we guess each other's woe?
My land, my love, be generous to forgive
my nomad rovings down the vagrant streets:
return to me, sometime be wholly my own
so you secure me entire, entirely your own.

Johannesburg   1962

A troubadour, I traverse all my land
exploring all her wide-flung parts with zest
probing in motion sweeter far than rest
her secret thickets with an amorous hand:

and I have laughed, disdaining those who banned
inquiry and movement, delighting in the test
of will when doomed by Saracened arrest,
choosing, like unarmed thumb, simply to stand.

Thus, quixoting till a cast-off of my land
I sing and fare, person to loved-one pressed
braced for this pressure and the captor's hand
that snaps off service like a weathered strand:
—no mistress-favour has adorned my breast
only the shadow of an arrow-brand.

                                                      1963

Take out the poetry and fire
or watch it ember out of sight,
sanity reassembles its ash
the moon relinquishes the night.

But here and here remain the scalds
a sudden turn or breath may ache,
and I walk soft on cindered pasts
for thought or hope (what else?) can break.

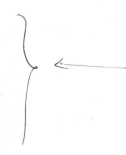

1963

Part 2

From Exile to International Activist

I must lug my battered body
garbage-littered
across the frontiers of the world,
recite my wear-shined clichés
for nameless firesides
and fidget, a supple suppliant, for papers
in a thousand wooden ante-rooms;
wince, in the tense air of recognition
as the clean-limbed, simple and innocent grow hostile;
—in my baggage I bear the ticking explosives
of reproach, and threat, and challenge.

Epping, Sydney   1970

Dennis Brutus's exile from South Africa in 1966 propelled him into a prominent role in the effort to internationalize the anti-apartheid movement. In the wake of repression after the Sharpeville massacre, the main organizations resisting apartheid, such as the African National Congress (ANC) and the Pan-Africanist Congress (PAC), were driven underground. With Mandela in prison, Oliver Tambo took over the leadership of the African National Congress and took the anti-apartheid movement to the world stage. Brutus's effective work on the South African Non-Racial Olympic Committee (SANROC) led to one of the first great victories in what would become, by the 1980s, a broad effort that involved a cultural boycott, and, finally, crippling economic sanctions against the racist state.

The story of the struggle over apartheid sports comprises the first section of Part 2. Brutus's memoir includes his encounters with International Olympic Committee President Avery Brundage and several other prominent figures in the sports world, including Jackie Robinson, the pioneer of desegregation in baseball; Muhammad Ali, the boxing legend; and Don King, the boxing promoter.

Part 2 also covers Brutus's emergence as an internationally renowned poet. The first published book of his poetry coincided with his imprisonment. By the time he was expelled from South Africa he was hailed as a major new voice in African literature. Brutus's views on the connection of his poetry to his activism, and the dynamics of culture generally, are explored in this section through interviews, speeches, and articles from the 1960s and 1970s. For example, his speech to the first Pan-African Cultural Festival, sponsored by the Organization of African Unity in Algiers in 1969, reflects not only a high point in the African and Third World national liberation movements, but also a critique of their limitations in confronting imperialism in the postcolonial era.

Brutus's memoir in this section, alongside selections of his liter-

ary criticism, highlights his prominent role in African literature. Brutus, along with his longtime collaborator Bernth Lindfors, helped launch the African Literature Association within academia, helping open the way for what would become the academic field of postcolonial studies.

The final section of Part 2 covers a range of Brutus's activity in the anti-apartheid movement from the early 1970s to the last bitter phase of struggle in the late 1980s. The watershed in the South African struggle in this period was the Soweto Uprising of 1976, whose best-known leader was the writer Steve Biko, a founder of the Black Consciousness Movement. This rebellion spurred an international solidarity campaign—including college student activism in the U.S. with which Brutus was heavily involved. Another wave of campus protest in the U.S. came in the mid-1980s in response to the township rebellions in South Africa during that period.

The material gathered in Part 2 is from diverse sources and aimed at different audiences. This material includes several of Brutus's best-known poems from—and about—the period spanning most of his exile. As in much of his work, these poems interweave themes of exile, political commitment, and personal intimacy. The narrative provided by the collection of these poems runs parallel to the stories told by the articles, speeches, and interviews in this section. Brutus's own personal struggle against the U.S. government's efforts to deport him are also detailed in his memoir. Throughout these varied selections, common themes emerge: the necessity of exposing, and opposing, the U.S. and Western support for the apartheid regime; the centrality of mass resistance in South Africa itself; and the linkage of the struggle to liberate Southern Africa to a wider international movement for social transformation.

L.S. and A.K.

Memoir
Isolating Apartheid—
South Africa and International Sports

One of the first major controversies about apartheid and sports concerned a proposed tour of South Africa by a cricket team from the West Indies in 1959, which took place as we were inaugurating the South African Sports Association (SASA).

The West Indies had the greatest cricket team in the world at the time, but they had never had a black captain. The captain had to be a white man, always, although they had some of the greatest batsmen in the world, who were black. At that time, C.L.R. James, who was editing a great political journal in Trinidad, *The Nation*, also was their sports columnist. He declared that a black man had to be captain of the West Indies team, and wrote articles attacking the inefficient stooges the West Indies Cricket Board was making captain. It didn't matter how lousy he was. The captain had to be a white man, because of "leadership" and all that.

In 1959, Frank Worrell, who was black, was a candidate to become captain of the West Indies team. He made the mistake of agreeing to tour South Africa as captain of the West Indies team and play ten matches—West Indies blacks vs. South African blacks—while the white South Africans were playing against England. This was a sop to the black players. Their argument was: "You can't play against whites, but we'll actually bring in a black team to play against you guys, while we're playing against our guys." I challenged this. I said, "This is being done to consolidate apartheid." Here C.L.R. and I were on opposite sides, although I was not really aware of it at the time.

Suddenly we were plunged into a debate about racism and sports in a very serious way, because there were blacks who accepted the idea of consolidating apartheid in sports, and blacks who opposed it. I came in as the South African Sports Association secretary—not as the president, but as the secretary who really wields the power. I was able to mobilize a campaign over the next six months, and there was an exchange of letters to the newspapers on the issue. There was a shift from a majority arguing for a tour by the West Indies team to a majority arguing against.

The story was in the newspapers every day. I had a Jewish friend, Myer Kaplan, who owned a little pharmacy where the Special Branch—the secret police—would go for free medicines and prescriptions. He was located on the edge of the ghetto where they were patrolling, and they would always drop in there. One day, while the police were there, Kaplan said to the head of the Special Branch, "Do you think this cricket tour is going to take place or not? I'm reading about it every day in the newspapers, back and forth. Blacks are talking about it. What's going to happen?" The man gets real mad and says, "Why don't you go and ask fucking Brutus?" It really was an admission that I was pivotal to that debate. The real irony is that when the tour was cancelled, it was because of a young man who belonged to the Indian Youth Congress, Essop Pahad, who said, "If the West Indies team comes we're going to set the stadium on fire." He became a minister in the post-apartheid government, under President Thabo Mbeki.

It was only later, in 1968, that I learned that C.L.R. and I had been on opposite sides of this controversy. We were at a conference together in Havana with the intellectuals of the world—*de todo el mundo*. Robin Blackburn was there. So was Eric Hobsbawm. We were having a wonderful time. But C.L.R. was hopping mad at me. We disagreed instantly, and in fact we never managed to agree. Although I had read his book *Black Jacobins* and I had a high regard for him, we were poles apart on cricket. He thought Frank Worrell should have been allowed to play in South Africa, because it would have improved his candidacy. If he could captain a black team in South Africa, then they could not keep him out of the captain's seat in the West Indies.[1] I argued that I didn't want to see apartheid consolidated by sports people agreeing to have two separate events.

A return to activism

My international activism in sports resumed after I was released from prison and forced to leave South Africa in 1966. But not immediately. For I was released from Robben Island in July 1965 and put under house arrest in Port Elizabeth. I was given a new banning order covering the next five years, but after one year I was granted an exit permit. I departed from South Africa at the end of July 1966 and arrived in London in time for the World Cup football final at Wembley, which I attended courtesy of the BBC—as arranged by Chris de Broglio.

After I moved to London, I got an invitation to speak to the Young Liberals on South Africa. At first I turned them down. But when I looked at it again, I noticed it's to the Young Liberals branch in Stratford-upon-Avon, which of course is Shakespeare's home. Shakespeare has always been very important to me, and I couldn't resist the invitation to go to Stratford-upon-Avon, really for literary reasons. About that time I applied for, and accepted, a job as a high school teacher.

Three things happened to get me involved again. First, I went to the Anti-Apartheid Movement in Britain and offered to work for them for free. They decided that they didn't want me—I am not sure why. Perhaps it was a simple ego thing; that they thought that I might become too prominent. Now, the ANC didn't want me either, because the ANC was very tight with the Anti-Apartheid Movement, and I was not, so there's point two. Three, John L. Collins, who was then canon at St. Paul's Cathedral and president of International Defense and Aid for Southern Africa, comes to me and offers me a position. When I tell him that I've already agreed to become a teacher, he says, "If I pay you the same salary that they would pay you as a teacher if you become an organizer, would you?" That's how I got the Defense and Aid job, although I was already excited to be a high school teacher again.

The organization had been launched in 1960 as the South African Defense and Aid Fund to support political prisoners, but was declared unlawful in 1966. It moved to London and became one of the beneficiaries of a United Nations trust fund established to help the victims of apartheid. I became its organizer. Defense and Aid was in some ways political, but it was really a non-governmental organization, an NGO, that didn't take sides in South African politics—a humanitarian thing. It was an organization that did not require me to toe any political line. In fact I was never hired or paid by any political organization. I was able to assist people from all the various South African political groups.

Exile in London allowed me to resume activity with SANROC, the South African Non-Racial Olympic Committee. It turned out that if you were part of an Olympic committee and wrote to the IOC, they were supposed to respond to you. A lot of people wouldn't have dreamed of even attempting that, because you must remember that people internalize their inferiority when they're told they're inferior.

Around 1958, I had sent out a note asking for more information about the IOC, and sure enough, I got the IOC Bulletin, which had a list of all the member countries, their postal address and everything. So immediately, I had a tool. And I even got a copy of what is roughly equivalent to the IOC charter. So I could tell them what's in their own charter, and this becomes a perfect weapon. The president, by the way, was Avery Brundage, a multimillionaire in Chicago, who at that time owned the LaSalle Hotel and an entire floor of the hotel was his office. So I was in correspondence with Brundage and I began to develop a strategy for this Olympic issue. My strategy was to assume that people meant what they said, always. If you said, "racism is wrong," I'd believe you meant that— that you didn't mean "except here," or "except there." That approach was key to the Olympics issue, since the IOC charter prohibited racism—by implication, initially; later, explicitly.

I visited the U.S. in 1968, a few months before the Mexico City Olympics, to raise the issue of excluding South Africa. I met with Jackie Robinson, the pioneer in desegregating baseball. He was no longer an athlete by then, but a spokesman for Chock Full o' Nuts, the coffee company, which targeted the African American market. More importantly, I met with Jim Bouton, a pitcher for the New York Yankees who had been in the World Series, who later accompanied me to the Mexico City Olympics. I had met him through George

Houser, executive director of the American Committee on Africa, the most important lobbying group on Africa in the United States.

I found myself being criticized from the left. In the black movement in the United States at that time, the late 1960s, you had the Martin Luther King line and the Malcolm X line. And the two lines in a sense were also being debated in sports. In particular, a black professor in California, Harry Edwards, became a spearhead of the debate. The boxer Cassius Clay became Muhammad Ali. You also had the basketball star Lew Alcindor, who became Kareem Abdul-Jabbar. So racism and sports wasn't a theoretical issue—it was a very specific issue for activists. Now it's interesting that when the African American athletes took their case to Brundage, they lost. He just cleaned their clock, wiped the floor with them. Whereas, I could go in and win. What was the difference?

The African Americans said you have to debate this issue in the terms of the ghetto, and say: "This is about joblessness and homelessness and police brutality." But Brundage simply said, "It's not in the Olympic charter." You must remember that Brundage, as head of the U.S. Olympic Committee, had defended Hitler in the 1936 Olympics, when Hitler had discriminated against Jews, and successfully argued against a boycott of those games.

Interestingly, I was attacked by my allies in the U.S., who said, "why don't you talk about Soweto, why don't you talk about Mandela." But I would not have won if I had gone that way. There are times you have to demarcate the area of struggle, where you have to almost allow your enemy to define the parameters, and then fight within those parameters. So my approach was to say: "Your own Olympic charter prohibits discrimination" and threaten a boycott unless South Africa was excluded.

My role as honorary president of SANROC gave me an opportunity to pull the whole continent of Africa together on the question of boycotting the Mexico Olympics if South Africa participated. This was done through the Supreme Council for Sport in Africa, which was established in Bamako, Mali, in December 1966—I wrote the constitution. I was assisted in this effort by Chris de Broglio, a white South African weightlifter who became SANROC's treasurer and a great ally. The meeting in Bamako was pivotal. It meant that there was a united body for sports in Africa that could take unified action.

This was to be important in the next Olympic year, 1968.

I then met with representatives of Caribbean and the South American countries in Havana and got them together. Then I went to Europe, to the socialist countries, and to Asian countries at a meeting in New Delhi. Eventually, we had a package of about sixty countries in favor of a boycott. That gave me the clout to go to Brundage.

I first met Brundage at his office in Chicago in 1967; I then met with him in Grenoble at the Winter Olympics in 1968, prior to the Mexico City Olympics the following summer. So when he instructed Mexico to invite South Africa to the 1968 Olympics, I could say, "It's either South Africa or the rest of the world, because we are now going to organize a boycott." And in fact we had about sixty countries whose representatives had said, "If South Africa is there, we will not be there." So it came down to a very clear choice. In response to the threat of a boycott, Brundage made a statement to the effect that, if he is the only spectator in the bleachers and South Africa is the only country in the stadium, the games will still go on. Then he goes to South Africa, allegedly to see animals in the game parks. I think he was trying to pull the chestnut out of the fire, and it didn't work.

By the time the Games came up, the Mexicans still had not invited South Africa. When Brundage demanded to know why they were not invited, the Mexicans replied that, "Well, maybe it got lost in the mail, or something. We don't know what happened." So the South Africans were not there in Mexico City. They were in Texas, so that some of them could just hop across the border, if they got in at the last minute. They had already made the team selections.

I was in Mexico City with Jim Bouton, the baseball player, whose book, *Ball Four!*, would later be denounced by the commissioner of baseball, Bowie Kuhn. Bouton got to meet the U.S. Olympic Committee members, who said to him, "Are you here on Moscow gold?" The South Africans had sent out a brochure to the various embassies in which I was labeled a communist, and told them "don't pay any attention to this guy." So if the communists were funding me, and Bouton was my ally, the commies must be funding him, too!

In the meantime, black Americans were conducting their own fight with Brundage. People like Kareem Abdul-Jabbar were boycoting the Mexico City Games. Remember, this is also the Games where the African American athletes Tommie Smith and John Carlos gave the Black Power salute on the podium when they were being awarded medals. I was working with them, but you can see there was some disagreement between our strategy and theirs. I think that mine was the one that worked.

Stopping the Springboks

Besides the Olympic boycott, I was also involved with the International Committee Against Racialism in Sport (ICARIS), and other organizations to kick apartheid South Africa out of international sports. I also took up the issue as part of my work as campaign organizer for International Defense and Aid, and spoke in Belgium, Canada, France, Italy, the Scandinavian countries, and elsewhere.

One of the most important actions was the Stop the Seventy Tour—the campaign to keep South Africa's Springboks rugby team from touring Britain. I was able to mobilize all across Britain to the point that the tour was cancelled. The South Africans had organized a cricket tour in 1969, and we had made it so rough for them they decided that they couldn't come for rugby. But in 1970 they decided to try again.

The climax of the campaign was when we put about 18,000 people on the streets in London to protest the Springboks. They went from London to Twickenham, where the Springboks were going to play England in a match. They had to surround the entire rugby field with cops holding hands, facing the stands, not the players, because they feared for the smoke bombs coming out of the crowds. And the match was stopped about three times.

But perhaps the best episode was at Aberdeen, Scotland. The students at Aberdeen had devised their own strategy—our strategy was based on letting the local people choose their own strategy. We never told them what to do. We just said, the "Springboks will be here next, do what you have to do."

In Aberdeen, the students started a fight among themselves. The cops ran there to stop it. And while the cops were over there, students invaded the pitch from another end. Then they all ran into the center of the field and piled on top of each other. There was this huge mound of bodies. And then, by agreement, everybody clutched everybody else. So when the cops dragged out a body, they got about six bodies attached to it. Best of all, while this was happening, guys climbed the goal posts and stood on the crossbars and gave the Nazi salute—a marvelous photograph for the press. About 100 of them were arrested and charged with the crime of public disturbance. So we went to John Lennon, and he said, "What's the total?" And he wrote the check, for about 1,000 pounds sterling.

In another case, the South Africans were going to play Oxford University. It was to be a great match, nationally televised. For the South Africans, this was prestige—really big. So I went out to Oxford from London, where I was still working at St. Paul's Cathedral on the campaign for political prisoners. The sports thing was a second vocation. I met the guys in a pub—the student anti-apartheid committee. There were about four or five of them smoking pipes and drinking sherry. And I said, "Hey, what are you guys going to do? This is terrible. I've come here for a meeting and there's nothing happening." I think I made them feel bad enough. So I went back to London and told everyone, "There's going to be national television, but no protest, nothing."

Then, on the day of the match, it's cancelled. The reason? The night before, some of the students had gotten onto the pitch. They poured huge drums of weed killer to paint on the grass, in eighteen-foot letters, "Oxford Reject Apartheid!" But it was invisible. It was only about an hour before the match when the grass turned brown. So you had these huge letters that were going to be televised all over Britain! They cancelled the tour halfway through shortly after that, and this was one of the things that just ruined it for them.

There were also campaigns around South Africa's participation in tennis. I was arrested in Wimbledon in 1971 for sitting on center court to disrupt a tennis match involving Cliff Drysdale, a white South African. The case was appealed to the House of Lords, which ultimately ruled in my favor. The reason was that the police had mistaken me for my brother, Wilfred, who had been detained to "keep the peace" for a protest in Trafalgar Square.

At the same time, the apartheid government tried to get athletes to come to South Africa to try and achieve legitimacy through sports that way. Most importantly, there was an attempt in 1975 by the South African authorities to get Muhammad Ali, then heavyweight boxing world champion, to visit the country. Clearly for the South Africans it would have been a coup if they could have gotten Muhammad Ali there. I wrote to Jersey Joe Walcott, a former heavyweight world champion, to ask for his support to convince Muhammad Ali not to go to South Africa. And I remember Jersey Joe writing to me, saying, "I am going to keep punching until we beat apartheid." So you had this nice fighting talk from a boxer.

In the case of Ali, I met with the boxing promoter Bob Arum who had connections in Israel and South Africa. I admit I'm guessing here, but my hunch is that the Israelis were trying to help apartheid by being in some way helpful in arranging for Ali to go there.

Arum was very powerful in the boxing world, doing what Don King was going to do later. He would own both fighters, so he could really decide if it was going to be a draw, or who was going to win and who was going to lose. And I had to take on Arum over Muhammad Ali. I met him in New York, where I said, "Look we're going to beat you on this one," and he said, "You can't beat me." He was arrogant.

We sent information and appeals to Ali through various contacts. When we learned that Ali was going to be in London on business, I got in touch with Omar Cassem, a Muslim cleric from South Africa who was living there. Cassem was a stalwart member of SANROC for years in South Africa, and had gotten an exit permit in 1966. Cassem got in to see Ali at the Park Lane Hilton—right in past the bodyguard—and talked Ali into backing out of the South Africa deal. There's another story concerning Muhammad Ali. In 1974, I got a call from Richard Durham, author of a biography of Ali. He told me that IBM was making a bid to promote a fight between Ali and George Foreman at the Astrodome for the heavyweight championship of the world. Durham wanted to keep the fight out of the hands of IBM, and told me that Mobutu, the dictator of Zaire (now Democratic Republic of Congo), was also making a $10 million bid for the fight. He asked me if they could trust Mobutu. I said, "No, tell them to put the money in an escrow account." The amount of money was confirmed and transferred.

Then, Don King, the fight promoter, asked me to go to Kinshasa, Zaire, to make sure they had a functioning satellite uplink to televise the fight—it was new technology then. Since I was already planning to attend the Pan-African Congress in Dar as Salaam in Tanzania, King agreed to pay for the air ticket from there to Zaire. When I was in Dar as Salaam, I was attacked by Amiri Baraka for collaborating with Mobutu to set up the fight. But the way I saw it, I was keeping it out of the hands of IBM. I didn't attend the fight, however. (I usually didn't attend sporting events—I left Mexico City before the Olympic Games, for example. To me, the politics was the important thing).

Another Olympic showdown

South Africa was formally expelled from the International Olympic Committee in 1970 as the result of pressure from the boycott. I was part of the committee that made the case for expulsion in Amsterdam in 1970. But the struggle around the Olympics was not over.

At the Munich Summer Games of 1972 we had a team arrive from Rhodesia—later Zimbabwe—which had unilaterally declared independence from Britain under the white minority regime headed by Ian Smith. They had a new flag, a new anthem, and a place in the Olympic Village. I raised the question, "How did they get in?" Legally a colonial country can only become a member of the Olympics if it is sponsored by the metropolitan country. That is, the parent country has to say, "OK, these guys are now nominally independent, they can have a team." That's how Rhodesia had gotten into the Olympics in Tokyo in 1964. But the team that was in Munich was not the same team as the British had sponsored then. This was a wholly new country, and all this worked against them— in fact, they were illegitimately inside the Olympic Village.

Then two very interesting things happened. One, the Harvard rowing team refused to row in the warm-ups with the Rhodesians. And interestingly, the Venezuelan team refused to do workouts on the track with the Rhodesians. So already there was tension. And when I raised the question of the illegitimacy of the team, this of course added to the mess. The top sportswriter of the *Times of London*, Neil Allen, did an interview with me, in which I predicted that if the Rhodesians walked onto the track, all the others were going to walk out. He had a lot of clout, and did a major story for the *Times*, which was being flown from London to Munich, where all the Olympic country delegates got a complimentary copy shoved under their door. They got up for breakfast and saw: "Walkout threatened." Cuba had already announced publicly that they would walk out if the Rhodesians were there. The Venezuelans made a similar statement. Brundage was forced to announce—and he was practically weeping as he went to the microphone under the spotlight—to announce that, under pressure, the Rhodesian invitation had been withdrawn. For me, it was really a major success—one where I had quite an important role in putting the whole case together. This, of course, was also the Olympics where the Israeli athletes and Palestinians were killed, which overshadowed all other issues.

The next Olympics fight was at the Summer Games in 1976 in Montreal—the outcome of which made me very unpopular in Canada.

Here's the story: South Africa was out. Rhodesia was out. What's more, the IOC had called on every country—because we had put a lot of pressure on them—to have no relations with apartheid South Africa.

But New Zealand decided to send their rugby team to South Africa to play a series of matches just before the Olympics were set to begin. This, mind you, was in 1976, when the students were being shot and gassed in the Soweto Uprising. So we said that New Zealand should just give us a pledge that they will not continue relations with South Africa in sports. We weren't even asking for a cancellation of the tour. I was staying at the same hotel in Montreal as the New Zealand Olympic delegates, and we were in arguments about this.

The president of the International Olympic Committee was no longer Avery Brundage, but Lord Killanin—an Irish lord who was then on the board of Irish Shell, the oil company—and fairly reactionary. He came to me and said, "Can you help solve this thing?" And I said, "Sure." All the New Zealand Olympic team has to do is to contact their prime minister, Robert Muldoon, and say, "Look, promise you won't do this any more. We know the rugby team is in South Africa now. But since the IOC has asked us not to do it in the future, we need to sever relations with South Africa in sports."

But Muldoon had won an election the previous year where he

was being backed by farmers—a reactionary bunch in New Zealand—and he wanted to win the next one. He was willing to go along with the South Africa rugby tour because it helped him appeal to his political base. He refused to sever relations with South Africa in sports.

So on the first morning of the Olympics, during the opening march into the stadium, twenty-five countries from Africa were missing. Another from the Middle East—Iraq—had pulled out in support of the African position. So the Olympics for the Canadians was virtually a financial disaster. For example, the Kenyans, who were the best distance runners in the world, were not participating.

I had put that together—but it was a failure. Because if it had gone the way I had planned it, New Zealand would have been out and the twenty-six countries would have been in. That's what had happened in Mexico City and again in Munich. And the irony is that it was the South Africans, I believe—my colleagues from my own committee of SANROC—who were responsible for this failure.

The Cubans had asked the African countries, "Do you want us to join you in a boycott?" The Cubans were absolutely vital to this. But a member of SANROC by the name of Samba Ramsamy, then the acting chairman, advised them not to pull out. Then the Yugoslavs came and asked the same question. Remember, this is the old days of the "socialist bloc"—if you pull out one, you pull out all of them. Again, Ramsamy told them, "No, this is an African struggle, you don't have to get into it." This was a complete mistake, because if we had put together a package of sixty countries to threaten a boycott, New Zealand would have been out. We could have had it. We lost it to our own treachery—and I don't use the word lightly.

The political situation in the next two Olympics was very confused, very messy. President Jimmy Carter pulled the U.S. out of the 1980 Olympics following the Russian invasion of Afghanistan and was pushing for a Western boycott, so many countries stayed out. The Moscow Olympics were a flop because of the absence of the West—just as the 1984 Olympics in Los Angeles were a flop because, of course, the Soviets and the other countries of the Eastern bloc stayed away. This was all about the Cold War. The South African issue was sidelined; it was not a major issue of debate.

There was, however, a South African component to the Los

Angeles games, which is very interesting. Prior to the Olympics, the *San Jose Mercury News* ran a story that South Africa was going to be re-admitted to the games. It's the only paper in the country that carried the story, reporting that Julian Roosevelt, who was a member of the U.S. Olympic Committee, together with the chairman of the committee, William Simon, former secretary of the treasury under Nixon, were planning to introduce a motion in the IOC calling for South Africa to be admitted by the Executive Committee. And if it was adopted in the executive, then it would be simply rubber-stamped in the IOC congress. That way, South Africa could get in through the back door. So I called a guy who was with the *New York Times*, Bill Rhoden, who wrote major pieces on the sports pages. I kept working on it, and eventually the *Times* ran the story. And you had these guys admitting that the matter was going to come before the Executive Committee. Remember, this is during the administration of Ronald Reagan, who was pushing a policy of "constructive engagement" with South Africa.

I contacted people in Watts, and we started organizing a protest outside the Biltmore Hotel in L.A., where the committee was meeting. Ironically, the same guy who had been in Canada, Ramsamy, talked to Richard Lapchick, whose father Joe Lapchick was a famous basketball coach. Lapchick, who wrote a Ph.D. and book on race, politics, and international sports, worked together with me on several issues. But Ramsamy called Lapchick, telling him that the protest outside the Biltmore had been cancelled. And so a lot of people stayed away who might have been there, because they were now getting two contradictory instructions.

At that time I was calling for a boycott and a demonstration to prevent South Africa being readmitted into the games. Yet someone else was saying, no, the protest is off. But there were enough people at the Biltmore with slogans and banners, mainly out of Watts, some students from UCLA, and so on. Eventually, Simon had to come out of the hotel and meet with me as the representative of the protesters. And in the presence of someone from the *New York Times* and TV cameras, he had to assure us the United States would not vote for South Africa to be readmitted into the Olympics.

After that, things got very messy in the Olympics struggle. I became active on other issues, for example the campaign calling for

divestment from companies doing business in South Africa. I didn't
see a necessity to be at the 1988 Olympics in Seoul. There was no
real campaign. I still think that it was the CIA that rigged the vote
for the Olympics to go to Seoul, because South Korea had the
whole political confrontation between the North and South. There
is no evidence, but I am generally suspicious about it.

There came the final, and very interesting, episode, the 1992
Olympic Games in Ga. This was the period of transition following
Mandela's release from prison. The South Africans were bound to
change their political structure, and Mandela would be elected, of
course, in 1994. In fact, the first transition took place in sports. It's
very revealing: The ANC agreed to vote for South Africa to reenter
the Olympics without asking for a change in the white-dominated
structure first. The first compromise with the old regime took place
there.

They'd had a meeting in Lusaka, and the ANC had sent some-
one to come talk to me about the plan. And I suppose they saw me
as pretty powerful, especially after L.A. So I said, "OK, let's talk
about it." I happened to be in Los Angeles, I was getting an award
from Jean-Bertrand Aristide and from the people of Haiti, for my
contribution to the Haitian struggle. But after the reception I met
with the ANC guys, and they said, "OK, we want your advice.
Here's the deal. The next Olympics are going to be in Barcelona in
'92. The major meeting is going to be in Birmingham, in England in
'90, and we propose to lift the boycott. There's a cultural boycott
on South Africa, we're going to lift the cultural boycott; that means
South Africa can get into the Barcelona Olympics."

I said, "What are the terms? How far are you changing the
structure? As of now, everything's white, run by whites, white
schools and gyms, the stadiums, they're all segregated, and the
money's there. The black kids are playing on fields with broken
glass and beer cans. What's going to happen to that?" They replied,
"Oh, that will come afterwards." I said, "No, that has to come be-
fore. Otherwise, no deal." And so we debated this. Then I got a
call from Donald Woods, the South African editor known for his
work with Steve Biko. He had been part of the discussion. I said,
"Nope, this deal is no good. First, they change, then they get into
the Olympics. Because if they're in, there'll be no incentive for

change." He said to me, "You're wasting your time, Dennis, it's a done deal. The ANC has already OKed it."

Sure enough, they had. So I made an effort to go to the Birmingham meeting of the IOC congress, prior to the Barcelona games, to present the alternative position. Membership can only be readmitted at the full congress. Interestingly, the police in Birmingham were instructed to keep me out. So I was not even able to enter the building where the congress was taking place. I talked to a few of the media people, but the South Africans were really not interested. You can understand—white South African journalists were so happy because they were back in the world of sports. It was just an incredible achievement for them. So, that's really where it broke down. I also presented a letter to Mandela at the time of the ANC congress in Durban, arguing no compromise on the issue.

There's an ugly little footnote that should be added as well. I got a letter from Samba Ramsamy, who was vice chairman of SAN-ROC, advising me that I'd been expelled from the organization. He was acting as chairman because his offices were in London and I was living in Pittsburgh, Pennsylvania. So I wrote back and asked, "When was the meeting that decided this, and who voted for my expulsion?" I never heard back—no reply, ever. There aren't even minutes to show where there was a meeting where this expulsion took place. I have never been able to get satisfaction on this.

I raised the matter of my unauthorized expulsion with the ANC, since they were cooperating with Ramsamy, but they refused to act. It was a forerunner of the many other compromises that were to follow. In fact, I raised the matter with Mendi Msimang and Wally Serote, the ANC representatives in London, with Nelson Mandela and Walter Sisulu in Johannesburg, and with Samba Ramsamy at the Carlton Centre in Johannesburg, and with Govan Mbeki—the father of President Thabo Mbeki—in Port Elizabeth.

After the letter of expulsion from Samba Ramsamy, we had a meeting of SANROC committee members in London; Omar Cassem, Stephen Tobias, and James Cooke attended. I believe Chris de Broglio and Basil Bhana were absent. We agreed to try to meet with Ramsamy and go to his home in Hampstead Heath. His wife answered through the door, urging us to go away. We failed to meet with him.

Ramsamy later became head of the National Olympic Committee of South Africa. Ironically, I had nominated Ramsamy to run SANROC because I was coming to the United States. My own hunch is that the ANC had chosen him as the man who could avoid embarrassment for them in the world of sports. The South Africa team in Barcelona in 1992 was predominately white, because really very few blacks had come up to that standard in terms of conditioning and training. Worse, at the 1996 Olympic Games in Atlanta, we still had a predominately white team, and all white in sports like yachting and marksmanship. Under apartheid, blacks were not allowed to own guns!

[1] Frank Worrell was the first black cricketer to captain the West Indies cricket team for an entire series.

Documents

"Certain countries are determined to protect South Africa"

United Nations Special Committee on Apartheid Hears Mr. Dennis Brutus, March 23, 1970

NOTE: On March 23, 1970, the Special Committee on Apartheid granted a hearing to Mr. Dennis Brutus, South African poet, teacher, and former political prisoner. Mr. Brutus is president of the South African Non-Racial Open Committee for Olympic Sports and campaign director of the International Defense and Aid Fund. The testimony concerned apartheid in sports, the conditions of political prisoners in South Africa, and the International Year for Action to Combat Racism and Racial Discrimination, 1971. The Committee requested the Unit on Apartheid to publicize his statement as widely as possible.

This issue, published in pursuance of that request, contains a condensed version of his statement and his replies to questions by members of the Special Committee.

Opening statement

I may say by way of preface that it is not insignificant that we are meeting while our minds are still fresh with the memory of the commemoration of Sharpeville and the massacre which took place there. I hope that my submissions will lead in fact to greater concern with the policy which gave rise to Sharpeville.

Today in London, one of the major sports bodies in the world, the International Lawn Tennis Federation, is meeting to consider precisely the question of racism as far as it applies to sports, with special reference to the recent episode which involved an American citizen, Mr. Arthur Ashe, who was refused admission to South Africa on what were clearly racist grounds. I hope that this gives a special urgency and a point to my submissions this morning and the deliberations of this committee with regard to those submissions.

I propose, Mr. Chairman, to make submissions mainly under two heads and I make them in terms of my two specific functions as the campaign director of the International Defense and Aid Fund for the victims of apartheid and as president of SANROC, the South African Non-Racial Olympic Committee....

Racism in sports in South Africa

I have already referred, Mr. Chairman, to the emergency meeting this morning in London of the world tennis body which has been confronted by one more example of South African racism in sports.

What applies in tennis, in fact applies in all other sports. Sports in South Africa are divided strictly on racial lines and how strict this division is can be seen by the fact that if a black South African were to play tennis with a white South African, he could go to prison for that. The mere act of playing a game of tennis could incur a prison sentence. There are people who have been arrested for playing football and charged in the courts. They happen to be white South Africans who were prepared to defy the law and play with black South Africans, and they were charged with the "crime" of having played in an area set aside for blacks.

I, myself, was arrested for attending a committee meeting where the question of the South African exclusion of blacks from the Olympic team was being discussed. I spent a period in prison on Robben Island because I had been guilty of opposition to apartheid and racism.

When Arthur Ashe, a leading American player in tennis—he is also a black man—applied for permission to play in the South African Open Championship—and the word "Open" is ironic—he was refused. One of the arguments put forward was that he had made statements against apartheid. Indeed, if this were a crime, there are not many who have not been guilty of that crime. In fact, the position could simply have been tested by any other black man, one who had been speechless, applying for permission to play in the South African Open Tennis Championship. He, too, would have been refused because it is contrary to the South African doctrine of permanent white supremacy which they insist must apply in every field of activity. To allow a black man in to play, and perhaps beat, a white man would have been a contradiction of the concept of white supremacy. In fact, merely for a black man to play in terms of equality with a white man, whether he won or lost, is still not permissible because this too would undermine the doctrine of racial supremacy—white supremacy.

The refusal of Arthur Ashe demonstrates the nature of the real problem. South Africa wishes to be a part of the international family of nations, at least as far as sports are concerned, while at the same time violating the international code of sports which says "there will be no racial discrimination in sports." They have this peculiar dilemma: on the one hand they wish to have racial discrimination and they enshrine it in their constitution, and, on the other hand, they wish to participate with the rest of the world on the basis of equality while they declare that they are committed to a policy of inequality.

Protectors of South Africa

The problem, in fact, arises because of the peculiar way in which certain countries are determined to protect South Africa from the logical consequences of her action. It should be obvious that the South Africans have disqualified themselves from participation by contravening the international statutes, but there are certain countries which are determined to preserve their links with South Africa and to protect the South African racists from the penalty they deserve. The reasons are not to be found in the area of sports: they are to be found in the realms of economics and politics. But it is a fact that Great Britain has consistently, in the international councils of the sports world, been a major defender, the bulwark, which has prevented effective action from being taken.

They don't have a veto in the sports body, but they sometimes have a loaded vote. When the world tennis body meets in London today, there are five countries which enjoy twelve votes each, but there are other countries which have no votes at all, and there are other countries that have one vote or two, and sometimes five. Britain, France, the United States, Australia, and South Africa have twelve votes and their combined sixty votes are sufficient to block any attempt at effective action. And so, the outcome at today's meeting will depend on how sincere the United States is. They say that they are dismayed because a United States citizen has been excluded from South Africa because of his color, but the real test is whether they will use their twelve votes today to take effective action. If they do not, then we will know that their concern for civil rights, for equality of citizens as far as sport are concerned, is hypocrisy.[1]

The position which obtains here where you have a country contravening the statute of the international body, deserving to be expelled and escaping expulsion because it is protected by allies, applies in every other sport. The occasions where we have been successful have only been in those sports where there is voting on the basis of one country, one vote. Where there has been a democratic structure, we have been able to achieve a considerable measure of success. In sports such as football, in which countries like Algeria and Ethiopia played a leading role; in sports such as table tennis where there is one country, one vote; in boxing where Ghana played a very important role; and in the Olympics, notwithstanding the fact that there is no democratic structure there, we have been able to achieve a very important measure of success. I should say, Mr. Chairman, that in the case of the Olympics, because there is no democratic structure, we might well have failed in 1968 in Mexico when we tried to have the racist body from South Africa excluded. But we were able, through the combination of the forces of the countries of Africa and Asia, the socialist countries, and some of the Western countries, particularly Italy, to exert a combined pressure which was so powerful that the countries which had hoped to bring the racist body to Mexico were compelled to bow to that pressure.

Total exclusion of South Africa from international sports by 1971

I believe that that kind of unity was instructive. If we can achieve it again till 1971, we can in fact achieve a major breakthrough and by the end of the year there can be the total exclusion of South Africa from international sports.

There are certain specific sports that we ought to consider and one of them is certainly golf where you have the peculiar position that men who support the policy of apartheid are able to travel all over the world, and take part in sports in the United States and elsewhere, at the same time that it is public knowledge that other black sportsmen are not allowed to enter South Africa. When a man like Mr. Gary Player says, as he has said repeatedly, "I am a loyal South African, I support my government, and I support the policies of that government, and the policy of that government is apartheid," when you have such a formal declaration, then one must consider the implications of accepting the exclusion of a black citizen of the United States from South Africa while at the same time a white South African who supports apartheid is welcome to participate in events in this country. There are other countries that have followed the lead of the United Nations and have consistently declined to have anything to do with the racist bodies in South Africa. But as long as some of the major bodies in the world of sports continue to support that racism, it will continue to flourish and, therefore, Mr. Chairman, I wish to make one new and very serious submission.

I believe that the countries that have taken a stand against South Africa in sports must now go further, and they must make it clear that not only will they break off relations with South Africa but they will break off relations with the countries which continue to strengthen and support the South African racists. If this means no longer participating at White City, London, or at Madison Square Garden, New York, I believe that countries have to go to that point of saying, "If you will support racism, then we are no longer prepared to associate with you." It is a high price to ask sportsmen to pay, to ask them to sacrifice international competition and the opportunity to achieve their maximum development, but in the name of the human rights we all believe in, and those human rights imply the highest development of the human personality, it is not too high a price to pay to ask a man to take a stand. I am convinced that it will not be a stand taken in vain and that such coordinated action will, in fact, achieve its effect. It will compel those who at present are still associating with South Africa to choose between the minority of racists in one corner of the world and the rest of the world which is combined in its opposition to racism.

Political prisoners in South Africa

I would like to pass from that, Mr. Chairman, to the other and far more profound concern in the field of human rights which for a long time has been my concern, and I know is the concern of this committee, the subject of political prisoners, the conditions under which they are kept, and the campaign for their release. I must say Mr. Chairman, frankly, that although after my release from prison and my coming from South Africa as an involuntary exile, there was a great surge of international concern about political prisoners, there has been a falling off in our activities in this field.

That concern had certain very considerable effects in restraining the South African government, in placing it on the defensive and in exposing the conditions under which the prisoners were kept. The South African government issued a series of glossy and very expensive publications in an attempt to whitewash the facts and did in fact admit Red Cross investigators. It is true that for a time there was certain material improvement in the conditions under which men like Nelson Mandela, Walter Sisulu, Ahmad Kathrada, and Denis Goldberg were being held under life imprisonment. I hope that in 1971 there will be a fresh intensification of action.

In recent months, twenty-two South Africans have been charged in the courts with subversive activity. They included the wife of Nelson Mandela, Winnie Mandela. These people, after being held for months and subjected to a considerable amount of ill treatment, were brought to court and charged, and acquitted. But they were, in the same courtroom, rearrested and are now being held under the Terrorism Act which permits the South African government to hold people in prison without charging them. They are held incommunicado: they are not permitted to communicate either with lawyers or with their families.

How desperate their conditions are, Mr. Chairman, can be seen by the revelations earlier this year when an inquest was held into the death of Imam Abdullah Haroun. Imam Abdullah Haroun was a leader of the Muslim community in Cape Town. He was held under the one hundred and eighty-day law without ever being

tried, and after he had been held for four months, it was an-
nounced that he had died of "natural causes." Subsequently it was
announced that he had died after complaining of a pain in the
stomach. But at the inquest earlier this year it was revealed that his
body had been extensively damaged, bruised, and mutilated. And
the explanation was given that he had fallen down some stairs. He
was never charged, he was never convicted of any crime, but he is
dead, and there is no doubt that he died at the hands of the South
African secret police and that he was tortured by them.

This is just one instance, Mr. Chairman, of the conditions
which now, this day, obtain in South Africa ten years after
Sharpeville. It seems to me that unless we intensify and redouble
our efforts to achieve the liberation of South African political pris-
oners and the total isolation of the policy of apartheid and mobilize
opposition and resistance to it, there will be many more Imam Ab-
dulah Harouns in the prisons of South Africa.

[1] It was reported that the International Lawn Tennis Federation de-
cided on March 23, 1970, to exclude South Africa from the 1970
Davis Cup competition and to review the situation in 1971.

Open letter from the South African Non-Racial Olympic Committee

August 3, 1966

Precious McKenzie wears an English blazer as a member of the
English weightlifting team in Jamaica.

Few people are aware of the fact that Precious McKenzie has
been the best weightlifter in South Africa since 1960, but because
Precious is a colored South African he was never able to compete in
a South African championship and never represented his country—
finally he was forced to emigrate to Great Britain in order to be
able to compete in international sports.

Within a few months he was shattering the British records in
his division and is now the British champion.

This sad state of affairs is the consequence of racialism in South
African sports which has penalized many fine sportsmen.

We call on all sportsmen everywhere to help us in our fight

against the color-bar in South African sports. Demand the expulsion of color-bar South African sports bodies from all international sports federations, and the admission instead of non-racial bodies.

Object to participation against South African teams which are not fully representative.

Dennis Brutus, President, SANROC
Olympic Games Participation for All
Without Racial Discrimination

Memoir
The Artist as Political Activist

How does one become an artist at the same time as becoming a political activist? It seems almost contradictory. no
It began very early. I was fortunate. Both my mother and my father were teaching English literature and the English language in primary school, run by Catholic missionaries. But my mother came out of another missionary tradition, which ironically had an American element to it, which is how she came to be educated at a college, run by American missionaries in a town called Hankey.

My father, who was born in Jamestown on St. Helena Island in the South Atlantic, came from Saldanah Bay near Cape Town. He presumably went to a missionary school—although I never talked to him about this. But he actually studied for a B.A. by something called Correspondence College at the University of Cape Town. There were no black colleges of course in those times. Because he was studying Tennyson and Blake and Browning, he would quote them as he shaved in the morning. And I overheard him, as a kid playing on the floor right next to him. And I quoted poetry back at him, because I heard him quoting poetry.

My mother washed the dishes at night, and talked to my brother Wilfred, who's four years older, about his work at school. He talked to her about what he'd learned in English and he recited some poetry—and she'd already taught that. She was washing the dishes, and I was drying the dishes, and I was hearing quotations from Wordsworth and Shakespeare, and so on. So I grew up at least with an ear for sounds, for language, and words.

I started writing poetry at high school. Actually I only wrote one poem, so it really doesn't count. But I saw the moon rising over the lake, and I liked the image—so I tried to capture it in four lines. That's the first poetry I ever wrote. But I already had an ear for the sounds of the language, and images. So it came together.

As a teenager, at high school and later in college, I had your usual crushes and wrote love lyrics and so on. You go through a teenage poetry writing stage. In my case probably a little more sophisticated than the average teenager because I had some knowledge of poetry already. I went to Fort Hare, I wrote a couple of poems there. These were very much in a hybrid Victorian or Elizabethan mode, because that's what I was being exposed to, rather than South African ones. We didn't have a South African literary tradition, let alone an African literary tradition.

When I became politically active, I quit writing poetry. Because I couldn't stand the way that poetry is just literary, you know, out of touch with reality. I didn't feel I could go on writing poetry. I actually quit. And then an interesting thing happened. While teaching W.H. Auden, a major English poet, I observed in him the ability to merge the private and the public, the aesthetic and the political. And I went back to poetry, because I saw a way that you could make a political statement, simultaneously and honestly—you know, it's not manufactured sloganeering. This is genuine poetic expression, which merges political comment with personal comment, including love lyrics.

My first book of poetry was first published in Nigeria in 1963, while I was in prison. Prior to that I was having a very intense love affair. And the woman for whom some of the poetry was written actually sent some of my poetry to Nigeria. And it was on the basis of that that they invited me to send a manuscript. It was actually more complicated, because prior to that, there had been an announcement in the major radical monthly journal. In it was a call for a poetry competition organized in Paris, in which only Africans were allowed to enter. So I wrote a critique of this, and said poetry is not about ethnicity. The editor wrote a response, defending the decision to make it exclusively for Africans—in Paris, mind you. And I then said, "Well, I'll enter the competition and win it, and then reject the prize." So I entered the competition and won the Mbari Prize—and then wrote to Paris and said I don't want the check, and returned it.

Later, it turned out that the organization that gave the prize was the Congress for Cultural Freedom, a CIA front. They were subsidizing a journal in London called *Encounter*. But I had, without knowing that they were CIA, rejected their prize.

Then the publishers in Nigeria requested more poems to publish on the basis of the four poems that my female friend had sent on my behalf. I told her, "Select whatever you like, whatever you think is good, send it." So I just gathered whatever was around, and I think someone hand-carried it to London on a plane and then flew it to Nigeria, where it was published as *Sirens Knuckles Boots*. The title was selected by the publisher.

As a result, I was charged in prison with the crime of publishing a book of poetry. Had I been convicted, I would have gotten a much longer sentence. Because of the banning order, it was illegal for me to publish anything. Any editor who published me would go to prison as well. And anybody who quoted from me would go to prison as well. These were all crimes. Even citing the poetry in a review essay.

I was asked about the book in prison. They showed it to me and said, "Did you have this book published?" I said, "Yes." I was going to plead guilty—I was going to accept a longer sentence. But the curious thing was, in framing the charge against me, they had to specify the dates when I had smuggled the manuscript out, but I couldn't remember. And the case actually collapsed. I know it sounds absurd.

Sirens Knuckles Boots deals with life in the ghetto—life under apartheid. Later there was a new book of world poetry that included me, which is quite a distinction, because it's perhaps 300 poems—with Brecht and Auden of course—and then I am in there.

After being released from prison, I was granted an exit permit, and left South Africa for Britain in 1966. I was invited to read poetry in England at an international poetry festival in Edinburgh with W.H. Auden. He and I did an interview for the BBC in which Auden was asked about the fact that he destroyed some of his own poetry and withdrew it from publication—and a lot that was political. And his explanation was that as he matured he realized that poetry makes nothing happen. Poetry doesn't change anything. And I said, "Well, you know you are so wrong." And I read some of my own poetry that had been influenced by him. I actually restarted as a poet as a consequence of Auden. And he was pleased.

So we got on well. We had some disagreements, but he invited me to stay with him in Austria, so clearly we could have been good friends. But he died shortly after that.

I think it's worth saying that I never saw poetry as a deliberate, strictly political instrument. It was political because my landscape was political. It was inescapably political. There was racism around me. I went to Robben Island, and saw people beaten and urinated on. I saw all that happened, and you couldn't exclude that from my reality. I always make that point—because there are people who think I set out to be a political poet, and I have to say that that was not my approach.

After being forced to leave South Africa, I consciously shut out of my mind the awareness that I was in exile. I have a poem about that in *South African Voices*, edited by Bernth Lindfors of the University of Texas. It seems to me that lots of people become exiles and then begin to wallow in their predicament. And one of the consequences is that they become alcoholics. They drink away their awareness of their misery, or they drown their misery. So clearly I had to keep the awareness of exile at bay, because I was aware of what it can do to you if you become too conscious of it.

Now here's the interesting thing. Through that screen, periodically the awareness drifts, but it drifts in really specific ways. For instance in Boulder, Colorado, I was doing a lecture once with Allen Ginsburg, in a tent where there was grass. There I saw the identical wildflower that I saw in South Africa, and I wrote a poem in that instance that connects this wildflower in Boulder with that wildflower in the ghetto in South Africa. So the awareness of exile would penetrate, but it would penetrate in an instant and in very specific ways. What appears in my poetry about specific details of South Africa in that period are things that succeeded in getting through the screen that I set up to protect myself from the awareness of exile.

Culture and resistance

I first experienced discussions about the relationship of culture and politics as a student at Fort Hare University. There was an underground curriculum there, but my own political awareness at that stage was less than those who participated, although I had had some exposure to politics in high school through my teachers, who were Trotskyists. At Fort Hare, the students' views were rather heavily influenced by a black nationalist opposition to white-imposed segregation. The whites were incredibly overt in their racism, determined to keep the blacks in their place. This is beyond even what blacks in the U.S. South experienced. It was colonial whites coming in to deal with "savages."

Black resistance to that overt white racism naturally drew from their own rich African cultural experience. This was a collision of cultures—the result of a long, ancient, rich culture now being derided and denigrated. I came out of the colored community—a segregated colored community that, while very humane, did not have the kind of cultural richness you had among Africans. They had the chieftainships—extended families, the marvelous values, and a way of recognizing other people's humanity, a whole rich culture. You don't have access to that if you're in an urbanized ghetto.

Fort Hare was an important place of resistance, because while the racist pre-apartheid government insisted that universities must be exclusively white or exclusively black, Fort Hare had started much earlier as a black institution, one not imposed by the government. It did not exclude non-Africans, although it was predominantly African.

There was a political background to the debate about black culture and resistance. At the time, ANC membership was not open. Coloreds or Indians or whites were not allowed to join. Even now there are people who have this illusion that the ANC was always a democratic organization committed to liberation, and don't know about this whole notion of racial organization. The Trotskyists had always called for a non-racial South Africa; the ANC perspective was for a non-racial South Africa that would consist of the ANC for Africans, and separate congresses each for coloreds, Asians, and white democrats. Ironically SANROC, by being non-racial, was acting in opposition to official ANC policy. It was only later in the 1960s that the ANC became open to all. Of course, they've rewritten the history, so that one is no longer aware of that fact.

Africa, art, and anti-imperialism

Internationally, the relationship of culture to the politics of national liberation and resistance to imperialism was an important question by the late 1960s. A key point in that debate was the first Pan-African Cultural Festival in Algiers in July–August 1969. At this point you have in South Africa what we called the national liberation struggle. Within that struggle, however, was a failure to define what it was we were fighting for beyond national liberation—something that became critical after the fall of apartheid.

By the time I went to Algiers I had appeared before the United Nations on behalf of the South African liberation struggle and for the release of political prisoners. It must be remembered that the ANC and the PAC—and the Pan-Africanist Congress—were, at that time, peers, and equally recognized at the UN. The one was as important as the other. Gradually, the ANC very cleverly managed to marginalize the PAC, perhaps because it had the Soviet Union behind it. The PAC put their money on Beijing, so they were relying on Mao Zedong. Later, in 1973, when I went to China, I met with Zhou Enlai at the Great Hall of the People. He said to me, "Tell the ANC that we will give them anything they want, but they must ask for it." And so I went to Oliver Tambo, then head of the ANC, and told him so. The Chinese said that the ANC had to ask for help, because the ANC had already made a commitment to Moscow not to ask for help from anybody else—ruling out Beijing. The ANC thus chose to continue its alliance with the USSR.

I did not represent any particular group at the Algiers conference. At the time, I was working in London for the International Defense and Aid Fund, supported by the United Nations' Trust Fund for South Africa and accredited to the UN via UNESCO, the UN Educational Scientific and Cultural Organization. In that work, I could not distinguish between the ANC, the PAC, the Trotskyist groups in the Non-European Unity Movement (later the Unity Movement), or any other group. One had to be evenhanded. In fact, I preferred it that way. So in Algiers, I was part of the liberation struggle, but in an undifferentiated way. I was neither ANC nor PAC, but something in between. I was also, of course, supporting FRELIMO, the liberation movement coming of out Mozambique, and the MPLA in Angola.

The Algiers conference was sponsored by the Organization of African Unity (OAU). The OAU, which was full of reactionaries, insisted that only one person was allowed to speak for all the liberation movements. The movements elected me to speak on behalf all of them, which was a high compliment. It was also evidence that they trusted me to be impartial, nonpartisan. I wasn't going to back any one of them while they were fighting each other. They could trust me to simply put the case for the liberation struggles straight.

At the time, we didn't know it, but the CIA had infiltrated the OAU and actually was sending the minutes of the OAU meetings to Washington. Perhaps even more significantly, the secretary general of the OAU at that time was the Guinean diplomat Diallo Telli[1] sometimes called DT, who was subsequently accused—rightly or wrongly—of being a CIA plant. So at Algiers, there were all kinds of tensions. The CIA was there. Mossad, Israel's spy agency, was there. And we know that the Soviet Union had some KGB people there. Algiers, therefore, was really a conference for the Cold War struggle. I came in initially as a poet, and then the liberation movements asked me to speak for them.

An accidental academic

I lectured in the U.S. on apartheid and prison conditions, including forty-two lectures in forty-two days for the American Committee on Africa, later part of Africa Action. Soon afterward, I was accredited to the UN as the representative of International Defense and Aid, and got invited to various seminars and to testify at the UN about conditions for political prisoners on Robben Island—no one had ever come off the island before then. And I did some poetry.

On the basis of that, I was invited to Denver in 1970 to stand in for the South African writer, Es'kia—Zeke—Mphahlele while he left the U.S. to apply for permanent residency. He was teaching English at the University of Denver, and I filled in for him as a visiting professor. It's a pure accident—I was really just doing someone a favor. I returned to Britain after that. But on the basis of my teaching in Denver, I got about a half a dozen offers from other universities in the U.S. and Canada. I consulted Oliver Tambo— then head of the ANC—in London. He left the decision to me.

I eventually settled on Northwestern University in Evanston, Illinois. I did two important things there. One was introducing African literature into the overall curriculum. Possibly for the first time anywhere in the United States, novels by Africans were intro-

duced into English M.A. and Ph.D. courses. I used novels like
Chinua Achebe's *Things Fall Apart*. So I think that was an impor-
tant innovation, and of course I really helped establish African lit-
erature as a category—not African literature in English, but as a
category within the whole curriculum. The second important thing
was the formation of the African Literature Association (ALA) in
Chicago in 1975, which took place the year I was a visiting profes-
sor at the University of Texas at Austin.

When I was at Northwestern, the black students called the
white academic at the head of African studies, Gwendolyn Carter,
"the lady of the plantation." It defined a slaveholding relationship.
When you went to visit her you would have a black student who
would take your hat and coat and hang them up. You were back in
the Deep South in Evanston. Here's the really interesting thing: A
few blacks had actually become part of running the plantation, as
kind of overseers. When we tried to form the ALA, they opposed
it. They said, "We've got African studies and it's being really well
run!" So when people tried to start the ALA, they were opposed. I
become the catalyst only because I was not aware of the history of
conflict. I came in like a bull in a china shop and I said, "We need a
literature association." I was not aware that there had been a fight
to prevent its coming into existence.

There were really several debates going on in academia at the
same time. There was the issue of "stupid white men"—of women
being kept out of high positions. So there was a women's thrust.
Then you had an African American thrust that revolved around
black studies, and the whole notion of the creation of programs
and degrees in black studies. African studies were secondary to
that, or even tertiary. But at the same time, there was still a struggle
against colonial attitudes in academia, which blew apart in 1968 at
the African Studies Association conference in Montreal, where
there was actually a split. The black Americans pulled apart and
formed their own organization, the African Heritage Studies Asso-
ciation. In some ways it was a mistake because it ended up ghet-
toizing black studies. I was part of these discussions, but not
significantly. It was one element in a larger struggle. I didn't get
into the gender issue. I was fighting for African studies.

Peculiarly, African studies were dominated by whites with colonial attitudes. They decided which blacks got promotions. If you didn't stay in line you didn't get a promotion. Interestingly, they preferred Africans to African Americans, because they thought we were more easily disciplined. We were coming from other countries; we didn't have a base. So they actually encouraged fission between African Americans and Africans, and would promote Africans in preference to African Americans. But this did not, surprisingly, produce a very docile group of Africans.

At the African Studies Association meeting in Chicago in October 1974, we decided to form an African Literature Association. I was elected chair of the steering committee because I had a lot of experience organizing committees in the resistance in South Africa. And of course when I became chairman, I saw no reason why we should continue to be on the plantation. By coincidence, I had already decided that at the University of Texas I would host a symposium of South African writers in March 1975; we decided to use the occasion to form the ALA.

Another South African writer, Willy Kgositsile, and I, were the nucleus. The other South African writers were Mongane Wally Serote, Oswald Joseph Mtshali and Zeke Mphahlele. I also invited people from Ghana, Nigeria, and elsewhere to participate in the symposium as discussants, but the leading speaker was always a South African. Two of the discussants were from Ghana, Kofi Awonoor and Ama Ata Aidoo, a woman who's done a lot of novels about women and gender. It was the biggest concentration of African writers ever, anywhere in the world, in one place. So the ALA, by coincidence begins there, because I had a program already in place for a Sharpeville Memorial Day. It turned into an African writers' symposium, which in turn became the ALA.

Now here's the interesting thing. My daughter Jacinta, a very shy little girl, was at the conference, sitting reading a textbook in the corner. She overheard six people come in and plot how to destroy the ALA before it started, and told me. Oddly enough, they had different reasons. Some wanted to protect the plantation. And others were black nationalists who really thought that anything that's African should keep out Americans. So it's really a chauvinistic line, as well. The third reason for opposing the creation of the ALA was astonishing. It came from Zeke Mphahlele, who argued that if you created an ALA separately from African Studies, the ASA, it would be taken over by the CIA. Of course, I couldn't take this seriously, but it was being presented as a serious argument. And unfortunately there were Africans from the rest of Africa who, of course, would take the line the South Africans took, and Zeke was a senior South African, so they were going to back him, even if they didn't like what he was saying.

Fortunately, I was prepared for people to counterattack before the meeting started. So I circulated a statement asking those who favored the formation of the ALA to indicate yes; those who opposed no—and only those who favored launching the organization would have a right to vote on its proceedings. That settled it. Still, those who were against got up to speak. One was a black guy from California called Adam Miller. He was sincerely a black nationalist at that time, so his opposition was based on that. I was saying this would be an open organization and he was saying it should be a shut one—closed to whites.

Now this was a period in black America when there was a very strong hostility, even to white liberals. There was a feeling that you didn't want white allies—you wanted to do your own thing. And unfortunately, they had a good reason for feeling that way. In too many cases, white liberals would simply take over and start running black organizations. Blacks, of course, were upset—here were your white allies running you. Already there had been a pivotal event in academia in this country in 1968, in Montreal, when the split in the ASA had taken place between blacks who were supported by radicals and whites who were conservative—the colonial types. Montreal was very important, and we were still inheriting the residue, even in 1975, which was much later.

At the ALA meeting, I was elected chair of the steering committee and eventually I became the first president, and wrote the constitution. For the first time for any academic organization, the constitution said in the opening clause that we were committed to the liberation of the African peoples. That phrase is still there.

Until the formation of the ALA, African literature did not exist as a category—it was not in the syllabus. The ALA legitimized this field of study, so that people could get promotions, recommendations, publish work, and do a whole range of things as a consequence of having an association that has intellectual and academic credibility. A lot of the pursuits over the years in African literature come out of the sheer fact of the establishment of the association.

The controversies over African and African American studies programs continued. In the 1980s black students at the University of Pittsburgh mobilized to stop the closure of the Africana Studies program there. The administration agreed to keep it open and support it if the students could find someone of international standing to run it. They asked me, and I accepted. I left a tenured position at Northwestern in 1985 and took the job, with a pay cut.

The language of struggle

While I was at Northwestern, I really existed in two worlds. I lived in Evanston, which is very white, dominated by academia, but I was active on the South Side of Chicago, where most blacks live. I was working with African Americans doing some quite useful things on politics and the arts, like poetry readings. I also spent time at Mundelein College, which then had a heavily black student body.

At Northwestern I started the Steve Biko Memorial Committee, which included regular poetry readings and discussions. Then I began working with a young black man, John Bellamy, to start an annual Steve Biko memorial event, with poetry and cultural events. I also worked with a black theater group called Kuumba, run by Val Ward. I also helped form the Africa Network (AN), of which I become chair. It anticipated the potential of the Internet by creating a national organization with the help of a woman named Y.B. Holly. The AN had annual awards, for which we nominated a black author, or poet. We didn't have money for prizes; we just listed the winners as honors.

It was in this period that I was a cofounder, with the Nigerian author Wole Soyinka, of the Union of Writers of the African People in 1975; I was also a vice president. Soyinka was secretary; the Ugandan writer Taban Lo Liyong was also a vice president. The president was Leopold Senghor, the poet who was then president of Senegal. The other cofounders were the Ghanaian writer Ayi Kwei Armah and the Kenyan author Ngugi wa Thiong'o. It didn't take off. Soyinka, who had been the prime mover, won the Nobel Prize for Literature and got busy with that. Recently, lamont b. steptoe, the Philadelphia poet and publisher, and I have tried to keep it going.

In African literature, as I see it, there are two things taking place. There are people writing about what's happening in Africa with a marvelous naturalism, doing it very well. Yet there's a huge piece left out of the narrative, although there are others who supply that missing piece.

For example, the largely anglophone novelists in West Africa, in Nigeria or in Ghana take the problems of Africa as if they are generated in Africa. But simultaneously, in East Africa, Ngugi, who's also an Anglophone novelist, is saying that neocolonialism is the problem. He's identifying the continuity of oppression under the colonial system with the oppression of today—the postcolonial, if you like, but I prefer neocolonial—phase. In his novel *Petals of Blood*, you find him talking about the role of the International Monetary Fund and the World Bank and what he calls the bedbugs—the corporations that are bleeding the people to death. On the other hand, very early in francophone African literature, the novelist recognizes the colonial influence. The authors identify the fact that the oppressor, if he's black, is really the inheritor of power from the white oppressor. They can see continuity between the two. I am thinking particularly of Sembene Ousmane's novel, *God's Bits Of Wood*.

Another key debate in African literature has been on the question of language—in fact between Chinua Achebe and Ngugi, who says, you are not an African if you don't write in an African language, which is as categorical as one can be. Of course he's supported by some very bright people, including someone like Chinweizu, who in my opinion is one of the best theoretical writers in Africa. A Nigerian, Chinweizu is author of *The West and the Rest of Us*, and contends you are only an African writer if you write in an African language. And that's it. Achebe says, "Too bad. I write in English because I'm comfortable in English." And so you have two very clear schools of thought.

Where do I fall in those schools? It's really not a simple answer, because I grew up in a trilingual community. My mother and my father spoke English and Afrikaans, but we were living in a community prior to apartheid, before 1948. We had segregation, but separation was not yet enforced by law. So I could grow up speaking English, Afrikaans, and a little Xhosa, which was the African language in my area. It didn't bother me at all. You knew a little of all of them, but gradually society became more and more English. Or you went to school or you went to a community where more English was being spoken and so on and you were comfortable with that. In school we were learning English and Afrikaans. African languages were not part of the syllabus. For me, for one thing the choice was imposed. So when I am asked to take sides between Achebe and Ngugi, I say I am on the side of both. But I can see how the colonial language has an enormous influence in shaping the colonial mentality. That's why Ngugi's great book is called *Decolonizing the Mind.* Because if you have enslaved the mind, you don't really need chains after that.

I am sympathetic to those who are opposed to the colonial language, but I don't condemn those who use the colonial language, particularly under the circumstances that gave it to them. On the other hand, you have someone like V.S. Naipaul, a writer who buys so completely into the colonial mindset. There's an article for which he's interviewed by Elizabeth Hardwick in the *New York Times Book Review*, and she asks him, "What is the future of Africa?" And he says, "Africa has no future."[2] That is absolutely classic. So when I encounter people who see V.S. as a guru who helps you to understand the colonial world, I remind them that this is the man who said Africa has no future!

Despite the prominence of Third World literature in academia today, these arguments are still there. Speaking on a panel at the ALA conference in Egypt in 2003, I was surprised at the amount of hostility I got in making a tribute to Edward Said at the new library in Alexandria. There were people from Egypt and North Africa who were not at all friendly to me because I was speaking highly of Said, mentioning not only his book, *Orientalism*, but a very important essay in which he talks about expanding the canon in English literature studies. Some people said, "No, no, that's old hat," or "That's not applicable." I suppose one shouldn't be surprised, because Egypt is so much in the pocket of the U.S. that some people didn't want to be seen as anti-Western.

There's also an argument to be had at the other end of the spectrum. In 2005 I attended the European Association for Commonwealth Literature and Language Studies—EACLALS—in Malta. It's very prestigious. It used to be pretty much Commonwealth literature—Canada, Britain, Australia, and New Zealand—Anglo-Saxon, really. But as the European Union has grown, so has this organization. The conference was all about postcolonialism. There are marvelous texts now, and most of their politics are postcolonial. There are a massive amount of new book titles. By comparison, the ALA is nowhere near it.

When I got up to speak, I told them that they're all out of date—which was very unpopular. I said, "We're not in post-colonialism anymore. We're in post-postcolonialism. We are now dealing with a global agenda to create an empire." I talked about Paul Wolfowitz, Iraq, the preemptive war strategy, and all that. Then I went on to discuss Africa and say, "Here's NEPAD, the New Partnership for Africa's Development—the global agenda in its African manifestation. This is South African President Thabo Mbeki functioning on behalf of George W. Bush as his point man, carrying out a subimperial agenda in Africa."

I was trying to move them past the stage they were at. I was saying, "You've got to take a leap into the present, because you're still in the past."

[1] Diallo Telli, also known as Boubacar Telli Diallo, was a Guinean diplomat and first secretary-general of the Organization of African Unity, serving between 1964 and 1972.

[2] Elizabeth Hardwick, "Meeting V.S. Naipaul," *New York Times Book Review,* May 13, 1979.

Documents

Somehow tenderness survives
Dennis Brutus talks about his life and poetry with Bernth Lindfors, 1970

The interview that follows was tape recorded in London over a period of two days in August 1970. All questions and nonliterary statements have been edited out in the interest of providing a consecutive autobiographical narrative on a single theme.

I think the earliest literary influence on me was my mother, who not only recited nursery rhymes to me as a child, but had herself a love for poetry. She was a schoolteacher who had taught, as teachers do in South Africa, the whole range of the junior curriculum and had been educated by English missionaries who created a taste for her in literature. I suspect their own education was not terribly good in terms of literature—the things they encouraged her to like were things that I grew out of in time. As a student teacher she learned and later taught things like, "Under the spreading chestnut tree the village [smithy stands]," and Colley Cibber's appalling poem, "The Blind Boy," and Wordsworth's "Lucy Gray," which I think is a very bad introduction to Wordsworth. It is a poem of considerable sentimentality. At any rate, this is "memorable" poetry—easy to remember, with all the features which poetry normally has in a rather exaggerated form, so that one knew rhyme and rhythm and imagery. And there was a Longfellow, about the wreck of the Hesperus: "It was the schooner Hesperus,/that sailed the wintry sea..." and things like that. Fortunately also some good things—Wordsworth's "Daffodils" [and] Thomas Gray's "Elegy in a Country Churchyard," which in some ways is regarded as a touchstone of English poetry. If one knew these, one had a fairly good entry into English poetry. I learned these from her, and heard her recite them and read them to us, rather earlier than the average schoolboy—white or black—and certainly earlier than the mass of the black schoolchildren around the country.

In addition, my father was also a schoolteacher (at one time studied for an arts degree—B.A.—with the University of Cape Town by correspondence) and would memorize poetry and recite it preparing for his examinations. So I was hearing bits of poetry all around me. One which I remembered all my life is Tennyson's ode on the death of the Duke of Wellington, "Bury the Great Duke," which has since become an element in one of my very few poems relating to him. This is the picture of the kind of beginnings I had. In addition, my mother had a great love for the Arthurian legends and used to read the stories of Sir Galahad and Sir Lancelot and the Round Table in secondhand books, cast-off books given away by white families—at various times she took in washing to augment the family income when she wasn't able to teach. Married women teachers were discouraged in the educational system. My father also disapproved very often of her being out of the home teaching.

My brother, who is four years older than myself, went to one of the better nonwhite missionary schools run by Anglican nuns; it was one of the few nonwhite schools at that time which had the vestiges of a library, often secondhand and cast-off books from white schools. He would bring one home once a week. These included, again, things which contained Arthurian legends and similar stories. My mother would read these to us in the evenings or on a Sunday afternoon. Most of this is pre-school, for a rather odd reason. I don't quite know how it happened, but at some stage, I not only damaged the bridge of my nose—possibly cracked a bone in it as a boy—but I was also a bleeder, with an excessively sensitive nose which bled heavily, and this prevented me going to school. In addition, because I didn't like going to school, I would sometimes irritate my nose to the point where it bled as a pretext for not going to school. So by the age of seven and eight, at the time when most other boys of my age had started kindergarten school, I had had two interrupted spells of starting school and then quitting again and was much at home and spent a lot of my time reading—I had no real companions at my age. So these are, if you will, the earliest literary elements that come together.

When I did go to school, I found myself in a rather peculiar position. I was then about ten, or close to eleven, when I seriously began schooling, but I was beginning at kindergarten level, which is six year olds and seven year olds, because I hadn't done any of the previous years. But possibly because of my reading on my own, I was very rapidly promoted. This meant that while I had an advantage in some subjects, in fact was ahead of my class in them, in others—like arithmetic and history and geography—there were enormous gaps in my knowledge of the basics, which all the others had acquired. The shape of the world, for instance, and how many oceans there were—things that I had to discover by flying around the world. It meant a very unequal kind of education. And going to a school where people spoke a very bad kind of pidgin English, the average colored person grew up knowing both English and Afrikaans, but both badly, with possibly a smattering of one of the African languages, depending on his area.

I went to a school where there were Irish nuns teaching, who themselves had no training as teachers—they were do-gooders, who came out to the missions to educate the poor blacks—and they couldn't speak Afrikaans, nor could they teach it. So one received an education without one subject which was compulsory (by law you had to know both English and Afrikaans).

So one had an extremely uneven and spotty kind of education, and this left you with a tremendous handicap when it came to writing, at the senior level, an examination which was standard for the whole population.

I don't think I wrote poetry until about the age of fourteen or fifteen. When I did, I think it was an entirely spontaneous impulse. As far as I remember, the first thing I wrote was for a full moon in August and really wasn't bad, even looking back at it now. It had a rhythm and an image and a good vocabulary. And it lies around somewhere; one might still find it.

It was 'round about this time that my brother went off to college to become a teacher—he would be nineteen—and when he came back during the holidays, I discovered that he had acquired a mastery of Afrikaans. This annoyed me very greatly, because I hated to be outdone by him in anything. And when I learned that he had written some Afrikaans poetry for the school magazine, I felt I ought to write as well. So it's very likely that the second poem I wrote was an Afrikaans poem; I'm not sure. I think there was also an English love lyric—I was having one of my adolescent crushes—certainly there was this Afrikaans love lyric about this time; chiefly because I felt I ought to compete with my brother. I discovered, when I went to high school, which is standard seven—the equivalent of junior high school, I suppose—that there were other chaps in the class who were messing around with bits of verse. And we had an excellent science teacher who was an anarchist, who encouraged us to set up a student publication to attack the staff, and I found myself being made the editor of this. Often it turned out that there were no articles for this publication, so I'd have to sit down and write several to fill the pages, and so I wrote some poetry, as well as an amusing essay—at least one.

I'm never good at dates, but if I remember correctly, I would have gone to junior high 'round about 1939 [or] 1940. Certainly after the outbreak of the war. And I know that in 1942 I had completed junior high and was going to senior high, so, that places us fairly easily. There is a junior certificate and then senior certificate, which is the equivalent of matriculation, and then you go on from there to university.

When I wrote matric, which is the university entrance [exam], of [the] fourteen who wrote (and this is in a town of over 200,000; there could be only fourteen nonwhites writing the university entrance!) only four passed! And of the four who passed, two did not get a university pass, they got a school-leaving pass. So we ended up with two people in the total nonwhite population of the area who might go to university, if they had the money!

In my case, there was a scholarship from the city council, a municipal scholarship, which I managed to win. I was placed first in the whole district, which I suppose was a distinction, though one I hadn't worked very hard for. But it was sufficient to pay for three years at university.

I should add that had I not won the university scholarship, there was a Catholic Irish priest who had told my mother that he thought

I was sufficiently promising and that he would pay for the first year at university—at least—and see what could be done thereafter. This was because my mother was a devout Catholic and so was I, and I was the top altar boy, server, and things like that, and I am quite sure I had been marked down as a potential priest, who would go to the seminary at some stage. So they would encourage my education. But it was a nice thing to do in any case, and the kind of thing, which didn't happen to many nonwhites—and if you didn't get this kind of opportunity, then you were just lost. You just became absorbed into the labor pool or the system, generally.

I began studying at Fort Hare College in 1943 or 1944 and went on [until] 1947, but the reason why I took an extra year—I could have finished by 1946—was that we had run out of money in the family, and if you had done two years of a degree, you were allowed to teach. So I took a year off from university to teach in a little village in the Karroo, a place called Ft. Beaufort, chiefly known for having the biggest lunatic asylum in the country. I taught there for a year and did some study and then went back to college the following year.

I remember now that in the year when I broke off from university to teach—I was staying on my own, in a little place attached to a church—I wrote a great deal of poetry, which I collected in a thing called "The Gray Notebook," retitled "Green Harvest," because it was all immature stuff. There would be about a hundred poems there, I suppose, which are probably lost now.

At the university, I was one of the editorial staff of the student publication, and I know they printed a poem—something about a cavalier, a sort of a sonnet—in the student annual, which was really quite selective in what it would print. But we got ambitious, as usual, and tried to produce a monthly, of which maybe three or four issues came out. In one of them, I did a terrible review of James Joyce, an essay on *Ulysses,* which appalls me now, looking back on my straight-laced Catholic solemnity. I also wrote a remarkable short story in the Joycean idiom, a stream-of-consciousness short story, which really was very good. And many years later, in prison, when I was with other prisoners who wanted to be entertained, I'd tell them this short story. And they were delighted. I was forced to repeat it on several occasions. I don't know where it's got to. The journal was just called SANC—South African Native College—which was what Fort Hare was then. The newspaper was *The Fort Harian*, for which I did a lot of potboilers, reviews of films and books and so on.

It would be very interesting if one could recall all I was reading at that time. I was reading, for instance, *Horizon,* a literary thing, which was really quality literature. Quite the best stuff being produced in Britain during the war came out there. You wouldn't find Ezra Pound elsewhere, or Elizabeth Bowen. Major writers, who have since emerged, began there. It was one of the best journals going. These were thrown out of the university library, and I collected an armful and read through them on my own—and what I found there excited me and presumably influenced my thinking and whatever I wrote at that time.

My favorite poets at that time? Well, as a high school boy, I'd been recognized as an expert on Browning to the flattering extent that a teacher would sometimes ask me to take on a difficult Browning dramatic monologue. I had been told that Browning was the most difficult poet going and, very fortunately, having said this to a science master, he said it wasn't true, people just put you off. Once you believed it, you were in trouble, but if you didn't believe it, you were okay. I accepted his word (he was teaching physics!) and, sure enough, I found I could work my way through Browning. Then I got to university, and for the second-year Arts English course, Browning was a prescribed work. You really had to know Browning. And there, too, I found other students doing the course coming to me for coaching in Browning.

As far as my other favorites are concerned, I think I really got interested in John Donne after about three years of teaching, as late as that. At the university, I suspect that we were required to know Donne. Our teacher didn't know him, so one wasn't really taught him. I think I knew very little Donne at university—but again, I may be wrong. I'm not too sure.

I do know it was after I left university that I discovered Eliot, who wasn't taught, and Yeats, and Hopkins, who weren't taught either. We were taught the old-fashioned English syllabus, where if you knew the Elizabethans and the Victorians, you were okay. That's where literature ended; nothing much happened after that.

Fort Hare was not really a university. It became a university

Browning and Donne

college, which made it a subsidiary of Rhodes University. But at the time I was there, it wasn't even a university college, it was a "native" college, which was a rather special breed of thing. But the degree I did there was on a par with the university degree.

I set out planning to do three courses in English and three in Afrikaans or Dutch. I was going to major in those, but I messed around in Dutch, and so instead of majoring in Dutch, I only took two courses there and took psychology as a second major. I also took things like education and politics, history and geography. You took two majors. Doing a degree in English, I specialized in Webster, in drama—out of cussedness—as opposed to Shakespeare, which everybody was specializing in. And I got a distinction in English, which was pretty rare, and for which I think you had to get over 66 percent on each paper you wrote. I missed it in psychology, chiefly because I got tight very unwisely the night before I wrote one of my last papers. The professor of psychology, a Norwegian named Jensen, was quite a distinguished man who subsequently went to the white university in Natal to teach philosophy, and he thought I was one of his brightest scholars. I could probably have concentrated on psychology. Having got a distinction in English, this in fact qualified me for another scholarship to do an M.A., but they found some peculiar pretext—apparently Catholics were disqualified; so I never did get the scholarship for an M.A. Had I got it, I'd probably not have taken it, because I had to go out and earn.

After leaving the university, I taught for a short while and then threw it up. I didn't like teaching. I taught partly at the school where I had been educated myself, which is Paterson High School, where I had done my junior and high school education, and then went to a Catholic high school called St. Thomas Aquinas–both of these were in Port Elizabeth, where I grew up.

I should perhaps mention that when I was teaching at St. Thomas I had a marvelous love affair with a girl who was a student but whom I religiously left alone until she left school. I felt, as I always have, that it's unethical to date your students and so I didn't go near her, as long as she was in my class, although she was absolutely adorable. But once she'd left school, I then felt free to take her out, and I might well have married her.

For her, I wrote perhaps a hundred poems, which are since lost.

But a lot of them were collected in a little red notebook, which I called "the red book." So if one could find that, one would have quite a lot of poetry. It would be Wordsworthian, Shakespearean sonnet stuff because one grew up thinking of Wordsworth and Shakespeare as exemplars of poetry. And I should think Browning would have influenced this sequence, too.

One of the poems I wrote for her has been salvaged and I think it's primarily influenced by Hopkins. Her name was Dulcy, and I wrote little things about "Dulce," which is Latin for "sweetness." And I called her "Sweetness" and, sometimes, "Sweet." In my poems I would just call her Sweet, and the last poem in *Sirens Knuckles Boots* is a poem from that period which says: "So, for the moment, Sweet, is peace...." I'm talking to her, so it's with a capital S. But it's invariably printed with a small s, so people think I'm saying that peace is sweet, when I'm really saying to her, "My Sweet, there is peace," which is quite a different thing. If there are any others of that quality, then they couldn't have been too bad, although now I tend to be rather contemptuous of that group. I doubt if they were any good.

The Dulce poem, as far as I remember, took thirty versions—at least thirty. Others, perhaps a dozen, maybe twenty. The more clotted they were, the more hard work there was, but normally some of it would come to your mind whole. An entire sentence or phrase would come straightaway, and this would establish the idiom for you. Then the rest would be pruning of a multiplicity of ideas, to make them function simultaneously.

I remember, on one occasion—and this is in the early 1960s, possibly 'round about December of 1961—having to write a Christmas card to someone with whom I'd had a love affair and it had just broken. Probably the most important event, or series of events, in my life. It's had a lasting impact. Writing for her (she was white; our whole affair was illicit and we could've gone to prison dozens of times; she also worked with me in the underground, in the political movement) writing for her—I think this is how it happened—I found I couldn't write a Christmas card that said what I wanted to say, so I wrote a little lyric instead, which had been taking shape in my mind for some time, and which I think was influenced by Auden's poem: "Lay your sleeping head, my love, human on my faithless arm...." I'm not sure, but I think that influenced it. This was the first of my "Nightsongs," "Nightsong: City," in which I achieved magically the simultaneous writing for South Africa and a particular woman. So, then, I could be talking to her and, at the same time, about the country. When I took the pen to begin writing this Christmas card, this was what the poem was going to be. At the moment I started, I didn't yet know what was going to happen. It was in the process of writing it that I discovered one could do the simultaneous statement, which I've done ever since. It's always a private as well as a public statement. Many of the love lyrics are also political, if one would read them that way, and many of the political poems are in fact couched in intimate, personal terms.

You know, when *Sirens Knuckles Boots* was put together, it was another woman who said she would dig up what she could find from my papers. She came to consult me and I said, "I don't care a damn what you take. You see what you want and take it." And she gave the bunch to Mbari. Some of the poems she took were written for her, but she also found the older ones, and found among my papers the one which had been written in the 1950s for Dulcy, which really belongs to a period ten years earlier. The things which I wrote for her in 1961 and the things I wrote for Dulcy in 1950—you can see the gap is ten years—I would say that in fact my style hadn't changed all that much, but that, I think, is because I always had several styles. There was a simple, direct statement, generally lyrical and rhyming and strictly metrical, often in stanza structure, but there would also be the kind of complex Hopkinsian stuff, and there would be a kind of colloquial, conversational, unadorned poetry, which I picked up from Yeats. Some of Yeats is wonderfully direct and simple. I think I was writing in all these styles, but at the time, for me, the ideal was a kind of fusion of Donne/Hopkins/Browning, which I would work towards at my highest pitch. But I could be writing at the other levels as well.

Today I think I'm reverting to the less ornate approach, but as the idea comes to me first—if it comes in essentially simple, conversational terms—I will then work it out in those terms. But if it comes to me as an idea which has been germinating, and when it takes shape in verse, comes in a complex form, then I will go on developing it as a complex statement. But very often I wish that my best poetry would be a simple, singing kind of poetry, so I may postpone an idea because it doesn't come in that form. Or I may dismiss it altogether. Or, as now—last night, going home after a political meeting, a wonderful evening, a portion of a poem came straightaway as I came out of the tube into the night. But a fraction of a second after that came the remembrance that I'm not writing poetry anymore, so I dismissed it. Whereas, if I had been writing, I would have begun to explore the idea, walking all the way home. By the time I'd been able to sit down and write, the poem would've been almost complete. This is normally how it works. The idea is developed in the elaborations and you hear the rhythm in your head and sound them out, and so on, for the final shape—which may still, of course, take redrafting and reshaping. But if it presents itself as a complex notion or image initially, I tend to accept that. Sometimes the whole form comes. Not only the diction, but actually the structure of the poem. Some of them, which consist of a statement and then the recapitulation or exposition, are always in the sonata form: for instance, "This sun on this rubble after rain," which is then developed in three refrains, each of which develops the initial theme. When you end: "Like the sun on this debris after rain," you've modulated into a statement that is richer than the first one, because you've worked it out in the exposition section. But the whole poem may come like that.

Of course, I've also gone through mystical phases, when it seemed to me immoral to write poetry, so for a whole year I would stop writing. I find that it is impossible for me to simply take a decision not to write. This doesn't mean that I've stopped thinking poetry or that ideas don't come to me, but I simply refuse to put them down. And when they come—when I'm walking the street or in the tube—if I am prepared to look at them closely, I will discover the ramifications of the idea, and the images will leap to mind and so on and I will have a poem. But when it comes as it normally comes first—as a kind of insight or perception or a musical phrase—if I dismiss it, then that's the end of the poem.

Now why do I do this? Normally, simply when I begin to develop a guilt about an accumulation of work and I realize that I may not do the work, but to give myself the possibility of doing it, I must cut out poetry. So that if I have spare time, rather than turning to verse (if I turn to anything) it will be to unfinished projects that I'm working on. Poetry is still a dreadfully occasional thing for me.

What is worse, as long as it's occasional, as long as one is a dilettante, one's not a craftsman. I've always said a good poet is like a good carpenter: if you made a table, the four legs would be square—you know, they would stand even on the ground, the thing wouldn't wobble—so that one would plane and chisel and hammer away until it was a well-wrought piece of carpentry. And it seems to me that if I ever made such a commitment—to be a craftsman in poetry—inevitably, the other things I'm doing would suffer, because I think you would have to be prepared to abandon yourself to some measure of impulse, because I think that this is in the nature of poetry. It's true Keats used to sit down every morning at ten o'clock and write for two hours solid, and he would know it was coming. He said that "Poetry has to come as naturally as the leaves come to a tree," and he could sit down and do a stint. I know other poets who say, "I do forty lines a day—no nonsense." And I think one can do that, because a lot of one's notions about writing poetry are merely sentimental. I think one oughtn't be romantic about being a poet, but I do believe that some of the writing of poetry is by impulse.

In order for me to make a total commitment to poetry, I would have to remake myself. This is not impossible, in the sense that I could wholly shut out, say, my political activity, my organizing work, my sports, the kind of chores which I do from day to day with this and that committee, and so on. I think it would not be impossible, but I think it would be immoral. This is what really stops me: that a total commitment to the craft of poetry, with the kind of integrity which that implies, would do damage to what I now regard as essential to integrity for me. Which means social concern. Specifically, social concern with my own country, to which I have a particular—largely sentimental—obligation. It seems to me that what you do in Britain on race is as useful as what you do in South Africa on race. I think it's extremely valuable to be working on it here, except that you mustn't spread your fire. There are good people working on the British scene; there are a few on the South African scene. That is where my knowledge, my expertise, my own experience lies, so it makes sense to do that.

On the other hand, I should think that if I got a year as a

writer-in-residence or something, I would probably do all the other little things I'm doing now, or some of them, because there would always be time for them, but my kind of relentless pursuit of what I was after would be of such a measure that I would be free of the sense of mere dabbling, of slipshod work, or just plastering and wallpapering over cracks, and that sort of thing.

To tell the truth, there are very few of my poems I can go back to without dissatisfaction, very few, and in fact the closer I look at them—and this is why I don't often do it—the more dissatisfied I become. I can see alternative choices, a clumsy jointing of images where they just don't fit smoothly, or where one might have fit several more things in the same phrase by a rearrangement or the choice of another adjective. And very often, of course, I fail, not through doing too little, but by attempting too much and succeeding badly. So one is conscious of the defects all the time.

In fact, my most productive periods are very often simply an expression of dissatisfaction with my verse. I'm really reworking themes, because I feel I've stated them incompletely. So several poems may often just be oblique attacks on a central idea, which I haven't elaborated fully.

There are very few of my poems I would rate as quite finished, and oddly enough, the one or two which I think I could not do any better on—though they are not perfect yet—are poems which are almost generally condemned. This is very amusing, because it seems to me "Longing," in its way, is nearly perfect in what it sets out to do. Now maybe it sets out to do the wrong thing, but having set out to do something, it came very close to achieving it: a fusion of very high-powered intellection, a series of purely abstract notions making a certain argument, but this argument building up also to an emotional intensity where the intellectual part is not lost, but reinforces the emotional part. But I don't think I've met more than maybe half a dozen at most—possibly three or four is more accurate—people who said, "Now, that is a good poem!" And I don't mind terribly, but it does make me cautious, because supposing one were to make this total commitment, and supposing, in fact, you set out to do these rather ambitious things—the world might agree that you are a bad poet!

Much of my poetry is written late at night or in the early hours of the morning, chiefly because my days are so busy. I'm only alone from midnight, perhaps, because the whole day has been tied up with talking and interviews, telephones, etc., particularly when you are on the road. You speak at a public meeting which ends at eleven, and then you have to have coffee with people until midnight and so on. If you're not alone, of course, you can't write. Unless, as I sometimes do at meals, I can cut off my associates from me and write a poem on the menu or something of that sort. But normally, once you're in company, it's impossible to write.

But it's hard to know what environment is congenial, because often I write under the most uncongenial circumstances. One explanation for why I can write so easily in so many places may be that it is my way of asserting, subconsciously, the difference between what I was in prison and what I am now, a kind of celebration of pseudo-freedom—not real freedom—but to celebrate the contrast between confinement and this new kind of mobility. I find I can write in a jet plane with great ease. I can go into a totally new and sometimes even alien, hostile environment and still find the capacity to write poetry, perhaps because I'm celebrating this kind of leap-frogging that I'm doing.

At other times I write because I find so much in my daily work that is frustrating. You go to an embassy to raise an issue on South Africa or even to get travel documents to enter a country and you kick your heels in corridors for days on end. When I am very angry or frustrated and I don't want to get mad—because then I would lose a grip on the situation—I turn inwards, and I write poetry instead, rather than blowing my top.

There are less compelling situations which provoke my poetic impulse, too. I may get a notion in the tube and find that I don't have a pen or I don't have paper, so I don't write it and then I forget it, but perhaps going to bed it may come back to me. Or on some other occasion I may see the same advert, or whatever triggered it off initially, and the notion may come back—often in a quite different form. I may then write it, or scribble the opening line on my newspaper. If I throw the paper away, then that's normally the end of the poem, if I don't keep it somewhere and go back and work on it.

But often, say, if you get a notion in the morning you forget it during the day. Going home, it comes back—and you don't feel

like writing. So you toy with it in your mind, you explore its possi-
bilities or its ramifications, and if they become exciting enough,
you can then write the poem. Or you may let it go. Or you may
find visitors at home or the telephone ringing or something and it
will disappear again.

On the whole, I try to avoid "occasional poetry," because I
have a guilt about it. So lots of things happen which seem to be an
occasion for a poem and I don't write it, I resist writing it. I should
think that I could have written a great deal more of elegiac poetry
but I don't. Those I write are almost always sufficiently immediate
and compelling. They also tend to be very bad poetry, because—
another reason—I write without conviction, conscious of this occa-
sional nature.

I should add that I make a very clear distinction between per-
sonal and poetic commitment. I believe that the poet—as poet—
has no obligation to be committed, but the man—as a man—has
an obligation to be committed. What I'm saying is that I think
everybody ought to be committed and the poet is just one more of
the many "everybodies." His commitment may or may not come
through in his work; I don't think this means writing on specific
political themes. I think it is immoral for an artist to import propa-
ganda into his work. It shows a lack of integrity. But I am con-
vinced that we all have a role; we've all got a job to do in society,
chiefly in the transforming or even in the destroying of a given soci-
ety. This happens, not because we're poets, but because we're peo-
ple living in the society. It may be that the poet, by virtue of his
talents or perhaps because of his sensitivity, may either be able to
see things better or say things better, but he has no obligation be-
cause of his poetic function. I don't think one must say to poets,
"You've got to be committed because you're a poet" any more
than you should say to a carpenter or a man in a trade union he's
got to be committed. I think the poet is just another man. True, his
concern is with ideas, where the carpenter's might be with lumber,
so his criticism would be on the level of ideas, possibly, because this
is his plane just as for the carpenter it would be on the level of bad
housing, because that's his plane. So, he must do his thing where he
is, but I would hate to go around the place telling people, "You've
got to be committed because you are a poet." I'll say to them, "We

ought *all* to be committed, because we are people, we're all part of the same human environment."

I've always been committed, but my commitment has taken many forms. When I was a social worker, my concern was with social rehabilitation, social welfare. This was my involvement in the society. As a teacher, I was opposed to discriminatory education, because that's where I was. When I was active in church work, for instance, in the slums or wherever, this was not an absence of commitment to a cause, nor of an obligation in the society. It didn't show in my poetry; there were no social messages, but I'd like to think that even now all I'm doing is commenting on the environment. And when the environment made no impact on me the way that prison, say, made an impact, or house arrest, or bannings, I did not reflect it, because it wasn't hitting me in that way. But, the moment it began to hit me, I reacted to it—not because I imported it, but because it was now the stuff of my existence, it was part of the fabric of my existence. To reflect what I was, was to include it.

It seems to me that certain themes which I was working on in the past, or which have run through my work consistently, are still there. There's a kind of religious questioning, which in fact has intensified after prison, and which I still continue now, whether it's in Algiers "On this anniversary day," or whether it's in Denver "Living a poem," or whatever—I'm still asking certain questions about the nature of my existence and certain theological concepts, if you like, religious concepts. That is still there. I still write the kind of intimate, personal, lyrical poetry—generally love lyrics and things like that or for nature or for South Africa—which tend not to be wholly egotistical. They're not only about me, but they tend to import bits of the South African situation or the South African predicament into my work. That, I think, is still there. In essence, one is still being tender about the loved object, but one's relation with it is different because it's now not mere nearness. It's not the violated, ravaged landscape that I lived in, but looking at it from a distance.

It strikes me sometimes that the world is so small today, and the areas of the world—in what is important—differ so little, that one needn't attach oneself to a particular area to the exclusion of all other areas. Also, I often suspect patriotism of being mere sentimentality, this kind of "my country right or wrong" nonsense, when in fact it's the world we're living in and not countries. And it is true that South Africa is in no way unique in the kinds of people that are there, in its climate, in its geography, in its mountains, in what is attractive. Having roamed, as I have, most of the world, I know how much South Africa is like so many other parts of the world. It's got unique political characteristics, but these really don't affect the quality of the human beings there; they're pretty much like people elsewhere. So how does one justify this sentimental attachment to an area no different from areas in Algiers or around Carmel on the West Coast of the United States? It seems to me one cannot justify it as an emotional response.

But when I was in South Africa, in a very large South African community—and a very narrow one, with a terribly ghettoized mentality—one of the ways I managed not to become ghettoized myself, so that I never became the typical subservient black man or, for that matter, the typical rebellious and frustrated black man, but something in between, was because I said, "In fact, I am a citizen of the world. I can go anywhere and I can meet anybody and I do not accept this kind of limitation on me, either the sub-man or the man confined in a particular locality or location defined for him by the state, with boundaries that he could not go beyond." I felt I was not localized, I couldn't be kept in my place. And this meant that one transcended a local patriotism.

So now, I ask myself: If, in South Africa, you were not a patriot, how do you justify now being a narrow patriot? If I am one now, then I suspect it's merely a sentimental posture. It gives me a persona as a particular poet with a particular voice—the exiled poet—but how phony is it? And then, I think the answer is really: You must do what you can do where you are. Although it is fine to fight for humanity, one must always see "humanity" in terms of real persons. One's reaction to good or evil is a reaction derived from real experience, so that the evil I must fight is the evil I know. The people I must fight for are the people I know. It's fine to fight for blacks in Britain, and I do what I can, but the blacks I know best and the situation I know best are the blacks of South Africa and the situation in South Africa.

In terms of geography, of landscape, I've seen mountains as fine in the Rockies. I've seen beaches as fine in Algiers and on the West

Coast. So that I suppose, in a sense, one sees people in a landscape, and then one knows that landscape, and it is dear to you not because of what it is intrinsically, but because of its associations. So it's a special landscape relating to special people; otherwise, it seems to me, there's very little justification for being sentimentally and narrowly attached to a particular strip of the earth, because our concerns more and more are global. It's one family; "one world," in Wendell Willkie's words, which I read long ago. I've always accepted it as one world. So we ought to be patriots of the world rather than of a country, but to get a focus, I think you need a place and you need people. So my greatest commitment—personal as well as poetic—is still to South Africa.

Protest against apartheid: Alan Paton, Nadine Gordimer, Athol Fugard, Alfred Hutchinson, and Arthur Nortje
1969

I speak only partly as a writer—a very occasional writer—one who does bits and pieces whenever he can, and therefore is at a distinct disadvantage when discussing literature. The fact that I come from South Africa lends, I suppose, to my writing and the writing of others in South Africa a certain special interest. This becomes even more interesting, I hope, if I tell you a little about the circumstances and the details of the situation there in terms of the writer's existence.

My case is not an extreme one, so it might be as well to start with that. I was banned from writing and I was banned from publishing anything. These two bans were not directly served upon me. As the result of an Act of 'round about 1961, which was designed to punish people who committed sabotage, and as a result of the interpretation of this Act, I was banned from writing. In a strictly legal sense, even to write was construed as sabotage. Therefore, I was, in that sense, banned from writing. But after I was released from prison in 1965, after I had been on Robben Island, the bans which had been served on me were all lifted the day before I was released and I was served with a new set of bans which ran until 1970. These bans included three, which almost certainly will strike you as curious. One was that I was banned from writing at all. This meant that I did not have to be published—merely to write was a criminal act. But, in addition, I could not even draft anything that might be published. In fact, my Banning Order (which has Mr. Vorster's autograph!) specifically forbids me to compose slogans; so that, in fact, even a string of words could have been illegal. Then there is a further one which says that I may not write, publish, or prepare anything which might be published.

All this is very complicated. But you can understand that if you want to write, and if you feel occasionally that you ought to write, it introduces a rather special urgency or intensity into your work. I have met Alex La Guma's wife recently. He was working on a novel while he was under house arrest. She told me how the pages, as he completed them, would be deposited under the linoleum so that if he were raided while he was writing, the Special Branch or political police would find only one page in the typewriter but wouldn't find the others.

Perhaps this is a rather oblique way of approaching my subject, which is really: Protest against apartheid in writing. I think one may say in all seriousness that to write at all once you are banned from writing—and it doesn't matter whether you write well or badly—constitutes a form of protest against apartheid in South Africa. The consequences of this are perhaps even more serious in that they extend beyond the particular person. It means that a large number of articulate people who could write, who would have things to communicate, are cut off from the community. They may not speak to it, address it, or express their thoughts. It works the other way as well. Not only may they not speak, but those who want to listen cannot listen—it cuts both ways. I think (and I hope) that this gives you an idea of the kind of sterility, the barrenness that is being created in South Africa in cultural terms. It might interest you to know that I was only able to read Alex La Guma's novelette for the first time after I came to Britain. If I were found with it in my possession in South Africa, this too would be a criminal offence.

This is stating the position of the writer in rather extreme terms, but I think it is worthwhile beginning from that point. When in literary form, people protest—as they do in South Africa—against apartheid, they come from every section of the population. They include Alan Paton, Nadine Gordimer, as well as people like Alex La Guma and Arthur Nortje, and a host of others who are probably unknown and are likely to remain unknown because they dare not be published. They may write, they may circulate their manuscripts secretly, but to publish would be to expose themselves to police action very promptly.

But my interest at the moment, I should say, is in trying to define the ways in which South African writers express their protest against apartheid. This is the question that intrigues me, and it is a question which, I hope, other people will consider as well. Because I have only lately begun to consider it, I find I can only give tentative suggestions, tentative definitions. I don't think I am competent yet to state dogmatically what I think is happening.

I should like to start with someone like Alan Paton who represents one extreme of protest literature in South Africa, and then work slowly over to someone like Alex La Guma who represents the other extreme. In between, you will find today people like Nadine Gordimer and, in terms of drama, Athol Fugard. I would also like to spend some time on someone whose work unfortunately is not known, but which does deserve to be known, a young man called Arthur Nortje,[1] a poet who has degrees from South Africa and Oxford and is now teaching in Canada.

Now, Paton is interesting because he started what seems to me almost a new era in South African writing. What is interesting about it is that other people had written not much less competently the sort of thing that Paton wrote in *Cry the Beloved Country*,[2] but somehow they did not set in motion the kind of cycle that Paton did. If you know *Cry, the Beloved Country*, you will know that it is a rather simple story. It is a narration of a black man in contact with a society which he doesn't really understand—a society in which he finds himself either unable to cope, or he finds himself sucked into the worst elements of that society. He ends as a criminal, and the society is accused of having made him a criminal. All this is really very straightforward and, in a sense, almost trite—and I don't think Paton himself would mind if one described it in these terms.

One must not think in color categories, but it is very difficult to resist thinking of Alan Paton as a white man, a sympathizing white man standing outside South African society with all its complexities and dynamic tensions and reducing it to what is almost a parable, a simple little tale told with a certain lyricism which I think is sometimes false because it is almost like a kind of poetic prose; but telling a story which moved people, and caught people's attention. It became a film, it became a play, and, among other things, it touched certain springs in the feelings of white South Africans. It is almost as if a serious novel on the theme of the disintegration of African culture and society, a serious novel on the misfits in our culture, would not be accepted or would not be understood; but reduced to these simple, almost fabular, terms, it was intelligible and it made an impact.

Paton, as you probably know, has had imitators who deservedly are not known outside South Africa. I have seen many botched novels, short stories, and long stories that try to relate pretty much the same story of the African, the simple African who comes from the reserves, who is sucked into the complexity of an urban location—life in the shanties among the *tsotsis* and the *skollies*, the hooligans and ruffians—and who finds himself a victim of this kind of society. If you had the time, or if you could spare (or even waste) the time, you could turn to the Afrikaans novel, the novels written by the Afrikaner, and you will find literally hundreds of novels that tell what is very much the same tale. The simple *boerenooi*, the young girl from the farm, who goes to Johannesburg where her morals fail. Usually, she ends up as a prostitute in one of the sleazier white suburbs. But it is the same story of a person failing to come to terms with a complex and tough society. This has been repeated over and over again.

Paton seems to have stated certain simple truths, and, of course this is Paton's protest against apartheid. This is his protest. Whatever he has said elsewhere in terms of the novel, I think has never matched this simple direct attack which he made in *Cry, the Beloved Country*. I don't think that Paton's best attack was in *Cry, the Beloved Country*. I think we should read a little pamphlet that he wrote when people were being moved out of their homes, a thing which he calls "The People Wept," which is movingly beautiful, a most poignant document far surpassing *Cry, the Beloved Country*. It may be that Paton's forte is really pamphleteering rather than writing novels.

Nadine Gordimer is, of course, everything that Paton is not. Her books are infinitely more complex, just as her characters are more complex. They are, as you know, extremely sophisticated people. Their emotions, their perceptions, and the problems that confront them are wholly of another order. But Nadine Gordimer, too, is making her protest against apartheid. This is her theme, and so her last book, *The Late Bourgeois World*,[3] has been banned in South Africa. There is a fairly simple explanation for this: that the principal characters, both black and white, at the end of the novel are on the edge of not merely an emotional but a sexual experience. And, while the South African government might not frown on black and white people having emotional relationships (I am not sure whether they would: probably they would frown on that too), certainly, sexual relations are forbidden. People have said that *The Late Bourgeois World* has been banned because Nadine Gordimer suggested the possibility of a sexual relationship. I don't think this is true myself. I think the whole novel is, by implication, a criticism and a condemnation of white society in South Africa today: of its ruthlessness, of the lack of feeling, of the lack of communication not only between black and white, but also between white and white.

I think that Nadine Gordimer has tried to say in *The Late Bourgeois World* that white South Africa is becoming dehumanized, that it is afraid to live and feel as human beings do because it has agreed to live by a set of rules which are themselves inhuman, and that once it has accepted that premise, it must watch its own humanity withering away. Some atrophy must set in. This, I think, is her criticism; this I think is her protest. There is this disadvantage, that I am afraid that Nadine Gordimer would find the same lack of humanity in other societies. This is because there is in her the kind of impersonality that you find in a microscope. She does not herself react to feeling. In her books even the emotional relationships are forced, are conjured up, are synthetic. Though Nadine Gordimer would say that she is condemning South African society for being dehumanized, I would say that Nadine Gordimer, who is one of our most sensitive writers, is also the standing, the living example of how dehumanized South African society has become—that an artist like this lacks warmth, lacks feeling, but can observe with a detachment, with the coldness of a machine. There is in her, herself, no warmth and feeling.

Now midway between them, to my mind, is Athol Fugard. I have never seen his play, and I think it is worth making this comment that when *The Blood Knot*[4] first played in South Africa, it showed in some centers for white audiences only. Subsequently, an arrangement was made to have separate nights—one night for blacks after a week for whites. I was then invited to go on one of the "white" nights, and sit with the man who worked the lights. This was a concession which was made to me, and which I rejected. Thus I have not yet seen *The Blood Knot*. I suppose I will have to wait until it is again put on in Britain. But, of course, this is not the problem now. What we want to see is to what extent Athol Fugard protests against apartheid.

Paton chose a simple narrative form. Gordimer's is a complex and sophisticated form which amounts to an oblique attack on the whole value structure of South African society. Fugard's is, of course, dramatic. He wants to present the whole problem of apartheid (and it is his overriding problem, the one that dominates his work) in terms of a clash. He has in *The Blood Knot* cleverly approached it from both angles—it is both conflict and unity—for the white and the black are, as they often are in South Africa, blood brothers. One has turned out to be black, and the other one has turned out to be white. In terms of the society, they are expected to live in different worlds and have completely different sets of values. The problem for the two brothers is how to reconcile themselves knowing that they really belong to different worlds. They discover the conflict that is implicit in both of them. They discover, too, a kind of bond that they cannot break. They must fight, they must beat each other, but they must also love each other—and this is the knot that ties them together.

Fugard has, of course, deliberately reduced this by such a symbol to a purely physiological association. It is a blood knot. Dan Jacobson has presented this same problem with infinitely more subtlety in his *A Dance in the Sun*[5] where he shows the immense and quite beautiful dependence of the black servant and the white master on each other. A much more complex presentation altogether, but Fugard's is dramatic and, as in much drama, the solution is a purely dramatic solution. It says nothing for the society. It offers the society no solution except that there will be this perennial drawing apart and drawing together. This is the knot that ties them.

These are three ways in which people have protested against the spirit of apartheid. I could, if you wished, recite a long list of pamphlets, articles, and even books which have been written, which are explicitly "nonliterary" or noncreative denunciations of apartheid, of which the finest ever to come out of South Africa was Alfred Hutchinson's *Road to Ghana*.[6] This had pace and momentum, simplicity and directness, and best of all, a freshness of language, a new minting of idiom and of image which I have never seen paralleled in any other writer who came out of South Africa. Regrettably, he seems to have lost much since he came to Britain. Perhaps this too close contact with the English language has blunted his ear, his tongue. I don't know. Certainly, and very regrettably, the freshness has gone, for I thought he was, at the time of *Road to Ghana*, the most promising writer we had in South Africa. I thought he would fulfill himself in Britain, but as yet nothing has really happened.

I should like to talk about Arthur Nortje. We both won Mbari prizes for our poetry at the same time (with the difference that I returned the money because I objected to accepting prizes on a racial basis—it was a competition for blacks only). We have this much in common—that we both won Mbari prizes, and also that he was my student once as a high school boy—but this is quite irrelevant.

I think he is far and away the best poet to come out of South Africa. What is particularly interesting is that his best poetry is being written in Britain and has been written only recently since he has decided that his hopes of returning to South Africa are almost nil. It seems that ever since he came to Britain roughly a year and a half ago, he wrote keeping himself well in check because he was afraid that if he spoke out and then had to return to South Africa, he would go to prison—as I am sure he would have to. Now he has resigned himself to not going home. Since he made this acceptance his poetry has acquired a tremendous freedom. But even before it reached this new capacity, it was already of such freshness and power that I seriously consider him to be the best poet to come out of South Africa. What he is doing at present is immeasurably better than what he did before. Nortje focuses in himself and in his work the essence of the protest against apartheid, and of the problems that confront the man who seeks to protest against apartheid. In Nortje you have the man of talent—and it doesn't matter whether he is black or white—the man of talent who dares not allow himself to develop because to do so, to look truthfully at South African society today, and then to describe truthfully his reactions to that society, can only land him in prison.

For many people the position is much sadder. There are people in South Africa today who have come to terms with apartheid, who accept the society and therefore whatever they write (and there *will* be writers—they want to go on writing whether it is poetry or prose) is limited. Whole areas of expression are shut out for them and these are things they see around them. They will see a man being beaten at the nearest bus stop because he doesn't have a pass on him, but they mustn't react to this because this is the part of society about which they may not speak. It is an area they cannot traverse in their work and, therefore, they cannot permit themselves to allow it to enter their experience, their perceptions, because it would demand to be expressed, or at least to work itself into their writing.

So we find a society almost barren of worthwhile writing and barren because people have accepted certain values in that society. I know there are all the old questions about commitment and involvement and engagement, and I prefer to shy away from them. I think it is simply true that an artist, a writer, is a man who lives in a particular society and takes his images and ideas from that society. He must write about what he sees around him and he must write truthfully about it, or he must come to terms with what is ugly in it, and pretend that it is not there or that it is not bad. Having done that, he cuts himself off from large areas of experience, large areas of expression. This is the price that he must pay because he has cut himself off from his fellow men. He has denied himself access to their feelings, the ability to enter into their experience and sympathize with them. Once he has deprived himself of this, his work must suffer as a consequence.

And this is why there is protest, in writing, against apartheid, and why we must go on protesting.

[1] Some of his poetry is published in *Seven South African Poets,* edited by Cosmo Pieterse (Heinemann, 1971); cf. also a small group in

Modern African Poetry, ed. Beier & Moore, new revised and enlarged edition (London: Penguin, 1968, 1970); an extended selection of the work of Nortje, who died in Oxford in 1970 while he was a student for the M.Litt. degree, is being prepared by Dennis Brutus.

[2] Alan Paton, *Cry, the Beloved Country* (London: Jonathan Cape, 1948).

[3] Nadine Gordimer, *The Late Bourgeois World* (London: Gollancz, 1965).

[4] Athol Fugard, *The Blood Knot* (Johanisburg: Simondium, South Africa, 1968).

[5] Dan Jacobson, *A Dance in the Sun* (London: Weidenfeld & Nicolson, 1956).

[6] Alfred Hutchinson, *Road to Ghana* (London: Gollancz, 1960).

African culture and liberation

Speech at the First Pan-African Cultural Festival, Algiers, July 1969

At this great cultural gathering—the first of its nature in the history of Africa—there will be many contributions of profound significance, offered by some of the most distinguished thinkers on the cultural problems of Africa. To these contributions I am content to offer merely a few marginal footnotes on aspects of culture in Africa which I believe it is necessary to take into account in any comprehensive discussion. I must add that it is my belief that there are many distinguished intellectuals in Africa whose views need to be added to those submitted to the symposium, if we are to have the fullest and richest understanding of the tasks which await us.

I speak deliberately of "tasks which await us" for I believe that it is no cliché to say that Africa is in the process of rediscovering and redefining herself and her culture, and that the greatest part of this task lies before us, and stretches in an immense vista into the future.

It is as a contribution to the preparations for these tasks of the future that I offer these footnotes.

It is, I believe, essential for us that we should, in preparing for our journey, strip ourselves of all unnecessary lumber—particularly of such procedures and attitudes as we have taken over from, or have had foisted upon us by, the colonial powers throughout Africa. It should not be necessary for us to create such stiff and complex procedures that it is difficult for the artist to speak to the people for whom his work is done; nor should he find, interposed between himself and his audience, a hierarchy of bureaucrats or functionaries through whom his message and his experiences must filter; above all, we must not be guilty of the restraints and silences which have been imposed on us by our oppressors—let Africa be distinguished by the freedom it gives for the artist to reach his full creativity, whether as a poet, as dramatist, or as an editor—in a freedom truthfully and honestly defined which is not debased by sensationalism or commercial exploitation.

Not less important is the need for freedom from alien cultures or, more precisely, the imposition of their standards of value. The ideal for an African is NOT to be a black Frenchman or a black Englishman, nor anything else but to be, at the greatest height of his powers, an African. Those who teach otherwise, whether they are foreigners or Africans, if they accept these alien standards are not the friends of Africa or of Africans.

This is true in a much more serious way in the area of politics and economics—areas which we know as Africans, cannot be artificially separated from other aspects of culture, just as we know the artist must not be artificially segregated in his society. The involvement of non-African countries in African economic and political life, in some areas, continues at an ever-increasing rate. This involvement is frequently to the detriment of Africa, and especially in the area of current greatest involvement, Southern Africa. British and American investment in the racialist oppression of apartheid shows no sign of decrease; the reverse is true. And the economic and military strength of apartheid grows to monstrously dangerous proportions which threaten the freedom of all of Africa. To ignore this threat, or to discount it, would be to do a grave harm to Africa and to the cause of African liberation.

If Britain and the United States are the leading partners of racialism in Africa, propping it up and strengthening it in South Africa and Rhodesia, and, through NATO arming the Portuguese oppressors in Mozambique, Angola, and Guinea-Bissao—if these are the leaders, they are not left far behind by France, West Germany, and Japan. By their support for and involvement in apartheid, these countries are acting against Africa. France, for instance, may claim to be the friends of some states in Africa, but as long as she sells Mirage and Mystere jets and Alouette helicopters to South Africa, and helps her to set up a system of ground-to-air missiles, who can say that she is the friend of Africa? And who can say that Africa should remain silent when France is arming the enemy of Africa and the African people?

These are not matters of art. Some would even say these are not matters of culture. But we have come to the Pan-African Cultural Festival understanding that there is a clear role for culture in the liberation struggle and that there can be no true culture where there is no freedom.

It is for this reason that I must reiterate—and I come from the area of conflict in Southern Africa and have been a political prisoner of both the oppressive regimes of Portugal in Mozambique and of South Africa, and have known the denial of all freedoms—that the freedom of Africa is imperiled by the growth of the monster of apartheid oppression, bloated and swollen by support from outside Africa to which I have already referred. The threat to Africa which is developing in Southern Africa can only be neglected at our peril. It needs the grave and urgent attention of us all. In our challenge to this threat we can draw inspiration and encouragement from the heroic example and glorious history of the people of Algeria and of this great city, Algiers, which is truly the capital of African freedom, won through revolutionary struggle. There are two further considerations, with implications which extend beyond the boundaries of our great continent, which I believe deserve the consideration of us all.

The first is that the gap between the affluent world, which derived so much of its affluence from others, and the "developing world" grows rapidly greater. Those who have, will have more. Those who have little, will have less. This is a matter of declared and defined policy, evidenced in such studies as the recent one by Duncan of Rio Tinto[1] in which the "Third World was discounted" and certain areas selected "for the greater future concentration of efforts and resources." The great expenditure on the exploration of the moon must also be seen in this context. While we salute, as a triumph of Man's intellect and of the human spirit, this great achievement, we must also be conscious of this turning towards mechanical and material concern as a turning away from the urgent and immediate human problems, which are crying out for solutions. What might not the money spent on the moon probe...have done to relieve the agony of black Americans? What might it not have done in social engineering to alleviate the agony and racialism which disfigure the United States: they can boast about their achievements on the moon; they cannot boast about what they are doing in their own country. Nor about what they are doing in Africa.

The second consideration of global significance is the increasing emergence of racialism in areas of the white world. The United States situation is sadly familiar to all of us; that of Britain, with characteristic humbug, is still in large measure concealed or disguised. But these symptoms in Britain and the United States are only part of an unfolding pattern, of which other parts can be seen in areas as distant as Australia and New Zealand. There is developing a most terrifying alignment of racial loyalties.

There is evidence of unthinking and automatic lining up of people—sometimes even those who believe themselves to be "liberals"—on the side of their kith and kin. A division of the world on the line of color. It is this blind loyalty to race and color—this coalescence of the centuries of racial oppression by different white nations in different parts of the world into a single global lineup on the basis of pigmentation—which some of us see with great dread, looming in the future.

It is here that Africa, particularly in this cultural festival, has a special role to play, a special gift to give to the world. It is for us to assert the singleness of the human race, and the primacy of human values. We are on the side of humanity. It is this assertion, this declaration, that we must send ringing round the world—to save not only Africa but all the peoples of the world, and to ward off this catastrophic conflict, which some, in their blindness, their folly, and their avariciousness, would thrust upon the world. I trust that of the many and important assertions that the festival—and all of African culture—will give to the world, this declaration will be paramount: Africa declares itself for the full freedom of Man and the family of Man.

[1] A mining company with extensive operations in Third World countries.

Cultural liberation and the African revolution
Speech in Montreal, May 1974

The title for this panel is "The roads to cultural liberation," and what I hope to do is to indicate the kind of road that is being traversed in Africa. I must start by saying that I propose only to give you some kind of descriptive rather than analytical account of what is happening, of the road currently being traversed, and the directions that it might take. I should also say that my association with the liberation movement in Southern Africa is essentially that of an activist and not a theoretician. And so I will not attempt a rather learned discourse that some of my colleagues have been able to present. I would like to assume, though I realize that there are disagreements in matters of definitions, that we are broadly in agreement on the two elements of the subject: what constitutes liberation and what constitutes culture. And in some of my remarks, I think, the content of these terms in Africa will be brought out.

All of Africa is confronted with a similar problem. The degree of dependence may vary, but there is no part of Africa which is not exposed to pressures, to imperialist designs, which is not enmeshed in the imperialist strategy, and therefore all of Africa is confronted with the problem, found also in other parts of the world, of having to deal with the existence of hegemony, of control by superpowers. One would have to distinguish between the situation as it is found in Southern Africa and what is loosely called independent Africa. The areas of the continent which are still engaged in an armed struggle against colonial powers, or against a kind of domestic colonialism as in the case of South Africa, where the settler and the colonized coexist, differ in many ways from those parts of Africa which technically enjoy autonomy, but which in fact through economic and political manipulation are still subject to influence from other powers.

Although Southern Africa is the area I know best, I will limit myself to just two elements of its situation that seem to me distinctive. In Angola, in Mozambique, in Zimbabwe, in Namibia, in South Africa, in all of those areas, you have people committed to armed struggle. And this is not true of areas of independence or pseudo-independence. The other element which seems to me is significant is that you have there, in terms of cultural oppression, a systematic attempt through apartheid, or the educational systems devised by the ruling minorities, not merely to deny the indigenous people liberation but to subvert their very aspirations. These are programs directed at creating in them an acceptance of dependence, and the notion that this is a permanent and God-willed situation in which they find themselves. That seems to me to distinguish those areas from say a Nigeria, or a Ghana, a Kenya, or a Uganda.

But there are also certain elements of the struggle for cultural liberation in Southern Africa which coincide with elements being found elsewhere in Africa, and I thought it would be useful to enumerate a few of those. One of the most powerful influences in the thinking of Africans, particularly African intellectuals, has been that of Frantz Fanon, and the notion of psychological colonization, which implies the need to decolonize not merely the body and the state, but the mind as well. I would say that there is in Africa now no notion more pervasive, and no notion that seems to me to possess a greater dynamic at this time. There is one other that approximates it, given the concept of pan-Africanism, which enjoyed a great vitality at a given period in Africa, and which may well not be due for revival. Fanon would count as one of the most important influences operating on the African mind, on the African intellectual, in setting a direction to (and the recognition of the need for this direction) the decolonization of the mind.

At a gathering similar to this, a colloquium la Brazzaville, in a gathering of African intellectuals, this was taken for granted. It was assumed that this was understood by everyone. And instead a new stage was undertaken, a re-examination of the choices being offered to Africa between a Western capitalist system, ideology, set of values, and a Marxist communist system on the other hand. And after much discussion, much analysis, the consensus was, and I am sure this is familiar to many of you, that for Africa there did not exist this either/or choice, or that it need not accept this either/or choice, that it would be possible instead to find a third, an African way, an African solution. There had been hints of this, of course, in Kwame Nkrumah, the notion of an African personality, of African socialism. There had been an elaboration of these ideas through Julius Nyerere, the concept of Ujamaa, of what is now being refor-

psychological (decolonization)

mulated I think as Tanzanian rather than African socialism (so that it does not seem a panacea for all of the continent, so that each area might develop its own characteristic economic and social system, derived from the cultural roots and the history of the people).

The question of pan-Africanism advocated by many—and specifically by Nkrumah, the notion of a Union of African States which gave rise to the Organization of African Unity (OAU)—is being re-examined very much at the present time, and I believe will be the focus, the central issue in the Congress next month in Dar es Salaam, [at] the Sixth Pan-African Congress. And already in the preliminary discussion and the papers which have circulated, a very interesting point is emerging, the idea that the OAU is a contradiction of the concept of pan-Africanism. I think that this is so important that perhaps one ought to spend a little time in showing how this sense of contradiction is arrived at. Among the elements in the argument is the fact that the OAU simply stabilizes and consolidates a state of affairs which is a false reflection of African societies, that nation-states, as at present constituted, exist as a result of artificial and arbitrary boundaries, some of them deriving from the partition of Africa, some of them from subsequent developments. But in this consolidation of states and the formalization thereof in the OAU, we are in fact agreeing to attempt to develop from a series of false premises, that if the initial premise was wrong, development derived therefrom must be wrong as well, and inimical to the future development of the continent.

It is I suppose a truism that the people who live in Zaire, and the people who live on the banks of the Congo River, are one people, though there may be some confusion now that the river is called both the Congo and the Zaire. But certainly the barriers which were drawn by colonial powers, whether they were French, English, German, Portuguese, or Belgian, that these are in fact a false reflection of the real situation. It has another important component. The argument is that the idea of pan-Africanism implies a rejection of the colonial system, the colonial powers, and of the present neocolonial relationships which exist. And the leaders of African states are seen as simply an elite to whom power was transferred by the colonial powers as an extension and a continuance of their influence in these countries. I'm reluctant to make a kind of detailed diagnosis of the ills that beset Nigeria, Ghana, Uganda, Kenya, and the others. I trust I can leave that to you. But I ought to say, just to offset that, that many Africans see the developments in Tanzania and Guinea as a counterpoise, as a motion in the opposite and correct direction, that ultimately the cultural liberation of each African nation-state will be based on the kind of premises of equality and an economic and social system derived from the history and culture of the people, a natural outgrowth of that. And, in passing, I should say that, in this ambition, many Africans believe that there is a great deal to be learned from China, and that the example and influence of China must be seen as a growing force for the future.

Where do the cultural practitioners fit into this? What is their specific contribution? I am thinking of creative artists, writers, and filmmakers. They seem to me to fall into several categories, and I might isolate three of these.

The notion of "cultural diplomacy" has a special reference in Africa. We understand the role of imperialism, of cultural imperialism, and in the deformation of minds, in the process of preempting, of coopting people into the system and making them collaborators in the system. But particularly in independent Africa the term cultural diplomacy has a different signification, and this is the notion that the artist, the cultural producer, should become the apologist of the system, the unofficial roving ambassador whose function is to project a good image and whose role is to defend the system. This has not worked out because most of the intellectuals have ended as the opponents of the status quo. The outstanding example, I should think, is Wole Soyinka of Nigeria. I would mention specifically his book, *The Man Died*, with its devastating attack on Gowon and the present regime.

But on the other hand, and this is the obverse, one has an Achebe writing in defense of the Biafran cause. The failure here seems to me to be an inability to identify the root causes of the conflict. To explain the Nigerian conflict in terms of tribal rivalries and antagonisms is one level of superficiality, but to say as Soyinka says that it was more than that, it was a collapse of humanity, of human beings behaving in some atavistic fahion seems to me merely another level of superficiality. Any failure to take into account the rivalries, the economic rivalries of the multinational corporations, of the oil interests, of Western powers, causes one to end up with a superficial interpretation. Fortunately there are writers, both critics and creative writers, who have penetrated beyond that and who see the African predicament, or tragedy if you will, in terms of this kind of manipulation of political and economic power for strategic reasons, whatever these reasons might be. I refer to other creative artists, people like James Ngugi [Ngugi wa Thiong'o] from Kenya, Peter Nazareth from Uganda, whose basis for judgment is sometimes overtly Marxist, sometimes a vague kind of socialist judgment, but who at least can discover the underlying forces operating against African liberation, cultural liberation, or indeed the larger whole of which cultural liberation is only a segment, the liberation of a people in every area of their existence.

The writers of South Africa among whom I'm included—a La Guma, an Mphahlele, an Nkosi—cannot return to their countries, but in a sense the position is no less difficult for a Soyinka in Nigeria or an Achebe or indeed a Kofi Awooner from Ghana. For all of us, the moment we become the gadflies in the society, the moment we become the critics and the commentators on what is projected as an ideal situation...we must expect to find ourselves in conflict with the situation.

I want to return to the liberation movement. I might have talked about Senghor and negritude as one of the minor little by-paths in the process of cultural evolution, cultural liberation, except that for most Africans today it is either passé or in fact pernicious, something which is harmful to cultural liberation. My last point rather is to say that the significance of the Southern African liberation movement is that it goes beyond resistance. It is not resistance to oppression; it is not even liberation merely in the sense of freedom to govern yourself. It has penetrated beyond that to an understanding that what we are engaged in is a struggle against imperialism. It is not a local, nor even a national struggle. We see ourselves as an element in the global struggle against imperialism. This seems to me the truly revolutionary element in our struggle for cultural liberation.

Literature and commitment in South Africa

Speech at the African Literature Association meeting,
University of Texas at Austin, March 1975

I WANT to examine the essence of commitment and, continuing in the vein of Willy Kgositsile,[1] reiterate one of the points he made. Before doing that, however, I propose to make some prefatory comments, look at certain aspects of commitment as expressed in the writing of blacks in South Africa, examine the relation between those writers who are involved in protest and the others who are part of the system, and conclude with some general observations which I think have useful lessons for our audience and particularly for critics in the field of African literature. (I do not propose to get involved in the debate this morning about my own work; I think I should abstain from that discussion.)

The essential point to recognize, and one Kgositsile has made, is that there is no uncommitted writing. It has been said in America in much simpler and sloganistic terms: "If you are not part of the solution, you are part of the problem." You have to decide which side you are on: there is always a side. Commitment does not exist as an abstraction; it exists in action. This is what it is about: Everything we do is either functioning within the system as it exists, or challenging the system. It is as simple as that. So when one examines literature, or when one creates literature, one is either following an established order and functioning within it, or one is bucking that order, challenging it, questioning it. It may be a useful aside to point out that the weariness, the irritation, the dissatisfaction which African writers feel when they are subjected to Western criticism is symptomatic of something much deeper. It is not just the rejection of a set of literary values, it is a questioning of a whole social order, of the Western way of life and its values. So the criticism expressed by Africans which exists within the literary field must be seen in a very much larger context.

I think in Africa we are trying to discover, painfully and often unsuccessfully, a way of recovering our humanity, and in that process we find that what the West has to offer is a deformation and a mutilation of humanity. Fortunately we are not alone. There are people in the West who themselves feel this profound dissatisfaction and are engaged in challenging the system; the people who demonstrated on this campus yesterday and a week ago on issues of racism (Sharpeville and discrimination against minorities) were the embodiment of that dissatisfaction.

On the South African scene, we find a long history of writing which is writing in protest against the existing order. If we turn to a poet like Samuel Mqhayi (perhaps still the greatest poet to come out of South Africa and who is little known in the West), we see in his famous satirical poem addressed as a welcome to the Prince of Wales that marvelous double level of meaning which functions as official salutation and at the same time as the most profound expression of disgust and contempt for those who can read the signs. We see the same kind of thing in Jolobe's writing about the making of a servant equated with "how an ox is broken," and in the fiction of a later generation—Peter Abrahams in *Tell Freedom, Path of Thunder, Wild Conquest*. That generation is followed by people like Ezekiel Mphahlele and Willy Kgositsile, and I would like to count myself and people like Alex La Guma and others in that group—all of us in opposition to the system, in conflict with it, and, inevitably in the process of conflict, being hurt in some way or another. That we accepted as the price of our activities.

One should perhaps look briefly at some of the white South African writers, who seem to me to fall into two broad categories: the Lionel Abrahamses and the Nadine Gordimers, who stand for liberal values (and I will examine that concept in a moment); and then there are the functionaries, the lackies, the butlers—and I include Guy Butler here—who are functioning within that particular context and really are subservient to the system.

But I want to look at that rather curious group which is regarded in the West as consisting of the most distinguished voices of the liberal tradition in South Africa and which forms a subgroup of the first group, and I choose two examples: Alan Paton and Athol Fugard, both of them mistakenly regarded as heroes in the West, both tired and defeated and, in the case of Fugard, now an accomplice of the system, a man who goes on television in London and New York and appeals for the playwrights of the United States and Britain to allow their plays to be performed in South Africa. Men like Arthur Miller, Tennessee Williams, and Arnold Wesker had taken a stand and said, "Either all our plays are performed for everybody or they are not performed at all; we will not allow them to be performed for white audiences only." Today Fugard is pleading that those men should accept the apartheid system, function within it. And Paton, who comes to Harvard for an honorary doctorate—and that itself says something for those of you who understand the system—he comes here to say that apartheid exists, we must learn to live with it, we must learn to function within it. And those two men, mark you, are regarded as the stalwarts of the liberal cause in South Africa.

Then we come to a younger generation of black poets, whom I salute: the Pascal Gwalas, the James Matthewses, the Joyce Sikakanes, and two people who are with us today, Oswald Mtshali and Wally Serote, whom I salute for a special act of courage yesterday which did not take place in this auditorium but out in the open air on the Main Mall, when they spoke in the Sharpeville commemoration. The reality of the South African situation is such that when they return to South Africa, both of them will be faced with the prospect of arrest and imprisonment for something that happened in Austin, Texas.

The question which naturally arises in some minds is: "What is the relationship between the writers who function within the system and the writers who challenge the system?" And there are several points to be made here. The first one to note is that there is almost no dialogue at all, no communication at all—with negligible exceptions—between these two groups of writers. This absence of communication in itself is worth looking at, because they speak and use the same words, but the words do not have the same meaning. If you spoke to a white South African he would assure you that South Africa is a democracy. Every white man and every white woman in South Africa has the vote. For them, indeed, South Africa is a democracy. So when a black South African speaks of hoping to achieve a democratic society, it baffles the white South African, who says, "But we have it already." They are using the same terms, but it is clear they are not even communicating with each other.

But even more fundamental than that failure in a shared language is the failure to share values. They really are talking about different societies, and therefore, even when they use the same words, what they are about is something so different as to be unintelligible to the other. And that point might well be borne in mind. I will return to it when I speak of its relevance for the critic and the interpreter of African literature.

It seems to me that one of the things we are doing is to engage ourselves in the struggle to recover and rediscover our humanity, and in that struggle there are a great many people who can't understand what this is about. They fail to see the necessity; they ask, "What are you going on about?" And that is because they've already accepted us as we are, as if that is the only way we can be, and that they cannot imagine us any other way. On the subject of commitment, Chinua Achebe said long ago in an interview here on the University of Texas campus, "Commitment runs right through our work. In fact, I should say, all our writers, whether they are aware of it or not, are committed writers." And he went on to say, "I believe it's impossible to write anything in Africa without some kind of commitment, some kind of message, some kind of protest." But obviously, if what we are striving for is something which is unintelligible to people, then they are going to have extreme difficulty in being able to interpret us, simply because if they cannot perceive our goal, then the whole process of working towards it is unintelligible to them.

I would like to quote something from Louis James which comes from a paper by Dr. Romanus Egudu and which had escaped my attention. He says, "In situations as explosive as that of Africa today, there can be no creative literature that is not in some way political. Even the writer who opts out of the social struggles of his country and tries to create a private world is saying something controversial about the responsibility of the artist to society." Where does that lead us? If the kind of challenging remarks made by Willy Kgositsile and the kinds of things I'm trying to say now trouble you at all, I will be very pleased. But I hope that I will do more than trouble you, for I want to suggest at least a few guidelines or pointers for the direction in which interpretation and criticism of literature might go.

I will conclude with a few points stated rather starkly which I hope you will, at your leisure, give some time and consideration to. I apologize for their simplicity, but it seems to me that truth very often is simple, though my critics, I know, are irritated sometimes by my simplicity. Let's start with something quite basic. Literature is about life and about people. That's what it is about. And really sometimes we have to remind ourselves that that's what it is about. And the consequences that flow from that. "Who are the people? Who are these people we are writing about and writing for?" Well, they could be a great many things. But I want to assure you that if you think it's the *New York Review of Books,* or professors of English at this campus or any other, or the critics of the *Times Literary Supplement* it may be obvious but I need to say it: You are wrong. Those are not the people.

And indeed, one would find a very interesting and revealing statistic, if you looked at a novel widely acclaimed by the critics as a serious artifact and you compared its sales with that, say, of *The Love Machine* by Jacqueline Suzanne. The critics and the elite—note the words—may be reading John Gardner's *Sunlight Dialogues,* but millions of people—thirty million people—have read Xaviera Hollander's *The Happy Hooker,* and that says a great deal about the society. In one dorm on this campus I guess two hundred people read one copy until it fell apart, so you have to multiply your thirty millions by some other figure—that says something about what is being done to people, these people about whom literature is being written and for whom literature is intended. I suspect, I fear very much, that we are not troubled when people are fed that garbage. It doesn't trouble those of us who are involved in the business of literature. And yet if thirty million people or more read *The Happy Hooker,* that's where literature for people is happening. One ought to ask questions about a society and a social order in which that kind of thing occurs, because that is a deformation and a mutilation of the human mind and the human personality in its commercialization and merchandizing of the human body.

So, if literature is about people and for people, let's look at two classic comments which are sometimes adduced in terms of the function of literature. There is the notion that the origins of literature, of all literature—its direction, its purpose, everything—flow out of a love of humanity. Well, this will not do. For if humanity is the reviewer in the *Times Literary Supplement* or the *New York Review of Books,* we are really writing for just a segment of humanity, a narrow and privileged segment, an elite. We are excluding from our concern and from our responsibility the mass of the people. Mao Zedong had an interesting thing to say about writers and artists in his lectures on art and literature at the Yenan forum. He says that the writer or the artist tends to play the hero; he thinks he's important, he thinks he's somebody special, but he must understand that the more he plays the hero and the special person, the more the people will not accept him. The writer distances himself from them in the process of making himself a special person, because special persons remain only a segment, an elitist segment, of the society. What I am saying may seem a kind of reversal, a turning upside down of a whole series of widely accepted values within a particular culture. If that is so, let me assure you that that is precisely what I intend.

I will conclude with one comment. In my view, and I believe in the view of the bulk of the writers coming out of Africa (this is especially true of the works of South African writers like Abrahams, Breytenbach, Can Themba, Gwala, Kunene, La Guma, Matthews, Nkosi, Rive, and Mphahlele), cultural activity is only one front in the struggle for the liberation of humanity in Africa and in the rest of the world, in an attempt to achieve our full potential, our full dignity, our full humanity.

[1] The South African poet whose comments preceded Brutus's in a panel discussion.

Meeting of African writers
Accra, Ghana, June 8, 1975

We have resolved at this June 1975 Accra meeting, to form a Union which shall be called Union of Writers of the African Peoples (Union des Ecrivains Negro-Africans). The following is a list of decisions, resolutions, and projects undertaken by the union:

A. 1. That the union will be, as far as possible, self-sustaining. We shall be free to seek and accept aid wherever possible but first the union will establish itself and its independence by the contributions of its own members. To this end it had decided:

    I. That all members shall pay a membership fee of the

equivalent of U.S. $20.

II. That all members shall pay to the union a minimum of five percent of all royalties accruing from their writing and publishing, in whatever media.

III. That associate member unions shall pay ten percent of their group membership fee.

2. It is the decision of this union to establish its headquarters in Accra, Ghana, in close collaboration with the hosts of the present meeting, the National Association of Writers, Ghana, who are, in this connection, hereby assigned the responsibility of interim Treasurers until the full congress of the union in Dakar, February 1976.

3. Membership shall be by application, invitation, or recommendation. The coordinating committee[1] of this union has been assigned the responsibility of future membership until the full congress of the union.

4. The coordinating committee has also been assigned the task of presenting a draft constitution to the full congress along the lines already established at the Accra meeting, the said constitution to be circulated in advance to all members, and modified as needed from positive suggestions, in order to minimize a waste of words at the full congress.

B. 5. We find that the establishing of an African cooperative publishing house is indispensable to the healthy development of African literature and educational texts; to the development of indigenous publishing houses; the protection of African writers from further exploitation and, the general promotion of an authentic literary culture. We consider also that the most favorable location for such an enterprise is Senegal. To this end, the Senegalese members of the union have been delegated to approach President Leopold Sedar Senghor with this proposal, bearing in mind the various aspects which have been emphasized as essential to this project; a strong continentwide distribution system; a low-priced sale policy to remove the stigma of privilege in literacy and culture; a translation bureau, bearing in mind the existence of and possible collaboration with the Ghana Institute of Languages and its School of Translators; insistence on an All-African copyright; collaboration with smaller indigenous publishers; full control over an integrated, modern printing press; assurance of royalties at all stages to its authors; reprint of African classics in translation, etc. It is our collective responsibility to persuade African governments, cultural and technical organizations, international organizations such as UNESCO, etc. to give vital assistance to this project which is essential to the cultural progress of the continent and to the world Humanities in general.

6. To undertake the publication of a regular journal of literature and criticism and the humanities.

C. 7. This union finds it regrettable that twenty years have been wasted since the Second Congress of African Writers in Rome recommended the adoption of one language for the African peoples. Resolved to end this state of inertia, hesitancy, and defeatism, we have, after much serious consideration, and in the conviction that all technical problems can and will be overcome, *unanimously* adopted Swahili as the logical language for this purpose. We exhort all writers to apply every strategy, individually and collectively on both national and continental levels to promote the use and the enrichment of Swahili for the present and future needs of the continent. In this connection, we have resolved that the proposed African Cooperative Publishing House shall adopt the policy of translating every work it publishes into Swahili. We exhort all schools to accelerate this process by substituting the study of Swahili for the least viable subject on their curriculum such as European ballet, la Civilization Francaise, English, social History, etc.

8. The Union of African Writers, aware of nameless atrocities perpetrated on Africans in Africa by external forces as well as by African authorities hereby expresses its vigorous condemnation of such atrocities wherever they do occur. This union wishes to stress its profound indignation against all attempts at the denial of human dignity, freedom, and security as is currently the situation in Uganda and South Africa, not to mention the other concentration camps on the continent.

This union therefore strongly urges all member states of the OAU to abandon the present plan of making Uganda the venue for the next meeting of the organization. We ask this in the name of common humanity and from a sense of being inseverably bound to the fate of African peoples everywhere.

[1] Ayi Kwei Armah, Eduard Maunick, Cheik N' Dao, Jean-Baptiste, Tati-Loutard, Dennis Brutus, Ngugi wa Thiong'o, Wole Soyinka.

English and the dynamics of South African creative writing

From *Opening up the Canon*, Leslie Fiedler and Houston Baker, eds., 1979

My discussion of the predicament of the creative writer in South Africa is essentially an examination of the context in which that writer operates and the factors at work on him or her—particularly those that inhibit creative work.

"The influences that operate on the creative writer" would more exactly describe what I am trying to do. Because South Africa is a strange society—in the sense of peculiar—it is helpful to look at the forces in the society that function either to promote or to inhibit creative writing. To do this, however, is to look also at the society and indeed briefly to sketch the development of writing in English in South Africa.

South Africa is currently independent, and began its existence, in European history, anyway, first as a Dutch, and then as a British colony. Writing in English in South Africa began in 1854 with Thomas Pringle, who was one of the settlers brought to South Africa in a large contingent at the end of the Napoleonic War. Pringle brought with him something of the English liberal tradition to the extent that within four years he was being forced out, forced back to Britain because of his criticism of the colonial administration. That exercise of power by an autocratic governor is, perhaps, as good a note as any on which to begin the history of English literature in South Africa. Since then, a few figures have won some international recognition. They include Alan Paton; Nadine Gordimer, probably South Africa's most distinguished novelist; and Athol Fugard, who has achieved an international reputation as a playwright. Before that we had a few rather less well-known names on the international scene: Olive Schreiner, with her novel *The*

Story of an African Farm, and William Plomer, whose precocious novel *Turbott Wolfe* was written when he was only nineteen. For those of us who follow black writing in Africa, there are also those names that are known all over the world in terms of black literature, such as Alex LaGuma; Mazisi Kunene, who writes in Zulu; Peter Abrahams, long exiled from South Africa; and Ezekiel Mphahlele.

The white South African writers, who enjoy advantages in publication and facilities and contacts not known to blacks, tend to be better known. South African society consists of two principal colonial streams: the English settlers and the Dutch settlers. The latter developed their own form of Dutch, called Afrikaans, a kind of patois that derived from it and is less well known. The Afrikaners have a much narrower audience. One of them, the poet, Breyten Breytenbach, has achieved some degree of international recognition. This recognition may, however, be the consequence of his antigovernment activities. He is currently serving a nine-year prison sentence in South Africa, and this, rather than his distinction in poetry, may be the basis of his reputation.

It is useful to look at some of the salient features of the South African context of society as they affect the writer. Following is some fairly crude information: roughly 25,000 books have been banned in South Africa and declared illegal. Possession of these books, reading them, and quoting from them are all criminal acts. Some fairly obvious books, such as obscene publications, are banned on the grounds of pornography. But many of the banned books would be considered harmless, if perhaps radical, elsewhere in the world. As of now 750 persons in South Africa are banned from publishing in South Africa or from having their work read or quoted in South Africa. They are also forbidden to attend any gathering where more than two people are present. (I myself fell into all of these categories when I was living in South Africa, and my work continues to be banned.) Most of the major writers, both white and black, are in exile at the present time. And perhaps a more dismaying statistic is that at least three major Afrikaner poets, and twice as many black writers according to some reports, committed suicide in South Africa in recent years.

Toby Moyana, in a lengthy essay titled "Problems of the Creative Writer in South Africa," contended that the government was literally legislating literature out of existence, that it was becoming impossible for people to write. It might be worthwhile to mention some of the legislation. One of the blanket laws that permits much of control legislation dates back to 1927; it is called the Bantu Administration Act. Since then the South African government has passed the Entertainment Censorship Act of 1931, the Unlawful Organization Act (1960), and the Publications and Entertainment Act (1956). In 1969 a great kind of umbrella law that makes virtually everything illegal if the state *deems* it to be illegal, called the [General Laws Amendment Act] was passed.

The mechanism by which these laws operate is instructive. Since about 1963 South Africa has had a Publications Control Board; this board determines what is fit for publication. It creates a real problem for publishers because the banning decisions often take place only after publication—after the publishers have already committed themselves to production. When the book is about to go on sale, the government issues a ruling that the publication is illegal, and this can cause great financial hardship.

It is sometimes said that repression may stimulate activity and that therefore there is a kind of paradoxical merit in being put under the pressures that are placed on South African writers. Oddly enough, there may be some evidence that confirms this theory in the society. It is true, for instance, that in 1976 when there was a massive uprising in the ghettos, especially those in the South West Townships that are lumped together under the word "Soweto," there was an incredible efflorescence of writing in the ghetto—particularly of poetry. Even more exciting has been the appearance of a kind of improvised theatre, an open air or guerrilla theatre with improvised poetry, much of which is not committed to paper. The poets seem especially to be responsive to the new tensions, the new pressures that are developing in the society.

It should be said the blacks in the ghettos see the affluence and the wealth of the apartheid society as being directly dependent on the sustenance it receives from outside countries, particularly Western countries. The massive injections of capital, and the transfer of technology to the apartheid society, are seen very clearly in the ghettos as factors that enable a minority regime to remain in power. Perhaps the greatest support that the West has given to South Africa (there is little more that they can give in addition to this) has been to provide South Africa with the capability of manufacturing nuclear weapons. This has been achieved through the assistance of the United States, France, and West Germany. It seems there is not much more that can be done except to continue as before. Many blacks feel that the West has made its ultimate commitment to the white society, and this commitment extends even into the realm of the arts. In literature, in the theatre, in ballet, and in music, the racist and repressive South African society continues to draw sustenance from the West. The blacks see this as simply one more dimension of Western support for a racist minority.

I should add at this point that very soon the United Nations will be launching new initiatives aimed at an embargo of South Africa; this will include a cultural embargo. There are people in the United States who could, I believe, make a significant contribution by supporting a cultural embargo.

How have the blacks responded in South Africa? How has creativity been expressed in this repressive society? And how would one answer the question raised by Houston Baker about the new insights that are brought into the English language by writers whose first language is not English? We may have a different world view and a different cosmology. I spent some time pondering this and came up with what may be a disappointing reply: I cannot see a great deal that is significantly new or inventive. If there were time, I could catalogue some of the minor variations, particularly in African perception of a creator, a universal force that tends generally to be female. I could tell you that the African sense of time is circular, and that the living and the dead coexist in the same kind of human fabric. I think these are incipient rather than developed features. They are implicit in some of the writings and, given an opportunity, may become more evident. There may, in fact, be an explanation for the failure to come up with new perceptions through communication in English. We are dealing with a society where communication between people is illegal, a society that creates a battery of laws that makes communication between people from different cultures or from different groups a criminal act. It can be a crime in South Africa for two people of different races to drink tea together, or to be in the same restaurant together.

One example, my favorite, is drawn from the area in which I was most deeply involved in South Africa—that of sports. A black athlete running on the same track with a white athlete could be arrested, or a black tennis player on the same tennis court with a white tennis player could go to prison. There are very blatant forms of discrimination imposed by the legal system, for which there are sanctions. Those who attempt to communicate are punished. It may be that in such a society one can neither come up with insights and perceptions into another culture nor with new ways of expressing what already exists in that culture.

The substance of the writing, particularly the new poetry, is first of all an attempt to articulate a community experience, to convey what is in the society rather than in the individual. Of course, in the African artistic and literary traditions, especially in the oral tradition, there is so much that antecedes the expression of ideas and the feelings of the community as opposed to the feelings of the individual. We have currently a completely new batch of young poets coming out of the ghettos, and their themes are pretty much the same: anger at the cruelty and the injustice of the system, and an attempt to articulate that anger, to go beyond it, and to function as rallying points, as interpreters of the feeling of the society. The titles of the works are revealing. One of the most important, banned almost immediately after publication, is called *Cry Rage;* it was a joint venture by James Matthews and Gladys Thomas. Another, published shortly thereafter with the work of nine poets in it, was banned immediately—that was called *Black Voices Shout.* In addition to books, magazines, many of them ephemeral, are also banned; some of them are banned by issue rather than by a blanket ban. A magazine like *Staffrider,* which is a vehicle for black writers, had its first issue banned, but the second, third, and fourth issues are still available. Perhaps it, too, will cease publication, as many of the others have. The writing is now published mainly in magazines and periodicals; these are often joint ventures by whites and blacks who are opponents of the system. Books of this kind have become rare.

It is important to remember, I think, that because of the colonial history of South Africa, every educated black is exposed to the mainstream of the English literary tradition. Blacks begin learning

Shakespeare and Wordsworth in junior school ("Daffodils" is learned in almost every school). In high school blacks begin to read what might be called classics: Dickens's *A Tale of Two Cities* and Cooper's *The Last of the Mohicans* are included in high school reading. They might even read an early Shakespeare comedy. By the time one goes to university, one is exposed to three years of English. If you are going to major in it, you go through the traditional kind of syllabus, beginning with Chaucer, through the Elizabethans (and perhaps the Metaphysicals), on to the Romantics and the Victorians, and perhaps reading a few of the modern poets as well. This pretty much is the range of exposure for an African being educated under a system inherited from the British university system. The example of the commitment by English writers, and the criticisms of society by such writers as Milton, Wordsworth, Blake, and Shelley, strike responsive chords in the African writer. Indeed, some African writers have been criticized for a too-slavish imitation of their English models.

The break, it is evident, comes in the very recent past; it is a move away from traditional form toward a very conscious attempt at immediacy, at direct and unadorned communication. This, I fear, would suffer if it were judged by any academic canon, for it hardly conforms to accepted notions about the craft of poetry. They would reply, quite frankly, that they are not interested in creating works that will endure, that they are not interested in creating works that will pass muster in the university; they would say instead that their preoccupation is with immediate and effective communication with the people around them. That may be not an unworthy goal.

The writer suffers, however, not only from the restraints and limitations imposed on him by the legal system, but by a whole new set of pressures that flow from convention and prejudice rather than from the law. These restraints, these pressures on black writers and writing are due to the arrogance of the literary critics and the contemptuous handling of black writers by established literary persons. It seems to me to be so pervasive that I am beginning to wonder whether arrogance is not an occupational hazard for all critics. Of course, I ought to give some examples of this, and I offer something that is of fairly recent vintage and this is typical. The South African critic A.G. Wyett, who has taught English literature in Kenya, Rhodesia, and Swaziland before coming to South Africa (those were his credentials), discusses the dilemma of black South African poetry in an essay. He says the black poet has to determine how he is going to make meaningful use of a centuries-old, culturally enriched language in the relatively undeveloped cultural environment in which he finds himself. He finds that the black poet often falls into the trap of pretentiousness, writing flat and clichéd lines, while believing that his lines are really successful poetic creations. Wyett does, however, balance this comment with something else, which may be a redeeming comment (I don't know, because what he concedes is the following): "The poet may create some remote possible line, but this achievement may be attained more by chance, by fortuitous ignorance of style, idiom, imitation and so on, rather than by deliberate artistic intention. For one thing, the black writer has to remember that the part chance plays in the creation of poetry in a language belonging to a foreign culture has yet to be explored. Perhaps we ought to hold off until exploration is complete." Perhaps Wyett himself would undertake to be a trailblazer. Wyett goes on to say that the evidence may yet be found to support his belief that good lines written by the black poet in a language not his own are the product of accident, rather than choice.

Wyett goes on to criticize African poetry for another weakness: the poet has become too committed, too much of an engaged poet. Here Wyett can cite W. H. Auden's authority; Auden said (and I think that this has become, unfortunately, almost an article of faith), "Let a poet if he wants to, write engaged poems. But let him remember this: the only person who will benefit from it is himself. The evil or injustice will remain exactly as it would have been if he had kept his mouth shut." I think Auden underestimates his impact on his own, and on future, generations. I believe he *has* moved others through his sense of concern for humanity. So, he may have judged his own work too meanly.

We return to our critic Wyett, who says: "If poets recognize the enormously healthy potential open to them in a poetic rebellion, they will eventually create notorious poems. At present the prevalent critical emphasis on the sterile and toxic impotence of resentment is engendering a poetry characterized by immaturity." Now you can see paternalism beginning to show its ugly head. For he goes on: "Yet we must not be too severe in our condemnation of it, just as we should not always be severe on the young. And there by the same token, we must not be unduly indulgent, otherwise the healthy young tradition may well grow warped or stunted."

There is a great deal more of that kind of reasoning, but I am inclined to pass over it. I wish, however (to balance that), to quote a correspondent who wrote to the journal *Contrast* protesting the condescending and arrogant attitudes of critics. H. Davis says that the insensitivity and incompetence of Wyett is underlined by his admitted failure to grasp the meaning of a poem that he quotes. Perhaps Davis might have been left in possession of the field, but the editor of the journal (and *Contrast* is a fairly authoritative journal by South African literary standards) comes to the defense of the journal: "I think it is correct to say that no member of this magazine's editorial board has ever looked back or judged for acceptance a manuscript of a poem or any other work in the light of the race or skin color of the contributor. It therefore comes as news to me that ten or a dozen or whatever number of black poems have been published in our pages. Good for the poets. If these poets are black Africans writing in English, which is not their mother tongue, then their achievement is all the more impressive." Davis goes on to say, "Since this periodical first appeared in December 1960, and they have had ten or twelve blacks since 1960, it has stuck to the original concept of the founding group that its policy is to have *no policy*. "Of course, it can be asserted that *no politics* is also politics, and that in the South African context, it is well nigh impossible to open one's mouth or to take up a pen without being committed to a political act." Having made that statement, the editor makes no effort to rebut it, a situation that I found curious, to say the least.

In order to take the issue just a little further afield—or perhaps to bring it a little nearer home—I am going to refer to another critical aberration, but not one that is limited to South Africa. Chinua Achebe, the distinguished African novelist, gave an address at a welcome reception, which was given for us by the mayor of Berlin, at a festival intended to open dialogue between Africa and West Germany, or indeed, between Africa and the West. In the course of responding to the welcome, Achebe made the remark that Africans are interested in dialogue on the basis of equality, that they are *not* interested in the kind of partnership that is that of a rider and a horse. Achebe talked about Joseph Conrad and expressed alarm at the determination of the West to have Africa explained to it by Western experts, and at the way the West very deliberately excludes Africans, who themselves are attempting to interpret their culture and their country. He says that Europe's (and America's) reliance on its own experts in reporting on the true nature of Africa would not worry anybody if it did not, at the same time, attempt to exclude the testimony of Africans. But it often does. He quotes an expert who says that "the real African" lives in the bush, goes around naked, and tells fairy stories about the crocodile and the elephant; and he adds wryly, "As the pace of change quickens, there won't be many authentic Africans left around. Certainly not any with the wholesome and unquestioning admiration of white people, which was the chief attraction of the bush African. In any case, the businessman who is in Africa for profit today isn't going to consult a witch doctor for his opinion on an investment first."

He then brings it even nearer home. He discusses a recent article in the *New York Times Book Review*. Elizabeth Hardwick interviewed V. S. Naipaul on the publication of his new book, *A Bend in the River*. Hardwick commented: "Naipaul's work is a creative reflection upon a devastating lack of historical preparation, upon the anguish of whole countries when peoples are able to quote." She quotes, according to Achebe, with apparent glee and approval from the growing corpus of scornful work which Naipaul has written on Africa, India, and South America and from his report on his Congo travels, where he sees "...native people camping on the ruins of civilization" and "the bush creeping back as you stood there." This is Achebe's comment: "Reading Elizabeth Hardwick's interview, an absurd or rather pathetic picture rises from the printed page. An old American lady lapping up like a wide-eyed little girl every drop of pretentious drivel that falls from the lips of a literary guru who is smart enough to fill his devotee with comforting myths." Her last question, predictably, was "What is the future of Africa?" His part and equally predictable reply was: "Africa *has* no future." This new Conrad figure, says Achebe, neither European nor African, will have his day and pass on, leaving the problem of dialogue, which has plagued Afro-American European relations for centuries, unsolved until Europe is ready to concede total African humanity.

Again, let me redress the balance just for a moment by pointing to some very distinguished American critics who have written with perception and sympathy on African literature. Perhaps it is invidious to single out particular pieces that I found especially valuable, but I do wish to mention Wilfred Cartey's book, *Whispers From a Continent,* and Paul Theroux's excellent early essay, "Voices from the Skull," on poetry in Africa.

As we leave the seventies and enter the eighties, I think it might be helpful to attempt a prediction about the literature being produced by English-speaking white South Africans and the English-speaking black South Africans. We might also look at those who are writing in Afrikaans, the other official language. There is, of course, an enormous body of material being turned out in the African languages themselves: Zulu, Xhosa, Sotho, and others. Some of it is oral, some of it is improvised and passed on. Some of it is committed to paper. There is a very special bind here, though, that I ought to explain. Because the apartheid government—the minority white government—has tried to revive the old tribal structures and to force the Africans back into those structures in order to prevent them from participating in the present political processes, the Africans tend to be suspicious even of their own languages and literary vehicles. They are fearful that these might be turned against them and used as one further pretext to force them back into a tribal mode within a broad policy of what are known as the Bantustans—a strategy that is aimed at forcing black Africans back into tribal structures. But nevertheless there is a great deal of literature being created. The English writers, I fear, will probably go on like Wyett and the editor of *Contrast:* not only arrogant but blind—or blinkered to their own arrogance. It may well be said that South Africa is not the only part of the world where a certain arrogance is exhibited toward minority writers.

The Afrikaners have an interesting opportunity, because as of now, political power is vested in the hands of the Afrikaans-speaking minority (although they hold their power with the collaboration of the English-speaking group). It may be that if the Afrikaners can reach their own people and persuade them that the issue is not survival, as they contend, but rather the question of the surrender

of privilege, they can perform an extremely useful function in the
society and actually help to change the direction of its history,
which seems now headed for inevitable disaster.

It seems to me that the black African writers can only become
more defiant and intransigent; that they will continue to be, as they
have been in the past, rallying centers around which groups form
in opposition in their resistance to the system. Nadine Gordimer, in
an extremely penetrating essay on the myths in the literature of
South Africa, has pointed to two myths that seem to help in under-
standing the white literature. She finds, particularly among the
Afrikaans writers, a tendency to blame the British imperial power
which crushed them at the beginning of the century, to blame that
power for the ills of the present, and to say, "We ourselves were
rolled over by the British imperial Juggernaut. We cannot take re-
sponsibility for what is wrong in society as of now."

The other myth, which is fairly closely related to it, is that more
and more (and a specific example is a quite brilliant work called
Dustlands in English), by an examination of the behavior of other
societies, particularly the killings in Vietnam, or genocidal activities
in New Zealand, Tasmania, or Australia, or among the American
Indians in this country, parallels can be found for the behavior of
the South African regime, which enables them to say, "We're as
bad as everybody else, but no worse." Therefore they can continue
doing what they are doing now.

Gordimer suggests that these are two of the most important
myths that enable white South Africans to live comfortably with
themselves. I suggest that the one that will emerge more strongly is
the argument that white South Africans can deny black South
Africans political rights, and indeed even South African nationality,
by offering them instead some kind of dummy citizenship in a little
client or satellite state, carved off from South Africa as the country
is dismembered by the process called the Bantustan Policy. They
will then be able to argue, "We have not really denied them rights;
we have simply substituted other rights for those we have deprived
them of."

In this context, the process of creative writing for both white
South Africa and black South Africa becomes much more difficult.
You have the battery of laws to contend with; you have the preju-

dices in the society; you have the myths that justify continued op-
pression in the society. You have, unfortunately, the money still
being pipelined into South Africa from outside to keep the regime
solvent and, indeed, prosperous. And so we roll on to an agonizing
and inevitable destructiveness.

I would like to close by harking back to a point I made earlier:
it may be that those of us who have a concern about creative writ-
ing, about creativity, and beyond that, about the simple business of
being human—that all of us can be involved in the process that re-
duces the aid currently being given to the South African regime. By
doing what we already do a great deal more, we can actually mini-
mize the area, the extent, the duration, and the scale of the conflict
that must come to South Africa, and in that way we can make our
own humane contribution.

Memoir
Fighting Deportation from the United States

In the early 1980s, the Reagan administration tried to deport me from the United States. In 1981, I got a letter from Elliot Abrams ordering me to leave the country. He was then Undersecretary of State for Human Rights—this is the man who would later be convicted in the Iran-Contra scandal but who returned to serve in the George W. Bush administration. Soon after, he sends a follow-up letter wanting to know when I would leave the country—an exact date.

My friends in Chicago, including my colleague at Northwestern, the Guyanese writer Jan Carew, started the Dennis Brutus Defense Committee, which eventually had groups in various cities around the United States. So we went into court and said that U.S. law says you cannot deport a person if he or she will be killed when they return to their country. So we produced a letter from a former member of the South African secret police, BOSS, named Gordon Winter, who said that Brutus is on BOSS's top ten hit list. The judge told the government, "You can't deport this guy." Then I got a new deportation order. It said that, "Since you were born in Zimbabwe, we order you to return to Zimbabwe. Let us know what date you will leave. Otherwise we have to send the federal marshals."

One comrade had been killed in New York on a train platform, we think by the South African secret police, but we can't prove it. Another guy I had worked with, Ahmed Timol, had been thrown from the seventh floor of the building in which he was being interrogated. So we again went to court, this time to challenge my deportation to Zimbabwe. We produced a letter from a member of the Zimbabwean government, saying that, "We do not advise Brutus to come back, because of cross-border raids. The South African army is coming in to carry out assassinations and we can't protect them." Again the judge said, "You can't deport this guy."

Sure enough, I got my third deportation order. It's again from Elliot Abrams. It says that, "Since you came to the U.S. from Britain, we will now deport you to Britain. Please advise us as to when you are leaving." Next we wrote to the British Home Office, and got a letter from Prime Minister Margaret Thatcher, saying effectively, "Mr. Brutus won't necessarily be welcome." That's because I had caused a lot of trouble already, having been arrested at Wimbledon for stopping a tennis match. So I was not deported to Britain. Now the funny thing is that the head of the Northwestern Program of African Studies attended a banquet and sat next to Elliot Abrams. She said, "Why are you trying to deport one of my faculty?" He said, "Oh no, we're not deporting anybody. She said, "His name is Dennis Brutus." He said, "What! He's still here?" So they gave up.

The fight against my deportation took place as the divestment and boycott campaign gained momentum and the apartheid system went into crisis.

Documents

Letter from Joel Rogers, acting INS district director, to Dennis Brutus
June 25, 1981

FILE: CHI-N-17784
CHI-N-11893
A17 351 223

I have determined that your failure to file a timely application for extension of stay was the result of circumstances beyond your control and as such is excusable; however, since you are not employed in the United States as a visiting professor on a temporary basis and you have not been granted a current waiver of the bases for exclusion that are applicable in your case, your motion for reconsideration must be denied.

ORDER: IT IS ORDER[ED] THAT the applicant's request for reconsideration of the denial of his Application to Extend Time of Temporary Stay be and same [sic] is hereby denied.

JOEL L. ROGERS
Acting District Director
[Immigration and Naturalization
Service]

Letter from Senator Howard Metzenbaum to Elliot Abrams, assistant secretary of state

January 19, 1982

Dear Assistant Secretary Abrams:

In the near future, an application for political asylum on the part of Professor Dennis Brutus, a noted poet and an outspoken opponent of apartheid, will come to your office for review. I urge you in the strongest terms to act favorably upon this request.

As you know, Professor Brutus was recently declared deportable by a Chicago Immigration Court as the result of a complex series of events beyond his control. The INS, whose Chicago office misplaced his file for a period of six months, has formally agreed that Professor Brutus was not at fault for the violations of the immigration laws that brought him to his current status.

Far more is at stake, however, than providing relief to an individual who ran afoul of the INS bureaucracy. To deport Professor Brutus would, I believe, send to the world a message of sympathy on the part of our government for the South African regime that imprisoned him for the "crime" of opposing that nation's racist system. In addition, there is ample reason for concern that forcing Professor Brutus to return to Southern Africa could render him vulnerable to reprisals.

If this nation is to remain, as it has always been, a haven for those who have stood against oppression, I do not believe that we can discriminate between friendly and unfriendly oppressors. Professor Brutus has been a spokesman for basic human rights in South Africa. As such, he deserves not only our hospitality, but our gratitude as well.

Very Sincerely yours,
Howard M. Metzenbaum
United States Senator [Ohio]

Letter from Thomas P. O'Neill, speaker of the U.S. House of Representatives to Elliot Abrams

February 22, 1982

Dear Secretary Abrams:

I am writing to support the request that Amherst College Professor Dennis Brutus be granted political asylum in the United States. Professor Brutus is an internationally acclaimed advocate of human rights. His stance against the apartheid system in South Africa is important in eliminating the stigma of racial discrimination throughout the world.

Professor Brutus's position as instructor of African literature in the United States serves important academic and literary needs.

I hope you will do all you can to help meet Professor Brutus's request to suspend his deportation proceedings and to grant him political asylum.

> Sincerely,
> Thomas P. O'Neill, Jr.
> The Speaker

Speech before the United Nations Special Committee on Apartheid

1974

...There is an alarming indication of increasing support by Western countries for the bastion of racism and white supremacy in Southern Africa.

One of the clearest instances has been the recent visit to South Africa by a task force of nine vessels of the British Navy, which have engaged in operational exercises with the South African Air Force and Navy. The declarations of Mr. Harold Wilson's government inveighing against the evils of apartheid are reduced to hollow rhetoric as long as Britain continues to collaborate with the armed forces of oppression in Southern Africa. This does not come as a surprise to those who have examined the policies of the British government: It is to be hoped that the newly reelected government will mend its ways—or will be forced to do so by more vigorous and effective protest by the British people.

Even more significant and alarming [are]the recent disclosures of the secret tilt of the United States government in support of the white supremacists in Southern Africa—while at the same time with familiar duplicity contriving to give the impression of support for African governments and the legitimate aspirations of oppressed African peoples for self-determination and self-rule. This has been amply documented in the recent writings of Jack Anderson of the *Washington Post* and a secret memorandum from the State Department itself. A more specific instance of active military collaboration between the United States and South Africa is shown in the joint exercise (war games?) between South African paratroopers and an American team including military personnel, which took place in parachuting championships held in August at Pretoria's Wonderboom Airport. No doubt these were excellent preparations for future counterinsurgency activities and are an ominous indication of the future United States stance in the escalating conflict in Southern Africa between the herrenvolk[1] minority and the people's liberation struggle.

In the area of political and military support for apartheid, I believe that at the present time the country that requires most concentrated and immediate attention is France.

While there are no formal military alliances, since 1963 France has been the principal (and virtually the only) country supplying arms to apartheid. The arms have ranged from submarines to helicopters, missiles and jets. Most alarmingly, South Africa has announced in the past few weeks that it proposes to purchase an additional fifty Mirage [fighter jets] from France. The country that trumpets its belief in democracy and racial justice has become the merchant of death and the purveyor of the arms to defend racism. This fact is being increasingly recognized throughout the continent of Africa and will in time lead to the total repudiation by the African continent of French influence and the French myths, I would urge that the deeply felt opposition to French support of apartheid be translated into action, that the Special Political Committee issue a request to all sympathetic countries that they immediately protest to the French government and denounce the traffic in murderous weapons designed to repress the African people and to crush their legitimate struggles in Southern Africa.

¹ A term used to describe the Afrikaner section of the white minority.

Notes on the South African liberation struggle
Article from *The Gar*, 1975

In 1960, after Sharpeville, when unarmed Africans protesting against the Pass Laws were massacred, the African people announced that they could no longer continue a peaceful struggle in the face of naked aggression. They resolved to embark on other methods of struggle. The two main resistance groups are the ANC, African National Congress, and the PAC, Pan-Africanist Congress.

There have of course been other resistance groups, including ARM, a white liberal, white radical, largely student resistance group which organized sabotage, with considerable success. There has also been a Unity Movement, or Trotskyist group, also students, mainly nonwhite, forming their own resistance group.

The dominant group, both historically—it was formed shortly after the Union of South Africa—and numerically, is the ANC, which achieved its largest following probably under Chief Albert Luthuli, Nobel Peace Prize winner. He was banned, confined to a farm, and eventually died under mysterious circumstances. The leadership was taken over by Nelson Mandela, who represented the younger guard of the ANC, who had traveled widely in Africa and Europe, and under whom the ANC embarked on its new phase of armed struggle, setting up a separate wing called Umkhonto we Sizwe, meaning the spear of the nation.

At the same time, the PAC had developed its own militant squads, called task forces, whose strategy was essentially assassination and terrorism, whereas that of Umkhonto we Sizwe was an attack on installations, government establishments, rather than persons. The attacks were always on property. The PAC group was called Poqo—the word means "solo"—and it was an all-African resistance group, as opposed to Umkhonto, which admits whites, blacks, browns, all South Africans.

In 1960, after Sharpeville, there were a number of sabotage incidents. People left the country and went off for military training in other parts of Africa, particularly in Algeria, and traveled through Zambia and Tanzania. It was impossible to attack South Africa directly because it was surrounded by white bastions, and so most of the encounters took place on the banks of the Zambezi River in the region of Wankie. The most spectacular and the most serious military clash took place as long ago as 1967. Since then there have been sporadic clashes, but in fact, instead of an escalation of the conflict, there has been nothing to match the size of that one. Indeed, that one itself has come under serious criticism from members of the ANC and PAC who claim that the whole venture was ill conceived, badly planned, and suicidal.

Since then there have been occasions when guerrillas have crossed into Rhodesia (Zimbabwe) and been picked up by security forces, indicating that the South African intelligence had succeeded in infiltrating the training camps.

Intensity vs. ideology

It may be that one of our central problems is an ideological one, or one of people being insufficiently revolutionary in their outlook, insufficiently committed. For one has to say bluntly that the struggle in other parts of Africa that started later than the struggle in South Africa—in Angola, Mozambique, Zimbabwe, Namibia—has in fact overtaken the struggle in South Africa. The obvious reason is that the white South Africans are the most highly equipped, the most efficient, with superb intelligence and surveillance, so that this is always going to be the toughest nut to crack. There must be very few people from South Africa in exile who are satisfied with the rate at which the struggle is developing. Now that the Mozambique bastion has fallen and we see Ian Smith's stronghold in Zimbabwe crumbling it may be that 1975 will be the year for dramatic developments in Azania [the Pan-Africanist term for South Africa] as well.

It should be said that Namibia, which the South Africans have illegally annexed and which the UN has ordered South Africa to leave, has had considerable military activity over the past year. The two liberation movements have had frequent clashes with the South African security forces, especially involving land mines being planted.

Arms for liberation

Most of these liberation movements began with nothing but a few old discarded rusty guns. This is especially true of FRELIMO in Mozambique, where they started with almost nothing but sticks and stones. Their leader, Eduardo Mondlane, a graduate of Northwestern University and a former professor at Syracuse, came to the States to appeal to the U.S. government to cease assisting the Portuguese in oppressing the people of Mozambique. He appealed for arms for the people of Mozambique. This was refused. The U.S. government continued to supply Portugal through NATO. Mondlane announced that he would take arms [from] wherever he could get them. After that, the bulk of his arms came from China, some from Russia, and other arms were bought in the open market and some in the black markets of Europe.

South African liberation forces are reasonably well equipped: bazookas, mortars, Sten [machine] guns. We don't have helicopters or jets, of course. I think it is worth mentioning that when I was in China last year I spoke to Zhou Enlai, who expressed his support for our liberation struggle. Zhou pointedly said to me that they could not supply anything until it was requested. This seems to me extremely significant. I reported it to the acting President General of the ANC, Oliver Tambo, the man who has taken Nelson Mandela's place, since Mandela is now serving a life sentence on Robben Island (I spent some time breaking stones with him there). Tambo did not react to my report—I did not expect him to—but it seems to me that this is something that the ANC should take up and should decide that it will make use of whatever facilities are available to it.

Funds for struggle

A great deal of the money still comes from Western Europe, but not from Western governments, except money being paid into the UN trust fund for the victims of apartheid. The International Defense and Aid organization, which I represent at the United Nations, is the main relief fund. A good deal of the money is actually raised for arms by private groups, for instance students in Scandinavia. And there's now a little money coming from black Americans as well.

Socialist ideology

Almost every liberation movement in Southern Africa is socialist in orientation, is anticapitalist. But there are segments who attach themselves to the Western powers, or to whom Western powers attempt to attach themselves. I believe that the societies that will be built after reconstruction will be socialist. And my own suspicion is that the degree of militancy and activity in a given liberation movement depends on the degree of politicization which has taken place, that the more committed they are to the building of a new society, of a socialist society, the more committed they are to revolution, the more vigorously they pursue the armed struggle.

Labor protests

The picture must always be seen on two levels of resistance. Besides the armed struggle, there are the more overt signs of resistance—strikes, walkouts, protests, sit-downs. By law, blacks are forbidden to form trade unions. Thus, only sporadic strikes by pockets of labor are possible. In the 1950s we attempted a general strike. Then we attempted a national stay-at-home [action] when strikes were illegal. Then we moved on to a national day of mourning in protest of the Africans who were shot while on strike.

The country has been so fragmented, labor has been so carved up, that there is no possibility for unified mass action on a national scale. There can only be action in a given industry, in a specific plant, in specific areas. Last year I arrived in New York from Beijing on the very day when the news came of the killing of twelve miners at a gold mine in South Africa, at a place called Carltonville. I was able to appear before the Special Committee on Apartheid to ask for action.

This kind of labor unrest is hard to categorize in terms of whether it represents one more thrust of the liberation movement or whether it is operating independently. Either way, all labor unrest leads to a heightening of political consciousness. But obviously it would be important if one could say that this represents one of the initiatives of the liberation movement. I would think that these were largely spontaneous, generated by local working conditions.

Often labor protest is simply a way of achieving reform within the system. Indeed, the South African government has moved rapidly to raise wages in order to quell black protest, at the same time allowing a dramatic increase in the cost of living. Real wages remain static. In some areas wages in real terms are where they were in 1911; in other instances real wages have declined.

Numbers

It's impossible to say how many there are within the liberation forces, and anyway, this figure is not given out. Normally the camps are quite small, about twenty, sometimes up to 200. Membership of the ANC is also difficult to determine. PAC was quite popular until 1960, right up to Sharpeville, which was a PAC rally, where sixty-nine people were killed and 200 injured when the police machine-gunned them at a peaceful demonstration. A segment of the South African population must certainly be pro-PAC. However, most people would deny any association with either the ANC or PAC, since both are proscribed organizations. To be a member of them, to work for, or simply to have in your home a photograph of any member, even if he's dead, is an offense for which you can be imprisoned.

There are probably now about 8,000 political prisoners; perhaps the figure is higher. At the time I was in prison on Robben Island, the figure was 8,000, although the South African government denied they were political prisoners. There were about 1,300 prisoners, including 1,100 political prisoners. The other 200 were life-time criminals, convicted of murder, rape, or other crimes. They were used by the warders to control the other prisoners.

Fragmentation

The blacks are split into what are called "homelands" or "Bantustans," each led by a stooge. The South African argument is that the nation consists of not one nation, but nine, a white nation and eight black nations (if one includes the coloreds and Asians you'd have more). The result is they are now trying to create nine states within a state, one a Whitestan, eight Bantustans. Regrettably, there are many in America and elsewhere who see the black stooges who collaborate in running the Bantustans as the real challenge to apartheid. By splitting the black population into tribal "nations," the white South Africans are trying to have no black nation larger than the white nation.

This is interestingly seen in sports. The South Africans insist that in time there will be something like seven or nine national teams. And to carry the absurdity further, each of these national groups will be admitted to membership in the UN. But all legislation passed in the Bantustans will still need to be endorsed by the white government at Pretoria.

Responses to Balkanization

We now have a strong student political movement, SASO, South African Student Organization, radical, militant, all black, which has deliberately broken with white students. SASO has been responsible for the development of an extremely important black consciousness movement, open to all those who are not white. It's working against the governmental attempt to split the oppressed nonwhites into separate groups, by setting up a united black power movement. Men like Sonny Leon, political leader among the "coloreds," have also done a very significant job in resisting the attempted fragmentation.

I think I have had a hand in this process too, because historically the first organizations in South Africa that completely smashed the color barrier within the black groups was the sporting organization. SASA, South African Sporting Association, created in 1958 gave birth in 1963 to SANROC, South African Non-Racial Olympic Committee. I was secretary and founder of SASA and became president of SANROC in 1963 and still continue to function as president.

There is also a conscious effort among intellectuals, academics, and clergymen to resist the Balkanization.

Role of exiles

There are three categories of exiles. There are those who immediately go into military training with the intention of returning; these are mostly young men and women: coloreds, Africans, Indians, and indeed, whites as well.

Others have a political function. The ANC has offices in London, Algiers, in New York at the UN, in Dar as Salaam and at Lusaka, right near the scene of action. Here the function is essentially mobilizing international support. And they raise money and make the necessary propaganda. Their function is to determine the rate of escalation of the struggle. People sometimes question whether you can run a struggle from London, when it's taking place in Pretoria. Of course, if we did have a leadership group there, we would not be able to say it. But there is little evidence that there is such a segment there now.

Reconstruction and ideology

Then there is the important issue which I fear is either being given little thought, or thought only by a small elite, the latter would worry me as much as the former. I do not see serious thought as to the problems of reconstruction, nor do I see serious study of the process of politicization, equipping people with the necessary ideology, which directs the whole planning. You have to know what kind of society you plan to rebuild. I see inadequate work being done, both in ideological instruction and hard blue-printing. Economic planning, study of resources, manpower, foreign investment and what you do about it, problems of nationalization. All these are spelled out vaguely in the Freedom Charter. The charter says the land shall belong to those that work the land. So in a vague way as long ago as 1956 when South African blacks adopted the charter they were spelling out a vaguely socialistic direction. But clearly you're never going to win on vague ideas. My hunch is that such study is being done by a small hand-picked group. I am not entirely happy about that. The decisions should be made by all the people.

So successful has been South African propaganda that Americans often ask, "Do black South Africans really understand what is happening to them? We always see smiling black faces." This of course is crap. In South Africa everything that happens to you happens because of the color of your skin. You pass a cinema and you see they're showing *The Godfather*, and you know you can't go in because it's for whites only. No black South African is unaware of it. So what you have is people full of resentment, potentially a powderkeg that can blow up at any time, but which way it will blow and how you put the pieces together again—for those things you need more than an awareness. You need political conscious-ness, political instruction. That we do not have enough of.

Neocolonialism

Many countries in Africa have become independent. And what's happened? Oppression, corruption, exploitation and ineffi-ciency. Nearly all of those that were given their independence by the West have gone back to the West and are now firmly in the pocket of the West. The wealth of Kenya, Nigeria, [and] Senegal flows into the West. All over Africa where countries have achieved independence it's turned out to be pseudoindependence. Power in the hands of a few blacks, poverty and exploitation for the major-ity. In each instance there's been an elite, and the white masters when they've left have simply transferred power to the black elite who continue to function on behalf of the white masters on the outside. The profits still go into Paris, London, and New York. So, what we have is neocolonialism.

Frantz Fanon has discussed this, in great detail, in *The Wretched Of The Earth*. But Fanon's understanding of the problem has not changed the situation. People read Fanon, and nothing happens! But in the countries where independence was fought for, not just given by the West, you have a revolutionary situation and the building of a socialist society. This is generating tension in the pseudo-independent countries that have chosen capitalism. So the revolutionary struggle in the South is having a revolutionary im-pact in the rest of the continent. The struggle is the struggle of the oppressed against the oppressor.

If we had won quickly we would now be sitting there merrily like Ghana or Nigeria saying, "Great! We got our freedom, the hell with the rest!" But when the struggle takes a long time, like in South Africa, we say, "We're going to build a whole new system." So we're into a whole new society in Africa. It's a whole new ballgame!

What then are the prospects?

Dramatic events are already unfolding in Rhodesia [Zimbabwe], Mozambique, and Angola. All these intensify the pressure on the heart of racist exploitation in South Africa. I cannot believe that the South African situation can remain unchanged. Black students have been organizing rallies in support of FRELIMO. They have been beaten, banned, and jailed; some have gone underground. The most unpredictable element is the role of the black stooges, whether they are going to play along with [South African Prime Minister B.J.] Vorster, [and] accept his new thrust for a reformed apartheid.

On the whole, I am pessimistic. My fear is that the ANC, which is not effective within South Africa, which functions in exile, and which sees protest developing in South Africa independent of it, that the ANC will decide it cannot back a thrust if it cannot predict the outcome. What we need within the ANC itself is that those who feel dissatisfaction with the rate of progress assert a demand for mean-ingful action. We need a nucleus of committed people who will say that the time for temporizing is past. If we lose this chance, if Vorster can come to terms with black majority rule in the new countries around South Africa, he can probably survive with his white govern-ment in South Africa. The fault will have been ours. It will be a long time before we can find another opportunity as crucial as this.

A footnote on detente:

In recent months there has been a new and significant develop-ment: a movement for "detente." This has included meetings be-tween Vorster and heads of black African states and a new call for dialogue. The essence of the plan, which may have originated with [Henry] Kissinger, is to create a new climate of "reasonableness," with Vorster promising concessions, and the black African states promising to relax their pressures on apartheid. Events in Mozam-bique, Angola, and Zimbabwe have forced this new strategy, de-signed to prolong the life of apartheid. But detente is likely to prove, as it has in other areas, wholly phony.

Steve Biko: In memoriam
Speech at Steve Biko Day, San Antonio, Texas, June 16, 1978

I believe that my message has already been delivered to you by the film you have just seen, which tells you what is happening in South Africa. All I can add to that is to tell you that the struggle con-tinues. The killings are still going on, the torture, the brutality, the murder. This night, in the ghettos of Southern Africa, that oppression continues. The resistance continues. And the people of South Africa will continue their struggle until they have reached a victorious conclusion. We will fight until we win. We will fight, and if necessary, we will die. But we will not stop until we have won the victory.

My message tonight to the people of San Antonio is twofold. I want to thank all the wonderful people who have been part of this event, who are listed as the sponsors and all the other nameless people who have contributed to this event in memory of Steve Biko. On behalf of the struggling people of South Africa, who cannot reach you tonight, I say thank you to all of you, and please continue with your efforts to help us, because the struggle must continue.

Since that film was made, over 600 leaders of the people have been arrested. The twenty organizations that were the voice of the people, which represented their aspirations, their anger and determination to achieve justice and democracy, all those organizations have been banned. It is a crime to belong to them. They have been driven underground, and the struggle continues underground— with one important difference. The people of South Africa have decided that they are no longer going to meet brutality with nonviolence. They are no longer going to meet machine guns and tear gas with bricks and stones, with broomsticks.... That they have been pushed to an armed confrontation—that there is no other way to achieve victory. And so the struggle must continue, by building an armed struggle until we achieve victory.

I have asked you tonight to remember the images you have seen, and to keep those images printed on your brain—to remember, and to let them help you in your determination to assist us in our struggle for justice. And I will ask you especially to form in your mind the image of one young man, a student in my hometown, Port Elizabeth. A young man kept naked in a prison cell, chained like an animal to the floor, beaten by the police, his body covered with burns from electric shocks when they interrogated him. And that meant sixteen days on the floor of that cell, then being thrown naked and unconscious into a jeep, and driven 700 miles from Port Elizabeth to Pretoria, and dying there, with his skull beaten in, with his brains smashed: I ask you to remember, especially, Steve Biko. And to remember him as a symbol of the courage and determination of the people of my country, and as a

symbol of the brutality, the oppressiveness, the vicious racism of the
minority apartheid regime in my country. And now, in tribute to
Steve Biko, I would like to interrupt my address before I make three
other points, to read to you a poem written in tribute to Steve Biko.

> The dusty roads
> from Peddie to King
>
> the yellow river
> choking with silt
> draining to i'Monti
>
> the dust-filmed bluegums
> poised and dreaming
> in the arid air
>
> the parching dust
> harsh in the throat
> and hurtful on the eyes
>
> the crude teutonic towns
> Hamburg, Berlin, Hanover
> with their ominous echoes
>
> —all these he knew
> their roads he traversed:
>
> they fired him with resolve
> and smoldering anger
>
> their racial hate seethed round him
> like the surge of shimmering heatwaves
> and laid a thousand lashes
> on his taut flesh:
>
> here he planned, dreamed,
> waged his struggle
> and hardened his will
> to confront the butchers
>
> to challenge their terror
> —even if they robbed him of his life.

After we have mourned Steve Biko, and after we have paid tribute to his courage, we have to ask, "What else can we do?" And if Steve Biko was here tonight, he would have a message for the people of San Antonio. He would say, "Out of this city have come murderers, in Africa, in Southern Africa." And he would say, "I accuse this city, and I accuse your Major Mike Williams, and I accuse the other mercenaries who have been recruited from this city and from Texas and from the United States to murder men, women, and children in Africa."

And not only to accuse those mercenaries. The United States has a constitution, and it has laws. And two laws are of special interest. There is a law that says, if you recruit people in this country to be mercenaries, to fight in a foreign country, you are committing a crime. There is a law that says if you serve in the army of a foreign country and you are an American citizen, you are committing a crime. But hundreds of Americans—Vietnam veterans, many of them—are now mercenaries in Africa. And in Chicago and other cities in this country, they sell openly a magazine called *Solider of Fortune,* which advertises for mercenaries in Africa. Why has not one single person been prosecuted in this country for being a mercenary in Africa? Why is not one single person prosecuted for recruiting mercenaries in Africa? Where is the Justice Department? Where is justice in this country if it is not concerned with those who can leave this country to murder in another country? I will say I accuse the United States government and the Justice Department of complicity. I accuse them of being accomplices in the murder and torture of people in Africa. And if Steve Biko were here tonight, that would be part of his presentation.

This country has made a commitment. It is a commitment that has traveled all over the world. It was a commitment that was made by President Carter when he stood in the rostrum of the United Nations and pledged that the United States would demonstrate an active concern for justice for majority rule, for self-determination, for democracy, for human rights—all over the world. Sounds very good. And what is happening in Southern Africa? Why are there mercenaries from the United States killing and murdering in Zimbabwe, going with gunships with napalm in helicopters, shooting up villages, murdering, torturing. Why? What has happened to the commitment to human rights?

I say—and I believe Steve Biko would say—that President Carter is guilty of hypocrisy. I accuse him of hypocrisy. I accuse him of being a hypocrite. I accuse him of being two-faced. And I believe that that situation will not change until sufficient people in this country demonstrate their concern, their determination, and ask these difficult questions, and continue to ask them until we receive the right answers. We cannot cease. We must go on. The struggle continues. The American corporations—all 495 of them—who are profiting from the blood, the sweat, the corpses of people in South Africa—on behalf of the people of South Africa, [to them] I say, "this must stop." And I ask you to join me and to support us in our struggle.

For the struggle for human rights, for justice, is one struggle. Our oppression is part of the oppression here and elsewhere in the world. The struggle for our freedom is also the struggle for freedom in other parts of the world. And that struggle must continue. And with all the sincerity that I can command, on behalf of the people of Southern Africa, I thank you. I beg you to continue. And I remind you: the struggle must continue.

Statement by Ad–hoc Group to End Northwestern [University] Investments in South Africa (AGENISA)
1981

The Rockefeller Commission Report, *U.S. Policy Toward Southern Africa*, must be condemned as a thoroughly bad document. It is outdated in that it has already been overtaken by events, it is biased in its findings (most of the members were associated with the corporations whose behavior in South Africa they were supposed to judge), it is self-serving in its recommendations, which will confer a cloak of respectability on those who are profiting from the oppression of millions of blacks, and it is pernicious in its effect, which will be to justify continued United States support for the racist minority apartheid regime.

It is significant that the issues which most exercise the opponents of apartheid oppression in the United States, divestment of holdings in corporations active in South Africa, and support for the liberation struggle receive considerably less attention than others: the millions in the United States, in churches, trade unions, community organizations, and on over one hundred university campuses will not be fobbed off by this attempt to defuse their anger and energy. They will continue their demand for divestment until complicity in South African oppression is ended.

Even more significantly, there are no statements from the most important body of opinion in and outside South Africa—that of the liberation movement. No doubt this was done to ensure that the publication could be distributed in South Africa where official documents of the liberation movement are proscribed, but more than anything else it demonstrates how pusillanimous the commission was and how little credence can be given to it.

> Dennis Brutus
> Co-Convenor
> AGENISA

The escalation of resistance in South Africa
Speech at the Third Unitarian Church of Chicago, June 1, 1986

A political voice is what the people of South Africa are trying to get; to express how they want to run their lives, what kind of laws they want to write, what kind of parliamentary system they want.

Because I'd like to assume that most of you know what is happening in South Africa and have a sense of the picture, I thought the most useful thing I could do is to select a few features of the South African situation; those with which you may not be familiar because the media is doing an incredibly bad job on South Africa. They are guilty of a gross neglect of something that affects their very own livelihood, their own rights.

In South Africa, as we know, a television cameraman, a radio man, [or] a newspaper man can be told you cannot go into that town, into that province, into that ghetto and if you go, you'll go to jail. The media, all sources of information, are controlled by the government and the police. Now, I assure you, if that happened in Havana, or in Managua, or in Warsaw, you'd have them screaming their heads off. Yet here we have the entire spectrum of the media of this country not raising a voice of protest at the denial of their own freedom, their own right to go where they wish and to report what they wish. Of course, in South Africa, if you had a story printed without clearing it with the police you would go to prison for that as well.

We have the most massive censorship. We now have women being whipped in the streets of South Africa; we have children tortured in the prisons of South Africa. Where is the media? Where is the coverage of these events? This is one of the things I thought I should raise with you. But then, to go on and to cover some of those things that are either not being reported or are being badly reported or only being reported in one or two places.

And so, I'm going to select a couple of features which seem to me especially important at the present time. They are important because these are the elements that are going to shape future events in South Africa. When you understand them, you will have a better understanding of the events which are now about to unfold in South Africa; the pattern that is developing.

I take it you all know of the raids South Africa conducted recently—sending the air force, sending commandos into three states, Zimbabwe, Zambia, and Botswana; killing people in their beds—ironically, none of them members of the African National Congress which was why [the South African forces] allegedly went in. And in one case, at least, blowing up the house in Harare where I would probably have been living if immigration had succeeded in getting me deported to Zimbabwe. It was the house where a friend of mine who was in prison on Robben Island with me, Joe Gqabi, was killed as he came out of the house with eight bullets into him. But now the house itself has been blown up by South African commandos.

But that strike at the neighboring countries, which is an important factor if you want to understand why the United States supports apartheid, why the United States supports Pretoria, why Reagan is determined that no significant action should be taken against apartheid. When you understand that South Africa is seen and has been recognized as such by Chester Crocker speaking on behalf of the State Department; that South Africa is recognized as the regional power that must do more than simply control its own population but control the entire area and all the adjoining coun-tries as well, to become the dominant regional policeman. And that is the function of apartheid in Southern Africa.

But in addition to the attacks externally, the apartheid regime has now launched and is preparing to launch more of the most vi-cious attacks in the history of its system against the African people. And as a prelude to that, they've done two very clever things. First you had a state of emergency declared. Now when a state of emer-gency is declared, it's roughly equivalent to martial law. It gives the army and the police complete power to do whatever they please. In addition, a law was passed to ensure that no citizen could sue them, whether it was for wrongful arrest, or having your son killed in the house, before your eyes, or people being tear-gassed in the churches of South Africa—whatever it was, you cannot sue the government, you cannot sue the police, you cannot sue the army. They are in-demnified for all their actions.

Now they announce the lifting of the state of emergency which was welcomed by the Reagan administration, among others. We now have progress. But the fine print says that while the state of emergency was lifted a set of laws was being introduced which were the equivalent of the state of emergency, which gave those same powers to the police and the army, but instead of the state of emergency being declared by Parliament, the power was now given to a single man called the minister of law and order and, more sig-nificantly, he can declare a state of emergency in any town, or vil-lage, or township, or ghetto. The moment it is declared in that area, it becomes a crime for the media to enter and it becomes a crime for the media to report anything that happened in that area even if they heard about it from someone else.

So you now take the issue out of Parliament and put it in the hands of a single man. You then allow the police and army com-plete freedom to act in secret so that there is no information being disseminated about it. So you have the state of emergency lifted, but in fact the state of emergency in a new, more subtle, more com-plex, and in fact more effective form. But that is something of which we'll see a great deal more. I don't know how much we'll ac-tually see or hear, but more will be coming.

The other extremely important development and very alarming

one is that the stage has been reached in apartheid South Africa
where you have four million white minority versus your roughly
twenty-four million nonwhite majority, but your four million white
minority has found in the ranks of the blacks sufficient allies so they
can use them and arm them to destroy the resistance. So the attack
on the blacks comes now not so much from your white army. They
go into the ghetto, they're fully armed, they have automatic
weapons, but they don't do the killing. They only stand by to protect
those who do the killing, so that there can be no counterattack and
no attempt at self-defense. Most of these are blacks who during the
day are wearing a police uniform and in the evening, plain clothes.

They call themselves vigilantes. They go out and seek those
who in the ghettos are organizing the resistance against apartheid.
And so, we have now killings by blacks, killing other blacks on a
scale we have not seen before and the most alarming element of it
is, we now have a black man whose salary is paid each month by
the government, who is supplied with an armed bodyguard with
automatic weapons and who goes around in a bullet-proof limou-
sine. His name is Chief Buthelezi, mark the name. This is the man
who has sworn to destroy the resistance so that it is no longer nec-
essary for the apartheid government to attack the supporters of the
ANC, the African National Congress, or the supporters and the
members of the UDF, the United Democratic Front; Buthelezi has
vowed that he will destroy them. And he is being permitted to arm
his supporters with automatic weapons and to go into the ghettos
and to kill whoever they please with the army standing by so that if
there is any attempt to resist, the military can move in.

And so, you have a situation of far greater intensity than you
had before and far greater danger than you had before.

But there is a third element which we must look at. That is the
interesting one. Throughout the country, in the ghettos, the govern-
ment has appointed its own black city council, not elected, ap-
pointed by the government to run the ghetto for the government.
And all of those have collapsed. There is not a single government-
appointed city council in any ghetto across South Africa. Those
who have tried to work the system on behalf of the government
have failed. Some have been killed, some have had their homes
burned down, and the majority have resigned and refused to con-

tinue to collaborate with the apartheid system. And out of that has come a second interesting development.

Now in these ghettos, people are setting up their own peoples' councils to run the ghettos themselves. They have their own police force, their own garbage collectors, they make their own rules, they have their own punishment and these are areas that the police and the army do not enter. These are now "no go" areas where the people are running their own lives and rejecting the whole apparatus of the apartheid system. Occasionally, the military will drive through in armored cars and drive out again. They don't run the area. They can enter and retreat. The people are running their own lives. And across the country now, we see the appearance of these self-governing institutions set up by the people.

Unfortunately, this has been very badly reported in the U.S. press, so most of you know nothing about it. The first story was broken by a man called Don Connell, writing for the *Christian Science Monitor* after he had been to South Africa and in fact had made use of contacts I'd given him in order to enter the townships and the ghettos. After his story appeared, other journalists began to pick up on the story. But even now it is something that is not clearly understood.

On the one hand you have the escalation of repression. On the other hand, you have the escalation of resistance. And now we enter what may be the most fateful month in the history of apartheid and the history of the resistance. There is no way of telling how it will come out. I'm not going to attempt it. I'm only going to spell out for you the forces that are involved, and I have already done most of that. But on June 16 of this year, the anniversary of the massacre of students in Soweto on June 16, 1976, when over 1,000 high school students were killed, we will see the most massive strike, most massive demonstrations, most massive boycotts that apartheid has ever seen in its history. People are mobilizing across the country to paralyze the entire society—the buses, the transport, the factories, the railroads—bring everything to a standstill. And, course, the government knows that.

And, of course, the government knows that. And so it is doing two things. It is not only deploying the military in preparation for June 16, but it is already arresting thousands without admitting any charge against them, because these are the people who are seen as the potential organizers. There is a law in South Africa, which I'm sure you know of: the preventive detention law which allows you to be held for 180 days in prison without any charge being brought against you. It is preventive detention. You are detained, not for a crime, but in case you might commit a crime. And so this is being invoked to jail thousands of people prior to June 16.

June 26 is what we call South African Liberation Day. It is the day when people rededicate themselves to the struggle for freedom. And so from June 16 to June 26, you will see probably, and I say probably, because it is possible that the government will succeed in jailing so many thousands of those who went through the mobilization that it won't take place. But my own hunch is that it will. And that we will see, this year, a bloody and terrible confrontation between the forces of freedom and the forces of oppression.

And so, when you see it happening, when you see in unfolding, particularly when you see an escalation of killing of blacks, by blacks, I hope you will bring to it a greater degree of understanding. But you can bring more than understanding to it. You can bring pressure to that situation. You can apply the force which will swing the balance of events either on the side of freedom or on the side of oppression. Power exists in the United States. It is the United States that has given to apartheid an extension of existence. Last year, when loans fell due by the apartheid economy to the World Bank and to American banks of $14 billion, the apartheid government said we can't pay. If we paid, we would be bankrupt. So the banks gave them six months more, five months more, and in February of this year, the banks met in London and they decided to roll over the $14 billion for another twelve months. And all the banks have to do is to demand the payment of the debt which is already due from an economy which is already bankrupt because they have spent their money on arms.

An economy which is in a deep recession because the unemployment in some areas is 60–65 percent. Where the growth rate has slowed down. Where there is conflict, even in the white society, about what to do and where to go. It is the banks that gave apartheid another twelve-month extension by rolling over a debt of $14 billion which has already come due. There are banks in

Chicago that are part of that consortium that allows apartheid to continue, just as the state of Illinois puts its money in those banks. The city of Chicago, I am told, is about to end that practice, but in such a weak fashion that it will take a lot more pressure. And it will take pressure from the people of the city of Chicago, people of the state of Illinois, and people of the United States of America.

There are three possibilities: to ensure that no money from Chicago goes to South Africa, particularly not in pension funds with the teachers, the municipal workers, and the others. To ensure that the state of Illinois stops buying South African steel, when the steel factories in Chicago are being closed down and people are being thrown out of their jobs because steel is being brought, under slave labor and oppressed labor in South Africa, to build the building of the state of Illinois in the city of Chicago and other buildings. Senator Paul Simon has just introduced legislation in the Senate asking for tougher sanctions on South Africa. So at the city and the state and the national level there are possibilities for you to take action, to exert pressure, and that pressure will help us.

The struggle in South Africa may be a long, protracted, painful, bloody struggle, or it can be shortened. We can end that vicious minority rule in the period of a year. The momentum is building for a showdown. But the key ace is not held by the people of South Africa. It is held by the United States. As long as the United States decides to send money and technology and arms to apartheid, either directly or through Israel or some other surrogate, so long as that happens, apartheid will survive. And apartheid will survive because the United States sees fit, and the government of the United States is the government of the people of the United States.

And so, you see, there is a way in which you can either help our oppressor or you can help us to be free. It is a very direct, very personal involvement. It takes a letter or a postcard from you to Mayor Harold Washington or to Senator Paul Simon or to your representative in the State Legislature. These are the ways in which you can move events, so that you can contribute to the pressure on the side of freedom.

We come here in June, on a beautiful day in early summer. And in my hemisphere, it is winter. There are people in the Crossroads Townships who shiver in the rain. Some of them have little plastic shanties which they put up each night, just a piece of plastic on a couple of sticks. In the mornings when the bulldozers arrive, they take them down and sit in the rain all day, and then put them up at night when the bulldozers leave. But there are people now, 30,000 of them, who don't even have those plastic shelters. They were destroyed last week. And they were destroyed by blacks sent in by the army and in a single night 3,000 of those shanties went up so that in a single ghetto, Crossroads, there are 30,000 homeless people out there in the rain. That is the reality of apartheid, while we sit here on a pleasant summer day.

And the people of the United States have some responsibility to those who shiver in the bitter cold of South Africa. They have a responsibility, but they also have the ability to change that situation. And I hope they will.

Poems

I must conjure from my past
the dim and unavowed specter of a slave,
of a bound woman, whose bound figure pleads silently,
and whose blood I must acknowledge in my own:

fanciful wraith? imagining?
Yet how else can I reconcile
my rebel blood and protest
but by acknowledgement
of that specter's mute rebellious blood ⟵

historical foundation

1973

I yearn towards the heaving earth
to the mountain-mounds upthrust through cloud-veils
and the lace-fringed lilypad islands floating
in the calm lake of our blue Mediterranean:
all the world is mine and to love
and all of its humankind.

Across the Mediterranean: Cairo to Frankfurt   1970

What is the soul of Africa?
What is it?
Is there a soul of Africa?
Is it simply that we have
contrived to be what humans are

while everywhere humanity
was being deformed?
and in the new age of man
this lunatic unsublunary age
is it still valuable to be man?
to assert the old humanities?

1978

Only in the Casbah
in its steep, stepped and narrow ways
warrening in shops, homes and passages
past the refuse and the children
and the shrivelled tenacious dames;
only in the Casbah
where the bombed structures gape
in mute reminder of the terror of the French
is the tenacious, labyrinthine and unshatterable heart
of resistance
truly known.

Algiers   1970

And I am driftwood
on an Algerian beach
along a Mediterranean shore

and I am driftwood.

Others may loll in their carnal pool
washed by tides of sensual content
in variable flow, by regulated plan

but I am driftwood.

And the tides devour,
lusts erode the shelving consciousness
fierce hungers shark at the submerged mind
while the quotidian battering spray . . .

Even the seabird questing
weaving away and across
the long blue rollers coasting
from green shelves of shore-land
and rock-tipped banks,
even the seabird has a place of rest—
though it may vary by season or by tide
and a mate brooding with swollen nares and puffed breast
signalling nest-routes with tender secret cries
though it vary by season or by tide.

But I am driftwood
by some white Algerian plage.

And the riptides rip and tear
erode, devour
and unrest, questing, yeasts in my querying brain
and I beat on the fierce savaging knowledge
rampaging through my existence
accepting the knowledge, seeking design

For I am driftwood
in a life and place and time
thrown by some chance, perchance ←——
to an occasional use
a rare half-pleasure on a seldom chance

and I grate on the sand of being
of existence, circumstance
digging and dragging for a meaning
dragging through the dirt and debris
the refuse of existence
dragging through the diurnal treadmill of my life.

And still I am driftwood.
Still the restlessness, the journeyings, the quest,
the queryings, the hungers and the lusts.

(Though we know how clouds gather and have weighed the moon,
though we have erected and heaved ourselves   vm?
in some vast orgasmic thrust

to be unmundane and to trample the moon—
still the blind tides lunge and eddy,
still we writhe on some undiscovered spit,
coil in some whirlpool of undefinable tide)

Yet in the unmarked waters I discern
traceries of patterns like wisps of spume
where I have gone
and snailtrails in seasands on a hundred shores
[where I have dragged my sad unresting loins]
—tracks on a lunar landscape that suggest some sense—

And still I am driftwood
on some sun-soaked plage.

Club des Pins/Algiers/en route to Paris.   1970

[I am alien in Africa and everywhere:]

in Europe, outside Europe I stand and assess them
—find French racial arrogance and Teuton superiority,
mouldering English humbug:

arid in Africa one finds
chafing, through bumbling,
at the restraints of restraint,
brushing impatiently through varied cultures
in fruitless search of depths:
only in myself, occasionally, am I familiar.

Paris—Algiers   1970

To be thrown outward in a steel projectile
to hurtle outward in quivering uncertainty
to a cold fragment of a continental ledge
for huddling and perching and grubbing
and ultimately, unthinkably, to find settlement there

and huddling in this gray tubular box
to find a gathering of the dispersed frantic consciousness
a ragged and stretched fabric of torn anxious mind
no longer struggling to encompass a host of contingencies
but thoughts roosting, still fluttering, on the central branched mind

and anger congeals and becomes aware
partly as the conscious rationale for flight
and partly as the self-conscious indignant pose—
the wounded "banneling," the D.P.-type
who is our age's mendicant and jew

anger too that in its artifice holds off
the true deep wound that lies
like the dark bruised pulp at the heart of the fruit:
the agony the heart and mind hold in suspense
the whirling axe—or propeller-blade—whose fierceness
    makes it invisible:

then to alight on green placid earth
to normality and efficient unhostile people
the engines, and all throbbing straining stilled
and all things quiet, except the dull half-heard throb in the heart...

For James Cooke, arrived from South Africa on an exit permit.   1967

One guesses his occupation:
satchel and suit and pompous hat
and the sheen of spurious smartness

What does he do and what is his polish?
Then past the smoothness thrusts the truth:
This is the upholder of the law
(which is far from being the same as justice)
and so there is dignity and self-respect
and callous boots to trample decencies

but this is not what rouses fear and queasiness:
it is the sense of robot power with far beyond

the deeper sense of power arbitrarily unleashed
and this is the corruption at the vitals:
the glazed ripeness of rotten fruit

1978

For them Burness Street is a familiar entity,
it lies whole, like a snake,
in the landscape of their minds
with its length and intersections
its trees and pavements, corners, shops
drains and gutters, curbs and slopes:

but for me, apart from its known beginning-point
and the dim extensions this implies
it came to me, twice, as a sudden surprise
both in its middle, crossing a known tract
and at its sudden tree-marked end
with the double-storeyed red-painted house
the grassy verge and friendly shutters
and the lovely laughing courteous girl
with shoulder-bobbed hair and the regular lines
that catch the near-perfect beauty of symmetry—
and, afterwards the moving story
of her secret patient waiting forbidden love.

For them, all South End is the familiar map
of their existence, all their growth and lives
though for me it is mere knowledge, mere report:
yet even I can sorrow, knowing their loss
their uprooting from their homely paradise
and all their yearnings and their sense of loss.

(A note on the effect of the Group Areas Act:
South End is an area from which the nonwhites
are being forced to move as a result of this act.)

1978

In the dark lanes of Soweto,
amid the mud, the slush, the squalor,
among the rusty tin shacks
the lust for freedom survives stubbornly
like a smoldering defiant flame
and the spirit of Steve Biko moves easily.

December 18, 1977   1978

Remembering June 16, 1976
Student Uprising in Soweto

They are coming back:
through woodsmoke weaving from fires
and swirls of dust from erratic breezes
you will see
ghosts are returning
ghosts of young men, young women,
young boys, young girls,
students:
and if you look closely
you will see
many of them have torn flesh
have wounds bright with fresh blood:
and there is blood in the sands of Soweto
the ghosts are coming back
past barking police dogs
through shifting veils of smoke
those who oppose oppression are coming back
demanding dignity
challenging injustice
they return to join a new generation
they chant:
resume the fight, resume the fight,
resume the fight

October 2002   2004

June comes round again,
rains soaking Soweto's dust:
here the salvias bleed

June 6, 1989   2005

(156)

Spring
moves me to tenderness
I kiss the first shy blossom
of forsythnia:
"Golden rain" I murmur
remembering
its South African name.

                                                2005

Poem for Vorster's resignation

Crumpled monster Vorster
toppled to a misshapen heap
grotesque gladiator for incubus
race hatred speared by truth
now fallen in the fetid spill
of your own guts and excrement
that was no applause you heard:

that sound roaring
over the mine dumps and debris,
that was the voice of ghettos crying:
Amandla! Amandla!
that was the angry townships roaring
Amandla! Amandla!

June 4, 1979   1982

An old black woman,
suffering,
tells me I have given her
"new images"

—a father bereaved
by radical heroism
finds consolation
in my verse.

then I know
these are those I write for
and my verse works. ←————————

June 20, 1980   2004

Swatches of brassy music
skein through the fug
smoke, liquor, sweat
laughter and erotic undulations
        How shall we forgive them?

Men in the clutch of death
lust
in the last despairing gasp
of their animation
        Why should they need forgiveness?

This night
in the endless light
of Robben Island
the men lie
with lidless eyes
and stare down the glaring corridor of time
with an open coffin at its end
and frantically scrape
at the bare smooth walls of unyielding knowledge
seeking some moss of comfort
some lichen-particle of hope

that shows there will be some change
some hint that freedom will arrive,
break through these walls of life-in-death
life-till-death
    How will they forgive us?

A horror tumuluses in my brain
shoulders thought into incoherence;
oh men, oh managers
how can we dare to fail
how can we dare to choose to fail
    How can we hope they will forgive us?

And after that?
will unforgiveness spoil the pleasant rasp
of the tepid beer we quaff
thirsty after the dance's gyrations?
Being cursed
will we sleep less sound
in the sticky languor of spent limbs
the flesh limply swollen with satiation
will that long billow of sigh
gusting through the prison corridors
disturb our sleeping ears?
will the sparse tears
unwillingly wrung
from contorted faces, mouths, eyes
of men desperately fighting for strength,
control,
will a large hot tear
dropping on concrete
wake us with its soundless splash?
or men mouthing bitter curses
or twisting their racked bodies
to try to minimize some area of the pain,
will these men rise up
to confront us
as our bodies flush and harden
with the slow tidal surge of lust
and make us limp with guilt?
or in the drowsy repletion

of our sexual aftermath
will their wraiths terrorize us
into wakefulness?

Swatches of brassy melody
skein the revelling air
Men under grip of death || ← *lust*
lust for a final lust ||
in insensate assertion
of the guttering, soon-to-be snuffed vital spark

In a gloom of dazzling perennial light
the prisoners yearn
outward
their longing visceral, vulnerable
like an extruded gut or glans

Schemers weave,
oblivious,
devious,
perhaps for unseen, not-to-be-whispered goals
and my protesting anger
storms at my eyes
with hot salt tears

We, not being mobilized
in will,
what can we hope for?
how can we get forgiveness
—if indeed it is sought or needed—?
and what will we achieve?

Somewhere in the mind   ⎤
a stubborn kernel   ⎟
—obligation, perhaps—   ⎬ ←————
stubbornly persists.   ⎟
The mind devises action. ⎦

1978

Today in prison
by tacit agreement
they will sing just one song:
Nkosi Sikekela;
slowly and solemnly
with suppressed passion
and pent up feeling:
the voices strong and steady
but with tears close and sharp
behind the eyes
and the mind ranging
wildly as a strayed bird
seeking some names to settle on
and deeds being done
and those who will do the much
that still needs to be done.

June 26, 1967, South African Freedom Day   1970

?

thunder-heads

Over the thunder-heads of terror we may fly
as now I probe their structure from head to base
from the Thor-hammerhead of their crown
thrashing through their configuration
like a sexually masterful invasion:

and if there is power and grace for this,
then I dare believe there will be ways
to find so great a height and peace
without the thunderclaps and storms
that will burst my land with cataclysmic blood.

1971

Above us, only sky
below, cloud
and below that
cloud;
below that
sea;
land is abolished,
only the sky and air and light
a beatific approximation
achieved.

After this power
this conquest of brute reality
what can we not not do
not abolish?

Peace will come.
We have the power
the hope
the resolution.
Men will go home.

In flight over the Atlantic after leaving South Africa
August 5, 1966   1968

The *New York Times* reports they say they are hurt;
the telex carries news of an Australian decision;
in dorpies and plains in the Free State
the rugby-players writhe, running their hands
over the bruises of defeat in Britain,
West German friends renounce their neo-nazi posture,
a truncated tour mocks them with uncertainties
—everywhere the sportsmen draw in the robes
and withdraw, fearful of contamination,
while the foul ichor oozes from their wounds—
Indeed I flog fresh lashes across these thieves!
And they bleed...

                                                                    1978

Munich poem:
At the time of the Munich Olympics

A disgust nauseous in me
in a foul bulge of bile
here in the vaulted hall
among these lofty walls
with the blue sky, and the spired temple,
and the green woods beyond
through the arched and fretted windows:
nearby is Dachau.
And once long feathers trailed
of greasy and rancid smoke
from the chimneys industriously stoked:
I remember the murders and massacres,
the ovens, the torture, the screams,
and I who have of it all
with a detached observant horror
am suddenly gut-swollen with foulness:
murderers! beasts! I remember you.

August 25, 1972   2004

Sabotage, 1962

Here, thunderheads rear in the night
dominating the awed quiet sky;

on the quiet-breathing plains
fractured metals shriek abandoned wails;

my country, an ignorantly timid bride
winces, tenses for the shattering releasing tide.

                                                        1975

Through the midnight streets of Teheran
with labors waiting for me
labor and unassuagable desire
and loneliness
I spin out my fated web—
old Ahasuerus of unrevealed destiny—
reeling doggedly in the corridors of circumstance
impelled by an impersonally benign *why? who is his audience?*
uncaring supernal omniscience.

Teheran   1970

Prayer

O let me soar on steadfast wing
that those who know me for a pitiable thing
may see me inerasably clear:

grant that their faith that I might hood
some potent thrust to freedom, humanhood
under drab fluff may still be justified.

Protect me from the slightest deviant swoop
to pretty bush or hedgerow lest I droop
ruffled or trifled, snared or power misspent.

Uphold—frustrate me if need be
so that I mould my energy
for that one swift inenarrable soar

hurling myself swordbeaked to lunge
for lodgement in my life's sun-targe—
a land and people just and free.

July 3, 1966   1968

Shakespeare

Shakespeare winged this way using other powers
to wrest from grim rock and a troubled student-lad
an immortality outlasting all our time
and hacking out an image of the human plight
that out-endures all facets of half-truth:

Hamlet

here now we hurtle north-east from the westering sun
that follows, plucks out from afar
the wingstruts crouched and sunlit for a plunge:

O might I be so crouched, so poised, so hewed
to claw some image of my fellows' woe
hacking the hardness of the ice-clad rock,
armed with such passion, dedication, voice
that every cobblestone would rear in wrath
and batter down a prison's wall
and wrench them from the island where they rot.

Flying to Denmark   1970

Response
?

For Canon L. John Collins

Now that we conquer and dominate time
hurtling imperious from the sun's laggard slouch
transcendentally watching the Irish jigsaw
slip astream dumbly under masking cloud,
green England dissolved in history-gray
and fanatic old Yeats made mellow by height,

now that all canons of space-time are dumb
and obey the assertions of resolute will
and an intricate wisdom is machined to leash
ten thousand horses in world-girdling flight,
how shall we question that further power
waits for a leap across gulfs of storm;

that pain will be quiet, the prisoned free,
and wisdom sculpt justice from the world's jagged mass.

En route from London to New York, El Al Airlines
August 5, 1966   1967

Crossing the Atlantic

In London it is dark:
night settles on the city
while the West-End hurls
its garish pyrotechnics
into the ten-o'clock sky.
In Westminster, that place of shame,
spawner of slavery's system,
hoarse-throated still with lust
for Africa's rape,
they plot fresh perfidy,
emerge, smiling,
dripping their festering lies,
but we pursue the sun,
head westwards of the Atlantic,
cross a gray sea soft and rimpled as tripe:
ahead, a saffron sun smolders;
the rim of the sky, edge of cloudbank
bleed an anaemic blood:
but the will, body, spirit surge.

September 24, 1975   1979

Crossing the English coast
returning,
is a synthetic joy;
and synthesized:

the paper-thrillers
of those perennial English wars,
planes limping back to base
after the well-done mission—
wreaking unanalyzable destruction

battered ships
rigging torn and masts askew
salt with long voyaging—
pillage, carronading, slaving—
hove in some quiet fishing village

the sporting hero from the victorious tour
sighting the welcome coastline,
or the fortune-seeker seamed and scarred
returning to the country greenery
the family home half-hidden among trees:

romance and glamor stir—
'faint horns of elfland blowing'
synthetic, synthesized, amalgammed feeling
ringing in a phrase unshaped, unsinging,
that sings unbidden in my sounding head.

1973

In the dove-gray dove-soft dusk
[when the walls softened to frozen smoke]
and their rigidity melted
receding to miles,
when the air was alive and tender
with a mist of spray from the sea,
the air luminous
and the sky bright with the dulling glimmer
of cooling molten lead;
when the island breathed—
trees, grass, stones and sand breathing
quietly at the end of the long hot day—
and the sea was a soft circling presence—
no longer a tight barbed menacing ring:
in the dusk
nothing was more agonizing than to be seized
by the poignant urgent simple desire
simply to stroll in the quiet dusk:
as I do now:
as I do now, and they do not.

1971

I am the tree
creaking in the wind
outside in the night
twisted and stubborn:

I am the sheet
of the twisted tin shack
grating in the wind
in a shrill sad protest:

I am the voice
crying in the night
that cries endlessly
and will not be consoled.

1968

Fry's still sell chocolate
still glean the cocoabean
and the bean still coalesces a swollen gleam—
sweatdrops globed on salt black flesh,
lambent like blooddrops fresh and red

A factory sprawls in acres of verdant park
and the city squats as it anciently did
on its excremental guilt and dominance—
and a ragged refuse dump of spilled, screwed,
   dried, twisted, torn and unforgiven
      black lives.

Bristol   1970

Western exploitation?

Sirens contrail the night air:

Images of prisons around the world,
reports of torture, cries of pain
all strike me on a single sore
all focus on a total wound:

global
[R]

Isle of Shippey, Isle of Wight,
New Zealand and Australia
are places with a single name
—where I am they always are:

I go through the world with a literal scar,
their names are stitched into my flesh,
their mewedupness is my perennial ache,
their voice the texture of my air:

Sirens contrail the London air.

1978

I walk in the English quicksilver dusk
and spread my hands to the soft spring rain
and see the streetlights gild the flowering trees
and the late light breaking through patches of broken cloud
and I think of the Island's desolate dusks
and the swish of the Island's haunting rain
and the desperate frenzy straining our prisoned breasts:
and the men who are still there crouching now
in the gray cells, on the gray floors, stubborn and bowed.

1971

Blue pools of peace
high-basined in the snow-flung Alps—
beyond the cold, sharp and stony ridges,
the stony shouldered ridges:

another day,
another milestone-journey, milestone day,
a sense of expiring years,
of fated cycles, expired chances and lost grace:

and a dogged thrusting-on
to new places, new names and new marks:
so we carve structures,
so we leave striations in the rocks.

Crossing the Alps: London to Rome   1970

In the comparative calm of normalcy
my role is tension. ⟵———
As on this sun-silvered day
the shirt-sleeved leisured float
in a lucent crystal ambience
while strong tides viper through the placid sea.

Dubrovnik   1970

At Manila airport
transit passengers may not
look
at the
sunset:
beyond the glass doors
a man with a gun
orders you
"Inside."

                                                            1978

Here
on another island ⟵——— [R]
within sound of the sea
I watch the moon turn yellow
or a blurred Orion heel

And remember
the men on the island
on strips of matting
on the cold floor
between cold walls
and the long endless night.

Nelson, New Zealand   1970

The sand wet and cool
darkening from yellow
to where it was damp,
from a lioness-yellow
to darkness, like ash
or the shadowy underside of a mushroom

and to lounge in such sand,
by the sea, uncaring
scuffing bare heels in the seasand
with the hard ridge of the heel,
half-calloused, half-feeling the cold cool
in warmgold folds, over silkchill skeins

sexual

and here to thrust out the legs
to feel the jar in thighflesh and flanks
and through this breakthrough of thighs
to find true fuller freedom of loins and thews
a great freedom of the groin—
an unfolding upflowering of the flesh—

hair uncaring of sand, of shellpowder
broken twigs and dirt;
and to feel the keening of the cold
the ghost of the spray, the spume, the salt—
a cold glitter as of crystals and knives
in the brightness and vagrant warmth of the day:

one assents to the brightness of the day,
its perfection and warmth
acquiescing in the cold in its essence
sharp as a shell-blade and menacing
while the shadows grow long and gray and cold,
one accepts the voluptuous splendor of that day

of an imaginary day
and of an untrue innocent idyll
that never happened
and a perfection of sensuality we never knew
but which they created by report

by alleging this was our act and our guilt:

and straightway
by the evocation of their charge
it was real and true;
and we entered into that sensual idyll
that sunlit sensuous voluptuousness
of luxurious indulgence in lush-ripe flesh:

creating truth

we were guilty then
accepting the untrue as the real;
so our pursuers, our enemies
became our donors, generous friends:
one perfect sunlit day was ours:
the forbidden idyll became the real:
we had our beach, our sea, our sun,
the stolen sensuous carnal delight
and the spray-bright, spume-chill, bladed air.

January 19, 1970   1973

A simple lust is all my woe:
the thin thread of agony
that runs through the reins
after the flesh is overspent
in over-taxing acts of love:

only I speak the others' woe:
those congealed in concrete
or rotting in rusted ghetto-shacks;
only I speak their wordless woe,
their unarticulated simple lust.

December 1971   1973

November sunlight silvers my grimy panes,
suffuses the gruel-gray sky
and gleams on the cold woodwork;

such wan luminescence
might as well not be,
lacks all virtue, is devoid of warmth

while Southwards in a steady blaze
like a sheet of molten lead heat pours down
and the world glows, while here I pine.

1970

How are the shoots of affection withered at the root?
What lops the tendrils that reach out
and what blights the tender feeling buds?

All that I dreamed—and doubtless you—
and that we fondly hoped and planned
how was it poisoned and with what?

Blighted withered are the leaves
a foul miasma breathes
and rheumy exudations seep
and a wormwood bitterness surrounds

How are the shoots of affection withered!

1978

The slim girl—grace of early autumn trees
has an individual message too;
scatters of gaudy yellow—gold confetti
amid the febrile glitter of hectic green
confer, deceptively, the festiveness of brides:

thus the consumptive's frantic gaiety
before pneumonia's sudden puncturing,
and thus with an autumnal pang I see
the springing buoyance of my urgent stride
is galvanized by secret rottings at the root.

1978

Inscription for a copy of *Road to Ghana* by Alfred Hutchinson

Well, we have caged our bird
and he has sung for us
as sweet a song as any heard—
time now, we freed our bird.

Skylark or nightingale
who cares beyond delight?
For all birds fly a vagrant trail
and the music cannot stale.

Out of the blue he dips
unearned and unenslaved
to brush with his wing our wondering lips
and break our fingertips.

All life the timeless song
will pierce the crash of life
and if I call my bird for long   *English & European*
"Phoenix" will I do wrong? ←

                                                    1978

Tenement balcony

From here I see the shanties
and the indomitable trees:
and standing on the rubble of a thousand I's
I see these trees and far clear skies.

                                                    1975

Where the statues pose and attitudinize—
even the headless weathered ones—
on the garden terrace, overlooking the landscape,
weariness hangs,

droops over them in their centuries' stance
flap-dragging like limp airless flags—
thread-worn flags, their colors bleared and dim

And I weary with them, from their fourteenth-century stance
and know they do not know the peace I seek:
("The secret," the Greeks said, "was not to be born,"
and: "Call no man happy until he be dead.")
And the deepest attraction of death is its nothingness,
its promise of total unknowingness is bliss—
Then it will be nothing, but the promise is bliss.

To be restful like a potato, this is something
tho' growth or decay make tiresome demands—
birds pecking (eyes, hair, maid's nose) are nothing
are exterior, make no inner demands—
but better by far to be a stone;
blissfully insensible, oblivious, and better than that,
a stone, with totally insensible stoniness:

but to be a statue; this is too much—
up at Frascati villa, among the hills
where the sturdy-footmen olives cling to the hills,
in the splendour of Falconieri among its peers—
Aldobrandini and Mondragon heights;
here, in this opulence, still I shrink back—
to be a stone, not a statue, for this I yearn.

1978

Love; the Struggle

Now the dawn's attack announces:
Light thrusts a thousand salients
To probe our dark's defences;
Limply now the curtains posture
Too unmobile to repulse
The day's outflanking pincers:
Stairs and bathroom creak life's permanent alarms
—Ah Love, unshoulder now my arms!

Now shuttered silk-lids open, shudder
At scar-shadows light brands everyday:
Look long, last, dismiss each other;
Lips sleep-curved in acquiescent parting
Tighten to resolve, farewell:
This is leaving, dying, is departing
Bereft our night, marauded of obliviousness to harms
—Ah Love, unshoulder now my arms!

Our tenuous luke-warmed pool of silence
Time's battery rocks and salvoes
From its niche in circumstance;
Conched, contrapuntal our concord
Day's breath wracks our peace,
Our dreams disrupt in blustery discord
Buckling to winds' capricious buffet we desert our calms
—Ah Love, unshoulder now my arms!

Era, anger summon fairplay
Unardent to the arduous strife
Heart, my dour heart turns from fairness;
Seas confront with seethe and trouble
Cries assail and thongs defy:
I gird from nestling to advance the struggle
A clinic dialectic titrates, dispells our charms
—Ah Love, unshoulder now my arms!

One kiss in turning, last-another,
Here, where spinal vacuum recalls,
Implant your charge before the smother;
From skin milk-soft, milk-mild-tender,
Confiding throat, accepting arm,
Pluck pulsing cadences: now end it.
Stars blear, nightbreaths fust and rasp: a clash, glint, stench of arms!
Unshoulder, Love, unshoulder all my arms!

                                                        1978

This is a land
so vibrant and alive
that laughter will come bursting through
as imperious as the sun

and the spirit will survive
resilient as the soil.

1978

For my sons & daughters

Memory of me will be a process
of conscious and unconscious exorcism;
not to condemn me, you will need
forgetfulness of all my derelictions,
and kindness will be only yours
if you insist on clinging steadfastly
to some few small exaggerated symbols—
"This much he cared," or "Thus he did"
and "If he could, he would have done much more."

This I can understand, for my affection
enables me to penetrate the decades and your minds
and now I seek no mitigation—
would even welcome some few words of scorn;
but it might help if, reading this,
if after adult bitter years,
you are enabled then to say: "He really cared then?"
"Really cared?" "Our fictions have some substance then!"

I will not ask you then to add what I do now:
my loneliness; my failures; my amalgam wish to serve:
my continental sense of sorrow drove me to work
and at times I hoped to shape your better world.

1978

I would not be thought less than a man
in feeling or understanding
and so must balance my revulsion
with its implied offense
to those to whom it is affliction
or fulfillment of a richly personal need,
and so I place on record facts I know
which build a wholly other world—
the hints of tenderness and passion
not blazoned forth as the false and insincere
the genuine concern and anxiousness
between two men whom sexual bonds had linked: *homosexuality*
not all of it was evil it must seem
(we except of course, seduction, outrage, rape)
or some of it had graces that I know not of

                                                            1978

Stubborn hope

Endurance is a passive quality,   *endurance*
transforms nothing, contests nothing
can change no state to something better
and is worthy of no high esteem;
and so it seems to me my own persistence
deserves, if not contempt, impatience.

Yet somewhere lingers the stubborn hope
thus to endure can be a kind of fight,
preserve some value, assert some faith
and even have a kind of worth.

                                                            1977

I come and go
a pilgrim
grubbily unkempt
stubbornly cheerful
defiantly whistling hope
and grubbing for crumbs of success
out of all near-defeats

I shuffle through the waiting rooms
and the air-terminals of the world
imposing and importuning
while the politely courteous
acquaintances
co-operate
help arrange my departures
without any pang of greeting

I work my stubborn difficult unrewarding will
obtusely addleheaded clumsy:
some few things happen
and I plod or shuffle or amble
wracked with anguished frustrate hunger
and go on.

                                                          1978

Here, of the things I mark
I note a recurring hunger for the sun

—but this is not homesickness,
the exile's patriate thirst:

At home, in prison, under house-arrest
the self-same *smagting** bit me

now is the same as then
and here I live as if still there.

*Afrikaans for yearning   1978

Sequence for South Africa

1.

Golden oaks and jacarandas
flowering:
exquisite images
to wrench my heart.

2.

Each day, each hour
is not painful,
exile is not amputation,
there is no bleeding wound
no torn flesh and severed nerves;
the secret is clamping down
holding the lid of awareness tight shut—
sealing in the acrid searing stench
that scalds the eyes,
swallows up the breath
and fixes the brain in a wail—
until some thoughtless questioner
pries the sealed lid loose;

I can exclude awareness of exile *labels*
until someone calls me one.

3.

The agony returns;
after a crisis, delirium,
surcease and aftermath;
my heart knows an exhausted calm,
catharsis brings forgetfulness
but
with recovery, resilience
the agony returns.

4.

At night
to put myself to sleep
I play alphabet games
but something reminds me of you
and I cry out
and am wakened.

5.

I have been bedded
in London and Paris
Amsterdam and Rotterdam,
in Munich and Frankfort
Warsaw and Rome—
and still my heart cries out for home!

6.

Exile
is the reproach
of beauty
in a foreign landscape,
vaguely familiar
because it echoes
remembered beauty.

1975

Tourist Guide
For those "confined to the Magisterial District of X"

Port Elizabeth

This is a settlers town
of cockneys, upstarts, misfits—pioneers!
The parish pump and village gossip
are never very far from sight
and the prim culture of the corsetted
village librarian to whom Shakespeare
is an heirloom—like a cairngorm!
Yet L'Estaque and other drowsy villages
along the mellow urbane Middle Sea
are also part of this blue landscape
and Africa, the native continent,
is present with subdued insistent presence
in the hornied feet of gaunt docklaborers
and in shadows of the township's broken streets
like coffins or the corpses of Good Friday night*

Cape Town

A gateway of civilization, this
(to leave behind you at the gate!)
Siberia once for a Batavian half-repentant thief,
some trappings of humanity
cling to those who tavern here.

The trees assert a dignity and opulence
(saponify the Table's indigestibility)
and summon trills about the "Fairest Cape"
—fairness has another, deathly, pallor here!

Here only is a sense of reconciled senility why?
and traces of uncertain tracks to find
a humaneness to heal the slaver's whip.
And from the admissions of a common man
may yet emerge the clamant fact

of unity, asserted with the crisp
incisiveness of logic or a spear.

Durban

Sturdy British businessmen
made this town (and "Coolies"!)
Light-festoons along the beach
dribble away the nutriment
of glaucous hunger-swollen urchins;
proud men display perverse inverted pride
as carrier-beasts for lording colonialness;
the stairs are occupied by ancient odors
of curry, hospitality and insecurity,
and the image of incited rampage
is cherished like a rusted hunting knife
amid the bustle of rapacity,
uncertain liberals and pink gins.

Johannesburg

Hills and dumps and concrete piles
and ragged areas of untended veld

burrows and tremors pulsing underground
and females and fists in the warrened cliffs

but hints of sky and tree redeem the air
when thunder deluges the fug

and metal in the clank of teeming shacks
tocsins the surgeon's cleansing cleaver.

1963

* Police fired on a Good Friday procession, New Brighton, 1956

Part 3

From National Liberation to Global Justice

.

Forgive me, comrades
if I say something apolitical
and shamefully emotional
but in the dark of night
it is as if my heart is clutched
by a giant iron hand:
"Treachery, treachery" I cry out
thinking of you, comrades
and how you have betrayed
the things we suffered for.

August 23, 2000, 3:05am   2005

The fall of South African apartheid, capped with the 1994 election in which all South Africans could vote, has seen white minority rule banished and Nelson Mandela make the transformation from political prisoner to an elder statesman on a world stage. The rigid racial hierarchy of apartheid has given way to one of the world's most democratic constitutions.

The dismantling of apartheid, however, has not been matched by economic and social transformation. Rather, South Africa has undergone what author and social researcher Patrick Bond calls an "elite transition"—the transfer of top offices in the South African state to the African National Congress, while economic power remains firmly in the hands of major corporations and a nearly all-white minority. South Africa's politicians—most of them veterans of the liberation movement, have in fact spoken out against inequality fostered by the world economy—"global apartheid," in the words of South African President Thabo Mbeki. But the government's economic program conforms to what has been called the "Washington Consensus" of privatization of state-owned industries and public services, free trade and "flexible" labor policies that make it easier to lay off or fire workers. Poverty has actually worsened in the post-apartheid years, and the AIDS pandemic has had grave social and economic consequences.

John Saul, a Canadian academic and a collaborator with the ANC for decades, concluded that in South Africa, "a very large percentage of the population—amongst them many of the most desperately poor in the world—are being sacrificed on the altar of the neoliberal logic of global capitalism....[T]here is absolutely no reason to assume that the vast majority of people in South Africa will find their lives improved by the policies that are now being adopted in their name by the ANC government. Indeed, something *quite the reverse is the far more likely outcome.*"[1]

Dennis Brutus has been at the forefront of those criticizing such policies and organizing resistance to them—a stand that has earned harsh criticism from many of his old comrades. Dividing his time between the U.S. and South Africa in the post-apartheid years, Brutus has worked with a variety of grassroots organizations including Jubilee South Africa, which campaigns for the abolition of South Africa's debt and demands reparations from corporations that profited from apartheid. These campaigns, for Brutus, are part of the larger movement for global justice, which he helped to coalesce. As South Africa was set to hold its first democratic election in 1994, Brutus was helping to launch the 50 Years Is Enough campaign against the International Monetary Fund and World Bank, contending that the international financial institutions in their half-century of existence had used Third World debt to maintain and extend imperialist control by the wealthy nations.

The selections in Part III follow the threads from the anti-apartheid movement into a new phase of activism for the international Left, a movement which gained worldwide attention as a result of protests at meetings of the World Trade Organization in 1999 in Seattle, protests at IMF and World Bank meetings in Washington, D.C. in 2000, followed, in 2001, by mobilizations at the Summit of the Americas in Quebec City, and protests against the Group of Eight Summit in Genoa. Brutus's speeches, documents, and articles included here highlight his role in the movement as an analyst, strategist, and organizer as he approached his 80th birthday in 2004. Also featured is Brutus' support for the Palestinian struggle for liberation and his role in opposition to the U.S. war and occupation in Iraq, views based on the same political principles that informed his role in the South African struggle: the right of self-determination for the oppressed and opposition to imperialism in all its forms.

The poetry in this section crisscrosses several themes converging largely around a preoccupation with the limits of national liberation, and with a sense that the contemporary world situation demands the globalization of specific, local struggles.

L.S. and A.K.

[1] John Saul, *The Next Liberation Struggle* (Toronto: Between the Lines; Scottsville: University of Kwa-Zulu Natal Press; New York: Monthly Review Press; London: The Merlin Press, 2005), p. 195.

Memoir
Apartheid, Neoliberalism, Resistance:
Another World is Possible

W HEN THE apartheid structure collapsed, it did so for about five reasons. Inside the country, labor was the decisive force. When the workers organized, a law was passed to say it was a crime to incite a strike. So people devised other ways—a stayaway, a grandmother's funeral, whatever. But they could paralyze industry. So labor was the most important factor, internally.

The second factor was that the ANC had a small military wing, Umkhonto we Sizwe, headed until 1987 by Joe Slovo of the South African Communist Party. So you had an armed struggle. Third, in the townships, people were willing to break the apartheid laws in a series of mass revolts.

The fourth factor was the international cultural and economic boycotts. Students across the U.S. were crucial to this; about 100 colleges divested some of their funds in companies doing business in South Africa. By mid-1985 the pressure had built up to the point that the banks withdrew lines of credit to the South African government. This forced the P.W. Botha regime to default on $13 billion in debt, close the stock market temporarily, and impose exchange controls.

Along with these combined pressures was the fifth reason: The Soviet Union under Gorbachev was ready to make its deal with the West. So they told the ANC that a military solution was no longer an option, stating "We will not supply you with arms," which were coming from East Germany.

The ANC was ready to capitulate anyway. And the apartheid government was smart enough to enter into negotiations that allowed them to end up with a solution where political power is apparently transferred, but not economic power. De Beers' diamond mines, the gold mines, the banks, all the corporations, remain in the hands of the same people who benefited from apartheid, with a small privileged black elite being able to share that wealth. You have a cosmetic change. The whole process of transition is brilliantly discussed by Patrick Bond in a book called *Elite Transition,* where he shows wealthy whites transferring power to wealthy blacks, giving them a piece of the action.

Mandela came out of Robben Island announcing, "The people are going to own the wealth of the land." Three months later he was meeting with the Chamber of Business saying "We wouldn't dream of nationalizing the coal mines. We wouldn't dream of nationalizing the banks, or the diamond mines." The same man said this. South African business emerged virtually unscathed.

Why did it go that way? This is a very interesting question indeed. Once the apartheid government had capitulated and the ANC government entered into negotiations, the people surrendered all authority to the ANC. There was no demand for accountability. There was no demand to report back what they were negotiating. And these guys were giving away the store, saying, "We are not going to touch this, we are not going to touch that." Later it all came out. There is more to it, of course, than even Mandela making deals from Robben Island and sending a courier to Lusaka to tell the ANC, "Here's what I've decided." But you must remember he comes out of a chieftainly background, and has always had difficulty accepting criticism.

Thabo Mbeki is in fact the heir, the inheritor of the deals that Mandela made. Of course, Mbeki—whom Mandela nominated as his successor only as his second choice—takes it a stage further. Mbeki had been head of the ANC Department of International Affairs, and was a major player in the ANC's negotiations with F.W. de Klerk's apartheid government. As early as 1990, Mbeki had been working on post-apartheid economic policy with Geoff Lamb, an old friend from their student days at Sussex University in Britain in the 1960s, when both had been members of the South African Communist Party. Lamb had been working at the World Bank since 1980. Together he and Mbeki set up what they called World Bank "reconnaissance missions" to cover many sectors of research in South Africa.

The Bank wanted to start making loans to the de Klerk government, but the mass movement stopped that strategy. However, the Bank did play a decisive role during the early 1990s in setting the terms of debate, and began influencing policy in many areas. They even started a new unit at the World Bank, the "Knowledge Bank," for which South Africa became the pilot project.

By 1994, the Bank persuaded Housing Minister (and leading Communist Party member) Joe Slovo to ditch the Reconstruction and Development Program, which had been part of the ANC's 1994 campaign platform. Minister of Water Affairs and Forestry Kader Asmal took the Bank's advice on water a year later, which led to much higher prices for poor people and the beginning of mass water disconnections. The Bank called their role in this policy "instrumental." Then in 1996, Finance Minister Trevor Manuel invited two men from the Bank to coauthor the full-fledged structural adjustment program, called Growth, Employment and Redistribution (GEAR).

In fact, three members of the World Bank staff helped write it. The World Bank was not only delighted to accept GEAR; the minister of finance of South Africa, Trevor Manuel, became the chairman of the board of governors of both the International Monetary Fund (IMF) and the World Bank and later took over the World Bank's development committee. And Steve Biko's partner, Mamphela Ramphele, the mother of his child, became a managing director of the World Bank. The South African trade minister, Alec Erwin, served as "friend of the chair" in the World Trade Organization's (WTO) Doha round of negotiations that began in 2001. This is a new position, with the function of communicating between the chairman of the WTO negotiations and the heads of state in Africa to tell the latter what the chairman wants them to do.

Mbeki made this direction clear the moment he became president. His first meeting was with the union leaders in Congress of South African Trade Unions (COSATU) to discuss GEAR. He threw it down in front of them and said, essentially, "Call me a Thatcherite, I follow Margaret Thatcher. And you want to know about GEAR? It is non-negotiable."

It is in this context that Mbeki was reelected as president in 2004. Notwithstanding his success—the press reported that he won 70 percent of the vote—he in fact won about 56 percent of the *eligi-*

ble vote. Only about 38 percent of the entire voting population voted for the ANC, and at least half the populace that might have voted did not vote. That has to be taken into account. South Africans are profoundly dissatisfied with the failure to deliver on the promises that were made and that have been denied, and voter turnout reflected this. In the white suburbs, the water is spraying the lawns, and the swimming pools are filled up. Drive from there to the ghetto, and there are ramshackle houses. The water's been cut off. There is no water in the homes. It is not a theoretical issue. It is very concrete.

A lot of people have failed to make the connection that when the city councils cut off water, the decisions they are making are really coming from the government, which influences privatization policies. This in turn reflects the influence of the World Bank and the IMF. So the city councils sell off the water to Suez or Vivendi from France or they sell off the electricity to Eskom, the South African state power company due to be privatized. So what used to be a social/municipal service becomes a commodity. You buy it if you have money; if you don't, you can't. Of course there's the whole AIDS failure as well. What you are seeing in South Africa is alarm and dissatisfaction at the failure to deliver, and that dissatisfaction is growing.

Another major problem is that of the landless. Under apartheid black people were driven off the land—their fathers, their grandfathers and their great-grandfathers. They were mainly peasants. They grew corn, had cattle and sheep. Then the white government would come in and say, "this is a black spot" and clear it for white settlers. They would call the police, who would pile the people on trucks, drag them into the bush, and in would come bulldozers to demolish black houses. These landless people are one of the strongest voices in South Africa. And you also have the people who have had their water and electricity cut off.

Against global apartheid: The struggle continues

What I did was to go back to South Africa and put together— as I had done in sports—a combination of what already existed, without attempting to create anything new. The grievances were there, the activists were there. We created the SMI, the Social Movements Indaba, a kind of South African Social Forum. And that was the movement that mobilized against the big World Summit on Sustainable Development in 2002 in Johannesburg, when Mbeki wanted to present to the world a showcase of happy, smiling blacks. He hosted the summit because they were giving him a piece of the action. But he also wanted to sell to the world an image of the wonderful miracle in South Africa.

They had a rally in the stadium, and lied to the people, telling them that Yasser Arafat and Fidel Castro would be there. So they got 5,000 people. But we, on the same day and in the same stadium, organized about two weeks in advance, got 20,000. Because we were the angry ones, the homeless, the jobless. That was a very powerful demonstration—a rejection of the deal that had gone down.

When I speak about these issues internationally, some people are very critical. After one meeting, a woman came up to me in great agitation and said, "You didn't tell the whole story. Africans are so much better off now under the Mbeki government than they were under apartheid." I have to agree with her—partly. So I told her, "It is quite true there are people living in good homes and some of them are black, so I am not denying that some things have improved. Certainly the apartheid statutes are gone. But the structures of apartheid are still there." There are more homeless, more jobless, more teenagers out of school. Increasingly, people's water and electricity are cut off because of privatization. There are massive evictions and people put on the streets because they can't pay rent.

There's a personal story that highlights some of the contradictions of the post-apartheid government, even if it is slightly oblique. In April of 2005 I went to the cemetery in Pretoria, where they were reburying the ashes of someone who had been hanged under apartheid, John Harris, a good friend of mine. John had taken over as chairman of SANROC after I was banned; he was then banned himself. He was hanged for putting a bomb at the main station in Johannesburg. He had phoned the police and told them there was a bomb in the station, set to go off in forty-five minutes, so clear the concourse. The police allowed the bomb to explode, to kill and injure people, because they decided they needed it politically. So nothing was done. A woman was killed and John Harris was hanged. I was already on Robben Island at the time, in solitary confinement. However, because I was Harris's friend, I was interrogated. They thought I knew about it.

At the rededication of Harris's ashes, his sister and wife, now re-married, were there, and we're good friends. The program explained how Harris had been arrested, how the police had ignored his warn-ing, and how he was beaten up before he was hanged. It also said, of course, that Harris was running the South African Non-Racial Olympic Committee, stating, "He became chairman when the previ-ous chairman was banned, arrested and then shot in the stomach while trying to escape from police custody." But there was no men-tion of who that person was. My name was omitted from the pro-gram. My role in anti-apartheid activity is being suppressed, so my name could be left out. But Anne Harris, John Harris's widow, said that she insisted that I be allowed to speak—which I did.

The program was run by the ANC government. The man run-ning it was Mongane Wally Serote, one of those whom I had brought to Texas for the ALA. He's now the CEO of Freedom Park, where Harris is being reburied. But he didn't turn up. He sent a message to apologize that he couldn't be there. Briefly, he was deputy minister of culture. It's one of those little ironic touches.

There was an even more ironic touch, because at the cemetery speaking before me was Albie Sachs, a justice on the Constitutional Court of South Africa, the equivalent of the U.S. Supreme Court. In 1988 the South African secret police set off a bomb in his car that blew his arm off, so he walks around with an empty sleeve.

Sachs and I were reasonably good friends. But it gets very tricky after apartheid, because Albie was a member of the \ (SACP) for a time. At some point in the post-apartheid period, the SACP decided that some of its members would resign and other members should reveal that secretly they had been members all the time when it had not been known—they had been seen as ANC members. So Sachs resigned from the SACP. But, very troublingly, while he was in the SACP, he wrote a think piece—a position paper—that was circu-lated very widely in the party. It argued that in order for South Africa to move forward, all South Africans should forget the past—that there should be no writing about their experiences under apartheid. Surprisingly, it not only became an SACP document—something like a CP edict—but it also became an ANC document. And at the point when it's an ANC document, it's almost like one of the old Stalinist changes in the party line. So at the Harris memorial,

I spoke to Sachs. I told him that I believe his memo, asking people to obliterate their past, has been a blight on South African literature—and what's worse, no publisher will publish South African writers if they write about their past.

Sachs denied to me that he wrote any such memo. He said to me, "Go ahead dig up the old memos, and you'll find I never said it." So I reminded him of one thing: how the African American writer Sterling Plumpp arranged for the two of us to speak at Witwatersand University. At that meeting, Albie Sachs got up and said, effectively, "Dennis Brutus is going to hate me for this, but I am saying that South African writers must forget their past." When I reminded him of this at the Harris ceremony, he said, "Yes, I remember that." Obviously, he can't deny it—it's a very vivid memory.

What's more, the ANC, which used to fund young writers, now says, "Well, you know, you're in a free country. We were helping you when you were in the underground, but now you don't need anything from us." Here's the terrifying thing: When there was an attempt to revive the writers' organization, Congress of South African Writers, thirteen writers sent a letter to the press saying we see no need for a writers' organization. So when the ANC says there's no need anymore for a writers' organization, they literally are killing off the organization. There's no money for it, and there are no critical voices.

From global justice to socialism

Today I can see a steady growth of opposition in South Africa—not just to GEAR, but to neoliberalism, the whole concept of Western corporate globalization. It's now linking up with the global struggle. That is the reason that we will win. We will win because we are now building global movements. It is people applying pressure—first locally on their governments, then globally. So I am optimistic that we are on the right track. I think the World Social Forum and what it stands for is one of the most hopeful things of our time. That is why I spend a lot of time with it. There are the dangers of co-optation, of course. There are rumors that the South African government wanted to host the World Social Forum in 2007. We in the Social Movements Indaba said that if that happens, we will be outside in the streets, protesting.

There is a debate about the direction of the World Social Forum among the activists, as well. If we follow Arundhati Roy's ideas, it would become more of a cultural event and take place every four years like the Olympics. There would be the possibility of a much stronger cultural stream. But I am opposed to it, because I think the strongest stream should be the political one, and I think it should happen every year. We are now settling for every two years, unfortunately. So in 2006 there will be regional social forums in Bamako, Mali; and Caracas, Venezuela. The World Social Forum will be in Nairobi, Kenya in 2007. There is a lot of potential there.

In this context we need to talk about socialism. In South Africa, it is still so alive for the people in the ghetto. They still talk about it, still say, "This is what we want. This is what we said we wanted under apartheid, and we still want it." In another climate, in another suburb, people would be afraid to say it. But in the ghetto, people have not given up on it. Consider Cape Town, where parliament sits. The politicians are riding in Mercedes limousines with chauffeurs, and they are so comfortable. This is the same city where one-third of the population lives in slums—which are called townships, but what are really ghettos. The people are lighting tires in the streets to keep the cops from coming in. They're mad at the cops, because the cops will come in and support the guys who want to turn off the water, because of privatization. These people are really resisting the establishment, and trying to force their will on it. What's amazing is that when you are with the people in the townships who have the memory of struggle, and who are currently engaged in struggle, it suddenly revives your own connection with it. Because they've never lost their connection with it.

South Africa, of course, isn't the only example in recent years where activism has actually propelled a comparatively radical or liberal government into office, coming in on the backs of workers' struggle. When they get into power and make deals, the question is, "Were they pushed or did they jump?" Because some of them are willing to be corrupted, and others are forced by the stranglehold which the IMF and the World Bank have over them. These institutions can cut off governments from access to markets and all that. That is why we have to switch to a broad-front attack. No one country can win against the international financial institutions. That requires a broad counterattack—and that's what's happening. But how do we ensure that, having won a comparative victory, we don't lose the fruits of that victory?

We really must develop a complete shift and put forward alternatives to the crisis—on paper at least. One can go even further than that and say that what we really need is a reversal of values. The central reversal is from private property to socialized property. What we eventually have to have is a blueprint in detail. That is when it becomes persuasive. On the one hand, what you have today is a system that is corrupt and destructive; on the other hand you have what is sane and logical, an equitable society. When you get into that, you can head off failure.

I believe that we can achieve a new kind of world—that another world is possible, as the World Social Forum theme puts it. This will not be accomplished through armed struggle, but in fact through Gandhian principles that are more likely to be transformative. We must be willing to challenge injustice, even if it means withstanding the brutality of the cops, getting beat on the head, and gassed. We have to say, "Go ahead, we're not going to quit."

The elements are there. People are saying, "This society is all screwed up. We can't allow it anymore. It has become intolerable. Let's just get enough of us together and we'll change things." On February 15, 2003, the day of the international protest against the war in Iraq, you could see this Gandhian moment in action. Millions of people on five continents were saying, "We don't want war—we want peace."

We have to go for far more. But it is a beginning.

Documents

South Africa: Transition to freedom?

Speech in Denver, Colorado, November 19, 1993

I will focus on our topic, which is the Transitional Executive Council (TEC), and lead from that to the later development, the agreement to sign a constitution which will be a provisional constitution and under which elections will take place on April 27, 1994, and thereafter we will have an interim government for a period of five years until 1999. During that period the final constitution will be drafted. So that's broadly the area of discussion, and that will be the heart of my presentation. But it seemed to me I should mention a couple of things by way of preface to that and also attempt in conclusion to indicate the possible scenarios, what is likely to happen beyond the election in 1994 and of course in the interim period as well. I will try not to be dogmatic and say absolutely that this is what will happen, but instead outline a couple of possibilities.

It seems to me in order to do that we do have to say something about what has gone before and examine a little more precisely what is happening at present and then move from that into the future. I'm delighted to notice that right here in this church and in other churches across the country, movements are being made and organizations are being set up to cooperate with the organizations in South Africa which are attempting to create a new democratic society. So it seems important to stress that people in the U.S. have a role to play in building a democratic South Africa just as people in the U.S. had a role in the past and assisted in the dismantling of the apartheid structure. I think it's worthwhile pausing just for a moment to re-mind you that probably the final nail in the coffin of the apartheid system, which led to the process of negotiation, was an act of Con-gress in 1986 called the Comprehensive Anti-Apartheid Sanctions Act, which stopped investment in and loans to South Africa, and those corporations that were already in South Africa were not per-mitted to increase their investment in South Africa. There are three decisive elements to that act, and they're all important. But more im-portant is to understand how that act came into existence.

It came into existence when Congress found it could no longer ignore the people of the U.S. who demanded that action in very par-ticular ways. It started first of all as essentially a student movement that said, "We don't want our universities investing in and profiting from racism." There were student marches and demonstrations and sit-ins all across this country. Out of those protests came a second wave of protests which were taken up by the trade unions, the churches, black community organizations, the Women's Interna-tional League for Peace and Freedom, the American Friends Service Committee, all of these got in. We built up such a snowball, which grew into an avalanche, that the point was reached where Congress could no longer ignore the demand of the American people.

It seems to me there's a very important lesson to be learned from those facts. One, never underestimate our capacity to influ-ence events. Never take the students too lightly. Students have very often been the spearhead of the struggle in this and in other coun-tries. And the final lesson is to recognize that the power that we had in the past to make things happen we still have. Sometimes we feel, particularly in the so-called new world economic order, now that we are told that there is only one superpower, we begin to feel help-less, as though maybe the way things are going there's nothing we can do to change them. That is not true. Just as we won in the past, we can win again. But if we win, it will be because we put people power together. The South African case is a good example to prove that. I was involved in that process, in South Africa, in organizing in various fields, against racism in education, racism in housing, in jobs, working with the PTAs, the parents in the schools in the town-ships and the ghettos. When the law was passed called the Group Areas Act, so that blacks were forced out of the city, and if they refused to move, steamrollers and bulldozers would come in. People would watch their houses being flattened, even while they stood there. One of the protests I was involved in was organizing that.

But above all, it was challenging the apartheid system in sports, keeping black athletes off the Olympic team, because, as they said in Parliament, "We do not select our teams on merit. We select our teams on race. If you're not white, you don't get on the team." It was as simple as that. Organizing against that brought me to Robben Island. I escaped and was recaptured twice, so I clearly wasn't very good at escaping. On the second occasion it got to be very serious because I was shot in the back by a member of the secret police on the main street of Johannesburg at such close range that the bullet entered my back and came out of my chest, went straight through me as I was running. So I went to Robben Island, where I broke stones with people like Walter Sisulu and Nelson Mandela. So for me, it has been a long struggle. Last year and eighteen months ago I was able to go back to South Africa as a visitor to see Nelson Mandela and Walter Sisulu. I went to a birthday party where about seventy of the people at the party had been in prison with me on Robben Island and we had broken stones together. So it was a great reunion. I mention that by way of background before we plunge into our subject, which has two elements: The creation of the Transitional Executive Council and then the signatures to the new interim or provisional constitution. To do that, however, we need a little more background, although these may be things you are familiar with already.

The state we call the Union of South Africa came into existence in 1910 and became the Republic of South Africa in 1961 by a referendum in which, of course, only white South Africans could vote. Black South Africans have been excluded from the electoral process for over three hundred years. That's why April 1994 is so important. It will be the first time ever that black South Africans are able to participate in the electoral process. There were small variations, at one time in the Cape, for instance, blacks were briefly allowed to vote in the early days of the Union. But over the years instead of rights being increased, they were decreased and diminished. Eventually you have a society ruled by a white minority of under five million in a population where the total now is roughly thirty-six million. All political power is in the hands of the white minority, with the assistance, sadly, of a small section of the oppressed who have agreed to collaborate in the process of their own oppression. I'll come back to that because when we talk about scenarios we have to recognize that that problem still exists.

As I mentioned earlier, 1986 was an important year, after the passing of legislation in this country calling for and indeed enforcing sanctions. The pressures grew on the apartheid system, the system of minority government, minority privilege. South Africa became isolated, in sports, in culture, and eventually, most seriously, in the world of trade. Economic pressures were put on the country. So we go to the stage where the minority white government agrees to begin negotiations to discuss the future. It's very important to notice that when they talk of the future there are two different viewpoints on what was going to happen. While the African National Congress and the liberation movement as a whole talked about the transfer of power, the apartheid regime in Pretoria talked about power-sharing. There was an important difference. In a sense, the debate subsequently has been about the nature of the relationship. It reaches a new stage after 1986, when in 1989 some of the people on Robben Island were released from prison, where they had been imprisoned for their opposition to apartheid, their opposition leading the struggle. There was a wide spectrum there. The people who broke stones with me were from the ANC, but they were also from the PAC (Pan-Africanist Congress), the Unity Movement, they were colored, Asians, Africans, all there. Except no white prisoners, of course. The white opponents of apartheid were kept in their own prison in Pretoria. Even in prison we had apartheid.

In 1990, after the release of Sisulu and others in 1989, Nelson Mandela was released, in February. There was great jubilation at that time, some of it, I thought, ill timed. I remember being on television with Bryant Gumbel on one of the networks and he was saying, "Why aren't you cheering because South Africa is free?" I said, Not yet. Nelson Mandela is out of prison, but he is not yet a free man. He will be a free man the day he can vote. As you know, even now Nelson Mandela cannot vote. So in fact the mere release of political prisoners was only one stage in the struggle. Indeed, the more difficult stages were ahead. The stages of now negotiating some arrangement between the roughly three million minority and the thirty million majority. That is the process we're into now.

In order to arrive at the next stage, one of the things we have to do, and there are many stages I'm omitting because I don't have enough time to spend on the background, one was the need to create a body which could oversee change, to make sure that there was not a great deal of cheating and skullduggery and deception. This is where a body is created which exists alongside the government and which is called the Transitional Executive Council. Its function is to oversee this transitional process. The transitional process, of course, starts from now up to April and is governed by the provisional constitution, which is now being drafted and has been signed. But in this process of conducting the elections themselves and leading up to the elections, there are enormous possibilities for deception, for cheating. That is why one needs an additional body. You can't trust the apartheid government, which after all has been running South Africa since 1948 pretty much at the point of a gun, with thousands in jail and people being killed in the ghettos, in the townships, all over. Therefore, one needed this transitional body, which, to some degree, at least, is not tainted in the way that the apartheid government is tainted. It is not an entirely clean body, not entirely impartial. It is composed of representatives of the apartheid government plus the organizations which were created by the apartheid government, including what are called the bantustans, these little black satellite states which were created by the apartheid government, plus, of course, the African National Congress as the leading liberation movement, but also the Pan-Africanist Congress, and the white organizations which are most committed to the preservation of apartheid and who are in there to make sure that not the whole of the apartheid store is given away. They're still in there looking after their interests. They too are part of this TEC, the Transitional Executive Council.

But the most important function of this body, and it is a function in which people of the U.S. will be involved as well, is to make sure that when the elections actually take place and people go to the polling booths and cast their votes for whichever party they wish to vote for, that they are not intimidated, that they are not threatened, not bribed. We have heard of these things happening in New Jersey and other places. The importance is to make sure that these elections are free and fair. There have been elections in other places, for instance, the last time they tried to have elections in Haiti, people came with machine guns and shot people down as they were going to the polling booth. So that you have the danger of real violence, as distinct from mere cheating or stuffing the ballot boxes. There are very serious problems. That's why in that phase its going to be very important to make sure that there is no intimidation, no cheating. This is where impartial observers and pollwatchers from other countries will be welcome. They can assist in making sure that the elections are indeed fair. So again, people in the U.S. may participate.

But there is one element of this process which is not being fully discussed, and that's the one I want to address. Let me lead in by making one other comment. Because there are twenty million people in South Africa who have never voted in an election, one of the things that we need to do is to instruct people in that very simple process. If you are unfamiliar with it, then of course it becomes very difficult. I'll give you one simple example of how it can be misunderstood.

There are already people in South Africa who are saying, "If you don't like the apartheid government, you must vote against them. And the way to vote against them is to make an X. That's the way to show you don't like them." So you can see how very easily people can be deceived. That is why it is necessary for people to be instructed. I should add a cautionary footnote here: You can go into South Africa and do one of three things. You can teach people how to vote for the ANC, the PAC, or whatever the other parties are, you can instruct them how to vote for apartheid and the Volksfront and the AWB, Afrikaner Weerstand Beweging, the armed white resistance against change. But when you do that you must understand very clearly that you are taking sides in the electoral process. It seems there is a third option, and a very important one, that people should be instructed in what the nature of the procedure is so that they follow the correct procedure, but not attempt to tell them how they should vote. Once you get involved in this process by taking sides, you'll find yourself supportive of the one side, but also very seriously confronted by people on another side who see you as an enemy and not an ally. For me what is essential is that people be instructed in the procedure. If you're coming from outside and you claim to be neutral, it seems to me that you ought to have that neutral position. That by way of putting it aside.

Now to the main problem in my mind. It takes us back to the issue of [whether] we are talking of power sharing or we are talking of power transfer. What apparently is happening, and I have not seen the exact text of the constitution, but two of the things that have already been reported, one is there is likely to be a president elected by the party which wins the most seats, gets the most votes, and even that will be ambiguous because it will not be as it is here or in Britain, but based on proportional representation, rather than a kind of winner-take-all representation. There will be a president and probably two deputy- or vice presidents, one of whom, it seems, is going to be Mr. de Klerk, and that may be part of the question that rises. Three, there will be something similar to the present structure of the country as it is now, with provision for the preservation of the bantustans which were created under the apartheid system, except that they will be referred to as regional governments. But in a sense you're likely to have something very close to a federal structure as you have in the U.S., with state governments plus your central government in Washington, Congress. Around that issue arises the problem, and some of you may have seen the maps in the *New York Times* this week which indicate that the constitution is going to be structured around the regional structures, nine or ten of those. Natal will become Natal-KwaZulu, and the Cape will be divided into an Eastern Cape, a Western Cape, and a Northeastern Cape. And so on.

Arising from that comes a new problem. There are parts of the country which insist that there should be great regional power and weak central power, and therefore that laws could be made in the regional governments which could be either in contradiction to or resistant of [the central government]. You may remember the old days in the U.S. when there was a great debate about states' rights, with people like Lester Maddox and all the others who refused to accept the desegregation orders coming out of the Supreme Court and argued on the doctrine of interposition, that they could interfere.

These are some of the problems we have in South Africa, this question of regional divisions, the question of the power of the regions vs. the center, and more seriously, from extreme white elements in the society, you get the demand for the creation of a specifically all-white state. So that you may end up with an enclave that is really not so very different from the old apartheid structures, but now being sanctioned by a new constitution. Simultaneously, while we're getting this demand from a section of the white population, we're also getting a similar demand from a section of the black population. Some of you are familiar with the claims of a man named Gatsha Buthelezi, who claims to represent the Zulu nation and who claims to have the right to create a Zulu state. What's important to remember here is that Buthelezi is the man chosen by the apartheid government to head up the so-called Zulu nation. He does not in fact represent the Zulu nation. There are many Zulus who are opposed to Buthelezi and his Inkatha. There are many Zulus in other organizations, and indeed, the past president of the African National Congress who won the Nobel Peace Prize, Chief Albert Luthuli, was a Zulu from Natal. One of the top advisers at the present time of the ANC economic planning unit is Professor Magubani, who taught at the University of Connecticut, Storrs, and who is a Zulu. The first thing we must be clear about is that a) Buthelezi does not represent all the Zulu people, b) you have to be aware that he is the creation of the apartheid system. And we have the facts to prove it. When Buthelezi had to organize a rally to demonstrate how many people supported him, the government supported the empty school buses, which went into the villages in the rural areas and brought people into Durban to have this great rally. We have seen the receipts. We know that the money that paid for those busses came out of the South African Defense Force, the army. They have propped this man up. But you will still read about him frequently in the U.S. media as someone who represents the Zulu nation. In fact, he gets five million rand a year to run the so-called KwaZulu. If de Klerk were serious about ending the existence of the bantustans, all he would have to do is to cut that subsidy. Five million rand, which is about $3 million, a year to run this little artificial state called KwaZulu. But because Buthelezi is the creation of the apartheid system, he is as much interested in the preservation of the old system of control with now the added advantage that he has your far right, the reactionary white South Africans, now in alliance with your reactionary black South Africans. This presents a very serious problem for this run up to the electoral process.

When the constitution was signed, the white far right walked out. They announced that they were calling on their followers to start arming themselves. Buthelezi took his group and they walked out. He then made a statement saying he was going to make it his business to smash the election. It would not take place. Clearly, you have two very powerful pressures working against the electoral process. So we come into the question of scenarios.

What is likely to happen? I think there are two elements to that question. The first one is, will the elections take place at all? The second one is, if indeed there are elections and if there are victories, what will those victories be? What will be the content of the new program for the new society? That is by far the more difficult question to answer.

It seems that we must anticipate, unfortunately, and I say it with profound regret, an escalation of violence from now until April. Between February 11 of 1990, when Nelson Mandela was released, up to July of this year, 10,000 people have been killed in political violence. Some of it came from the apartheid government and its army, its hit squads, its secret police. Some of it came from Buthelezi and Inkatha. Some of it came from areas of the ANC organization where they reacted to attacks on them. But there is a real power struggle. You will still read in the papers about "black-on-black violence." We will hear about tribal violence, ethnic violence, Zulus killing Xhosas and Xhosas killing Zulus. In fact, it will have nothing to do with tribalism. It will be a power struggle between those who are interested in preserving some of the remnants of apartheid, so they don't have to give up all their power. Those who want to preserve the remnants of apartheid are white, but also black. Those blacks like Buthelezi who benefited from apartheid are anxious to see some of it retained, and indeed, they'd like to see their own apartheid enclaves, those satellite or client sectors being kept. So my fear is, and I'd like to believe and will be delighted if it turns out that I am wrong. But what we must anticipate between now and April is in fact an escalation of violence. One possibility is that in fact that escalation may be so great that the election may not take place. It may in fact be impossible to conduct it. Again, I hope that this is not true. I hope that the elections can be held.

If they are held, we will still have to ask, what is it that was won, and who won it? And how much power will they have? At least one possibility is that while the ANC may win, particularly now that the African National Congress has agreed to form a single slate of ANC members plus members of COSATU, which is the most powerful trade union body in the country, and the South African Communist Party. Because they were allies in the struggle, they will have a single platform, a single program, and a single list of candidates. At least, that is the position at present. They may win. They may even win a majority. De Klerk expects them to win a majority, but he expects that majority to be so small that he and his allies in that Parliament will be strong enough to block any significant political change. Any significant legislation can be halted because they have built into the constitution, and this troubles me a great deal, that you can only win a decision by a vote if you have 75 percent of the vote.

As we saw with NAFTA this week, if you get one more than half you win. In South Africa it's going to require a 75 percent majority to get legislation passed. That means that if the ANC does not have that majority, if it has 74 percent, 73, it will be unable to get that legislation passed. Therefore, already there is built into the structure a blocking mechanism which will mean that in South Africa if change comes it comes very slowly and only with the permission of those who are opposed to change. You can only get change when they cease to oppose it.

These are some of the very serious problems that arise. There is one other that I have to face, and I do so reluctantly, but I think it's one of the possibilities on the horizon. You have to recognize it in any scenario. Black South Africa from 1912, when the ANC was formed, to 1960, when people were shot down in the streets of Sharpeville, 1976 when students were killed in the streets of Soweto, to 1989, when people were machine-gunned in the ghettos of Sebokeng and Boipatong and other places. They have given their lives in a struggle to be free. They have given their lives in a struggle to become full human beings with the full dignity of human beings like anybody else in the world. If now the content of the victory turns out to be such that it does not give them what they have fought for and died for and what they had hoped they were going to achieve, if it turns out that they are getting less than they had struggled for, you may find a new wave of struggle emerging by those who say, "This is not what we fought for. This is not what we expected." And, I have to tell you, among the young of the country, those who are homeless, jobless, without education, without training, who are looking forward to a new South Africa in which somehow all their expectations are going to be fulfilled, for those people to have their expectations frustrated is to create a new a powerful anger in the country. So for those who conduct the election and fight and win the election, there will be a very heavy responsibility on them to achieve that new democratic South Africa.

Again, I say it's helpful to know of these possibilities, and I say again that people in the U.S. can be helpful to us in the struggle in South Africa. One of the ways, as I've pointed out earlier, is by participating, being a pollwatcher, going over and being an instructor. But there is a more serious obligation that rests on all of us, whether we go there or whether we stay. That is to look at the situation very closely and honestly and critically. If we can see from this end a retreat from the goals and the objectives that were set out in the future or in the past as a promise for the future, I believe we have an obligation to speak out, to say, I see what's going on and I'm pleased, or, I see what's going on and I'm displeased. We want solidarity, but I believe the best service you can give to us is critical solidarity.

They had a phrase in France in the days of the struggle over there. They talked of "les trahisons des clercs," the treason of the academics. I use it when I speak at the universities. I say, if you see something is wrong, don't be polite. Don't be nice to us. If you think something is going wrong you have an obligation to give us your solidarity, but it has to be critical solidarity. No betrayal of the cause, the goals that we fought for, struggled for, some of us have died for. We must go forward, but to a genuine democracy, not a cosmetic one which will please the corporations so they can say, "Well, it looks like they got a democracy over there. Is it a real one? We don't care. Where is the money? Still in the hands of a minority. Where is the political power? Still in the hands of a minority." That would satisfy the West. It cannot satisfy those of us who are committed to true freedom, true dignity.

I must stop at this point to give you time for questions.

The question is, What are the provisions for security, and I take it you mean both in terms of the TEC and the constitution, or are you thinking specifically of the TEC? The two really overlap, so let me address both of them. Very interesting situation. One, you will have your observers, of course, to make sure there's no cheating, but two, you will have both the military and the police available for protection, security, whatever. That's fairly straightforward. But the liberation forces of the ANC, called Umkhonto we Sizwe, the spear of the nation, are to be incorporated into the South African army. That's point one. Point two, they are already conducting joint exercises, the South African Defense Force (SADF), and Umkhonto we Sizwe, and point three, they have already jointly come to the U.S. for training. Members of Umkhonto we Sizwe and the SADF are now being incorporated into a single military force. There was an occasion on the East Coast where two speakers arrived on campus, one from the SADF and one from Umkhonto we Sizwe, and they were both going to address a student audience. But the protest was so strong that the meeting was cancelled. But what we have here is a very interesting development. Nelson Mandela made a statement yesterday, saying that, "Any talk of civil war will not be tolerated." This is very instructive. The South African army and the ANC army are now going to run the show and they won't allow any dissidence. It sounds like a strange echo coming from the West Bank, where Yasser Arafat has said that he and the PLO will deal with any dissidents from now on. The Mossad and the Israeli army won't have to do it, but the PLO will do it.

So you have a very curious situation there, and for some people a very troubling one.

[There was] a question about how to ensure that there is fairness in terms simply of accessibility. At least two things have been agreed on: there will be no polling booths in police stations. There was a time when that happened in the South. It was a way to discourage blacks from voting in this country. But they may be in

churches, in schools, in post offices. As of now, the general agree-
ment is to make sure [voting] is accessible. The second part of your
question is, what about the rural areas, where often there is no
transport, no busses? People have to walk miles. I believe many
people will walk miles. But there is going to be an attempt to pro-
vide transport for them. That in itself becomes a difficult issue.
Buthelezi has, for instance, said that there are parts of KwaZulu
that are no-go areas. Either you vote for him or you vote for no-
body. All the busses that come in can only come in with his permis-
sion. That takes us back to the question of security. It's going to be
important to make sure that you have a strong force in place to
make sure that the intimidation and all kinds of hostility are re-
moved so that people can vote freely. It is being addressed at the
present time.

I'm glad to have that question on alternative ideologies, philoso-
phies for South Africa. What is the way forward? And particularly,
how does one avoid getting South Africa's future hijacked or mort-
gaged to the IMF and the World Bank? That problem becomes even
more acute now that President Clinton has announced that he wants
to extend the free trade agreement all the way down to South Amer-
ica. George Bush or his speechwriter has come up with a phrase that
they will have a free market economy from the Arctic Circle to the
Antarctic Circle. In that context, which is really a global problem, the
South African problem becomes even more acute. It is compounded
by the fact that both Mr. de Klerk and Mr. Mandela have already
met with the World Bank and the IMF and already have commit-
ments from the World Bank of something like $280 million. If you
put that money into South Africa, but put it in the hands of the same
old corporations and the banking interests and mining interests who
ran the country in the past, all you're doing is making them bigger
and stronger, to go on exploiting and oppressing. You will have your
wages depressed, people getting slave wages, and both the ANC and
de Klerk have made this promise to the corporations. If you come in
your profits will not be interfered with. You can ship them back to
wherever you are based. That's part of our problem.

So to go very rapidly beyond that, it seems that South Africa is
going to be caught in the whole global process of the extension of
capital internationally and globally. The creation now of suprana-

tional economic structures which don't even take orders from the government where they are based, they just transcend those boundaries, what can we do? It does seem to me that the people of the world who are the victims of this process had better get their act together. It is time for us to mobilize resistance as much as oppression is mobilized against us. One of the alternatives is that in our time the notion of democracy as we've used the term up to now has been thoroughly discredited. Democracy serves the interests of the small, monied few, the privileged ones. Therefore we must look very seriously at alternatives that share the wealth of the country instead of concentrating it in the hands of the few. This, of course, is to look at socialism as an alternative to bourgeois Western democracy.

...I'll just repeat [the position of the IMF] quickly. The IMF tends to dictate to a country what its economy should do. When they make a loan they also dictate the conditions of the loan and exercise significant control. In Zimbabwe, for instance, they told the President, Robert Mugabe, you have to stop growing corn. From now on you have to grow tobacco. You can't eat tobacco. When people are hungry they now have to import food from South Africa. In the meantime Zimbabwean tobacco is being bought by the U.S. and sold to China, labeled "produce of the United States." So you get this whole vicious process going on. How does one resist it? You're quite right in pointing out that the position of the ANC, of Chris Hani,[1] of the Freedom Charter, is not to accept that kind of control. Whether the ANC may now retreat from its position is one of those things that must trouble us. I don't want to paint too bleak a picture, but I have to point out that in South Africa already people are talking of something that they call a rationalization process. The first thing, you have to fire a lot of people. Secondly, you have to devalue your currency. Thirdly, you have to depress wages. All these are dictated as conditions of the loan. This is being talked about in South Africa now by serious economists who are planning to run the country and are already talking of this rationalization process, which I think should trouble us.

I thought we might finish with me reading a bit of poetry. It was written after Mandela came out of Robben Island. I remember the days we were there breaking stones together in the white sea sands of the island. I'm also saying to him, the struggle is not over.

There are still difficult times ahead, crevices of deception and racism and deceit, but I express my appreciation for this wonderful, courageous man. That's what the poem is about.[2]

> Yes, Mandela—
> some of us admit embarrassedly
> we wept to see you step free
> so erectly, so elegantly
> shrug off the prisoned years
> a blanket cobwebbed of pain and grime:
> behind: the island's seasand,
> harsh, white and treacherous
> ahead: jagged rocks and krantzes
> bladed crevices of racism and deceit.
> In the salt island air
> you swung your hammer, grimly stoic
> facing the dim path of interminable years.
> Now, vision blurred with tears
> we see you step out to our salutes
> bearing our burden of hopes and fears
> and impress your radiance
> on the gray morning air.

Thank you.

[1] Chris Hani, a leader of the South African Communist Party, was assassinated in April 1993.

[2] First published under the title, "February 1990," in the collection *Still the Sirens*.

Martin Luther King Day:
Globalize the struggle for justice
Speech to the National Conference of Christians and Jews, Trinity Church, Pittsburgh, January 17, 1994

I am not going to attempt to say what I think Dr. Martin Luther King would have said on this occasion. I regard that as presumptuous. Instead, I will remind you of one or two of the things he said which seem to me to be of continuing relevance—things which perhaps can serve to inspire us in our own day-to-day experience and struggle. I also remind you that Dr. King understood very clearly that when you speak truth to power—when you address the problems of society in your time—you cannot expect to be popular with everybody. Indeed it may be that your function is to be not only prophetic, but challenging, and to compel people to reexamine their lives and their behavior.

One of Dr. King's most important documents, as I am sure you are aware, is a great, thoughtful letter he sent when he was in the Birmingham jail. We all know it as the *Letter from Birmingham Jail.* What we sometimes forget is that that letter was addressed to the clergy—to the heads of the religious institutions in Atlanta and elsewhere who had criticized him. Who had said that he was bringing dishonor to the church and to Christianity. It was in defense of his actions that he wrote that famous letter from Birmingham jail. He knew what it was to be unpopular. He knew what it was to speak out against the establishment. And he knew it was his duty to speak out about contemporary issues.

I am going to follow Dr. King at least in that respect, and part of my comments will be directed to the specific problems I see confronting us at the present time. Here, in the city of Pittsburgh, in the state of Pennsylvania, across the United States, there are problems that have become global in their dimensions, and will require a global response. And so I will address those as well.

But let me remind you first of Dr. King's words and our struggle for freedom. He said:

> When we allow freedom to ring, when we let it ring from every village and hamlet, from every state and city, we will be able to speed up that day when all of God's children, black men, black women, white men, white women, Jews and Gentiles, Catholics and Protestants will be able to join hands and to sing in the words of the old Negro spiritual, "Free at last, free at last. Thank God Almighty, we are free at last."[1]

If I may add a footnote to that, it seems to me that in our time, very often, we tend to think of those words as if they have become a reality. The truth of the matter is they have not. And Dr. King did not claim that they were a reality. He talked about *when* we are free, *when* we will be able to sing. He did not say we can now. He said the day must come, and that we must work for that day to come. I give you one other quote from Dr. King just as a kind of dig—to remind you of his own role, and of the role he expected us to play. He said: "Yes, if you want to call me a drum major, go ahead. If you want to say I am a drum major, fine. But say I was a drum major for justice. Say that I was a drum major for peace. I was a drum major for righteousness."

That is what his struggle was about. He was not afraid or ashamed to admit that he was willing to engage in a powerful and militant struggle in the cause of justice. It is true that he was inspired by the ideas of nonviolence, ideas that he had acquired in part from American thinkers like Thoreau, but also Indian thinkers like Mahatma Gandhi, who spent time in a prison in South Africa developing the notion of a soul force, of satyagraha, of an ability to change the world by one's own moral strength, one's own moral conviction. Gandhi was in the same prison in Johannesburg, incidentally, where I spent part of my time as a political prisoner in South Africa. Perhaps you will permit me just a moment or two of personal reminiscence here, specifically in relation to Dr. Martin Luther King. I mention just three issues here which may be of interest to you.

In South Africa in the 1950s and in the 1960s we developed a powerful movement for an international cultural, economic, political and sporting boycott, because of South Africa's policy of racism, which Dr. King denounced.

As part of our international protest, starting from South Africa and launched out across the world, we were able to get Dr. Martin Luther King to sign an international declaration against apartheid—against racism and racial oppression in South Africa. I was partly responsible for organizing that contact, and corresponded with him on this subject and drafted the particular document. Years later, after I had come out of Robben Island prison where I had spent time breaking rocks with people like Nelson Mandela, Walter Sisulu and Govan Mbeki—I went into exile, first in Britain and then to the United States. I worked in London at St. Paul's Cathedral, organizing a fund for political prisoners and refugees, and in the course of that, I wrote to Dr. King in Atlanta, inviting him to speak at St. Paul's, where we launched an international appeal for South African political prisoners.

Dr. King made one other, and rather daring, statement when he talked about South Africa and racism and apartheid. He looked not only at the problem and its manifestations; he also looked at the roots of the problem. He looked at it at a time when it was not very popular to do so—and this is what he said. The tragedy of South Africa is not simply in its own policy. It is the fact that the racist government of South Africa is virtually made possible by the economic policies of the United States and Great Britain, two countries which profess to be the moral bastions of the Western world. You can see Dr. King was tying the South African problem intimately to the behavior of governments in Britain and the United States. It was not a popular thing to say. But it was true—and he dared to say it, because he insisted on speaking truth to power.

And so when I came to Pittsburgh in 1986, I could raise the question of the United States' involvement in the oppression in South Africa, and indeed of the institution to which I was being appointed as chair of the department—to ask the awkward question about the involvement of the United States in the racism and oppression in South Africa. I am pleased to say that with the support of many people in this city, particularly of the clergy, and very particularly of faculty and students at the University of Pittsburgh, we were able to challenge that policy. It was an unpopular thing to do, but we did it. We did better than that. We managed to persuade the university that the right and moral thing to do was to divest of its involvement in South Africa. We had begun the struggle in 1952 in South Africa in conjunction with people like Jackie Robinson and Jersey Joe Walcott and the people in athletics; Harry Edwards, and Lee Evans, and the academics, who were able to bring it to a successful conclusion. This ensured not only that the United States ended its collaboration with apartheid, but also that the United States assisted in bringing us to the point where we are today, so that in April in this year we hope to have democratic elections in South Africa for the first time. Black South Africans, who have been unable to vote for 350 years, will finally be able to vote. When they do vote, it will be because of the pressures we exerted in South Africa, in the United States, and elsewhere, on that system— we were able to bring it to the negotiating table, and to move forward to write a constitution that included all South Africans, not just a minority of the people.

But the struggle, of course, must continue. That is why I see it as my duty to refer to the contemporary situation, and attempt to say what I think Dr. King might have said, and what I think should be said at this time, in this country, in this place.

Some of us last week had the good fortune to hear a brilliant and amusing address by one of the great literary figures of this country. Studs Terkel was in town. He said when he thinks of Pittsburgh, he thinks of all the great baseball players. Even as a boy, that's what Pittsburgh meant to him. But as he grew up, he became aware of the great city of the steel industry—the prosperity and the smog, of course, and the pollution. But then he said something that suddenly rang a bell and made me feel guilty. He talked about the struggle of the workers in this country—particularly those in the steel industry, and particularly in the period when the steel industry was shutting down in Pittsburgh and moving out of this area, and going into South Korea or South Africa or wherever. The people here were thrown out of work, and people were homeless.

There were a few of the clergy—and I had almost forgotten about it—who had the courage to challenge the process at that time, to denounce it. But they, instead, were denounced. They were condemned when they cried out and begged for compassion for those who were suffering in this country. Studs Terkel admitted that he hadn't really understood what was going on—that he felt bad now that he had failed to support those people when they were protesting. When he said that, it rang a bell for me, because I too— I had the excuse that I was new in the city, I didn't really know what was going on—I too had failed to support that protest by a handful of courageous clergymen. Maybe some of their actions were too extreme. I don't know. Maybe some of their statements were too extreme. Perhaps. But we do know that thousands were thrown out of work. There was a period of great hardship. And it was a calculated hardship on the part of corporate authorities who made those decisions.

That will bring us to the present. If Dr. King were alive today, I think—although I admit this is speculation, but reasonable speculation—I think he would be horrified to see how the struggle and the gains of the 1960s have been eroded. I think he would be horrified to see how few have gained and how many have suffered. And how for the mass of black Americans and indeed for other minorities as well—Asian, Native American, Chicano, Latino, you name it—things have indeed become worse. The evidence is in the streets, in the homeless, in those struggling to shelter against the cold, in those offering little styrofoam paper cups on the streets of Oakland and Pittsburgh, begging for small change. Things have become worse for millions of people in this country. I believe that would have deeply troubled Dr. King. And I believe he would be even more troubled if he could look into the future. I say this reluctantly. I don't want to sound excessively pessimistic. But in my own view, the situation in this country will get worse. It will get better for a few. It will get worse for many more.

You will ask me for evidence. You will ask me for my arguments. I offer you a process which you may accept or you may reject. But let me offer it to you anyway. There are three elements in it in the past, and a fourth element in the future.

One, we have had, after a great deal of fuss and debate in this country, the passage of something called NAFTA, or the North American Free Trade Agreement. That was followed by a summit in Seattle where I happened to be with my wife when Bill Clinton, President Clinton, met with the Asian and Pacific nations in APEC. Thereafter in Geneva, there was GATT—the General Agreement on Tariffs and Trade. Now there will be a fourth meeting in Washington in the spring, which will be called the summit of Western nations.[2] All of these developed a certain pattern. It is a pattern in which the rich get richer and the poor get poorer. The mass of the people will be exploited. Now I concede that this is my own opinion, my reading of the situation. You may disagree.

As the industries left Pittsburgh in the past, they will leave it again. There are already a thousand American corporations operating in Mexico. There's a report that 2,200 are planning to move south of the border, into the area called the maquiladora zone, where labor is cheaper, where there are no controls on pollution of the environment, and where men and women can be ruthlessly exploited. Giving jobs to people in Mexico is going to mean the loss of jobs in the United States. After NAFTA we go to APEC and GATT, which is a general agreement, not merely affecting Canada and the United States and Mexico. And if you were listening to the news this morning, you would have heard that Chile, down on the southern tip of South America, is now likely to become a partner in the NAFTA agreement. Then we move on to this larger, global operation in Washington.

How is it possible that this has happened? One could offer many explanations. I will offer just one at this point. In a curious way, many of us rejoiced in the fall of the Berlin Wall and the end of the Cold War. We talked of the peace dividend—how the money which had been spent on missiles and H-bombs and whatever was now going to be spent on homes, schools and jobs, and more treatment for health and more hospitals. We were wrong. Warren Christopher, the Secretary of State, before he left for GATT, said very clearly—speaking to about 500 businessmen, CEOs, in Washington—that there was a time when there were two superpowers. We had to worry about what the reaction was from the other superpower for whatever actions we initiated, whether in Africa or in Asia or in Latin America or the Caribbean. Those days are past. We now have the freedom to operate as we choose....He assured them that the business interests of the United States will be paramount. But in fact, even that is not true. Because what is happening now is the creation of supranational financial institutions. Your old multinationals and your old transnationals have reached a point where they can override the legislation of the United States or Canada or Mexico. That is what we have created in our time. It is a monster that will destroy many of us. And perhaps—and I don't want to sound like a prophet of doom—it may, in its ruthless greed and exploitation and its reckless uncaring for humanity threaten the very planet and its survival if we don't mobilize our own efforts and confront these issues.

This is not a time for silence. This is not a time for apathy. Particularly, we ourselves are reasonably comfortable and sheltered against the cold, and protected from the elements. If we have some modicum of security ourselves, the greater the obligation to act. We must become drum majors for justice, and for righteousness. We must mobilize whatever small struggling organizations we have which care for the homeless, for the hungry, for the violent, for those who are terrorizing us now, not merely in the ghettos but in the suburbs with the free play of guns, drugs and the enormous and dangerous frustration and bitterness and hopelessness which is confronting the young in this country. The solution is not to build more prisons. The solution is not to jail more young people. The solution is to give them the hope and the chance of a decent existence, of a decent life and training for a decent job. It is time for us to rise and confront these problems.

The National Conference of Christians and Jews is one group involved in challenging what is bad in this society. There are others—the NAACP, the Community of Reconciliation, organizations in this city, churches in this city. We need to come together. We need an alliance of those who are caring. And we need to form alliances with people in other cities across this country. If we are to face a globalization of oppression, a globalization of capitalism in the post-Cold War world, then let us be willing to prepare also for a globalization of resistance, a globalization of the struggle for justice.

I ask you to join in such a struggle, to be willing to take part. To send a resounding "No" across the world, when there's a summit in Washington where they plan a further extension of the process of domination, of colonialism reborn, of racial oppression and exploitation. The time to start is now, to work throughout the spring challenging this process. In the meantime there are people who continue this process in their own form, on their own terms, in their own way. Whether you follow the news in Algeria, where a government is being challenged, whether you follow the news in the Middle East, where an attempt at a solution is being worked out in the face of the opposition of many of the people. Down in South America, and in South Africa, where, if we have a solution that is not a just solution, there will be no peace. The struggle will continue until we arrive at a just society.

All of us can contribute to it, as the people of Pittsburgh contributed in the past to the struggle for justice in my country. I ask you to renew your commitment. To go forward, and to march with courage and with confidence, and accept the words of Dr. Martin Luther King. Let us all be drum majors for justice.

[1] Brutus has changed King's original text slightly.

[2] This is apparently a reference to the Council on the Americas' 24th Washington Conference in May 1994, which focused on the first Summit of the Americas, held in Miami in December 1994.

Africa 2000 in the new global context:
A commentary
Africa Today, October–December 1997

As we prepare to enter the third millennium, a new political and economic agenda is being designed for Africa that will deeply affect the lives of its people far beyond the year 2000. What are the contents of this agenda, its implications, and some of the possibilities it opens? Since the end of the Cold War, a new global vision has emerged with the shift to a unipolar world dominated by only one superpower. The presumed demise of the conflict between capitalism and socialism has so changed the global political landscape that Francis Fukuyama has even suggested that we are witnessing "the end of history."[1] According to Fukuyama, we are moving toward a world where major political and economic trends and patterns can be expected to remain essentially unchanged. I believe such a vision is a world where power will always be in the hands of those who now possess it, and the powerless will (unfortunately) continue to remain so—a world where the rich will get richer and the poor will get poorer. Politicians as well as academics are spreading this new orthodoxy.

This trend is upheld by the World Bank and the International Monetary Fund (IMF) according to guidelines that were established in 1944 at the Bretton Woods conference in New Hampshire, where policies were devised to prevent the type of political and economic disruptions brought about by World War II. These two institutions recently celebrated their fiftieth anniversary. Perhaps what they were also celebrating is their capability to impose the agenda that issued from Bretton Woods, which they were unable to realize during the Cold War due to the existence of a conflictual world dominated by two nuclear superpowers.

Glimpses of this agenda, particularly as it affects Africa and other "less-developed" regions, can be caught from a statement made in 1992 by Lawrence Summers, who was then chief economist of the World Bank and is now deputy secretary of the treasury in the Clinton administration. In an internal memo[2] leaked to the press, Summers proposed that the toxic waste of the "first world" be shipped to the countries of the "third world." He argued that the Third World has more space for such waste and that the cost of treating the diseases produced by nuclear waste is much lower in these countries.[3] Summers' views are typical of those who are shaping World Bank policies.

The World Bank asserts that the causes of Africa's economic bankruptcy are the corruption and inefficiency of its political class and its wasteful government spending, including that for education. What Africa needs, according to the World Bank, is not more educated people —professionals, people with managerial skills— but rather more people who have "practical" skills, whether in agriculture or industry. "Capacity," not education, is the key word in this context, and the World Bank has appointed itself as the agency to provide it, as we learn from their 1991 document "Africa Capacity Building Initiative."[4]

What the World Bank has recommended are both massive cuts in the education budgets of African countries—spending cuts reaching 50 percent for some universities (for buildings and salaries of staff and teachers)—and cuts in enrollment. Paul Johnson, a writer for the *New York Times Magazine,* describes such external initiatives in an article entitled "Colonialism's Back and Not a Moment Too Soon."[5] In this article, Johnson makes three points about African countries: (1) they are economically bankrupt; (2) they have discovered that they cannot govern themselves; and (3) they are now asking the colonial powers to return to run them. As unbelievable as these assertions may seem, they reflect the position of both the World Bank and the IMF as they extend their hegemony over Africa and other "less-developed" regions of the planet.

One of the central mechanisms by which this re-colonization process is carried out is the loan system through structural adjustment programs. Significantly, many of the countries that received loans from the World Bank have not seen their economies improve. Quite the opposite. Some are in a far worse economic position and more indebted than they were prior to taking the loans.

Once a loan is taken, paying it back can be a backbreaking matter. But this is only a part of the problem. Even more pernicious is that the World Bank often dictates how the borrowed money is to be spent, which is specified through a whole set of "conditionalities." One of them is the drastic reduction in public spending for higher education, which can be cut by as much as 50 percent. Other conditions include equally devastating cuts in the number of civil servants and massive currency devaluations that dramatically diminish the purchasing power of many Africans, while at the same time dramatically increasing the cost of imported products.

In the case of South Africa, which is still negotiating with the World Bank, such structural adjustment policies are referred to as a "rationalization" program. The implication is that there is something quite irrational—that needs to be corrected—about the number of university instructors and students who are in professional programs. While the debate continues in South Africa, some of the World Bank's conditionalities are already being carried out, including the sale of South African Airways. [6] The existence of a minimum wage is seen as a major flaw. In addition, the South African government, under Nelson Mandela, has been asked to promise that it will not allow workers to strike.

The end result of structural adjustment programs, such as those proposed for South Africa, can be a country that is even more bankrupt, more unable to repay its loans, and more impoverished, as its currency is devalued, its services are gutted, and its agricultural sector is turned upside down to produce cash crops for export rather than food for the people's subsistence. This has been the case in Zimbabwe, where the World Bank persuaded the government to shift production supports from food crops like maize to export crops like tobacco. Not surprisingly, malnutrition has increased and infant mortality has doubled.

It is hardly imaginable that anyone could knowingly devise such a ruthless, heartless system that is entirely devoted to increasing profit and largely indifferent to its human cost. This, however, is the system that is shaping life in Africa today, and it is the system that we must challenge. It is crucial that we do not accept the current academic wisdom that pretends that there are no choices or alternatives—a position one often hears rehearsed in South Africa today. The debate has been conducted within the African National Congress (ANC), where opposing sides have adopted the labels TINA and THABA, standing for "there is no alternative" and "there has to be a better alternative."

Alternatives do exist. [7] We have to challenge the assumption that structural adjustment is inevitably Africa's way to the future. A crucial condition is that African countries begin to cooperate with each other on a regional basis so that they are no longer forced to depend on the global structures and agencies that today try to dictate Africa's political and economic course. If this can happen, a better, more promising future can be envisaged.

What is certain is that we cannot accept the prospect of a world where the majority continues to become poorer and poorer while a few individuals continue to amass incredible riches. While the World Bank was celebrating its fiftieth birthday, demonstrators in the streets of Washington were declaring, "Fifty years is enough!" They were part of a strong Fifty Years Is Enough campaign that has been mobilizing across the United States and other countries. Along the same lines, during the G7 Summit in Halifax, Nova Scotia, 3,000 people gathered in the streets protesting the G7's global agenda and organizing a "People's Summit." Similarly, during the recent Summit of the Eight in Denver, an alternative people's summit, termed "The Other Economic Summit," was convened over a period of several days. In numerous workshops, the global agenda of the G8/IMF/World Bank was examined and challenged in Denver; among the distinguished participants were Vandana Shiva,[8] David Korten,[9] Kevin Danaher,[10] and Lisa McGowan and Njoki Njehu of the Fifty Years Is Enough campaign. Joining them were the homeless, women who are fighting against discrimination, and teenagers who know that there are no jobs for them and who have no hope for the future.

They all understood what structural adjustment involves, and not just in the Third World, for this program is being carried out not only in Africa, Asia, and Latin America, but also in Canada and the United States. In Washington, Halifax, and Denver, people recognized that there is a link between the re-colonization of Africa and other parts of the Third World, and the attack on workers' social and economic rights in the metropoles. They recognized the increasing homogenization of global rule as multinational corporations and multinational financial agencies such as the World Bank and the IMF increasingly control the economies of every country in the world. Most important, they recognized that the struggle for self-determination and human welfare must be a globally coordinated project. The future will decide whether this

project can be realized. But there can be no doubt that the answer
to this question will determine the course of African history in the
twenty-first century.

[1] Francis Fukuyama, *The End of History and the Last Man* (New
York: Free Press, 1992).

[2] See Catherine Caufield, *Masters of Illusion: The World Bank and the
Poverty of Nations* (New York: Henry Holt, 1996).

[3] "Let Them Eat Pollution (Excerpt from a Letter Written by the Chief
Economist of the World Bank)," *The Economist* 322 (February 8,
1992), 66.

[4] World Bank, *The African Capacity Building Initiative: Toward Im-
proved Policy Analysis and Development Management* (Washington,
D.C.: World Bank, 1991); Committee for Academic Freedom in
Africa, "The World Bank's African Capacity Building Initiative: A
Critique," *CAFA Newsletter* 6 (Spring 1994), 14–19.

[5] Paul Johnson, "Colonialism's Back—and Not a Moment Too Soon,"
New York Times Magazine (April 18, 1993), 22.

[6] See articles by Patrick Bond and others in *Southern African Report*,
427 Bloor St., West Toronto, Ontario, Canada.

[7] See, for instance, various studies on sustainable development, espe-
cially Ann Seidman and Frederick Anang, eds., *Twenty-first Century
Africa: Towards a New Vision of Self-sustained Development* (Tren-
ton, N.J.: Africa World Press; Atlanta: African Studies Association
Press, 1992).

[8] Vandana Shiva, *Biopiracy: The Plunder of Nature and Knowledge*
(Toronto: Between the Lines, 1997).

[9] David C. Korten, *When Corporations Rule the World* (London:
Earthscan, 1995).

[10] Kevin Danaher, *Fifty Years Is Enough: The Case Against the World
Bank and the International Monetary Fund* (Boston: South End
Press, 1994), and *Corporations Are Gonna Get Your Mama: Global-
ization and the Downsizing of the American Dream* (Monroe,
Maine: Common Courage Press, 1996).

Why I protested at the World Bank
Economic Justice News, April 28, 2000

After being shot by apartheid's police, imprisoned with Nelson
Mandela on Robben Island, and driven into exile for my efforts to
liberate South Africa from the tyranny of minority rule, I have
found on returning home that the triumphs of the last decade are
threatened by a new kind of tyranny, that of the World Bank and

the International Monetary Fund (IMF). It is that threat—plus the damage already done in the rest of Africa—that motivated me to go to Washington for the massive demonstrations on April 16 calling for an end to the abuses of these institutions.

The presence of so large and diverse a group of people from around the U.S. and around the world (and yes, there were many from Africa, Latin America, and Asia who managed to make the trip) convinces me that we are witnessing the birth of a new kind of international social movement, one which will reshape the global economy.

South Africa's economy is strong enough that it need not submit to IMF and World Bank "recommendations" the way the other countries of Africa have, yet our politicians seem vulnerable to the pressure mounted by the U.S. Treasury Department and multinational corporations to comply with the "Washington Consensus"—government austerity, allowing apartheid-era wealth to flee, and other pro-corporate policies.

On April 16, the U.S. public and the bureaucrats at the IMF and World Bank finally heard some of the anger and rejection of the global economic system that is welling up every day in much of the world.

A philosopher once remarked that the great ideas of history are first dismissed as ludicrous, then castigated as subversive, and ultimately regarded as self-evident. The demonstrations in Washington last week fill me with hope that for the second time in my life, I will see that progression come full circle. Before long, I trust, it will be commonplace to observe that twenty-plus years of the IMF and World Bank's "structural adjustment programs" have brought only more debt and increasing poverty for some ninety countries, and, not coincidentally, more profits for multinational corporations. Those who insist—backed up by economic theory but not economic reality—that it is mere coincidence that the IMF and World Bank have been present at (and presiding over) catastrophe after catastrophe will finally fall silent.

Most vital to the movement that has called the IMF and World Bank's bluff is whether these institutions continue to be granted coercive power over the economic policies that govern the lives of most of the world's people. The IMF's own review of structural adjustment and the World Bank's own assessment of its forest policies are just two recent examples of their own acknowledgement of failure. As the statements of support that were issued just before our demonstrations at the Havana summit of the leaders of 133 less wealthy countries confirm, this is not news to the people of Africa, Asia, the Middle East, and Latin America. We are not talking about "fixing" these institutions, but finally freeing the countries they have dominated from their failed economic philosophy.

Of course, even massive displays of opposition on their home turf are unlikely to persuade the IMF and World Bank to change their ways. The Jubilee 2000 movement, which has mobilized hundreds of thousands in repeated actions over the last five years to demand cancellation of the most impoverished countries' debts, has extracted concessions from the heads of the G7 countries but not yet managed to move the IMF and World Bank away from their insistence that any relief from debts owed them must be paid for by someone else and accompanied by more structural adjustment.

Fortunately, in the case of the World Bank, we have a viable weapon: on April 10, I helped launch a boycott of the bonds that finance 80 percent of the Bank's loans. These bonds are bought by institutions like churches, universities, pension funds, and municipalities. The movement that came to life on the streets of Washington will now replicate the success of the divestment movement that helped end apartheid. Students, workers, and others, learning about the impact of the Bank's policies, will apply pressure to their sources of support, make them unattractive to investors, and ultimately defund them. We will be stopped only when the Bank finally meets the people's condition: an irrevocable end to structural adjustment.

It's time for new confrontations
Mail & Guardian, July 21, 2000

Last Friday afternoon [July 14, 2000], I joined a demonstration that led to the disruption of the Urban Futures conference final plenary session at Wits University's Great Hall. The delegates are owed an apology, but the two lead administrators of Wits and Johannesburg Metro who were prevented from speaking are, on reflection, not.

I was in transit between literary and political engagements in Grahamstown and Okinawa. In virtually all such contemporary meeting grounds, the power of the market is now being popularly received with profound reservations.

So it did not surprise me that the heavily corporate-biased agenda that both the university and Johannesburg Metro are pursuing, in the Wits 2001 and Egoli 2002 plans, has generated such angst and resistance. The emergence of a Johannesburg Anti-Privatization Forum to link the two campaigns shows an awareness of "town-gown," local-global connections that people of conscience must applaud.

In fact, it is not stretching matters to draw a thread from Mahatma Gandhi and Martin Luther King, through the anti-apartheid struggle, through the civil disobedience that I witnessed at the World Trade Organization summit last November in Seattle and at the April World Bank meetings in Washington, and on through the Anti-Privatization Forum's actions this month: sit-ins and sleep-ins at administrative offices, water balloons playfully tossed into a pro-privatization Urban Futures workshop, and the nonviolent storming of the Great Hall stage.

They all cause discomfort, and in some cases they humiliate. But they are done with the idealistic intention of drawing attention to injustice. They are essentially nonviolent, even if annoyingly confrontational. And like fine grains of sand in the cogs of a terrible machine, the grating of such protest generates noises that can wake us all up. Something is not right. The machine must be stopped, even if bodies must be put on the line to do so.

Indeed, the days of thinking that enlightened elites generate progress in small committees are far behind us. Only such cries from below will eventually make enough of a racket to change society, the city, and the university, for the better.

That is why I am convinced that at stake last Friday was not, as might at first be assumed, freedom of expression for the scheduled speakers Colin Bundy and Kenny Fihla, who wield enormous power to market their message. What are sometimes faux-liberal notions of free speech run the risk, as in this case, of decontextualization. Thus tobacco advertisers have been told not to market their wares to children, and rightfully so.

A university is different, no doubt: a tranquil place where ideas intersect, a site therefore to uphold complete freedom of expression. But by last Friday, a newly-corporatized Wits had lost enough of this status to justify an interruption to the Bundy and Fihla speeches. (Regrettably, a very different speech by Xolela Mangcu was also jettisoned in the commotion.) For while Bundy pronounces eloquently that There Is No Alternative, through an array of university loudhailers [bullhorns], there were by Friday no practical possibilities of debating the fait-accompli defunding of arts and education faculties at Wits, or the fate of more than 600 workers recently fired or outsourced, and who now are without a substantial part of their pay packet, without benefits, without a chance for their kids to grow up and go to Wits.

That plan was, I'm told, inadequately consulted. When a group of the university's—and country's—leading industrial sociologists pointed out profound methodological flaws (not to mention cut-and-paste plagiarism and spelling errors!) in a R4,5 [4.5 million rand] million consultancy report on outsourcing, the Wits Council dogmatically refused to rethink the plan.

What Bundy, to his credit, did put on offer to those protesters was fifteen minutes to make their case to last Friday's plenary. But the offer was considered contrived and meaningless, a last-minute amendment that emerged only because of rumors of unrest. The university's strategy, protesters felt, was to channel, contain, sanitize, and snuff the passion for social justice that students, staff, trade unionists, and Johannesburg residents brought into the Great Hall.

What therefore is truly at stake in such confrontations is whether profound pain inflicted upon ordinary people by a new elite acting much the same as their predecessors, has an appropriate vehicle for expression. The well-paid administrators don't feel the desperate pangs of those whose very ability to feed their families is now in question. The demonstrators' goal was to make that pain more viscerally understood, and they succeeded marvelously.

Likewise, over the past eight months, in all corners of the globe, a great deal of nonviolent civil disobedience has drawn the world's attention to systematic "neoliberal" injustice: market imperatives ruining ordinary people's lives. Dramatic protest settings have included Seattle, Davos, Bangkok, Cochabamba, Washington, Chiang Mai, Bombay, Buenos Aires, London, Istanbul, Lagos, and Windsor. Mass strikes of millions of people, as happened in South Africa on May 10 and India the day after, reflect the demand for change.

My Friday afternoon was memorable because to my surprise, a spirit of resistance pervaded a university I remember with mixed feelings. A half-century ago, I learned some fine lessons at Wits, it is true, but these also occurred in a context of systematic pain. My own law studies were abruptly terminated by a spell at South Africa's other elite university, Robben Island.

Then, as now, a school that taught me much also left large gaps in my education. For then, as now, Wits leadership had a choice to join the struggle for justice; then, as now, it seems, the moral responsibility has been forsaken at the top.

But not at the bottom.

It's time for new confrontations.

Africa's progressive movements

An interview with Patrick Bond, ZNet, December 28, 2000

Good to see you back in Johannesburg, comrade Dennis, even briefly, in the midst of your travels. But the news today (December 27) is mixed, because it seems that some Washington sharpies have persuaded Nelson Mandela to lead a World Bank/IMF/ UNICEF conference on child poverty in London in February. You broke stones on Robben Island with Mandela during the mid-1960s. What's he up to, do you think?

This latest gimmick seems to be Washington's response to the sharp attack leveled at the Bank, especially their new managing director for human development, Mamphela Ramphele, at the Prague annual meetings three months ago. The Bank and IMF stand accused of contributing to 19,000 avoidable deaths of young kids every day. At one NGO-Bank discussion in Prague, a representative of the British trade union, Unison, really went after Mamphela, who as you know was Stephen Biko's partner before moving to Cape Town University. There, as president during the 1990s, she smashed the main trade union and cut lowest-tier workers' wages by half.

Then add to that, our finance minister Trevor Manuel's role as chair of the Prague meeting, which we protesters forced him to shut a day early. So it looks like some South African former anti-apartheid leaders are now playing the role of useful idiots for global apartheid. Maybe our allies in Britain can mobilize so that the tarnishing of Mandela's prestige by the IMF and World Bank doesn't go unanswered. A similar thing happened just over a month ago, by the way, when another South African, education minister Kader Asmal, hauled Mandela out to defend his two big Lesotho dams at the London launch of the final report of the World Commission on Dams, which Asmal has been chairing over the past two years.

It was most embarrassing. Across the Earth, megadams financed by the World Bank have been catastrophic, so much so that this commission report has to admit the vast extent of the damage. And yet there was Nelson Mandela being used to put a gloss on Africa's biggest dam—the sanctions-busting Lesotho Highlands Water Project—which community groups in Soweto and Alexandra townships, as well as displaced Basotho people and environmentalists, all agree is a corrupt fiasco. Last month, the progressive movements from both countries together called for a moratorium on the Lesotho dam, which of course was ignored by Pretoria and Washington. So you see the damage Mandela is now doing to social progress. It's tragic, really.

Well, although the African National Congress won the South African municipal elections very comfortably early this month, their leaders failed to inspire even half the population to come out to vote, and the ANC share went down from two-thirds in the national election last year, to just three-fifths. And they did quite badly amongst working-class "colored" (mixed-race) and Indian people, even losing the city of Cape Town to the old apartheid party. What do you make of that?

This is just one expression of dissatisfaction. There are many others. The point is, that disgruntled mass-based organizations and allied intellectuals in this country are more attuned than ever before to the need for an anti-neoliberal program. But not just here. Two weeks ago, in Dakar, Senegal, there was a most encouraging multilingual gathering of radical social, church, women's, and labor groups and movements from across the continent. Samir Amin, the great Dakar-based Marxist economist, opened the gathering.

I hear that the delegates joined 5,000 Senegalese for an anti-austerity march during the conference. It was supposed to culminate at the IMF/[World]Bank office in downtown Dakar, but the new Senegalese government of Abdoulaye Wade was too frightened to allow that. Still, this was a great marker of the growing energy and tight organization that exist in some African cities.

And the conference proceedings suggest a very tough reckoning of where African social justice movements are now, and where they need to go. This was the first time that very strong contingents from Anglophone and Francophone countries came together, along with several from Lusophone (Portuguese-speaking) countries. The Northern allies who came to observe reportedly learned a great deal and were most impressed.

In terms of programmatic and political thinking, what do you feel Dakar achieved?

From the conference material I've seen, and from what we've learned from South African participants' report-backs, there was a qualitative advance on analysis, consolidation of structures, clearer definition of goals and strategies, and alliance-building with other Southern and Northern comrades. The environmental debt that the North owes the South is now also a very important issue, recognized by all the participants.

Outputs [from the conference] included the Dakar Declaration and Manifesto, and an excellent statement advancing the African People's Consensus—the principles that stand in opposition to the Washington Consensus of the World Bank—which I suspect will soon be up on the various Web sites of conference sponsors. There was also a meeting of the Jubilee South network, which gathered all the main southern hemisphere campaigns.

The short-term debt-related demands coming from the Jubilee South network were extremely progressive, focusing on the notion of illegitimacy. This has become the basis for critiquing all outstanding debt. The way Jubilee South puts it is clear: "No conditionalities, no structural adjustment programs for new loans; immediate cancellation of illegitimate debts; and South governments should have a public investigation and audit of the debt, suspend payments until investigations have been made, and non-payment of illegitimate debts."

Some of the concrete strategies advanced include national people's tribunals on debt and structural adjustment programs across the South, following the extremely successful Brazilian model. By 2002, an international people's tribunal will be convened. I was particularly encouraged about two specific issues I've been following: our demands as a movement are maturing from mere debt cancellation to insisting upon reparations, and the role of the World Bank Bonds Boycott as a handle for local activists, to shrink the power of Washington from the bottom up. The boycott strategy gives readers of ZNet some good activist opportunities at home, between coming to all these wonderful protests at meetings.

By the way, big protests are likely to be at the Davos World Economic Forum in January, Buenos Aires and Quebec City for the Free Trade Agreement of the Americas, both in April, May Day in all kinds of places, a World Day of Action against Debt just before the Genoa G8 Summit in June.

And, of course, there's the annual meeting of the World Bank and IMF in September. That's back in Washington next year, and unlike last April when there were fewer than 1,000 official delegates at the A16/17 spring meetings, the cops are not going to be able to close off ninety city blocks and get their delegates in next time. Because the meeting is scheduled to be at the Sheraton Hotel at Rock Creek Parkway, we're going to outnumber their 20,000 delegates and have a real party in the park.[1]

Back to Africa, how about relations between states and civil societies? Is there any concrete possibility that governments in Africa will finally listen to the progressive forces?

In Dakar, there was much greater emphasis than there has been so far on relating to governments, but that includes challenging corrupt regimes, of which we have dozens on this continent. So, on the one hand, the African Jubilee groups and other social movements are going to forcefully agitate for their governments to ally with civil society on the demand for debt repudiation and cancellation, and even to form a debtor's cartel and build a reparations movement. And on the other hand, regarding the corrupt regimes, we will not only see Africans being more courageous in denouncing crooked rulers, but also demanding that Western financiers also take responsibility for their complicity.

Our Nigerian comrades, for example, are having success putting the heat on London, Swiss, and U.S. banks for bankrolling Sani Abacha and hiding his stolen funds. My friend Archbishop Njongonkulu Ndungane, who replaced Archbishop Desmond Tutu a few years ago, has challenged the World Bank, and Swiss and German banks and governments. Backed by Jubilee South Africa, he's saying they must repay payments made by South African society on loans to Pretoria during the apartheid era which upheld white power.

Do you have any reservations about Dakar? For example, I saw a vicious e-mail attack circulated by Ann Pettifor of Jubilee UK who questioned what otherwise seemed a very unifying process.

As usual, minor tensions developed when some renegades from Jubilee 2000 UK wanted to exert undue influence. I gather it stems from them losing control, and from their rather less ambitious campaigning objectives. Yet overall, the more radical Jubilee South positions were fully endorsed within the South-North meeting.

But I wish there had been more forward planning, in the light of some key points of global movement building. We're not only showing up at the enemy's meetings, you see, we're now putting our own gatherings together, like Dakar, and we must drive towards more inclusivity and programmatic work. The crucial session will be a vast meeting in Porto Alegre, Brazil, next month [the World Social Forum], where the Workers' Party, Movement of the Landless, and a huge collection of the best progressive forces in Latin America are bringing in activists and strategists from all over the world.

There'll be another huge event in Durban, South Africa, next August, by the way: the UN conference on racism. That conference will be an opportunity for Pretoria and the UN bigwigs to showcase South Africa as a model for solving racial problems. I believe that this would be a false image. We will instead be using the occasion to present a more honest picture of the failures of this government. Many of the gross inequities of the apartheid system—homelessness, lack of water, inadequate health services, the Bantu educational system, all originally based on racial distinctions—have actually gotten worse since 1994. The reason for that is, essentially, dictation by proponents of neoliberalism, especially the World Bank. Pretoria has pretty slavishly adopted the Washington Consensus ideology. And there's little or nothing to show for it.

OK, the best progressive forces in this country share that line of argument. But after Durban on racism next August, there's yet another huge event coming up, the UN's World Summit on Sustainable Development here in Jo'burg in 2002. This was announced a couple of weeks ago, just after Jo'burg successfully hosted the Persistent Organic Pollutants (POPs) treaty conference. I hear from people in the Ralph Nader circuits that they were fairly pleased with the outcome, because they exerted enough pressure to overcome reactionary positions by not only the United States but by the host, South Africa, which is, for instance, using DDT to treat malarial zones.

Yes, that World Summit is probably the point at which the work done in Dakar, Porto Alegre, and various other sites on alternatives to neoliberalism will come to fruition. ZNet readers should put Jo'burg on their agenda.

Hey, will they have finally changed the name of Johannesburg by then? The nineteenth-century land surveyor, Johannes Rissik, doesn't deserve it. I guess it'll be called Igoli, Zulu for City of Gold?

Renaming Jo'eys was another of the ANC promises in the municipal elections earlier this month. Don't hold your breath, though, Dennis. White big business interests say that it's a global brand name, now, and the neoliberals running the city will probably persuade the politicians to let it die.

Yes, like Seattle is a brand name to our comrades! From Seattle to Soweto, that sounds right. See you there in 2002!

[1] The meeting was cancelled following the September 11. 2001, atacks.

South Africa supports global apartheid
IndyMedia South Africa, August 26, 2001

"Nkosi sikelel' iAfrika." "God Bless Africa." We sang this song on Robben Island on Africa Freedom Day, the anniversary of the adoption of the Freedom Charter. Singing was forbidden. So was whistling. The punishment: three meals denied. A day breaking rocks on an empty stomach.

But on the anniversary of the Freedom Charter we would sing and go hungry. We sang in defiance. We were in prison because of our defiance. I was active in the sports boycott. When I was shot by the security police in Johannesburg, I lay in a pool of blood for forty-five minutes waiting for help. I remember seeing the head offices of the Anglo-American corporation above my head as I lay there. I asked myself: Is it to protect the wealth of these corporations that the government is using such brutal methods against us?

After my release, I spent several decades in exile working against apartheid. I returned only after we had defeated the regime which had ruled us so arrogantly. But each time I return, I wonder where the fruits of our struggle have gone.

Two weeks ago I addressed angry workers in the township of Wentworth in South Durban. Angry because they earn barely enough to feed their children. And angry because the oil refinery where they work treats them like spare parts in the machines—expendable, interchangeable. I saw the same thing as I remember fifty years ago in the colored townships of Port Elizabeth. Joblessness. Homelessness. Poverty.

In the new South Africa we are all equal before the law. But in material terms, we are moving further apart. South Africa has overtaken Brazil to become the most unequal country in the world. Look around you in Durban and you will see evidence of this inequality. In the ghettos of Chatsworth, where unemployment is around 50 percent since the clothing industry retrenched so many workers. Or the African townships, where cholera hit recently and where hundreds of families are without water as they cannot afford their water bills. Or the communities where workers' homes are engulfed in clouds of noxious fumes. Or downtown where beggars and sex workers abound.

By contrast, a small minority in Durban's affluent suburbs still control and enjoy the city's wealth. As world leaders meet in Durban to discuss racism, it is ironically the greed of corporations in their countries that keeps black people here poor. Why should investors in New York, London, Zurich, or Tokyo expect huge returns, whilst their plants and suppliers in South Africa or Indonesia pay workers a pittance? Why must we follow World Bank and IMF structural adjustment policies, which mean cutting services, privatizing, and putting up prices for the poor?

The answer, we are told, is globalization. The need to compete. To attract investment. This tale, like the story of the emperor's new clothes, seems to have hoodwinked our politicians. The investment never arrives, just more hardship. Our own finance minister, Trevor Manuel, seems to be in the pockets of the World Bank and IMF. He is doing their dirty work in South Africa and covering up for them by being the token African chair on their board. Legitimizing the global corporate agenda they support. I believe this is criminal. As the rich get richer and the poor get poorer, we are facing a global economic divide as profound as the racial divide which separated South Africans. This is global apartheid.

I don't expect the official UN conference will change much, especially as the U.S. government has demonstrated its ability to change the agenda to suit its interests. Even in the NGO conference, where I am speaking, our impact may be limited. It is on the streets when we march against global apartheid that we may make a difference.

Our protests in Durban will take up where the protestors in Seattle and Genoa left off. And after the WCAR [World Conference Against Racism], is long gone, the struggle will continue in Durban's townships. In prison in the 1960s we starved for a day to sing Nkosi Sikelel'. Now that this song is our national anthem, our people are starving whilst the politicians sing and the corporate bosses feast.

Enough is enough! Let us take to the streets! Down with global apartheid, down!

World Conference Against Racism: South Africa between a rock and a hard place
with Ben Cashdan, ZNet, July 11, 2001

If you were planning a holiday in South Africa's east coast resort of Durban before the warm winter season is over, you'd be well advised to steer clear of the city during the last few days of

August and the first week in September.

Unless that is, you are a government official, a UN bureaucrat, an academic, or a journalist with a burning desire to discuss racism, xenophobia, and related forms of intolerance. If you are one of the latter, you probably already have your hotel room booked.

If you are one of thousands of delegates coming for the official inter-governmental World Conference Against Racism (WCAR) you may well be booked into the Royal Hotel, with its splendid colonial-style accommodation. If you are a lowly NGO worker, you will most likely have to make do with the spartan Holiday Inn Garden Court.

Either way, your program will be very full, as you ponder the fight against racism in Durban's world-class International Convention Centre (ICC), conveniently located opposite the Hilton Hotel and a stone's throw away from the beachfront, rubbing shoulders with presidents, prime ministers, and luminaries such as Kofi Annan, Thabo Mbeki, Mary Robinson, Manning Marable, and Harry Belafonte.

During your stay in Durban you may take a stroll along Marine Parade, the beachfront promenade, to be confronted by a stream of Zulu-speaking hawkers (South African slang for informal street vendors) eking out an existence or Durban's incongruous rickshaw drivers desperately competing to pull you along in decorated two-wheeled chariots. As long as you stick to the official conference transport you won't be bothered too much by the beggars, pickpockets, and prostitutes.

It's highly unlikely that you'll follow any of these unfortunate folk back to their homes in the townships of Chatsworth, Cato Manor, or Umlazi where unemployment is up above 50 percent since the collapse over the past few years of the textile industry and other globally "uncompetitive" sectors. As South Africa has implemented WTO tariff reductions, these jobs have moved to East Asian sweatshops where wages are even lower than in Africa.

You will almost certainly not see the desperate living conditions of South Africa's poorest Indian community in the council flats in Chatsworth's Unit 3, known owing to its poverty as "Bangladesh." Last year Bangladesh hit the headlines when ANC-led Durban Metro Council evicted several families from their council flats for failing to keep up with their rents. The council is determined to ensure that rents are up to date in preparation for privatization of housing. The community resisted the evictions, with Indian grand-mothers in saris defending the homes of their Zulu neighbors from the municipal police, who resorted to tear gas and rubber bullets.

Thirty years ago these families were evicted by the apartheid government for being too dark in complexion. The ANC is now evicting the same families for being poor. Mandela's friend and bi-ographer Professor Fatima Meer labeled the council's actions "fas-cist brutality."

You also won't have time to visit the tiny and leaky matchbox housing, constructed by the ANC government under its reconstruc-tion and development programme (RDP) into which some of the destitute are being relocated along the Higginson Highway, far from jobs and services. You'll also miss the misery of the shackland that is Cator Manor. With your busy conference schedule you defi-nitely won't have time to take an hour's drive north along the N3 highway to Hammarsdale, a former KwaZulu homeland "growth point," its factories subsidized by the apartheid government to keep black people in the bantustans. Now the jobs are gone and the residents of Mpumalanga township just outside Hammarsdale are literally starving. No one is quite sure whether the twenty bod-ies in the morgue each weekend are victims of poverty, AIDS, cholera, or some combination. In Mpumalanga, former ANC and Inkatha Freedom Party (IFP) activists, once avowed enemies, are now united against a new enemy: Durban Metro Council. Their objection, Durban Metro's new cost-recovery policies. In Mpumalanga, many residents received subsidised water even under apartheid. Now the ANC government is installing water meters and cutting off services to those too poor to pay.

Cholera broke out in Durban and its surroundings last year, making 80,000 people sick and killing 180 across the country. At its center, a community who used to get subsidized water but was recently disconnected.

Just before you touch down at Durban airport, you may catch a glimpse of the township of Wentworth, where black workers re-cently struck against oil refineries owned by Shell, British Petroleum, and a Malaysian oil company after in the same week one worker was killed by exposure to hydrochloric acid and another was injured in a machine. In Wentworth, where workers live on the hillsides all around the plants, inhaling noxious fumes day and night, residents are eight times more likely to get asthma, bronchitis, and leukemia than the South African population as a whole. Protective labor legislation, won during the anti-apartheid struggle, is currently being rolled back in the interest of international competitiveness.

If you don't see most of this, you may not be struck by the poignancy and potential for irony of our ANC government hosting a world conference against racism in a city where the majority are black and poor, and a minority, mostly still white, continue to enjoy the spoils of the economy.

A question on many people's minds in the run up to the World Conference Against Racism is whether the economic forces and policies, both local and global, which continue to keep so many black people poor, will be up for debate in the conference at all.

Perhaps the clearest manifestation of this uncertainty is the behind-the-scenes tussle over one particular agenda item in the conference: whether the Global South, and people of color in the North (led by African Americans), deserve reparations for the crimes visited upon them by the largely-white North: viz. slavery, colonialism, and apartheid. African delegates meeting in Dakar in January to prepare for the WCAR highlighted reparations as the key issue for discussion in Durban. As recently as this week, the U.S. and some European governments are reported to have threatened to withdraw their funding or to boycott the conference altogether if the issue of reparations is to be included. U.S. Secretary of State Colin Powell warned supporters of reparations to withdraw this issue or risk "derailing" the conference. In South Africa, opinion appears divided. Jubilee South Africa has been outspoken in its support for reparations. Jubilee leaders such as Anglican Archbishop Njongonkulu Ndungane of Cape Town have repeatedly called on Swiss banks to pay back the profits they made from trading in apartheid gold and to compensate the victims of apartheid violence for the support the banks provided to Pretoria during the 1980s. In 1986, when P.W. Botha declared a debt standstill, Swiss bankers provided a major bailout.

Yasmine Sooka, a commissioner of the Truth and Reconciliation Commission (TRC) has argued that families of freedom fighters killed or injured during the struggle should receive compensation from the banks for prolonging apartheid.

Interviewed at the World Economic Forum in Davos, Switzer-
land, in January, Thabo Mbeki distanced himself from this call.
Whilst commending Jubilee 2000 for its success in promoting debt
relief, Mbeki said of the reparations campaign, "It's an NGO call.
As government we've never made such a call."

Granted Mbeki was in Davos to promote South Africa to in-
vestors as a safe and lucrative place to do business through his Mil-
lenium Africa Plan (MAP). A demand from the president that
foreign banks pay back profits made over a decade ago would
hardly have helped his cause. In line with Mbeki's reticence, top
South African officials appear reluctant to take sides publicly in the
debate over the conference agenda.

The differing views on reparations are associated with quite
different assessments of how racism should be approached at the
WCAR. Northern governments would generally like to see the dis-
cussion focus on racial ideologies and psychologies and the need
for education and tolerance. This personalized approach to dis-
cussing racism avoids an acknowledgement that Europe and the
USA built their economies through systematic racially-based ex-
ploitation and dispossession. "Civil society" groups in South Africa
such as organized labor and NGOs (whose contribution in Durban
is confined to a separate venue at a separate time) believe that the
WCAR must consider the systemic causes of racial inequality.
Amongst these are the historical legacy of slavery and colonialism,
the impact of the current phase of corporate-led globalization on
jobs and living standards in the Global South, and, last but not
least, the effect of domestic economic policies on the living stan-
dards of the black majority. With the help of the World Bank,
South Africa introduced its own home-grown structural adjust-
ment program in 1996, under the rubric, Growth Employment and
Redistribution, or GEAR. GEAR focused on macro-economic indi-
cators such as budget-deficit reduction, replacing the Reconstruc-
tion and Development Program (RDP), which had emphasized
meeting the basic needs of the population.

The South African government is caught between a rock and a
hard place. If it limits itself to the "personalized" approach, it risks
being co-opted into an agenda set by the North. Debt cancellation
would be off the agenda, as would most of the concerns being
raised by grassroots groups in South Africa.

On the other hand, if the South African government takes a courageous line against the racial disparities exacerbated by globalization, it risks throwing the spotlight on its own neoliberal policies. Since the introduction of GEAR, life has undoubtedly become harder for the vast majority of the poorest black South Africans. In 1990 South Africa was the second most unequal society in the world. After seven years of an ANC government, South Africa has won first place.

One option, of course, is to keep quiet and try to bask in the glory of the political "miracle" of the South African transition and the racial reconciliation it was built on. As conference hosts there will be plenty of opportunity for pomp and ceremony, and to promote Durban as a tourist destination. For those off the tourist track in Durban's black and Indian townships, however, it increasingly seems as if the struggle against racism is a struggle against our own post-apartheid government.

While the government bureaucrats meet in the ICC, and NGOs parley in Kingsmead stadium, community groups across the city are planning their own action. They will call for an end to cost-recovery in poor townships, an end to evictions, a halt to commercialization and privatization of services, and a renewed focus on meeting basic needs.

Their Concerned Citizens Forum, or CCF, formed two weeks ago by poor people of every race and religion is likely to make one of the most powerful statements against racism at the WCAR, although they may not be in a lavish venue, and the TV cameras of the world may miss them.

However, we urge all those international groups and activists on the way to Durban to make contact with grassroots groups like the CCF. We'll certainly be with them, and we promise to bring you the story from the grassroots outside the WCAR in future postings.

Reflections on Durban
with Ben Cashdan, *The Nation*, September 17, 2001

To some of us in Africa, it seems as if your new president is scared of getting involved. Whereas Clinton entertained us with his exploits, throwing apologies around liberally afterwards, Bush seems to prefer pre-climactic withdrawal. We are referring of course to the U.S. government's premature departure from the World Conference Against Racism. This was the highest-profile pullout ever staged by such a low-profile delegation. One wonders whether U.S. officials were sent there with the express purpose of being withdrawn in protest.

What Bush overlooked is that the damage has already been done, and the United States cannot dodge its responsibility by its absence. The damage we are referring to is the legacy of centuries of conquest, subjugation, and economic exploitation on the descendants of slaves and on colonized and indigenous peoples. Granted, Bill Clinton's apologies pale into insignificance by comparison.

In reality, the former colonial and slave-trading powers needed this conference more than the so-called victims. This was a unique opportunity for Western governments to look on politely while representatives of the poor and marginalized aired their grievances, and for those governments to make a symbolic gesture in the direction of their victims—infinitely preferable to the hard-core demonstrators on the streets of Seattle or Genoa.

The European Union recognized this. The Belgian foreign minister stayed an extra night in Durban, holding up an important EU summit in Brussels, in order to try to come up with a final conference declaration. "One of the main reasons we need this conference to be a success" he said at his press conference, "is to provide a reply to the 'anti-globalists.'"

The message Europe wanted to give to the anti-globalization movement is that Western powers are aware of their historical responsibility for creating poverty and inequality and are on top of the situation. Fancy footwork by Europe insured just this outcome. The conference declaration denounces slavery and colonialism and recommends remedies based on a "developmental partnership," such as "promotion of foreign direct investment and market access."

Presto! Western elites are absolved of the guilt they might feel for having built their economies on systematic racial exploitation, and, as if by magic, minor modifications to their present economic policies are offered as remedies. No need for wild calls like reparations, and never mind a fundamental rethinking of contemporary capitalism. And as a bonus, Thabo Mbeki and leaders of other African elites consent to the outcome. Not a bad result for Europe. Seems like Bush missed the boat.

Even greater legitimacy was accorded the UN conference by the presence of thousands of nongovernmental delegates at the parallel NGO Forum. Not only did African presidents endorse the conference outcome but those boisterous civil society types, who have developed a predilection for trying to sabotage international gatherings of world leaders, had their own meeting just a block away.

Not surpisingly, the NGO declaration contains much more radical language than the official UN document. It condemns the contemporary racist exploitation by states of groups such as the Palestinians, the Dalits (or "untouchables") in India, and present-day slaves in Mauritania and elsewhere. And it calls for direct financial reparations to be paid to the victims of racism. It also points to present forms of globalization as an ongoing source of racial inequality.

What impact will the NGO document have on the UN or its member governments? Perhaps the best indication of this is given by the response of the UN High Commissioner for Human Rights, Mary Robinson, to the NGO document. Her first, private reaction was apparently to reject it outright. Later, at a press conference, she said that while it contained some good ideas, she could not recommend it to the main conference. In particular, she felt that its reference to Zionism as racism was unhelpful.

Could it be that the whole multimillion-dollar event, including the NGO Forum, was a charade, designed to give the impression that the more enlightened elements of global civil society have bought into the empty promises of globalization? That certainly was the prevailing view in the third gathering, the unofficial "pavement conference" attended by 20,000 landless and penniless people from around Durban and elsewhere in South Africa.

Unable to afford the $100 entrance fee to the NGO Forum, Durban's poor held their own assembly and march. This was the largest political protest in South Africa since the demise of apartheid, outside of a labor-union general strike. A few U.S. conference delegates strayed wide-eyed into the gatherings. They may not have understood the slogans being chanted by the masses in Zulu: Ulawula ngobubanxa Mbeki, e-South Africa ("Hey Mbeki, you're messing up South Africa"); Wena wawutshelwua ubani ukuthi amanzi ayakhokhelwa? ("Who told you you could sell us water?").

But they couldn't have missed the placards: "Landlessness equals racism." "You promised us land: you gave us jail." "The landless of South Africa support the landless of Palestine." Since the demise of apartheid, just 1 percent of South Africa's land has been redistributed to the black majority. White farmers still own 85 percent of the land. Homeless families who recently put up shacks on unused land in Johannesburg to fend off the winter cold were promptly and mercilessly evicted by the ANC municipality.

Residents of Durban's still-segregated black townships also condemned the ANC's cost-recovery policies, which have led to thousands of people having their water and electricity cut off and 100,000 people contracting cholera in the past year. Thousands of workers marched to protest the job losses associated with South Africa's home-grown (but co-written by the World Bank) structural adjustment program. South African unemployment is estimated to be around 40 percent, and according to the UN Development Program, South Africa recently overtook Brazil to become the most unequal society on the planet.

Across South Africa, as elsewhere in the world, a new social movement is forming to resist the new economic apartheid, which comes in the form of structural adjustment, corporate excess, and debt-dependency. This is a global apartheid system felt almost as strongly in the ghettos of Western cities as in the sweatshops of the Third World. The "Durban Social Forum" was founded on the streets outside the World Conference Against Racism to challenge this system.

At Porto Alegre in Brazil in February 2002, the second World Social Forum will unpack an alternative vision for the world, in which peoples' basic rights are paramount. Later this month protesters will once again challenge the World Bank's dependency-creating policies in Washington, D.C. Then in November, thousands across the world will challenge the proposed new round of WTO talks to be held in the inaccessible state of Qatar. In September 2002, many thousands will return to Johannesburg to challenge the hype at the Rio+10 summit on sustainable development.

Together with the local struggles for jobs, homes, services, education, and healthcare, this is the real cutting edge of the fight against racism on a global scale. The World Conference Against Racism never provided a real opportunity for change. We are pleased that the U.S. government revealed its real interests by going home. At least Bush, unlike his predecessor, represents a more honest approach.

World Summit on Sustainable Development
Independent Politics News, Summer 2002

The World Summit on Sustainable Development—the WSSD—will be an event of major, indeed global significance. It is being held August 26–September 4 in Johannesburg, South Africa. In discussing sustainable development we are also discussing the fate of our planet. There will be over 100 heads of state, 60,000 registered delegates, multiple sessions, and much hoopla. But there will also be serious issues taken up. Some may dismiss the WSSD as just another talking shop, but the fact is that there may be truly serious decisions that will be sneaked by us if we are not careful.

Coming ten years after the last summit in Rio de Janeiro, the assessment of progress will be truly gloomy. Compared to the goals set out in Agenda 21 at Rio, the report sheet will show that that there has been little or no progress. The condition of the planet, the pollution of land, sea and air, has grown steadily worse. The corporations are still recklessly concentrating profits and resisting legislation which would try to curb them, and with most lawmakers comfortably bought via campaign contributions, they can safely defang laws which would try to restrain them.

Some examples of what is happening:

—A block of ice, a thousand square miles in extent, has recently broken off the Antarctic land mass, following another somewhat smaller piece, at astonishing rapidity;

—The oceans are rising; Pacific islanders have been forced to leave their homes and move elsewhere;

—Peasants in India are forced to give up lands and homes as the Indian government approves expansion of the Narmada dam.

The United States continues to be the greatest polluter of our world, so the U.S. will be a major target, especially after reneging on the Kyoto Protocol and cutbacks on pollution of the atmosphere. But for the continent of Africa there will be an issue of more pressing importance, an effort to foist on the people of Africa a new form of colonization called NEPAD—the New Partnership for Africa's Development.

NEPAD is something of a variant on the African Growth and Opportunity Act, what Jesse Jackson, Jr. called "the new re-colonization act." NEPAD is designed to tie Africa to the developed world in a relationship of dependence; already in South Africa some are calling NEPAD "kneepad"—it will bring Africa to her knees. Africa will need all the allies it can get from the rest of the world to resist this new cruel enslavement.

The brainchild of Thabo Mbeki, South Africa's president, he hopes that this act will give him the mantle of international statesman once worn by Nelson Mandela and make him the blue-eyed boy of the West. His cronies include Obsanjo of Nigeria and Bouteflika of Algeria, who hope also to benefit from the largess of the West.

Despite current fractiousness, the forces struggling for true freedom in Africa—as opposed to current cosmetics in South Africa and elsewhere—will get it together in time to mobilize for a people's grassroots summit—as opposed to the ministerial summit, to challenge this agenda and declare the people's opposition. August–September looks to be a lively time.

In all sincerity one can say that the fate of the planet itself will be under discussion. The heedless, destructive rush of the corporations for profits and the fierce destructive competition of the capitalist system which drives the present world order in what we broadly call the process of corporate globalization—this itself must be brought to judgement. There are some seeking pretexts to duck this confrontation, but all who care about the survival of our species, of all species, and of the planet itself, must seek to be engaged around these issues. There will be many ways to be involved: by helping others to participate, by sending messages of support, by contributing funds for those mobilizing in defense of us all. This is a rallying call, a call to action to defend Africa, to defend the planet. It's time to get involved.

Global agendas are set
by the usual suspects
IndyMedia South Africa, July 15, 2002

South Africa and the world are faced with critical ideological choices in coming weeks. What kind of case is the global Left making? The stakes couldn't be higher. When the World Summit on Sustainable Development convenes in Sandton in late August, it will literally be deciding on an agenda for the planet. When countries joining the Africa Union (AU) meet in Durban next week, the New Partnership for Africa's Development (NEPAD) will set the agenda for our continent. But in reality, much of the agenda for both these events has already been determined by the Group of Eight (G8) leadership in its mountain hideout in Canada.

George Bush, Tony Blair, Jacques Chirac, Gerhard Schröder, Jean Chretien, and the others serve as a sort of board of directors which promotes northern corporate interests. That is not good for the rest of us. This was proven at the Bali prepcom [preparatory committee] for the world summit in early June, when corporations pushed the privatization agenda via the G8, World Bank, International Monetary Fund (IMF) and World Trade Organization (WTO).

Frontline battles to save humanity and the environment have been waged often enough by people's movements against these institutions, from Seattle to Prague to Washington. And there are many other sites across the Third World that have hosted IMF riots against neoliberal (free-market) economics.

Now we find that we also must do battle with the United Nations bureaucrats and a global compact that, because of U.S. unwillingness to pay back dues, requires Kofi Annan to go begging to some of the world's most criminal multinational corporations. And now we learn too, that the host country for the world summit and the AU are apparently intent on selling out the continent under the rubric of a plan crafted by the same technocrats who wrote Pretoria's failed GEAR [Growth Employment and Redistribution] economic program, under the guidance of Washington and the corporate leaders of Davos.

It is past time for us to insist that President Thabo Mbeki rise off his kneepad and assume the dignity of an African leader, or face ridicule. In Durban at the launch of the Africa Union, social movements will remind the world that discredited elites cannot rename their club and continue to endorse the Washington Consensus.

Virtually all civil society commentators have complained that NEPAD is top-down, non-consultative, and so prone to neoliberal economic mistakes and that it must be tossed out and a new program started from scratch. *Time* magazine put Mbeki on its front cover on June 10, alleging incorrectly that he has made a U-turn on AIDS. The G8 elites need a rehabilitated Mbeki, and they insist that, as *Time* claimed, NEPAD "could be the continent's last hope for joining the global economy."

Yet Africa has joined the global economy, and that is the problem. For more than a quarter of a century, the revenue from our outputs—mainly cash crops and minerals—have fallen dramatically even though our outputs have increased, due to what economists call "declining terms of trade." Meanwhile, debt repayments and capital flight continue to suck us dry of finances we desperately need for investment.

So why then does NEPAD politely agree to repay debt under the Highly Indebted Poor Countries program that even the World Bank now admits has failed? And how can Mbeki in good conscience promote more "public-private partnerships" in Africa which do not work at home? The privatization of water, electricity, transport, and telecommunications by European, U.S., and Asian firms have all failed on their own terms, as well as in providing sustainable access to the masses of South Africans.

In the movements for global justice, our strategy is to endorse, attend, and create a series of progressive events at the AU in July and the world summit in August that will allow the voices of angry citizens to be heard. These include communities resisting evictions and water and electricity cutoffs, rural people demanding land reform, AIDS activists seeking antiretroviral medicine, environmentalists halting dams and dirty energy projects, women opposing patriarchy and violence, consumer organizations opposed to corporate domination of everything, and labor on strike against their oppressors in the private sector as well as municipal and national governments.

We expect all these movements will join a mass march on the

Sandton Convention Center at the midpoint of the world summit. Its aim is to nonviolently remind the elites that we don't trust them, and to remind society of the issues that the elites are doing their best to ignore.

Africa's struggles today

An interview with Lee Sustar, *International Socialist Review*, September–October 2003

Africa is obviously very poorly covered in the U.S. media, in particular during the period around the war in Iraq. What was unfolding in Africa was ignored except for the Liberia crisis— although once it reached a certain stage, it began to get some attention. Of course, the Bush trip to Africa shed some more light on what's been happening. You've been there for several weeks, watching things unfold from the African point of view. What can you tell us about the overall picture?

It's quite true that the Bush visit put an enormous spotlight on Africa when Bush traveled with his 600-person entourage, journalists, etc. In many cases media events were carefully controlled so that only the American press were allowed at the press conferences. In fact, there were long articles in the South African press about journalists who finally sneaked in to stand at the back of the hall and were told they were not allowed to ask questions. Bush goes to Senegal, he goes to Gorrei, which is the island from which slaves were shipped to the New World. He comes to South Africa and meets with [Prime Minister Thabo] Mbeki in Pretoria and significantly does not go to Maputo where the AU is meeting—the new African Union heads of state. Then he goes to Botswana which is very rich in diamonds, does Uganda very briefly for a couple of hours, and ends up in Nigeria, which of course is Africa's biggest oil producer.

But I would say for the whole of Africa, if they look at the total visit, the event that they would say is the most significant was Bush meeting with Mbeki and announcing that Mbeki is his point man. Specifically, of course, on the Zimbabwe issue, where Mbeki's quiet diplomacy the British have been screaming about is now endorsed by the U.S. government, which says whatever Mbeki does is OK. But more seriously, the process is a signal to the rest of the continent that they have to take orders from Mbeki. His sub-imperial role is clearly defined.

I should mention that wherever [Bush has] gone there were protests. In South Africa, we had huge protests. In Johannesburg the protests were directed not at Bush but at Mbeki's embracing of Bush. So you had loyal ANC [African National Congress] people, labor, workers, and so on joining in a march in protest against Mbeki's welcoming of Bush. But at the same time, ironically, the ANC put together a small protest saying, we're not protesting against our president, we are protesting against the U.S. president and the invasion of Iraq. So that you have a kind of tail attached to the protests. They come in with this little footnote.

The second issue I would focus on as being of major significance for me and for most Africans—apart from Bush's designation of Mbeki as his agent in Africa—was Bush's endorsement of NEPAD [New Partnership for Africa's Development] and saying this is the program which is being led by Mbeki and which has the U.S.'s endorsement. So simultaneously you have an allegedly African initiative together with a U.S. initiative coming together.

The two of them, of course, mainly focused on trade—doing two things and we should recognize both. On the one hand giving South Africa access to the U.S. textile market. Although interestingly, one of the conditions is that the manufacture of textiles has to be done with U.S. material. So you can manufacture the goods but the raw material has to be U.S. produced. So it's not really as advantageous even as it appears on paper.

The other more significant—and I think far more dangerous—element for the future is the creation of free-trade zones, where you would have U.S. manufacturers being able to produce without being taxed locally on the products. And of course within these free-trade zones labor controls on wages are removed. So there is freedom to depress wages to the lowest possible level in order to increase the margin of profit on the product. And there are already several areas in Southern Africa that are free-trade zones. In one case on the island of Mauritius, they've gone from making a region of the island a free-trade zone to the entire island becoming a free-trade zone.

So the last point I should make is that I was very impressed to hear people talking on talk shows in Africa. One of the things they're saying was that there is no country in Africa where there is not some opposition to NEPAD. So maybe just a word about NEPAD. The notion is that Africa becomes an equal partner in trade either with the U.S. or the developed West—Europe and the United States. But others have compared it to the partnership between a rider and his horse. You know the African does all the work and the partner (the U.S. or Europe) is in fact riding on the back of Africa. The whole thing is unequal and we could go into it in detail, but I might as well focus on the one issue in NEPAD that seems the most damaging. If you read the document called the "New Partnership" you'll find that it says very explicitly that Africa will be brought into line with the requirements of the IMF, the World Bank and the WTO. And that spells out more clearly than anything else the dependency relationship which Africa is being forced into. With South Africa leading that process. Now, as you know, Mbeki was the first chairman of the AU and in that way was directing the NEPAD process. But he's no longer chair as he's just handed over the chair to President Joaquim Chissano from Mozambique. But since there is a troika consisting of the three people who fathered NEPAD—that's Mbeki, Nigerian President Olusegun Obasanjo, and President Abdoulaye Wade of Senegal. The three of them really gave birth to NEPAD as we know it. They still are pretty much the power brokers, and although Chissano is the chair, the three of them still exhibit a very strong influence.

With NEPAD, is the view from the standpoint of South African capital and these three players to try to create a more economically unified Africa, to try to negotiate a position to play the U.S. and Europe off one another—to try to look for the better deals as opposed to playing separately?

My guess would have to be yes and no. Instead of regional agreements, you have one for a continent. But that's only half the answer because simultaneously there are agreements with Europe and the EU, including the Lomé Agreement. The catch here, why I'm kind of hedging my answer, is that when these three guys recently went to Evian to meet with the G8, and then they meet with the EU representatives, there is a sense in which what you suggest of them playing Europe against the U.S. is still going on. But it's almost as if the U.S. and Europe have already agreed on spheres of influence between themselves. So when the Africans go to Europe there are certain things they know they can get and certain things they can't get. Then they go to the U.S. for those.

I'll give you one example and a very dangerous one. In Evian, where the G8 met, they refused to give Africans anything. Even the promises they made in Canada, they didn't deliver on those. But guess what—they offered Africa $15 billion to set up a military force, an RDF. So Africa is going to have a Rapid Deployment Force funded by Europe. Not by the U.S. So it's as if Europe is getting into the act in one way. Of course this means supplies of weapons. You've got to update your weapons and all that. But at the same time that Europe is taking care of the military side, the U.S. is taking care of the economic side. So the colonization of Africa is really going to be a two-fold process. The attack comes both from the United States and Europe.

The other news that we did get in the U.S., however briefly, was that during the world conference on racism there were actually sizable demonstrations that brought some focus on different social movements and different trade union struggles in South Africa in particular. Can you tell us about that and how that fits into the overall opposition to this program?

Yes, I am glad that you mentioned that. Of course, there was the World Conference Against Racism in Durban, followed by the World Summit on Sustainable Development in Johannesburg. And you really should take the two together because the same forces are at work in both cases. You have your whole combination of government and corporations on one hand and you have the people in the streets. About 10–15,000 in Durban and over 20,000 in Johannesburg. And both of these really are the embodiment of the social movements we've seen in Seattle, Genoa, and Prague.

The focus in Durban was on the kind of glossy façade, which said racism in South Africa is over. Even while people are still living in shacks and their water was being cut off, electricity was being cut off. So you get the homeless and the jobless and people with AIDS and of course your activist movement, student movement, your labor movement coming together very powerfully in Durban. And as you may remember, one of the strongest elements in Durban was this demand for reparations, a demand for the cancellation of debt. So these two elements come into play in Durban. And then later they come into play in Johannesburg. Johannesburg was called the WSSD [World Summit on Sustainable Development]. And what is striking there is that Mbeki calls a rally in the stadium in support of the WSSD and gets under 5,000 people. And then the social movements—they group themselves under something called the SMI (Social Movements Indaba)—from the same stadium they put 20,000 people into the streets, marching from Alex (this is one of the worst slums in Johannesburg) to Sandton (which is your most expensive suburb).

Both of them, it seems to me—and I think you've made the point, I just want to reinforce it—reflect this kind of global opposition to the global agenda. It's taking on the corporate power and governmental power, the whole neoliberal project. The commodification of water, commodification of air, it all fits into this.

Can you tell us about the lineup of forces? Certainly from Mbeki fronting for NEPAD and an imperialist project in Africa, the prestige of Africa's greatest liberation movement is being used for these purposes. We have seen tensions in the Communist Party [CP] alliance, the ANC and the trade unions. COSATU [the Congress of South African Trade Unions] has been much more critical. How is the legacy of the national liberation struggle and the politics of this opposition playing out? How are people defining themselves and what are they trying to put forward as an alternative?

It's not easy but I'll try. I have to start by stressing that the new struggles all emerged as initially local issues. People's water being cut off. People's kids dying because they don't have food. People dying in the streets. More homelessness, more unemployment than there was under apartheid. The gap between rich and poor has increased. And South Africa now has become the number one country in the world with the largest gap between rich and poor by their own statistics. Very significantly, recently they showed that real earnings for blacks have gone down by about 15 percent in the past ten years, just as for the white minority and few elite blacks it has gone up by 16 percent. So the gap actually widens there. I think one has to stress that it's a response to lived experiences that people build a new movement and new struggle. And then it takes different forms—the homeless, the jobless, the landless, the people with AIDS, people with water cut off, with lights off.

All those come together. Now in that context you get a tension developing on the Left—in ANC, in COSATU, and in the NGOs. It takes two forms and it's a little bit difficult to explain and even I can't satisfactorily explain it for myself. For instance, people recognize that one of the reasons they are homeless and waterless and lightless is privatization. The social services have become commodities and they can't pay. So they understand that the whole process of their immiseration is driven by privatization. When you understand that you have to ask why is the government doing this? And then you get a split within the Left—those who defend privatization and those who attack privatization.

This is where we find the dilemma being crystallized. Jeff Radebe, who is a member of the central committee of the Communist Party, is the minister in charge of driving the privatization process. So you have a man who is both a member of the Communist Party—which denounces privatization—and is also the minister who is driving the privatization process. Of course we challenge him. And the explanation is, "Oh, if you are a member of the Communist Party and you become a minister of government your first loyalty is to the government." You can claim to be loyal to the party but your first loyalty is to the government. COSATU identifies very clearly that privatization is why they are losing jobs. A million jobs lost. And they say this is what privatization has done.

So what do we do? Every year, at what is now called the annual general meeting, they call a strike against privatization. Then they meet with the government and they call the strike off. It's a ritual annual strike: "We're not going to take it any more." Then the government says, "OK, go ahead but don't do it again." Until it happens next year. It really has become a ritual.

So that partly explains it. But of course the CP now has 50 members in parliament. And they get really nice perks. They get free airfare, free hotels for themselves and their families, and so on. The perks, I hate to say it, I think are really quite important. And the government, I think, has the ability to disperse all these advantages. The resources are there. There may be a few people if you read the left literature (especially the CP) you'll find them coming up with a kind of tortured logic, which says in any case we're not really free. Of course this is also what George Soros says, that the ANC is a captive of the World Bank and IMF. But there are people in the CP itself who say we don't really like what we're doing, but we're not really free not to do it.

There are many struggles. There is the beginning of protests but also an ideological challenge to this as well. How does the labor movement fit into this and the unions, the pressure from the rank and file?

Not yet. Not yet. There's talk of dissatisfaction. The way COSATU has dealt with it is rather clever. You do have these annual strikes of thousands in the street or you may have a stay-at-home or a one-day strike—and then after that there's just a massive shedding of jobs. The mines have just announced that another 18,000 are going be fired. And the mining union says we're going to go on strike and then they make some compromise. I don't follow those negotiations closely because they're so repetitious. There's talk and threats and little action.

Interestingly, I've met with the head of COSATU, but I didn't meet him on those issues. COSATU is an ally of Jubilee South Africa with which I serve in filing the case for reparations [from corporations that benefited from apartheid]. COSATU is our ally and is also an ally of the ANC as part of the tripartite alliance. When they came over to our side on reparations, they went back to the government to check if they could do it, and the government said we will neither support you nor oppose you. But since then, under pressure from (a) corporations and (b) the U.S. government at Davos [Switzerland, the site of the World Economic Forum], the COSATU guys backed off. Suddenly they are no longer our allies in the reparations fight, although they started out as our allies. Now, apparently this happened in Davos. The U.S. government and of course IBM and the banks said don't touch it.

Jubilee South Africa filed a suit in New York for reparations in the name of a collective of the homeless and jobless and it was OK'd by COSATU and by the churches. Suddenly the churches announce, "We don't like what you are doing." And this was quite remarkable because evidently Mbeki and people in the government contacted the churches and said get out of it. So at the moment it looks like Jubilee is alone in conducting the suit.

Now it's not really as simple as that because what they've said is not that they're getting out but that they don't like the way we're doing it and they'd like these changes and so on. So the fact of the matter is that they are trying to find a way of killing the action. They told us you can't have a conference so we went ahead and had a workshop instead. We had about 140 people coming from twenty-three to twenty-five organizations willing to buck both the churches and COSATU—saying in spite of those guys we'll go ahead. After that the churches and trade unions said go ahead, we can't stop you, so we'll go ahead and join you. My feeling is they'll either stack that one with so many church organizations that they'll either wipe us out or discredit us or maybe even instruct the lawyers to drop the suit. There is a whole range of possibilities. What we are trying to do of course is to mobilize our allies so we will be there in force. The dates are August 20–21. The government has filed a countersuit in New York in opposition to our suit for reparations.

We think we can sue for $100 billion. And we don't think we'll get it. But what we might get is a settlement out of court when we go after Ford, GM, IBM, Citibank, and these guys. They'll do what they did on the Holocaust issue. They settled out of court when they saw they were going to lose and the dirt was flying around. And we think that money should go into institutional reparations—schools, hospitals, clinics for people with AIDS, and so on. But the corporations have decided that they don't want to go into court and they want to kill this suit. And the way to kill the suit is not by themselves, but to get the churches and trade unions to say don't touch it.

In recent weeks we've heard about demands for Western military intervention in Liberia. Groups like the Congressional Black Caucus, which has been quite good on African debt are now calling for intervention in Liberia. What attitude should people in the global justice movement take toward that issue?

I was very interested in the debate that the Left has had on the future of the UN. I can understand people saying things like somebody has to do something in Iraq. And if it's not the U.S. then it better be the UN. And I say: Too bad. The one is as bad as the other. We'll have to find alternative ways to go in and clean up Iraq. But to ask the UN to do it is to ask it to go in as a surrogate for the United States. First of all, it's a U.S. mess you're asking them to clean up, and the UN has not demonstrated independence of mind or independence of values. Even if you ask why did the Security Council stand up to the U.S., you get a set of very mixed motives. The French and the Germans were worried they wouldn't get a piece of the oil. You get a whole set of reasons that have nothing to do with ethics. This is not morality we're talking about. I would say Africa is an enormous mess mostly generated by the West—its diamonds, its oil and its mercenaries. So when you get to a mess in Africa the wrong people to call for help are the people who caused the trouble. As desperate as the situation is, I promise you, if you get Charles Taylor out of the way, you'll get another American stooge, a Mobutu being installed to protect American interests—gold or diamonds or oil, or uranium. There are terrible killings and of course they must be stopped. But sending a killer to clean up the killing operation....

Twenty-five or thirty years ago I think that debate would have been answered by a Left in solidarity with the struggles. The idea of national liberation and self-determination was at the forefront. Now there's formal independence—the formal colonies are virtually all gone, although Iraq may be something different. How can we get that politics back on the agenda?

The reality is that Africa has been re-colonized. It is the neocolonial process that is now paralyzed. And it is that neocolonial process that generates those conflicts, internecine conflicts in Africa. Genocide and fratricidal killings of people even from the same community. One side paid by the other side. Armed by both sides. The South Africans are selling guns to both sides like crazy. They don't care as long as the money comes through. Black diamonds out of Botswana. Blood diamonds out of Sierra Leone. And who profits? They are now selling diamonds on the streets of Amsterdam.

So the short answer, again, is don't send in the killer to clean up the killing. Find alternative solutions among themselves. I think we are in a terrible mess, but we aren't going to solve the disease by giving the patient poison.

We have had the rise of a global social movement. Africa is increasingly vocal and important in that. How do we take the issues out into the movement?

Glad you asked that. I think this is where the social movement globally becomes significant for Africa. Alliances form because other parts of the world are suffering from the same imperialism. We have allies at the same time we begin to construct our own opposition. And usually the very simple lesson is that we fight the oppressor where we find him and we define our resistance in terms of that oppression. So it varies from place to place. Just for the record, we now have an African Social Forum. We have a Southern African Social Forum and in South Africa we have SMI. People are suspicious in Africa about things not indigenous to Africa and they want to know that we do it in our own way.

One of our curious problems is that at the moment, parallel to the uncertainty people have about the UN, we have uncertainty about the AU. You must remember that the AU is the replacement of the OAU [Organization of African Unity]. It is perhaps good in one area, which is the emphasis on decolonization, on African independence. That was its strong point. It was full of intrigue and dishonesty and was infiltrated by the CIA. They were corrupt people in there so it really wasn't very good except on the insistence of an independent Africa. And eventually, of course, we pretty much won that struggle after a fashion. Most of Africa is in some way or another independent.

Then, along comes the AU. And the AU is not about independence. Ideally, it's about "good governance" if you like. It's certainly about trade relations and international stature. There's talk about the African Renaissance and so on. But for the left, radicals in Africa have been unable to define their attitude towards the AU. And you can understand why. We do need a continental body. It makes sense. The disappearance of the OAU was not regretted...but once you have a vacuum you're in trouble. You need some sort of organization there. So we do need a coordinating body. Should it be the AU? The answer more and more is no.

Which is interesting because what people are saying is what is the AU all about? The heart of AU is NEPAD. Now if NEPAD is what the AU is about, it means we are going to be subjugated to the IMF, the World Bank, and the WTO. It means surrendering ourselves into bondage by believing that we were establishing an autonomous body. Interestingly, about two weeks ago when they were meeting in Maputo, the AU was discussing NEPAD, and there was a meeting with Bush in Pretoria, we issued a statement and for the first time we denounced the AU. We said as long as the AU has NEPAD as its backbone, we must regard the AU as suspicious.

And again, out of the African Social Forum we may have to develop an alternative to the AU. It may take some time, but the AU is not in our interest and we need to build a new one.

For those of us who were active in the 1980s, the South African struggle was a touchstone. Today, there are all these contradictions and difficulties. I'm not asking for inspiration, but it seems to me that the struggles are repeating and beginning anew and drawing from the past.

I like that and I'll give you an interesting little episode. Last year, just before the World Summit on Sustainable Development, we got together to plan an action. And the place we chose was a house on a farm in Johannesburg called Rivonia. Now Rivonia was the house in which Walter Sisulu and Nelson Mandela had met to plot the overthrow of the apartheid government. So when we met there I said this is the beginning of a new struggle and it's appropriate that we meet in the place where the serious challenge to the apartheid regime began.

Statement on the Palestinian campaign for the academic and cultural boycott of Israel
May 13, 2005

Since the Sixties until 1994 I have dedicated most of my time—apart from a spell on Robben Island Prison—to promote and enforce the boycott of apartheid South Africa. I have no doubt that international solidarity, particularly in the form of the boycott campaign, contributed to change in South Africa.

Despite the political changes in South Africa, apartheid lives on. It lives on in the oppression of the Palestinian people and their daily subjection to the racism of the Israeli state. The actions of the Israeli state are reminiscent of, and often even worse than those of the South African apartheid regime.

Apartheid South Africa also acted with impunity. It was supported by the West and, let us not forget, by pariah states such as Israel and Pinochet's Chile. It was only when people of conscience

and organizations around the world pressured their own govern-
ments and multilateral institutions, did we see movement toward
democracy in South Africa. Facile arguments against the boycott of
Israeli institutions are familiar to me. They were the same or simi-
lar to the arguments used against anti-apartheid activists.

Israel, like apartheid South Africa, ignores international law
and is supported in this by the major powers. The latest outrage is
the near silence on the grotesque and obscene Apartheid Wall
which the International Court of Justice condemned some time
back. This complicity, understandably, contributes to the despera-
tion felt by many in Palestine. The call from Palestinian academics
for a peaceful boycott campaign should therefore be embraced par-
ticularly by those who pontificate against violence.

In the spirit of moral consistency and resistance to all forms of
injustice I have no hesitation in supporting the call for the aca-
demic and cultural boycott of Israeli institutions. While I believe in
the comprehensive boycott of Israeli institutions, I applaud the re-
cent decision of the UK-based Association of University Teachers
as a step in this direction.[1]

I call on academics and scholars throughout the world to join
us in this action.

> [1] The AUT's endorsement was later rescinded under pressure from
> pro-Israel groups.

Africa: Can Blair and Brown deliver?
Speech at the G8 Alternatives Summit, Edinburgh, July 3, 2005

I'm glad to be a part of this historic occasion which, as I'm sure
you all know, is part of a much larger series of events taking place
here in Edinburgh and in Gleneagles [at the Group of 8 summit].

Our topic today is "Africa: Can [Tony] Blair and [Gordon]
Brown deliver?" I will attempt to respond to that, but it seems to me
that we ought to add an additional B to those two, because there is
one other B who is a part of this process, and opposition to him is
part of the whole struggle for social justice. So I would add another
B, and then we will go ahead and boo together, for the third B is, of
course, George W. Bush.

We boo because we understand that much of the problem here in Britain and particularly with Tony Blair as he tries to deflect people's attention, is about war, and people's involvement in war and about Britain's involvement in that war. And above all, it's about the dishonesty and the lies surrounding that involvement in war.

When we talk about Africa and can Blair and Brown deliver we must not forget Bush. We must not forget the whole issue of global justice for all the people of the world.

And so to the question, and as you know there are really two elements to the question.

The first is what exactly is being proposed and the second is what can be delivered from what is being proposed?

I don't need to remind you that in the run-up to these talks there have been discussions both here and in Washington of the possibility of 100 percent cancellation of debt. At the time of the sixtieth birthday celebrations of the World Bank and the IMF in Washington, and I was there as part of the protests against them, the discussion was quite serious of the 100 percent cancellation of debt.

They went further, both in Washington and in Britain. They researched and discussed. The result was that they said it is possible to arrange the 100 percent unconditional cancellation of debt and it would not make a significant impact on the global economy. Therefore it was entirely feasible to do it. This was their own research, their own findings.

But then it turned out that hidden in the detail there was an additional element—George Bush was asking for the 100 percent cancellation of the debt of Iraq. The argument was that this was an odious debt. In fact he failed to get 100 percent, but he did get 80 percent cancellation of the debt of Iraq. But, as we know, this is not what is on offer to others.

The countries of the Global South, whether in Africa or Asia or South America, have come together to take a position. If you do nothing else I would urge you to get the document that states the position of the Global South—here I will settle for reading you the opening lines. Jubilee South's response to the G8 debt proposal says, "Justice demands unconditional and total debt cancellation for all global South countries."

That is our position. I hope that you will take the document and you will study it carefully.

I would like to focus on the most significant aspects of this most significant occasion, the whole of the G8 summit and all of the people in the streets, all the declarations and all the denials—how does one sum it up?

Well firstly, in some ways it is a distraction from a much more serious issue, that this country, Britain, has been dragged into a war, and dragged into a war by lies. And I think we should go on nailing those lies.

Secondly, somehow another very serious issue, an issue of life and death—an issue that involves the lives of millions of people who are going to die because of this debt—[has been ignored, and] somehow the focus has turned to entertainment, to [Bob] Geldof and Bono, to concerts around the world and Live8. It's a very clever distraction from the issues of debt and of life and death. And we are all implicated because we can either be placid and accept it, or active and reject it.

The third rather striking aspect is that with the emphasis on slogans like Make Poverty History we have really been duped into an approach to a problem by offering a solution that is no solution. We are going to the G8 to ask them to help make poverty history.

And I have to remind you that the source of poverty, the engine and the generator of poverty, the system and the structures that have created massive poverty across the world emanate from the G8. They are the source. They are the source of our suffering, the source of our pain, the source of our oppression.

And so instead of making poverty history we should be making the G8 history.

Imperialism, sub-imperialism, and popular resistance in South Africa
Speech at the Brecht Forum, New York City, May 23, 2005

It seems to me, as I speak across this country and other countries—particularly for those who were involved in helping us to overthrow the apartheid system, challenging that system of racist minority domination—when you tell them about what's happening in South Africa today, they have great difficulty in accepting it.

They have been part of the struggle; they know we won the struggle. Nelson Mandela came out of prison on Robben Island; they wrote one of the most humane constitutions in the world, and everybody celebrated.

And yet, the reports coming out of South Africa, and the reports that I must communicate reluctantly, are of a very bad situation—and you find great difficulty in accepting that. It seems to me that on the other hand, once you've seen this video, once you've seen the people marching, once you've seen the police being marshaled and their force being demonstrated and the use of tear gas and the people in jail, it becomes less difficult to accept our reports that somehow things have gone horribly wrong in South Africa. That where we marched against the oppression of a minority racist regime in the past, we now have to march against the people we put in power. The people who were elected to serve us, are now serving instead the World Bank, the IMF, and the whole corporate global agenda.

And so we are now in the position once again, of having to march. And some of us will be beaten, and some of us will be jailed, and some of us may end up in prison, as I did on Robben Island, when I broke stones with Nelson Mandela many years ago. But some of us are willing to take that challenge and to confront an oppressive system with the understanding that oppression is not only about race, and oppression is not only about color, and you may as easily be oppressed by a black government as by a white government, and that you must be willing to confront that government.

I'm going to stop there. I hope you have questions about that, and we can engage in discussion about it, but I want to move on to just one more point which Patrick [Bond] suggested I mention. That is the fact that we are currently engaged in a huge struggle to confront this new oppressive regime, which serves the World Bank and the IMF and the corporate global agenda. Part of that is a very interesting initiative we've launched this year. In the curious way history has of repeating itself, the bank which financed apartheid and profited from apartheid is now going to return to South Africa and buy up 61 percent of the biggest bank in South Africa. Barclays Bank, which donated 10 million rand to the apartheid army, is now coming back to profit from the new South Africa—as they profited from the old South Africa—and we have said that this is not acceptable. We have decided to launch a challenge in the streets of Johannesburg and Cape Town, Durban and Port Elizabeth—wherever there are branches of a bank called ABSA, the Amalgamated Bank of South Africa, which Barclays Bank is about to take over by purchasing 61 percent of ABSA....You'll read about it in the papers, I'm sure—because we've had to launch a new challenge to a new oppression.

One interesting dimension of it is the fact that Barclays already functions in over eighty countries in the world. And it seems to us that when we challenge Barclays, we should challenge them not only in South Africa but wherever they are, across the world. And that means we're going to have to call for our allies to take to take to the streets in the way that they took to the streets in the good old days of the anti-apartheid struggle. The students, and the churches, and the trade unions, and the Quakers, and all the others, will have to be willing to lay their bodies on the line one more time. We are willing to confront this new oppression. In the old days this confrontation was pretty localized. This time it's going to be globalized. We are willing to take them on, all over the world, and to challenge them all over the world. When we do, its worth remembering that we're really taking on the global struggle against the global corporate agenda which is crushing people everywhere all over the world: the workers, the peasants, women, children, the exploited, the oppressed. We fight on behalf of all of them. And...we have to start all over again and build a whole new movement and a whole new struggle. And I hope that all of you will be part of it. As I said, a little later on we'll squeeze in some poetry, but we also want to have discussion and questions. So I'm going to hand it back to Patrick now and then, maybe we'll come back with some poetry after you've got some questions. Thanks. [Applause.]

Discussion

I think implied in one of the questions was this notion that in fact the image of South Africa around the world, even now, is a rather flattering one. For a lot of people there is the impression that after apartheid and the release of Nelson Mandela, there was the adoption of a very progressive constitution, and there is the assumption that South Africa is really taking good care of its people—

of its elderly, of its sick, of its infirm, of the victims of apartheid. I suppose in one area the truth has begun to come out—the issue of AIDS and the question of anti-retrovirals. The South African government is doing a very bad job, and most people know that, and they think that the Mbeki government has done a bad job in that area. But in other respects there is still the assumption that it is a progressive society. But off course we know how the spin doctors work. We know how, when I am in other parts of the world and I talk about a peace movement in the United States, people are amazed. You say there are people in the United States who are against the war in Iraq, and they say, "What? You must be joking!" Because that's how badly the protest movement in this country is reported in other parts of the world. And the impression is that most Americans are solidly in support of the war in Iraq. I'm just trying to kind of dispose of that fallacy, which is still being projected.

Patrick is raising other issues that I'm not sure we have the time to get into so I'm just going to go back to one I began with. That in fact in South Africa—you saw the images in the video, those of you who were here at the beginning—not only is there resistance to the new regime, but the new regime is willing to turn out the army and the police force, and stun guns, and to jail people....

[A] very dangerous, very sophisticated operation is in process. This whole idea for NEPAD, the New Economic Partnership for African Development, it's really about re-colonizing Africa. Re-enslaving and re-exploiting Africa on an unparalleled scale, with the collaboration of some of the heads of state in Africa willing to become part of this scheme. Because of course there are perks, and there are rewards, for those who are willing to collaborate in the scheme. But fortunately, it is true to say that all over Africa people are getting together, in fact are compelled to get together. The burden of debt, of hunger, of literal starvation—the lack of drinkable water, lack of food, is forcing people to mobilize, to organize, and to protest. And it will grow. What we need—and this is very important—is allies in other parts of the world, and when Patrick raised the question earlier, is it right for the North to be profiting and living well at the expense of the people of the South? This is really a question which we must ask ourselves and be challenged by....

The African Social Forum for me began all the way back in

Seattle, when people took the streets and confronted the World Trade Organization and the World Bank and the IMF plus the corporate powers, Bill Gates and Microsoft and all the rest of them— Boeing and the rest. But since then, 1999, at the beginning of the century, people have been in the streets, challenging corporate power and challenging the corporate agenda. So in Africa we've developed an African Social Forum, as there is a European Social Forum and an Asian Social Forum. And there is also the World Social Forum some of you may have attended in Porto Alegre [Brazil], and also in Mumbai, and we are getting it together. If there is global oppression, I'm glad to say there is also global resistance. And we are building steadily an African Social Forum as part of that. We met in Lusaka, we met in Bamako in Mali, we met in Dakar, in Senegal, and in the year 2007 we expect to be meeting in Nairobi as a World Social Forum. So all over the world, people are getting their act together, and we are mobilizing to change the world. The slogan of the World Social Forum, "Another World is Possible," is something we believe, and something we can do. South Africa, Ghana, Zimbabwe, Zambia, the rest of the continent—we're all coming together in the African Social Forum, which in turn is part of the World Social Forum.

We are building a world liberation movement.

Poems

Train journey

Along the miles of steel
that span my land
threadbare children stand
knees ostrich-bulbous on their reedy legs,
their empty hungry hands
lifted as if in prayer.

July 1962   1968

Picture of a young girl dying of aids

She looks out of the photograph
her large eyes say
she is conscious of her beauty
but they are shadowed with sorrow
at her young life ending soon:
"Look at me" her dark eyes say
"I am a lesson in faulted living
perhaps I can help you learn
I am dying young of aids":
she lives in the shadow
of impending, inescapable death.

October 2, 1991   2005
Pittsburgh, PA

Robben Island Holiday Resort

Where the bikinied bathers pat
soothing cream into sun-scorched limbs
or scuff swishing through silken sands
some of us will hear the slap of batons
slashed across wincing vulnerable flesh
or the rasp of chains dragged in the dust
by stiff creaking ankles, weary and stubborn

February 23, 1993   2005
Boulder Colorado

If you ever go visiting in Capetown
and look across that blue and silver bay
spare a thought for those who ploughed
the gray miles of water
salt and bitter as their tears
who stir in graves as restless as the surge
and wonder if they gave their lives in vain.

November 18, 1996   2005
Pittsburgh, PA

Abafazi

"Abafazi" in the Xhosa language is "women."
This poem is dedicated to Dulcie September (killed
at her Paris office by fascist agents), Ruth First, and
all the heroic fighting women of South Africa.

Where the shining Tyumie River
winds down through the
Amatola Mountains, blue—
shadowed in their distances
along the banks stand miles
of waving corn, the blade-shaped
leaves flashing as the wind rustles
through them and they throw back like spears

the shafts of light that fall on them:
the trees stand tall, aloof and dreaming in
the haze of the warm midday heat
except for the young blue spruces—
they seem alive and restless with magic
and a blue shade, as if moonlight
lingers there, is gathered around them.

All this grows from dark, rich, fertile soil;
through these valleys and mountain slopes
warriors once poured down to defend
their land and fought and gave their lives.

they poured their rich blood with fierce
unrelenting anger into this dark fertile soil:
and the men and women fight on,
and give their lives.
The struggle continues.

1989

September 20, 1989

Summer's last morning;
brightness suffused with tepid warmth,
already radiance fades from the marigolds;
in deepgreen darkgreen shadows
deepred darkred berries blush
to tumescence and burst with ripeness:
the growing cycle ends
the season turns to dying.

the cycle's chord of growth concludes

September 20, 1989   2005

Remembering

Wanda Cele, student and poetry enthusiast,
University of Durban—Westville

Under these low stars
this sky filled with a red glow,
does this spirit still linger?
is it near in this dusk?
do his eager questions still hover
in this unanswering air?
The gleam of his bright eyes
will find no reflection in this dark:
somewhere, perhaps, red blood turns brown
that oozed from your stab-wound,
your lifeless corpse, all animation gone,
cannot heed our sorrow
nor heal our pain and loss.

                                                        1993

Prison

The "Abyss"* is their word for time,
time in prison—any kind of prison
they can see time as a devouring maw,
a vortex that sucks away their lives;
but in that vision they assert themselves
seeing the abyss and themselves as separate:
so they take on, once more, human dignity.

*Also the name of the Newsletter published by Pennsylvania Lifers
Association in Huntingdon Prison. This poem is dedicated to them.

                                                        1993

Out of rain-gray mist
looming over rainwet asphalt—
yellow school buses

December 1994

2005

North and South our horses head
going nowhere
South and North our powers pull
inducing paralysis
contradiction must be resolved
that is clear
no glib formulations
must obscure
phantsi privatization phantsi
forward to socialism
our road is clear!

September 16–17, 2001
Capetown, Guguleto, South Africa

2005

Prose poem: Visiting my father's birthplace

The landscape is familiar: gently sloping hillsides covered with greenery—brown shrubs. I am going in search of my father in the country of his boyhood and though I'm in a car with family members, it is all intensely private—so private that I don't even allow myself the murmured converse I usually conduct with myself.

This green-shadowed landscape troubles me. The hills have been slashed open, of course, so that there are red-raw stretches all along the wide asphalt roads—and I cannot suppress the knowledge that these wide swift roads were planned to ensure the rapid transit of military vehicles to any area where there might be "trouble"— the euphemism for unrest provoked by police brutality or the ruthless enforcement of inhumane laws. There is another reminder of the iron land of repression—the miles of gleaming wire and cable that conveyed instantaneous alerts about these same "troubles"; that sent helicopters or armored patrols—scorpions, hippos, buffaloes (these vehicles had animal names, sometimes because they evoked a resemblance)—with screaming sirens and flashing headlamps into the "townships," as the segregated and menaced areas were called. They are a constant presence. And though they no longer carry the same menacing quality, they are a brooding reminder, a symbol not to be shaken off.

So it is with the load pressing on my mind that we enter the small fishing village where my father grew up, after stopping at an information cottage near the entrance and picking up some material from a helpful but somewhat perplexed attendant.

The sea stretches out, pale blue to silver at the horizon and the bay curves gently, with fishing boats in the foreground, and a bulky factory on the headland of the entrance. The town will, of course, have changed greatly, but the sea is the same sea, and this is pretty much the scene he would have looked out on. I try to see with his boyish eyes: try to feel what he felt, to enter somehow into the thoughts and feelings of the father who would never let me enter his mind. Nothing comes of it. Only the thought of that lingering military presence. And of the greed for profit that will bring more factories to destroy this landscape that can still tug at my heart.

2004

Exile, exile
you are a bitter word
I eat you with my bread
I drink you with my tea
you are the bitter word
that makes the world bitter to me

The stars look down
they see the world
they see a place
where I cannot be

Exile, exile
you are a bitter word
I eat you with my bread
I drink you with my tea
Exile, exile
you make the stars bitter to me

2005

Home-walking blues
late night gleaming on window panes
cold rain slashing my cheeks
mutters among blue-shadowed trees
a voice remembered in my head
murmuring bad news:
walking to a place called home
a cold bitter place called home.

Home-walking blues
heading east where the light has died
stray leaves drifting across my face
sighs from dead leaves crunched underfoot
a voice remembered in my head
murmuring bad news:
walking to a place called home
a cold bitter place called home.

October 1996   1999

In a country which denies that men
and women are human, where the
Constitution excludes them as sub-
humans, the creative act is an act
of dissent and defiance: creative
ability is a quintessential part
of being human: to assert one's
Creativity is also to assert one's
Humanity. This is a premise on which
I have acted all my life and it is
the premise I have offered to others
as an inspiration.

March 13, 1989   2005
Pittsburgh, PA

So neat they were, so attractive,
shapely with a jewel-like gleam,
but also so lethal, lying there quietly
in a detective's hand.
Having known a bullet in my back,
I regarded these bullets with respect,
knowing they might have plunged
blasted into my skull; "Fight! Fight!" was urged:
"A lucky escape," I thought,
but commended my self on my prudence:
inches deep in snow outside
O'Hare Airport, my feet tingling,
was still preferable to lying
a corpse staining new-fallen snow.

                                                                  2004

The sounds begin again;
the siren in the night
the thunder at the door
the shriek of nerves in pain.

Then the keening crescendo
of faces split by pain
the wordless, endless wail
only the unfree know.

Importunate as rain
the wraiths exhale their woe
over the sirens, knuckles, boots;
my sounds begin again.

1963

Mumia

He is surrounded by the shadows
The shadows of death row
They want to make him walk that valley
The valley Jonny Gammage knows.
But his voice is strong for justice
For freedom he is strong
Mumia, Mumia
You're never fighting alone
In your fight for justice
From death row
The fight for your release
From death row
And until there's justice
From death row
There will be no peace
Out of the shadows his voice echoes
Thousands of Black youth
And it shatters lies and silence
With the thunder of its truth.
Mumia, Mumia
Do you hear us march along
To your words that speak for freedom
And the courage to be strong

August 2, 1999   2005
Pittsburgh, PA

Sequence for Mumia Abu Jamal

I

Some voices must be silenced
they threaten the structures
of seemingly safe respectable lives
their clear vibrations
may shatter the crystalline shelters
that encase us from reality
shielding us from unbearable truths

but some may choose not to be deaf
they beat with broken palms
against the smooth impenetrable glass
of lies and comfort and power
and beg to hear the piteous cries
rising from the smoke and fire:
some voices must not be silenced

II

The smooth impenetrable glass
of indifference and uncaring
is cool and pleasant to the touch
like the stone heart of power
that conceals the rottenness within.

III

In the night
anger burns like fire
along the veins
in the brain
and at the core
of the anguished
unavailing heart.

IV

Red and orange and saffron
the fiery ghosts
rise in the night
to sear the dreaming brain
and blast the wakeful eyeballs
staring into the dark:
images of terror.

V

Red, bright red as blood
luminous with life
anger runs through the brain
anger against injustice
anger against pain
anger against impotence

And red, red as a rose
red as soft red velvet
red as a deep red rose
with shadows dark to black
red as poppies in sunlight
red as massed salvia
red as the blood of children
in the dust of Soweto
(come see the blood of children
in the streets of Soweto)
red as poppies in sunlight
with their fragile beauty
with their indestructible beauty
steadfast under battering rain
so strong, so red our courage:
we will not bow down
we will not submit to defeat
our courage will endure
our truth will survive.

2005

Winged Pegasus stands transfixed
on an oil-tank in Texas
and the plains extend around:

in the noise-fug of motors
where is the singing note
that will turn the stones to trees?

there is a harmony of will
that tremoring the fetid slag
patterns the impotent atoms.

New Orleans: October 30, 1971   1975

New Orleans

This is no city for old men;
air a-tingle with jazzy riffs
lithe thighs of nubile women
sculptured by ardent breezes
slow sensual flow of dark waters
past undulant delta slush
at night raucous laughter mingling
with saxophone's horny bray

once, by Hotel Sonesta, we parted
with acerbic rasping friction;
perhaps that too-blatant sexual flaunt
—publicly uncaring like birds copulating—
repelled, made our private desire obscene.

December 26, 27, 28
New Orleans Journey
Pittsburgh, Cincinnati, Pittsburgh   2005

"Freedom!
It's wonderful"
said the Ukrainian
on the train to Philadelphia.
"In the Ukraine
the Russians take away my freedom
but here I am free
to make sure the black man starves."

1974

The home of the brave
and the land of the free
to massacre:

the land of liberty
and freedom of choice
of subjection for others:

the land of plenty
and quality education
for people of quality:

Amerika the beautiful
cesspool.

1973

A terrible knowledge
*To the memory of Karen Silkwood, who died
on the road from Cimarron, November 13, 1974*

On the road from Cimarron
terrible knowledge squatted
like an unnatural monster
at the back of her brain

On the road from Cimarron
terrible knowledge pursued her
headlights lasering
the back of her head

On the road from Cimarron
terrible knowledge
of a mutilating death
rested with lethal casualness
on her sleeve

On the road from Cimarron
terrible knowledge impacted
on her brain
with the shattering crash
that smashed her car from the road:
they wished her to die
with the terrible knowledge
locked in her skull

terrible knowledge
of a nuclear holocaust

terrible knowledge
of a nuclear holocaust
clumsily unloosed
through carelessness
or greed

terrible knowledge
that even now
a few are dying

slowly
horribly
lied to
lied about
and she had the terrible knowledge

Behind her
out of the dark
hurtled a red glare:
baleful Moloch,
awesome fireball
glimmering:
terror
lunging to destroy

Out of the dark
behind her
a monstrous hound
lunging from Erebus
sharp fangs snapping
to extirpate her:
terrible knowledge
of impending death

Terrible knowledge
of the guilty ones
—cops, executives, agents—
who conspired to destroy her
and her terrible knowledge
and now conspire
to plead their innocence
their ignorance

Terrible knowledge
of our capacity to destroy
of our potential for destruction,
of our destructive greed:
terrible knowledge
Karen's knowledge,
our knowledge,
terrible knowledge

1979

"These plants produced enough plutonium
to end the world in one incandescent flash." *

I return to the seething earth
heading northward,
swinging from the South

(where Death, a golden timekeeper
squints telescopically at our vulnerability
and once erupted his logic
through our placid insanity)

swinging westward through an eastward loop
to the big love field
'Big D' boasting of a giant penis,
giant love

(where Death's fell missile darted
beamed on a telescopic focus of light
on a vulnerable nape, raying like light
in the proud defenceless meat

—for the potentially healing must die
lest they obstruct the midas-change
of all things to fatality
in this doomed micro-mini-universe)

and west and north to the range
the continental divide,
the upthrust complaisant mound
the outflung, submissive, earth;

further north the earth boils
and on the nearby flats,
the neighborly flats,
Death seeps—old Dis—from an unancient Stygia

and I head, having made my loop,
noose-shadowed, in bladed blade-gray air
in a guillotine ambience

to my burial,
to the burying-ground of us all

(we will not return the burial grounds,
the ancient, ancestral burying-grounds,
we will return to the burying-grounds
to the burial grounds that will not be there)

to my burial,
to the burial ground for us all—
for no-one
for there is no burial
no lasting city of death

we have here no lasting city,
no lasting city of death:
there shall be no lasting city—
only a drift of ash
where once was a fading incandescent spark

a handful of gray ash drifting,
dispersing,
in the lighted, sightless, universe.

Austin—Dallas—Denver   1973

*From an article in the *Sunday Times* (London) February 8, 1970, by
Cal McCrystal (New York) quoting from an article to appear in *En-
vironment*, the official publication of the Scientists' Institute for Pub-
lic Information. Further quotes: "'The most dangerous tombs in the
world.' Vast underground tombs in Washington State, Columbia,
holding as much radioactivity as would be released in a nuclear war,
are vulnerable to earthquakes, two geologists warn America in a
forthcoming report. The 140 storage tanks at the Atomic Energy
Commission's reservation at Hanford hold high-level radioactive
wastes with a life of hundreds of thousands of years…most of the
Hanford reactors are now shut down but, says *Environment*, during
their years of operation, 'these plants produced enough plutonium to
end the world in one incandescent flash'…The Waste Solidification
Engineering Prototype went into operation in 1966…by last June it
had processed…possibly less than one per cent. 'At this rate,' says
Environment, 'it will be centuries before the entire accumulation is
solidified.'" Other references in the poem are to a multiple shooting
at the University of Texas at Austin, the Kennedy assassination in
Dallas, and the Rocky Flats fire (Atomic Energy Commission plant)
near Denver.—D.B.

Your breasts under my lips
or your nipples brushing my chest—
"Vietnam!" the contact cries out

in the electric instant of touch
when our persons merge their reserve
self-identity breaking with crackle like ice
"Vietnam!" hangs in the space in my forehead
like a smudge, like flak, an exploding shell

all guilts, all anxieties
swirling sluggishly in the vortex of sense
with the sweet urgent pull of lust
the delight of intellectual interplay
the sensuous relish of light and scent and sense
knot to a thick cord of pain
that congeals from the confused flow

"Vietnam! Guilty! Murderess!"
my agonized awareness cries

Lovely and wealthy and comfortable,
innocent and uncaring
You too are guilty too;

past the soft breast, pink-nippled
the ripe mellifluous curve of thigh
I see torn pieces of flesh
torn as by beasts, or hacked by butchers

I see pieces of flesh scattered among ricestalks:
Vietnam! Vietnam! my body cries.

Evanston: June 4, 1972   1974

The new Middle Passage confronts us talk of a new Holocaust
how many thousands of our men and women must die in this new
Holocaust how many must be broken in mind and body brutalized
and broken in the brutalizing business of war limbs amputated body
disabled brain damaged haunted by images of horror and courage
haunted by bloody deeds and bloody dyings talk of a new Holocaust
confront a new Holocaust how many of our men and women must
confront a new Holocaust say no, say no, say no

February 17, 1991   2005

In this time in this air
to live is to be saddened
awareness of pain is
pervasive as the air
each labored breath draws
from a miasma of sorrow
the ribcage creaks pain
expelling, not expunging sadness:
still falls the rain of horror
the landscape is drenched with destruction:
"business as usual" goes the cry,
business of profits, of death and dying
how goes the world away
how goes the business of the war

February 17, 1991
Pittsburgh Airport   2005

Gull gliding against
gray-silver autumn sky
sees a vast miasma of greed
slowly encompass our entire planet
cries out to unheeding stars
to whom wails of children rise
in shrill unending caterwauls

Gull sees traps and snares
lethal pellets of noxious lead

noisome sewers of excreta
dribbling across continents
rivers of pesticide
oozing from lush golfcourses

Gull gasps, chokes on acrid billows
from rainforests rampaging fires
rancid with roasting flesh
ashen with cindered bones

Gull breasts with buckling wing
fierce gusts of questions
strives, resists against questions
slowly droops against questions
succumbs twisting against question
submits to extinction: Questions

October 18, 1995   2005

Bearer of life
and bearer of death:
What strangulation
clutching the throat
torturous throng, throng
circling gloom;
the impulse of life
Kills and is killing
horrific Cage to pace
as the steel bar, steel axe
clangs down, clangs down.

December 10, 1993   2005

Indian Ground
Navajo Reservation

A hot dry wind moves
over blown grass and bare ground
sighs a great sadness.

1993

Amerika

Wraiths are racing down Fifth Avenue
over ice-crystals ignited by streetlights:
spectres fleeing vainly their grisly deaths
and premonitions of the undead
doomed to be struck down tomorrow:
Amerika, Amerika, where will you find compassion?

February 8, 1987
Pittsburgh, PA
For Reading at Houston, TX
February 10, 1987   2005

Off to Philadelphia in the morning
after blueberry pancakes U.S.A.
with silver images of people
wrestling the racial problem
flickering on my retina-screen;

outside the shark limousines glide
past neons, glass and chrome,
on 42nd nudies writhe
their sterile unproductive lust;

off to Philadelphia in the morning
to rehearse some moulded and half-singing words,
remouth some banal platitudes
and launch-lodge some arrows
from a transient unambitious hand,
a nerveless unassertive gripe.

New York   1970

A mauve haze
the serried wintry branches make
at the end of the avenue:

I grow dizzy with lust
and yearning

soon age will add
another patina
to insulate me
against delight

and around me the tight-buttocked girls
romp, ogle and frolic

and still one burrows
makes a place
an impact,
in some crevice of the globe

To Indianapolis: November 17, 1971   1975

Zimbabwe

So to my neglected birthplace,
often disowned, sometime by me
—not scorn but skipping details:
here I first breathed African air,
my heart shaped by country's contours
my infant sensibilities stirred:
returning I sense deep discontent,
mealie fields rippling restlessly
stirred by half-concealed angers:
patient African children, staring
with trusting innocent eyes
how much longer must you hunger
how long before your nights are rent not
by cries: how long to wait for peace?

August 8, 2004   2005

Two Zairian soldiers

They are young and open
eager to speak their halting English
curious about the larger world
envious of its glamor:

they are trained for lethal acts
and coiled with a deadly efficiency
but their fresh-faced innocence
makes them admirable servants of an unborn world
of a new world yet to be born.

2004

Night sequence

I

Ships at night: Bosphorus

Sailing across dark waters
under low glimmering stars
with a burden of centuries
murmuring through breathing air:
years crowd in, achievements,
sorrows, joys foregone in vain:
well, we must endure past years,
await, crumpled, some uncertainties:
on dark Bosphorus waters

II

Darkness closes in:
portent of horrors:
there is reason to despair:
evil men work their evil ways
wreak terror on our earth:
miscall it "shock and awe"
blinded by arrogance

or drunk on ichor of hubris—
its reek, acrid fumes, or—
simply, perhaps stupidity
their combat-boots pound our world
while we cringe, defenses inadequate
turn our faces to the wall:
it is time, perhaps for despair.

2005

Welcome to Neptune Bar

Fishes swim amid friable statuary
in blue-green reaches of fabled waters:
an emperor-demigod splashed here
seeking survival in a fleeing ship:
a queen sailed by in an opulent barge
wafted by fragrant lyrical air:
all history swirls by in centuries
chants in incandescent snatches
how ephemeral, how fragile we all are

April 12, 2003
Neptune Bar
Helnan Palestine Hotel
Alexandria, Egypt   2005

Song
For the Sandinistas

I hear you singing
though the barbed wire tears
at your throat
and small wildflowers struggle
among the spent bullet casings:
and steady as starlight gleam
or gun-barrels
shines your resolve—
the Somocistas will never return.

1993

Isla Negra: For Neruda

*Written on the occasion of learning that
Pablo Neruda was to be reburied on
Isla Negra: where he lived.*

Now
the earth that loves you
and that you loved
welcomes you again at last
its dark brown arms
open to embrace you:

the crowds that swarmed the streets
at your funeral
shouting *"Chile is not dead"*
will shout your return
crying amid tears and laughter
"Presente!"

*"We were waiting for you here
on Isla Negra."*

The sea, the briny kelp, the seagulls
will know that a lover has returned
the scrawled messages to Pablo
on the walls of your shattered house
—all will fill the air with chants and poems

and songs that sing you home.

1993

Zocalo

It stretches for great distances
that enormous expanse,
harsh surface underfoot
immense, a great square
confronting a vast edifice;

(nearby, steps, a cathedral—
Maria Imperatriz, possibly
mothers, babes at their breasts
suckling, with begging cups):
this ground is sacred
soaked with heroic blood
of those who died for freedom,
sacred too, with footprints—
Villon, Zapata trod this square
now Zapatistas arrive
a fanfare of triumphant trumpet notes
flourish of banners, bandanas, masks
with banners that declare
"We are all Indians"
for all the world, they declare.

March 11, 2001   2004

Seattle
In the Tenderloin

Some last flicker
of defiant vitality
gutters in the collapsing husk
a despairing lunge
of shrinking sexuality
reaching with skeletal fingers,
disarticulated, arthritic,
for my frissoning skin
from a cavernous skull
shrunk to a calcined thinness
eyes glare, plead, twinkle
in appeal, denunciation:
halloween's pumpkin mask
of play, horror and grisly humor
All-Saints and the unavailing reprise
of All-Souls, doomed and damned.

September 20, 1996   2004

At night, after Porto Alegre; South African Airways 747

In this dim winged cathedral
soaring above oceans of silvery cloud
far beyond Atlantic's tumultuous heave
we move, star-girt, distant
from greed's debris, genocides, calcined bones
curled in our private shrines
or bent over light-pooled pages
to a new world, new earth, where finally
our dreams can be fulfilled.

April 1, 2001   2004

San Francisco: San Jose: Santa Clara

The perfume of freedom has burned my mind
with grief for my country
while I walk the ammoniac streets
reeking of urine and vomit
while shadows move in and out of shadows
gesturing with flapping empty trousers,
while gnarled and soiled both hands
thrust and receive with skeletal fingers,
dead eyes stare glassily, unconnected
to the hoarse whispered words of thanks
and I stare against the blank wall
of a despaired and despairing future:

the perfume of freedom has burned my mind
with grief for my country:
but I remember that seeming ultimate journey
to the bottom end of a continent
to an island graveyard of corpses and hopes
and an indestructible assertion
"We shall survive"

March 8–9, 1994
Ch'iu Chin = Chinese poet
The opening line is borrowed from her 1907 poem.   2004

Flying, after Seattle

Eastward, with wings sun-silvered
at sunset, flying after Seattle
we dip into encroaching gloom
a surge of joy irradiating darkness
as a new youthful song proclaims hope:
at a crux in time we made our choice
beat back predatory ghouls
who would devour our inheritance:
big-shouldered we thrust through dusk,
strong-voiced with deep throated snore
buoyant on wings borne on sweet air
after acrid stench, boots and concussions
our searchlight glare disrobes their putrescences
crouched under miasmas of confused lies.
Arise, you billions to assert our will:
We begin to construct a better world.

December 15, 1999
Pittsburgh, PA
(Flying to JFK November/December 1999)   2005

Silence in the still warm room
silence pressured from the silent street
snow-muffled, traffic-deserted:
the self, in the stillness, poised
a pivot around which nothing revolves
looks inward, finds itself in flight
from itself and the inexorable demand
for surrender to the ocean of selflessness:
this is what love is about:
and it resists, hugs fiercely
its self to itself:
is doomed to loneliness.
And still it cries out against aloneness.

January 14, 1997   2005

"Arm the homeless" shrieks
campus toilet graffito:
someone, somewhere cares

November 29, 1993   2005

A dream

Still, they come, stalwarts with
peaked faces shrunk by hunger
shoulders caved with hours of
labor, gathering to gather
energies for a never-ending
struggle, unobtrusively
I slip away, seeming akin,
my work known by few (my name
by even fewer) till someone
greets me, murmurs thanks mixed
with praise, imprint of a kiss
still woven on my hand as I leave.

May 4, 2003   2005

In a green dusk, shadows—
pale green of ripening apples—close in:
neons, fluorescents still twilight pale
loom or cluster or dissolve:
I gather my scattered selves for exile
but all city details remain a blur:
I wait for a wrench that signals parting
with grief or sorrow, only uncertainty:
in time a future, a new present will take shape

July 31, 2003
July 30, 1966   2005

I will be the world's troubadour
if not my country's

Knight-erranting
jousting up and down
with justice for my theme

weapons as I find them
and a world-wide scatter of foes

Being what I am
a compound of speech and thoughts and song
and girded by indignation
and accoutred with some undeniable scars
surely I may be
this cavalier?

1978

One world weeping

To those huddled figures
draped in cloths
young people, perhaps
even small children

moving through the shadows
and into the darkness of corridors

my heart follows you
impotent, in agony

my hands reach out to you
till my fingers are covered with blood

The world is filled
with soundless weeping.

1993

I am a rebel and freedom is my cause:
Many of you have fought similar struggles
therefore you must join my cause:
My cause is a dream of freedom
and you must help me make my dream reality:
For why should I not dream and hope?
Is not revolution making reality of hopes?
Let us work together that my dream may be fulfilled
that I may return with my people out of exile
to live in one democracy in peace.
Is not my dream a noble one
worthy to stand beside freedom struggles everywhere?

1975

Document Sources

Editors' note:

This volume gathers selections from nearly fifty years of Dennis Brutus's work—much of it never before published, some that first appeared under pseudonyms in defunct publications, and most of it long out of print. In addition, we have included previously unpublished material from the Dennis Brutus Papers at the Northwestern University Archives in Evanston, Ill., (referred to below as NU archives), the Dennis Brutus Collection at Worcester State College in Worcester, Mass., (WSC collection) and the Dennis Brutus manuscript holdings in the National English Literary Museum in Grahamstown, South Africa (NELM holdings).

The memoirs that begin each part and section of this book are based on a series of interviews with Dennis Brutus, conducted by Lee Sustar between April 2004 and November 2005. The memoirs were edited by Sustar in collaboration with Brutus. "You've come to Hell Island," Brutus's account of Robben Island prison that appears in Part 1, was edited by Aisha Karim and approved by Brutus.

Finally, for simplicity in the citations below, we refer to Dennis Brutus as D.B.

Part 1

Balthazar Johannes Vorster, Minister of Justice, to Dennis Brutus (n.d., 1961). In NU Archives, Box 1, Folder 2.

D.B. (under the pseudonym J.B. Booth), "Silent poets, strangled writers" (1963). In *Fighting Talk* (Johannesburg), January, 1963, copyright © 1963 Dennis Brutus. Used by permission of the author.

D. B. (under the pseudonym J.B. Booth), "Negritude, literature and nationalism: A word from South Africa" (1962). In *Fighting Talk* (Johannesburg), October, 1962, copyright © 1962 by Dennis Brutus. Used by permission of the author.

D.B. (under the initials D.A.B.), "In a Cape packing shed" (1961). In *Fighting Talk* (Johannesburg), August, 1961, copyright © 1961 by Dennis Brutus. Used by permission of the author.

D.B., "Sports: Threat to the security of the state" (1961). In *Fighting Talk* (Johannesburg), December 1961/January 1962, copyright © 1961 by Dennis Brutus. Used by permission of the author.

D.B. (under the initials D.A.B.), "Walking home to Mofolo" (1959). In *Fighting Talk*, May, 1959, copyright © 1959 by Dennis Brutus. Used by permission of the author.

D.B., "You've come to Hell Island" (1974). Transcription of autobiographical notes, 1974. In NU Archives, Box 10, Folder 6, copyright © 2005 by Dennis Brutus. Used by permission of the author.

Part 2, Section 1

D.B., "United Nations Special Committee on Apartheid Hears Mr. Dennis Brutus" (March 23, 1970). In United Nations Unit on Apartheid, Department of Political and Security Council Affairs, *Notes and Documents*, March 1970, copyright © 1970 by Dennis Brutus. Used by permission of the author.

D.B., "Open Letter from the South African Non-Racial Olympic Committee on Precious McKenzie" (August 3, 1966). In NU archives, Box 4, Folder 6.

Part 2, Section 2

D.B., "'Somehow tenderness survives:' Dennis Brutus Talks about his life and poetry," interview by Bernth Lindfors (1970). In *The Benin Review* No. 1 (Benin City), June 1974, pp. 44-55, copyright © 1974 by Dennis Brutus and Bernth Lindfors. Used by permission of the authors.

D.B., "Protest against apartheid: Alan Paton, Nadine Gordimer, Athol Fugard, Alfred Hutchinson and Arthur Nortje" (1969). In Cosmo Pieterse & Donald Munro (eds.), *Protest and Conflict in African Literature* (New York: Africana Publishing Corporation, 1969), pp. 93-100. "Protest Against Apartheid" copyright © 1969 by Dennis Brutus. Used by permission of the author.

D.B., "African culture and liberation." Speech at the First Pan-African Cultural Festival, Algiers, July 1969. Typescript, NU archives, Box 10, Folder 18. A version of this speech was published in *Africa Today*

(January-February 1970), p. 4, copyright © 1970 by Indiana University Press. Used by permission of the author and publisher.

D.B., "Cultural liberation and the African revolution" (1974). Paper presented in Montreal at a meeting of the Centre Québécois de Relations Internationales and the Research Commission, National Movements and Imperialism of the International Sociological Association, May 15-18, 1974. In Immanuel Wallerstein (ed.), *World Inequality:* (Montreal: Black Rose Books, 1975), pp. 152-156, copyright © 1974 by Black Rose Books. Used by permission of the author and publisher.

D.B., "Literature and commitment in South Africa" (1975). Presentation at the first annual meeting of the African Literature Association, Austin, Tex. In Bernth Lindfors (ed.), *Contemporary Black South African Literature: A Symposium (Revised and Augmented)* (Washington, D.C.: Three Continents Press, 1985), pp. 81-86, copyright © 1985 by the African Literature Association and Three Continents Press, Inc. Used by permission of the author and publisher.

Ayi Kwei Armah, et al., "Meeting of African writers, Accra, June 1975." *In Transition 50/Ch'indaba* 1 (Accra), October 1975/March 1976. Copyright " 1975 by Union of Writers of the African Peoples. Used by permission of Dennis Brutus.

D.B., "English and the dynamics of South African creative writing (1979)." In Leslie A. Fiedler and Houston A. Baker (eds.), *Opening Up the Canon: Selected Papers of the English Institute, 1979* (Baltimore and London: The Johns Hopkins University Press, 1981), pp. 1-14, copyright © 1981 by the English Institute. Used by permission of the English Institute.

Part 2, Section 3

Joel Rogers, Acting INS Midwest District Director to Dennis Brutus, June 25, 1981. In NU archives, Box 28, Folder 4.

Senator Howard Metzenbaum to Elliot Abrams, Assistant Secretary of State, January 19, 1982. In WSC collection.

Thomas P. O'Neill, Speaker of the U.S. House of Representatives to Elliot Abrams, Assistant Secretary of State, February 22, 1982. In WSC collection.

D.B., "Speech before the United Nations Special Committee On Apartheid" (1974). Undated typescript in WSC archives, copyright © by Dennis Brutus.

D.B., "Notes on the South African liberation struggle" (1975). In *The Gar* 32 (Austin, Texas), 1978, pp. 7-10, copyright © 1975 by Dennis Brutus. Used by permission of the author and publishers.

D.B., "Steve Biko: In memoriam" (1978). Speech at the Steve Biko Day commemoration, San Antonio, Texas, June 16, 1978. Edited transcript of tape in possession of the editors. Copyright © 1978 by Dennis Brutus. Used by permission of the author.

D.B., Statement by Ad-hoc Group to End Northwestern [University] Investments in South Africa (AGENISA) (1981). In WSC collection, copyright © 1981by Dennis Brutus. Used by permission of the author.

D.B., "The escalation of resistance in South Africa" (1986). Transcript of a speech at the Third Unitarian Church of Chicago, June 1, 1986. In NELM holdings, copyright © 1986 by Dennis Brutus. Used by permission of the author.

Part 3

D.B., "South Africa: transition to freedom?" (1993). Speech in Denver, Colorado, November 19, 1993. Originally broadcast on Alternative Radio; transcript available on the Alternative Radio and ZNet Web sites. Copyright © 1993 by Dennis Brutus. Used by permission of Alternative Radio and ZNet.

D.B., "Martin Luther King Day: Globalize the Struggle for Justice" (1994). Speech on January 17, 1994 to the U.S. Conference of Christians and Jews, Pittsburgh. Edited transcript of tape in NU archives. Used by permission of the author.

D.B., "Africa 2000 in the new global context: A commentary" (1997). In *Africa Today,* vol. 44, no. 4 (October-December 1997), pp. 379-384, copyright © 1997 by Indiana University Press. Used by permission of the author and publisher.

D.B., "Why I protested at the World Bank" (2000). Published on the Center for Economic Justice Web site, April 28, 2000, copyright © 2000 by Dennis Brutus. Used by permission of the author and publisher.

D.B., "It's time for new confrontations (2000)." Published in the *Mail & Guardian,* (South Africa), July 21-27, 2000, copyright © 2000 by Dennis Brutus. Used by permission of the author and the publisher.

D.B., "Africa's progressive movements," interview by Patrick Bond (2000). Published on the ZNet Web site, December 28, 2000, copyright © 2000 by Patrick Bond and Dennis Brutus. Used by permission of the authors and publisher.

D.B., "South Africa supports global apartheid" (2001). Published on the IndyMedia South Africa Web site, August 26, 2001, copyright © 2001 by Dennis Brutus. Used by permission of the author and publisher.

D.B. and Ben Cashdan, "World Conference Against Racism: South Africa between a rock and a hard place" (2001). Published on the ZNet Web

site, July 11, 2001, copyright © 2001 by Dennis Brutus and Ben Cash-
dan. Used by permission of the authors and the publisher.

D.B. and Ben Cashdan, "Reflections on Durban" (2001). In *The Nation*,
September 17, 2001, copyright © 2001 by *The Nation*. Used by per-
mission of the authors and publisher.

D.B., "World Summit on Sustainable Development" (2002). In *Indepen-
dent Politics News*, Summer 2002, copyright © 2002 by Dennis Bru-
tus. Used by permission of the author and the publisher.

D.B., "Global agendas are set by the usual suspects" (2002). Published on
the IndyMedia South Africa Web site, July 15, 2002, copyright © 2002
by Dennis Brutus. Used by permission of the author and publisher.

D.B., "Africa's struggles today," interview by Lee Sustar (2003). In
International Socialist Review 31, September-October 2003, copyright
© 2003 by Dennis Brutus and Lee Sustar. Used by permission of the
authors and publisher.

D.B., "Africa: Can Blair and Brown deliver?" (2005). Speech at the G8
Alternatives Summit, Edinburgh, July 3, 2005. Published on the Web
site of *Socialist Worker* (Britain), July 9, 2005 as "Dennis Brutus—
Don't get duped again," copyright © 2005 by Dennis Brutus and *So-
cialist Worker* (Britain). Used by permission of the author and publisher.

D.B., "Imperialism, sub-imperialism and popular resistance in South
Africa" (2005). Edited transcript of a speech given in a presentation
with Patrick Bond at the Brecht Forum, New York City, May 23, 2005,
copyright © 2005 by Dennis Brutus. Used by permission of the author.

Poetry Sources

"Prose poem: Visiting my father's birthplace," "Home-walking blues,"
"So neat they were, so attractive," "Poem for Vorster's resignation," "An
old black woman," "Munich poem: At the time of the Munich
Olympics," "Crossing the Atlantic," "Two Zairian soldiers," "In the dark
lanes of Soweto," "Zocalo," "Seattle: In the Tenderloin," and "At Night,
after Porto Alegre," from *Poems, From the Dennis Brutus Collection,
Worcester State College, Worcester, Massachusetts*, edited and introduced
by Ken Gibbs, copyright 2004 by Dennis Brutus. Used by permission of
the author.

"Amerika," "San Francisco: San Jose: Santa Clara," 'In this time in this
air," "Bearer of life," "Sequence for Mumia Abu Jamal," "Remembering
June 16, 1976," 'In a green dusk, shadows," "Gull gliding against," "'Arm
the homeless' shrieks," "June comes round again," "Spring," "Welcome to
Neptune bar," "September 20, 1989," "A dream," "Forgive me,
comrades," "Robben Island Holiday Resort," "If you ever go visiting in
Capetown," "North and South our horses head," "Exile, exile," "In a
country which denies that men," "Mumia," "New Orleans," "The new
Middle Passage," "when my mother talked to me," "Night sequence,"
"Flying, after Seattle," "Picture of a young girl dying of aids,"
"Zimbabwe," and "Silence in the still warm room" from *Leafdrift* edited
by lamont b. steptoe, copyright © 2005 by Dennis Brutus. Used by permis-
sion of the author and Whirlwind Press.

Further Reading

Books by and about Dennis Brutus

Dennis Brutus, *Sirens Knuckles Boots* (Ibadan, Nigeria: Mbari Publications, 1963).

———. *Letters to Martha* (London: Heinemann Educational Books Ltd., 1968).

———. *Poems from Algiers* (Austin: African and Afro-American Research Institute, University of Texas, 1970).

———. *Thoughts Abroad,* written under the pseudonym John Bruin, (Del Valle, Texas: Troubadour Press, 1970).

———. *Strains*, Wayne Kamin and Chip Dameron, eds. (Austin: Troubadour Press, 1975).

———. *A Simple Lust* (New York: Hill and Wang, 1973).

———. *China Poems* (Austin: African and Afro-American Research Institute, University of Texas, 1970).

———. *Stubborn Hope* (Washington, D.C.: Three Continents Press and London: Heinemann Educational Press, 1978). Augmented edition published by Three Continents Press, 1983.

———. *Airs and Tributes,* Gil Ott ed. (Camden, N.J.: Whirlwind Press, 1989).

———. *Still the Sirens* (Santa Fe, New Mexico: 1993).

———. *Remembering* (Camden, N.J.: Whirlwind Press, 2004).

———. *Leafdrift,* lamont b. steptoe, ed. (Camden, N.J.: Whirlwind Press, 2005).

Andrew Martin, *Poems of Dennis Brutus: A Checklist, 1945-2004* (Madison: Parallel Press/University of Wisconsin-Madison Libraries, 2005).

Craig W. Mcluckie and Patrick C. Colbert (eds.), *Critical Perspectives on Dennis Brutus* (Boulder, Colo.: Three Continents Press, 1995).

The struggle against apartheid

Jeremy Baskin, *Striking Back: A History of COSATU* (London and New York: Verso, 1991).

Robert Davies, Dan O'Meara and Sipho Dlamini (eds.), *The Struggle for South Africa: A Reference Guide to Movements, Organizations and Institutions,* rev. ed., 2 vols. (London and Atlantic Highlands, N.J., 1988).

Allison Drew, *Discordant Comrades: Identities and Loyalties on the South African Left* (Aldershot, England and Burlington, Vt.: Ashgate Publishing Co., 2000).

————. *South Africa's Radical Tradition: A Documentary History, Vol. 1: 1907-1950* (Rondebosch, South Africa: UCT Press; Cape Town, South Africa: Buchu Books; Bellville, South Africa: Myibuye Books; 1996–1997).

Baruch Hirson, *Revolutions in my Life* (Johannesburg, South Africa: Witwatersrand University Press, 1995).

Dennis MacShane, Martin Plaut and David Ward, *Power! Black Workers, Their Unions and the Struggle for Freedom in South Africa* (Boston: South End Press, 1984).

Nelson Mandela, *The Struggle Is My Life* (New York: Pathfinder Press, 1986).

Nelson Mandela, *Long Walk to Freedom* (London: Abacus, 1995).

Martin Murray, *South Africa: Time of Agony, Time of Destiny* (London: Verso, 1987)

————. *The Revolution Deferred: The Painful Birth of Post-Apartheid South Africa* (London and New York: Verso, 1994).

Edward Roux, *Time Longer than Rope: A History of the Black Man's Struggle for Freedom in South Africa* (Madison: University of Wisconsin Press, 1964).

Jack and Ray Simons, *Class and Colour in South Africa* (London: International Defense and Aid, 1983).

Sports and apartheid

Douglas Booth, *The Race Game: Sport and Politics in South Africa* (London and Portland, Ore.: Frank Cass Publishers, 1998).

Christopher R. Hill, *Olympic Politics* 2nd ed. (Manchester, England and New York: Manchester University Press, 1996).

Richard E. Lapchick, *The Politics of Race and International Sport* (Westport, Conn.: Greenwood Press, 1975).

Tom Newnham, *Apartheid Is Not a Game* (Auckland, New Zealand: Graphic Publications, 1975)

————. A Cry of Treason: New Zealand and the Montreal Olympics (Palmerston North, New Zealand: Dunmore Press Ltd., 1978).

South Africa after apartheid

Neville Alexander, An Ordinary Country Issues in the Transition from Apartheid to Democracy in South Africa (Pietermaritzburg, South Africa: University of KwaZulu-Natal Press, 2002).

Patrick Bond, Elite Transition: From Apartheid to Neoliberalism in South Africa (London: Pluto Press, 2000).

————. Unsustainable South Africa: Environment, Development and Social Protest (Pietermaritzburg, South Africa: University of KwaZulu-Natal Press and London: Merlin Press, 2002).

————. Against Global Apartheid: South Africa Meets the World Bank, IMF and International Finance 2nd ed. (London: Zed Books and Cape Town: University of Cape Town Press, 2003).

————. Talk Left, Walk Right: South Africa's Frustrated Global Reforms (2004, Pietermaritzburg, University of KwaZulu-Natal Press).

Thomas Bramble and Franco Barchiesi (eds.), Rethinking the Labour Movement in the "New South Africa" (Aldershot, England: Ashgate Publishing Co., 2003).

Ashwin Desai, We Are the Poors (New York: Monthly Review Press, 2002).

Sean Jacobs and Richard Calland (eds.) Thabo Mbeki's World (London: Zed Books and Pietermaritzburg, South Africa: University of KwaZulu-Natal Press, 2003).

John Saul, The Next Liberation Struggle (New York: Monthly Review Press; London: Merlin Press; Halifax: Fernwood Press; and Pietermaritzburg: University of KwaZulu-Natal Press, 2005).

Glossary of Acronyms

AGOA ◆ African Growth and Opportunity Act

ALA ◆ African Literature Association

ANC ◆ African National Congress

APEC ◆ Asia-Pacific Economic Cooperation

BCESL ◆ British Commonwealth Ex-Servicemen's League

BOSS ◆ Bureau of State Security

CIA ◆ Central Intelligence Agency

COSATU ◆ Congress of South African Trade Unions

FRELIMO ◆ Frente de Libertação de Moçambique (Liberation Front of Mozambique)

GATT ◆ General Agreement on Tariffs and Trade

GEAR ◆ Growth, Employment and Redistribution

IMF ◆ International Monetary Fund

IOC ◆ International Olympic Committee

MPLA ◆ Movimento Popular de Libertação de Angola (Popular Movement for the Liberation of Angola)

NAACP ◆ National Association for the Advancement of Colored People

NAFTA ◆ North American Free Trade Agreement

NLL ◆ National Liberation League

NEPAD ◆ New Partnership for Africa's Development

NGO ◆ Non-Governmental Organization

OAU ◆ Organization of African Unity

PAC ◆ Pan Africanist Congress

SACP ◆ South African Communist Party

SANROC ◆ South African Non-Racial Olympic Committee

SASA ◆ South African Sports Association

SOWETO ◆ Southwest Township

TINA ◆ There Is No Alternative

UN ◆ United Nations

UNESCO ◆ United Nations Educational Scientific and Cultural Organization

WB ◆ World Bank

WCAR ◆ World Conference Against Racism

WSSD ◆ World Summit on Sustainable Development

WTO ◆ World Trade Organization

Index of Poems

Index

Biographies

A biographical note on Dennis Brutus

While this book provides an overview of Dennis Brutus' life and work, some further personal details should be noted here. Born in Salisbury, Southern Rhodesia (now Harare, Zimbabwe) on November 28, 1924, Dennis Brutus grew up in Port Elizabeth in South Africa's Eastern Cape. Brutus married May Jaggers in 1950, and together they had eight children: Jacinta, Marc, Julian, Antony, Justina, Cornelia, Gregory, and Paula. His elder brother, Wilfred Brutus, who was also involved in the South African anti-apartheid struggle, was, like Dennis, also imprisoned on Robben Island, and later died in exile.

A graduate of what is now Fort Hare University in South Africa, Brutus has held a variety of academic posts in the U.S., principally at Northwestern University and the University of Pittsburgh. He has also taught at the University of Texas at Austin, the University of Colorado, the University of Denver, Worcester State College, and at other institutions.

Brutus has won numerous awards for his writing and activism. He was the first non-African American recipient of the Langston Hughes Award (1987). He also received the First Annual Paul Robeson Award for Excellence, Political Consciousness, and Integrity (1989). In 2004, Brutus was inducted into the National Hall of Fame of Writers of African Descent by the Gwendolyn Brooks Center at Chicago State University.

More biographical information on Brutus, as well as wide-ranging commentary on his work, can be found in Craig W. Mcluckie's and Patrick C. Colbert's invaluable *Critical Perspectives on Dennis Brutus* (Boulder, Colo.: Three Continents Press, 1995). A bibliography of Brutus' work is available in Andrew Martin's comprehensive *Poems of Dennis Brutus: A Checklist, 1945–2004* (Madison, Wis.: Parallel Press/University of Wisconsin-Madison Libraries, 2005).

Lee Sustar is labor editor for *Socialist Worker* newspaper and writes frequently on politics, globalization and the economy for the *International Socialist Review* and the Counterpunch and Znet Web sites. His writings on the labor movement have appeared in *New Labor Forum* and won a 2003 Project Censored award.

Aisha Karim received her Ph.D. from Duke University's Literature Program in 2004, specializing in postcolonial literature and theory. Her awards include a Mellon Fellowship for the Humanities, Woodrow Wilson Foundation, and research grants from the Harry Frank Guggenheim Foundation. She currently teaches at Saint Xavier University in Chicago and is co-editor, with Bruce Lawrence, of *The Chain of Violence*, forthcoming from Duke University Press.

About Haymarket Books

Haymarket Books is a nonprofit, progressive book distributor and publisher, a project of the Center for Economic Research and Social Change. We believe that activists need to take ideas, history, and politics into the many struggles for social justice today. Learning the lessons of past victories, as well as defeats, can arm a new generation of fighters for a better world.

We take inspiration and courage from our namesakes, the Haymarket Martyrs, who gave their lives fighting for a better world. Their 1886 struggle for the eight-hour day, which gave us May Day, the international workers' holiday, reminds workers around the world that ordinary people can organize and struggle for their own liberation. These struggles continue today across the globe—struggles against oppression, exploitation, hunger, and poverty.

Also from Haymarket Books

Subterranean Fire: A History of Working-Class Radicalism in the United States

Sharon Smith ■ This accessible, critical history of the U.S. labor movement examines the hidden history of workers' resistance from the nineteenth century to the present. *ISBN 193185923X*

The Dispossessed: Chronicles of the Desterrados of Colombia

Alfredo Molano, with a preface by Aviva Chomsky ■ Here in their own words are the stories of the Desterrados, or "dispossessed"—the thousands of Colombians displaced by years of war and state-backed terrorism. *ISBN 1931859175*

Women and Socialism

Sharon Smith ■ The fight for women's liberation is urgent—and must be linked to winning broader social change. *ISBN 1931859116*

Black Liberation and Socialism

Ahmed Shawki ■ A sharp and insightful analysis of historic movements against racism in the United States. *ISBN 1931859264*

Literature and Revolution

Leon Trotsky, edited by William Keach ■ A new, annotated edition of Leon Trotsky's classic study of the relationship between politics and art. *ISBN 1931859213*

The Meek and the Militant: Religion and Power Across the World

Paul Siegel • Examines the historical roots of religion around the world, it origin and persistence, and how it has acted as a bulwark of the social order, but also as a revolutionary force. *ISBN 1931859248*

What's My Name, Fool? Sports and Resistance in the U.S.

Dave Zirin • Offers a no-holds-barred look at the business of sports today. Zirin shows how sports express the worst, as well as the most creative and excitig, features of American society. *ISBN 1931859205*

Order these titlesonline at www.haymarketbooks.org or call 773-583-7884.
Haymarket Books is distributed to bookstores by Consortium Book
Sales and Distribution, www.cbsd.com.